Programming
Standard
COBOL

Programming Standard COBOL

Winchung A. Chai
Montclair State College

Henry W. Chai
Marcinko-Chai Associates, Inc.

Academic Press
NEW YORK SAN FRANCISCO LONDON
A Subsidiary of Harcourt Brace Jovanovich, Publishers

COPYRIGHT © 1976, BY ACADEMIC PRESS, INC.
ALL RIGHTS RESERVED.
NO PART OF THIS PUBLICATION MAY BE REPRODUCED OR
TRANSMITTED IN ANY FORM OR BY ANY MEANS, ELECTRONIC
OR MECHANICAL, INCLUDING PHOTOCOPY, RECORDING, OR ANY
INFORMATION STORAGE AND RETRIEVAL SYSTEM, WITHOUT
PERMISSION IN WRITING FROM THE PUBLISHER.

ACADEMIC PRESS, INC.
111 Fifth Avenue, New York, New York 10003

United Kingdom Edition published by
ACADEMIC PRESS, INC. (LONDON) LTD.
24/28 Oval Road, London NW1

Library of Congress Cataloging in Publication Data

Chai, Winchung A
  Programming standard COBOL.

  Bibliography: p.
  Includes index.
  1. COBOL (Computer program language) I. Chai,
Henry W., joint author. II. Title.
QA76.73.C25C48   001.6'424   75-26345
ISBN 0–12–166550–X

PRINTED IN THE UNITED STATES OF AMERICA

TO OUR PARENTS:
CH'U CHAI AND RUTH MEI-EN TSAO CHAI

Contents

List of Sample Programs xiii
Preface xv
Acknowledgments xvii

PART I FUNDAMENTALS

Chapter 0 Preliminary: Basic Concepts of Computers

- **0.1** The Computer System   3
- **0.2** Programs and Programming Languages   8
- **0.3** Flowcharts   10
- **0.4** Punched Cards   12
-          Exercises   14
-          References   14

Chapter 1 Introduction to COBOL Programming

- **1.1** ANS COBOL   15
- **1.2** COBOL System: Language and Compiler   15
- **1.3** COBOL Program Structure   16
- **1.4** COBOL Coding Sheet   18
- **1.5** A Simple COBOL Program (Sample Program 1A: Cards to Printer)   19
- **1.6** Summary of Rules for Writing COBOL Program   23
- **1.7** Sample Program 1B: Address Labels   24
-          Exercises   28

Chapter 2 Elements of COBOL Language

- **2.1** Basic Elements   30
- **2.2** Reserved Words   31

- **2.3** Programmer-Supplied Names 31
- **2.4** Symbols 32
- **2.5** Summary 33
- **2.6** Standard Notation for Format Description 34
  Exercises 35

Chapter 3 Identification and Environment Divisions

- **3.1** Identification Division 36
- **3.2** Environment Division 37
  Exercises 41

Chapter 4 Data Division

- **4.1** Contents and Basic Format 43
- **4.2** File Concepts 44
- **4.3** FILE SECTION: The File Description Entries 45
- **4.4** Record Contents: Group and Elementary Data Items 46
- **4.5** Level Numbers 47
- **4.6** Records or Data Description Format: PICTURE Clause 47
- **4.7** WORKING-STORAGE SECTION: Description 53
- **4.8** VALUE Clause: Literals 53
- **4.9** Sample Program 4A: Overdue Payment Notice 56
  Exercises 61

Chapter 5 Procedure Divisions

- **5.1** OPEN Statement 63
- **5.2** CLOSE Statement 65
- **5.3** MOVE Statement 65
- **5.4** READ Statement 66
- **5.5** WRITE Statement 67
- **5.6** ACCEPT Statement 69
- **5.7** DISPLAY Statement 70
- **5.8** GO TO Statement 72
- **5.9** STOP Statement 72
- **5.10** PERFORM Statement 72
- **5.11** Sample Program 5A: Customer Address Listing 74
- **5.12** Sample Program 5B: 80/80 Card Listing (ACCEPT and DISPLAY Statements) 77
- **5.13** Sample Program 5C: Page Heading, Current Date, and Page Number 79
  Exercises 83

Chapter 6 Editing and Data Manipulations

- **6.1** Editing Characters 86
- **6.2** Numeric Editing 87
- **6.3** Alphanumeric Editing 90
- **6.4** Permissible Moves: The MOVE Statement 90
- **6.5** Numeric Moves 91

- **6.6** Alphanumeric Moves 93
- **6.7** Group Moves 94
- **6.8** Sample Programs 6A: Weekly Charge Account Summary Report 95
- **6.9** Sample Program 6B: Minimum Payment Notice 98
  Exercises 101

Chapter 7 Calculations

- **7.1** ADD Statement 106
- **7.2** ROUNDED Option 108
- **7.3** ON SIZE ERROR Option 109
- **7.4** SUBTRACT Statement 110
- **7.5** MULTIPLY Statement 113
- **7.6** DIVIDE Statement 114
- **7.7** COMPUTE Statement 116
- **7.8** Sample Program 7A: Daily Sales Report 118
- **7.9** Sample Program 7B: Weekly Payroll Report 122
- **7.10** Sample Program 7C: Checking Account Report 126
  Exercises 129

Chapter 8 Conditions Statements: The IF Staement

- **8.1** Introduction 131
- **8.2** General Discussion of the IF Satement 132
- **8.3** Relation Test 136
- **8.4** Sign Test 139
- **8.5** Class Test 140
- **8.6** Condition-Name Test 141
- **8.7** Compound Test 142
- **8.8** Sample Program 8A: Weekly Payroll with Tax Routine 145
- **8.9** Sample Program 8B: Salesman Commission Computation 148
- **8.10** Duplicate Date Names 151
- **8.11** Sample Program 8C: Purchase Analysis Report 153
  Exercises 155

Chapter 9 Table Handling

- **9.1** Table Construction 161
- **9.2** Two- and Three-Dimensional Tables 164
- **9.3** Rules for Coding Subscripts 168
- **9.4** Sample Program 9A: Creating Hourly Rate Table from Punched Cards 169
- **9.5** Sample Program 9B: Salesman Commission Computation with Rate Table 171
  Exercises 173

Chapter 10 The PERFORM Statement

- **10.1** PERFORM/THRU Option 176
- **10.2** EXIT Statement 177

- **10.3** PERFORM/TIMES Option 178
- **10.4** PERFORM/UNTIL Option 179
- **10.5** PERFORM/VARYING Option 180
- **10.6** Nested Loops 183
- **10.7** Sample Program 10A: Depreciation Schedules 184
- **10.8** USAGE Clauses 188
- **10.9** Sample Program 10B: Student Test Scores Computation 189
  Exercises 193

PART II ADVANCED TOPICS

Chapter 11 Magnetic Tape Processing

- **11.1** Magnetic Tape Characteristics 199
- **11.2** Tape Density and Access Rate 200
- **11.3** Tape Records, Blocks, and Interblock Record Gap 200
- **11.4** COBOL Instructions for Processing Tape Files 202
- **11.5** Variable-Length Records 209
- **11.6** Sample Program 11A: Creating a Variable-Length Tape File 211
  Exercises 213

Chapter 12 Sorting and Searching

- **12.1** SORT Feature 215
- **12.2** Sample Program 12A: COBOL SORT Feature with USING/GIVING Option 217
- **12.3** Sample Program 12B: COBOL SORT Feature with Input/Output Procedure Options 220
- **12.4** Indexed Name and SET Statement 222
- **12.5** SEARCH Statement 224
  Exercises 227

Chapter 13 Program Checkout: Testing and Debugging

- **13.1** Compile-Time Errors 229
- **13.2** Object-Time Errors 232
- **13.3** READY/RESET TRACE Statement 233
- **13.4** Compile-Time Debug Packet 238
- **13.5** The Use of Dumps for Debugging 241

Chapter 14 Direct-Access Devices

- **14.1** Direct Data Sets and Files 242
- **14.2** Magnetic Disk Units 243
- **14.3** Direct Files 245
- **14.4** Creating a Direct File 248
- **14.5** Sample Program 14A: Creating a Direct File 249
- **14.6** Sample Program 14B: Updating a Direct File 251

14.7 Indexed Sequential Files   252
14.8 Sample Program 14C: Creating an Indexed Sequential File   255
14.9 Sample Program 14D: Sequential Access of Indexed Files   257
14.10 Random Access of Indexed Files   258
14.11 Sample Program 14E: Random Updating an ISAM File   259
  Exercises   261

Chapter 15   Report Writer Feature

15.1 Basic Concepts   264
15.2 DATA DIVISION: REPORT SECTION   265
15.3 PROCEDURE DIVISION   270
15.4 Sample Program 15A: Report Writer   271
15.5 Sample Program 15B: Report Writer with SORT Feature   273
  Exercises   276

Chapter 16   Additional Features

16.1 COPY Statement   277
16.2 GO TO . . . DEPENDING Statement   280
16.3 ALTER Statement   280
16.4 Subprograms   281
16.5 Sample Program 16A: COBOL Main Program to Call a Subprogram   282
  Exercises   286

Chapter 17   Structured Programming

17.1 Why We Need Structured Programming: Program Correctness and Readability   287
17.2 The Three Basic Control Structures   288
17.3 Basic Rules of Structured Programming   289
17.4 Sample Program 17A: A Structured Program   289
  References   291

Appendix A   ENVIRONMENT DIVISIONS for Various Systems

Burroughs 5500   292
Control Data 6400, 6500, 6600   293
Honeywell 200   293
IBM 360/370   293
IBM 1130   294
UNIVAC 1106, 1108   295
XDS Sigma   295
RCA Spectra 70   295

Appendix B   Job Control Statements for IBM 360/370 Systems

B.1 Job Control Statements for OS   296
B.2 Compiling and Executing a COBOL Program under OS   300

B.3 DD Statements for Processing Disk Files under OS   304
B.4 Job Control Statements for DOS   306

Appendix C COBOL Reserved Words   309

Appendix D Standard COBOL Statements for IBM 360/370 Systems   312

Appendix E Revision of ANS COBOL: COBOL 1968 versus COBOL 1974   317

Appendix F Operating the IBM 029 Keypunching Machine   319

Glossary   323

Solutions to Selected Exercises   331

Index   336

List of Sample Programs

I FUNDAMENTALS

1. 1A Cards to Printer 19
2. 1B Address Labels 24
3. 4A Overdue Payment Notice 56
4. 5A Customer Address Listing 74
5. 5B 80/80 Card Listing (ACCEPT and DISPLAY Statements) 77
6. 5C Page Heading, Current Date, and Page Number 79
7. 6A Weekly Charge Account Summary Report 95
8. 6B Minimum Payment Notices 98
9. 7A Daily Sales Report 118
10. 7B Weekly Payroll Report 122
11. 7C Checking Account Report 126
12. 8A Weekly Payroll with Tax Routine 145
13. 8B Salesman Commission Computation 148
14. 8C Purchase Analysis Report 153
15. 9A Creating Hourly Rate Table from Punched Cards 159
16. 9B Salesman Commission Computation with Rate Table 171
17. 10A Depreciation Schedules 184
18. 10B Student Test Scores Computation 189

II ADVANCED TOPICS

19. 11A Creating a Variable-Length Tape File 211
20. 12A COBOL SORT Feature with USING/GIVING Option 217
21. 12B COBOL SORT Feature with INPUT/OUTPUT Procedure Options 220
22. 13A Debugging with TRACE Statement 233
23. 13B Debugging with Exhibit Statement 234
24. 13C Debugging with ON Statement 240
25. 14A Creating a Direct File 249
26. 14B Updating a Direct File 251
27. 14C Creating an Indexed Sequential File 255
28. 14D Sequential Access of Indexed Files 257
29. 14E Random Updating an ISAM File 259
30. 15A Report Writer 271

31. 15B   Report Writer with SORT Feature   273
32. Setting Up a COBOL Copy Library   279
33. 16A   COBOL Main Program to Call a Subprogram   282
34. 17A   A Sturctured Program   289

Preface

This book is intended to be an introductory textbook on computer programming. It covers all the important features of Standard COBOL developed by the American National Standard Institute (ANSI). The text may be used in either an introductory course in business information processing as the language text or as a regular text for a course in the COBOL language itself.

The approach used in this text is to introduce the student gradually and systematically to COBOL. One of our primary objectives is to present the materials so that students can begin to write programs as soon as possible with a minimum of confusion. To accomplish this objective, we have presented two complete sample programs in Chapter 1. One program includes a line-by-line detailed explanation. The reader is strongly urged to study these programs, keypunch them, and run them on a computer as early as possible.

The book is divided into two parts. Part I (Chapters 0–10) covers the basic elements and fundamental features of the COBOL language, including data manipulation, editing, calculation, logic, table handling, and loops, with emphasis on punched-card input and printed-report output. The presentation is geared directly to beginners with no prior programming experience. As each element of the COBOL language is introduced, its nature is explained together with ample illustrations. This is further supplemented by thirty-four completed sample programs with written explanations. These programs serve as indispensable tools for digesting the text materials. One of the quickest ways to learn how to write a COBOL program is to study these sample programs and actually run them on the computer.

Part II (Chapters 11–17) covers a broad spectrum of more advanced programming topics, including magnetic tape processing, files on direct-access devices (for example, BDAM and ISAM), sorting, searching, COPY library, subprogram linkage, and debugging languages. These topics are organized as a collection of building blocks, and may be read independently.

Also included is a chapter on structured programming, which has become one of the most important topics in computer programming. However, since this is basically an introductory text, our discussion is concise and strictly from the COBOL programmer's point of view. The interested reader is urged to consult the references listed at the end of the chapter for further study.

Although Standard COBOL is designed to be applicable to any particular computer system, there are some COBOL features that are hardware dependent. In such cases the IBM System/360 and System/370 are used as the examples. Some hardware-dependent features are explained for Burroughs, CDC, Honeywell, RCA, and UNIVAC in an appendix. Also included in the appendixes are job control statements for OS and DOS operating systems, a complete reserved words list, ANS COBOL statement and instruction formats. A glossary is also included. These materials will provide a quick and comprehensive reference for the COBOL language.

Acknowledgments

The following information is reprinted from COBOL Edition 1965, published by the Conference on Data Systems Languages (CODASYL), and printed by the U.S. Government Printing Office:

Any organization interested in reproducing the COBOL report and specifications in whole or in part, using ideas taken from this report as the basis for an instruction manual or for any other purpose is free to do so. However, all such organizations are requested to reproduce this section as part of the introduction to the document. Those using a short passage, as in a book review, are requested to mention "COBOL" in acknowledgment of the source, but need not quote this entire section.

COBOL is an industry language and is not the property of any company or group of companies, or of any organization or group of organizations.

No warranty, expressed or implied, is made by any contributor or by the COBOL Committee as to the accuracy and functioning of the programming system and language. Moreover, no responsibility is assumed by any contributor, or by the committee, in connection therewith.

Procedures have been established for the maintenance of COBOL. Inquiries concerning the procedures for proposing changes should be directed to the Executive Committee of the Conference on Data Systems Languages.

The authors and copyright holders of the copyrighted material used herein:

FLOWMATIC (Trademark of Sperry Rand Corporation), Programming for the Univac (R) I and II, Data Automation Systems copyrighted 1958, 1959, by Sperry Rand Corporation; IBM Commercial Translator Form No. F28-8013, copyrighted 1959 by IBM; FACT, DSI 27A5260-2760, copyrighted 1960 by Minneapolis-Honeywell

have specifically authorized the use of this material in whole or in part, in the COBOL specifications. Such authorization extends to the reproduction and use of COBOL specifications in programming manuals of similar publications.

Our thanks to the IBM Corporation for granting permission to reprint Figures 0.1, 0.3, 0.4, 0.5, 0.6, 14.1, 14.2, 14.4, 14.5, E.2, and parts of the descriptions for Figures 14.6, 14.9, 14.10, 14.11, and 14.12; Hewlett Packard for permission to reprint Figure 0.2; and Interdata Corp. for permission to reprint Fig. 0.3c.

We also wish to thank Robert Smith, who contributed greatly to the chapters on debugging and direct-access devices; Lester Thierwechter, Frances Palmieri, Gary Scarcella, Thomas Fritsche, Glen Scabet, Mike Homaychak, Mark Fistes, John McGrath, and Tim Daly, who programmed various test problems; and Stan Benton, Donald Carver, George Gugel, Thomas McConnell, Gus Mutter, Steve O'Conner, Dale Washburn, Ted Williamson, Walt Westphal, and Vernon Zander, who have read individual sections of this book and given freely of their time for comment and criticism.

Finally, our special thanks to Sylvia Ann Chai for her encouragement and invaluable assistance, to the staff of Academic Press for their overall editorial assistance, and to Mrs. Mary Laverack and Richard Laroy for their efforts in typing the manuscript.

Part I
Fundamentals

0
Preliminary: Basic Concepts of Computers

Before one can learn how to write computer programs, he must have some basic knowledge about computers. This chapter provides the minimum background needed before actually starting to write programs. If the reader has some prior knowledge in data processing, he can simply browse through this chapter and go directly to Chapter 1.

0.1 THE COMPUTER SYSTEM

A computer, in a general sense, is a collection of electronic devices that can accept information, perform calculations or manipulate data, and produce results.

There are many types of computer systems, varying in size, speed, and application. Figure 0.1 presents a typical computer system—IBM system 370. However, regardless of the type of computer used, in general there are three basic components in a computer system:

input/output devices,
storage or memory unit,
central processing unit (CPU).

The functional diagram Fig. 0.2 illustrates the interrelationships of these components.

Input/Output Devices

The input/output devices are used to transfer information between the external world and the computer. Generally these devices can be classified into four groups:

unit record devices,
serial devices,
direct-access devices,
miscellaneous devices.

4   0 Preliminary: Basic Concepts of Computers

Fig. 0.1   IBM 370 computer system.

Unit record devices include card readers, card punches, and line printers as shown in Fig. 0.3. These devices are characterized by the fact that information is processed one unit at a time, such as "read one punched card" or "print one line."

Unit record devices operate at relatively slow speeds. For instance, the average card reader can process about 600 80-column cards per minute (that is, 48,000 characters per minute or 800 characters per second). Despite such slow speeds, punched cards still play an indispensable role in a computer system. The description of punched cards is presented in Section 0.4.

Serial devices include magnetic tape units and paper tape units. In a serial device, information must be processed in a specific sequence. For instance, in a magnetic tape unit, the computer must start from the beginning of a tape reel to access the desired record, even though such a record might be located near the end of the tape reel.

A magnetic tape unit as shown in Fig. 0.4 has been used by many installations as a faster medium of input/output than punched cards. Magnetic tape units read or write at speeds ranging from 15,000 to over 300,000 characters per second.

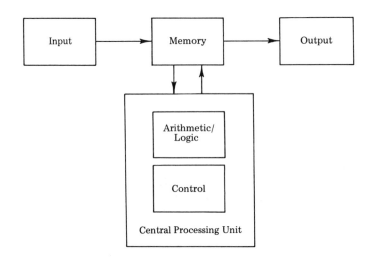

Fig. 0.2   Basic functional diagram of a computer.

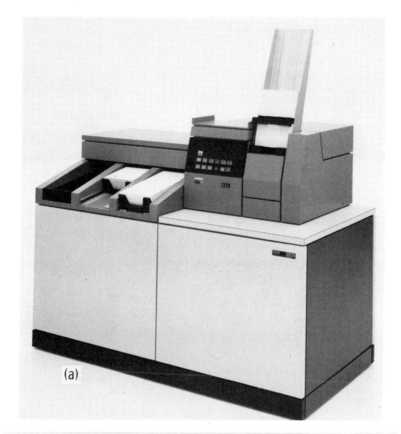

Fig. 0.3 (a) IBM 3505 card reader. (b) IBM 3525 card punch. (c) Interdata printer (courtesy of Interdata Corp.).

6   0   Preliminary: Basic Concepts of Computers

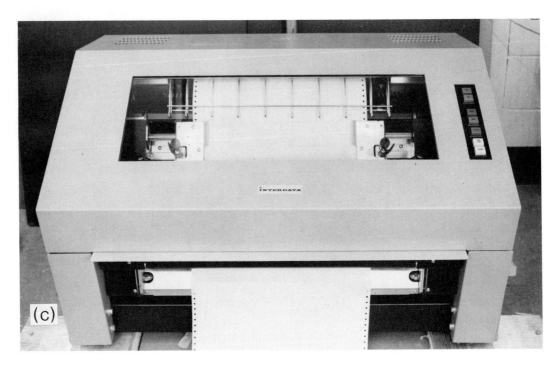

Fig. 0.3 (continued)

Fig. 0.4 HP magnetic tape unit (courtesy of Hewlett-Packard).

Fig. 0.5 IBM 3330 disk facility.

Direct-access devices include disk storage units (see Fig. 0.5) and drum storage units. These devices are characterized by the fact that information can be accessed directly by the computer regardless of how it was stored.

Direct-access devices have become increasingly the most common storage systems in use for processing a large volume of data. The real advantages of direct-access devices are speed in accessing records coupled with an almost "limitless" capacity (see Chapter 14 for a detailed description).

Miscellaneous devices include keyboard terminals, cathode ray tubes (CRT; see Fig. 0.6), and audioresponse units. Each device has characteristics of its own. The interested reader should consult appropriate publications for further information. (References are given at the end of this chapter.)

Main Storage—Core Memory

The main storage unit is used to store instructions or data while they are being processed. The most commonly used devices are magnetic cores, integrated circuits, and data cells.

The capacity of the main storage unit is the most frequently used measure of the computer's size. A standard unit of measurement is the number of bytes or number of words. Generally a byte can hold one character, whereas a word can hold several characters of information.

Modern computers can have a main storage unit anywhere up to 800 million bytes (that is, 800,000K bytes). Generally the larger the storage capacity, the more powerful the computer.

Fig. 0.6 IBM 2250 display unit.

Central Processing Unit (CPU)

The central processing unit (CPU) is considered the "brain" or "nerve center" of a computer system. The CPU is divided into two components:

(a) The arithmetic and logic unit, which performs operations such as addition, subtraction, multiplication, division, and comparison.
(b) The control unit, which monitors various input/output devices, the main storage (for example, that determines which instruction should be executed next), and the arithmetic-logic unit. The control unit essentially functions as a "coordinator" for the entire computer system.

Processing speed within the CPU is remarkably fast. The time required for processing instructions in the modern computer is often measured in terms of microseconds (one millionth of a second) or even nanoseconds (one billionth of a second). As a consequence, today's computers can solve the type of problems that would have been impossible twenty years ago because of the staggering amount of calculations involved.

0.2 PROGRAMS AND PROGRAMMING LANGUAGES

A program is a set of instructions that directs a computer to process data and produce desired results. A programming language is the notation in which a program is written. There are three types of programming languages:

machine languages,
assembly level languages,
higher level languages.

Machine languages are written in the machine code. The computer can interpret and execute these codes directly.

Since each type of computer has a unique set of machine codes, a program written in one machine language cannot be executed by another computer. Machine languages are difficult and tedious to learn.

Assembly level languages are similar to machine languages except that they are made up of mnemonics consisting of one through four characters. For instance, the number 16 may represent the machine code for adding. The same instruction in an assembly level language may be written as ADD or A.

Each computer has its own assembly level language. Programs written in one assembly level language for one machine usually cannot be executed by another machine.

Generally speaking, for a specific computer the assembly program is the most efficient type of program that can be executed. However, the greatest drawback of these languages is that they are machine dependent and rather difficult to learn.

Higher level languages are for the most part machine independent. Programs written in this type of language for one machine can be executed by another computer with a minimum of modification. In general, a single program statement in a higher level language generates many machine instructions. Thus, higher level languages are relatively easy to learn and allow the programmer to concentrate on the problem he is solving. Some well-known higher level languages are

FORTRAN,
COBOL,
RPG,
PL/I.

FORTRAN (*formula translation*) has been used primarily for solving mathematical or engineering problems. It is one of the oldest computer languages in use. FORTRAN statements closely resemble mathematical notations (see Fig. 0.7 for illustration).

COBOL (*common business oriented language*) is designed for commercial applications. The language is very similar to English. For example,

ADD NEW-INTEREST TO BALANCE.

is a typical COBOL statement that anyone can read and understand. Thus, most of the COBOL programs are self-documenting and easy to understand.

Higher level languages	Assembly level language		Machine code language		
	Instructions	Comments			
COBOL	L 5, M	Load register 5 with M	5850	CODE	0010
ADD M TO N, GIVING K.	A 5, N	Add N to register 5	5A50	C012	0014
	ST 5, K	Store register 5 to K	5050	C016	0018
FORTRAN					
	M DS F	Reserve a full word	0010		
K = M + N	N DS F		0014		
	K DS F		0018		

Fig. 0.7 A sample of program instructions.

RPG (report program generator) is designed to generate printed reports from the processing of large-scale business data with a minimum programming effort by the user. This language is suitable for routine business reports and small computers.

PL/I (programming language one) is a comparatively new language that incorporates a great number of features from both FORTRAN and COBOL. PL/I is a multipurpose language that can adequately handle both commercial and mathematical applications.

A program written in a higher level language or assembly level language is referred to as the source program. A source program must be translated into a machine language code program (which is referred to as the object program) before the computer can understand it and thus execute it. Such translation is done by a language translator, which is supplied by the computer manufacturer.

0.3 FLOWCHARTS

To develop a program the programmer must make a complete analysis of the problem to be programmed. This analysis is normally accomplished by developing flowcharts. There are basically two types of flowcharts: system flowcharts and program flowcharts.

System Flowcharts

The system flowchart provides a schematic diagram showing the input and output and the required processing from the point of view of what is to be accomplished. Figure 0.8 presents a system flowchart depicting the operation involved in a simplified version of a weekly payroll process. Notice that this chart indicates only the input (that is, employee time card), processing sequence (that is, sort first, then execute payroll program), and output (that is, weekly payroll report and employee paycheck). The system flowchart only shows what sequences of operations are to be performed, and not how these operations are to be performed.

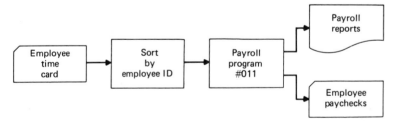

Fig. 0.8 System flowchart for a simplified version of payroll processing.

Program Flowcharts

The program flowchart is the "blueprint" of a program. It provides a picture of the problem solution and the problem logic that specifies the exact processing sequence.

Figure 0.9 presents part of a program flowchart for processing a weekly payroll. Notice that this chart is much more detailed than the system flowchart. In fact, the program flowchart is the final step before the actual programming. If the program flowchart is constructed correctly, the actual effort of programming is nothing more than writing on coding sheets what has already been specified on the flowchart.

0.3 Flowcharts 11

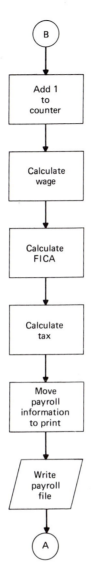

Fig. 0.9 Part of program flowchart for payroll processing.

Standard Flowchart Symbols

To promote standardization in flowcharts, standard symbols have been adopted by the American National Standard Institute (ANSI). The following is a list of symbols used in this text with their meanings.

System flowchart symbol	Meaning
▱	File: a collection of data records stored on punched cards
⌒	File: a collection of data records stored on on-line storage such as magnetic disk or drum

File: a collection of data records stored on magnetic tape

Report: printed by the computer

Computer program

Program flowchart symbol	Meaning
	Terminal point: beginning or ending of a program
	Process: a single operation or group of operations such as computation or data transfer performed by the computer
	Input/output: all input and output operations such as reading a punched card or printing on a line
	Decision: a question, decision comparison, or number of alternative paths for the program to follow depending on the result of the decision, question, or comparison
	Connector: the continuation of data flow to another part of the flowchart, or the entry point of a data flow
	Flow: the direction of data flow
	Conditional flow: the direction of data flow depending on the fulfillment of certain conditions
	Predefined process: one or more named operations or program steps specified as subprograms or procedures

0.4 PUNCHED CARDS

The punched card is the most commonly used input medium for data processing. It has played an indispensable role in rapid data processing ever since its invention in the late 1800s. There are several types of punched cards, the most commonly used being the 80-column IBM card.

0.4 Punched Cards 13

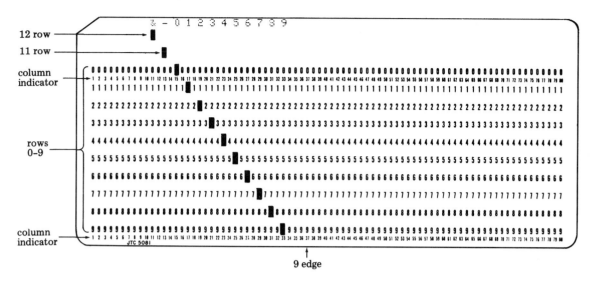

Fig. 0.10 IBM 80-column card.

The IBM cards contain 80 vertical columns, each of which has twelve possible punching positions. The top edge of the card is known as the 12 edge, while the bottom is referred to as the 9 edge (see Fig. 0.10).

Every card is divided into two major sections. The upper three vertical positions are known as the zone punches and contain holes in the 0, 11, and 12 positions of the column. (This is why the top edge of the card is known as the 12 edge.) The lower section of the card contains the numerical digits 0 through 9, known as the numerical punches.

The zone and numerical punches are combined to represent alphabetic characters or special symbols. These are illustrated in Fig. 0.11.

This method of combining different punches to represent characters in a punched card is known as the Hollerith code, after Herman Hollerith, who introduced the use of punched cards in the late 1800s.

In addition to the 80-column cards, IBM also uses 96-column punched cards. This type of card contains two sections. The lower section is the punch area, while the upper section is the print area. Ninety-six column cards are designed specifically for the smaller types of computer systems such as the IBM System/3 computer series. They are not widely used.

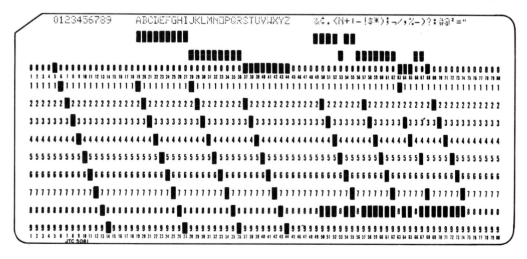

Fig. 0.11 Numerical and alphabetic characters.

EXERCISES

1. Briefly explain the various functional units of a computer.

2. Define the following terms:
   unit record devices
   direct-access devices
   serial devices

3. Name two devices that can be used as both input and output units.

4. What is a computer program? A programming language?

5. Briefly explain the difference between machine language, assembly language, and higher level language.

6. Describe briefly the IBM 80-column cards.

7. Explain the difference between
   (a) an object program and a source program,
   (b) a system flowchart and a program flowchart.

REFERENCES

Davis, G. B. "An Introduction to Electronic Computers." McGraw-Hill, New York, 1974.
IBM Corp. "Introduction to IBM Data Processing Systems," Student text No. GC20-168R-3. White Plains, New York, 1972.
Rothman, S., and Mosmann, C. "Computers and Society." Science Research Association, Chicago, Illinois, 1972.
Silver, G. A., and Silver, J. B. "Data Processing for Business." Harcourt, New York, 1973.
Weiss, E. A., ed. "Computer Usage Fundamentals." McGraw-Hill, New York, 1969.

1

Introduction to COBOL Programming

1.1 ANS COBOL

COBOL (Common Business Oriented Language) was developed under the auspices of the U.S. Department of Defense in cooperation with computer manufacturers, computer users, and universities.

The initial specifications for COBOL were presented in a report of the executive committee of the Conference on Data Systems Language (CODASYL) in April 1960. It was designed to be business problem oriented, machine independent, and capable of continuous change and development.

Since 1960, COBOL has undergone considerable refinement by the repeated efforts of the CODASYL committee. It has certainly emerged as the leading data processing language in the business world. In 1968, American National Standard Institute (ANSI), an industry-wide association of computer manufacturers and users approved a standard COBOL language. The standard language has specifications at three levels—low, middle, and high—so that standard COBOL can be implemented on computers of varying sizes. This standard is called ANS COBOL (American National Standard COBOL).

Despite the attempts at standardization, variations from one computer's COBOL to another's still exist. Most of these deviations are designed to take advantage of some feature of the hardware that is not provided for by the ANS specification. However, the trend is toward stricter application of the ANS specifications.

1.2 COBOL SYSTEM: LANGUAGE AND COMPILER

Every COBOL system consists of two main elements: the COBOL language and a COBOL compiler. COBOL language is one of the higher level computer languages. Since this language is problem oriented and relatively machine independent, it has little resemblance to machine language. Thus, programs written in COBOL (known as source programs) must be translated to produce machine language programs (known as object programs) before they can be executed by the computer.

Such translation is performed by the COBOL compiler, which is a special set of programs. It is usually written, supplied, and maintained by the computer manufacturer. The main function of the compiler is to translate a COBOL program into a machine language program.

1.3 COBOL PROGRAM STRUCTURE

Every COBOL program is organized into four separate and distinct divisions, in the following order:

IDENTIFICATION DIVISION
ENVIRONMENT DIVISION
DATA DIVISION
PROCEDURE DIVISION

IDENTIFICATION DIVISION

The function of the IDENTIFICATION DIVISION is to identify the program and to provide other information such as who wrote the program, when the program was written, and program descriptions. It is the simplest of all four divisions to write (see Fig. 1.1).

ENVIRONMENT DIVISION

The ENVIRONMENT DIVISION is the one division that is machine dependent. In this division the programmer describes the kind of computer he wants to compile and run (that is, execute) the program. This division also relates the program's data files to specific computer input and output devices (see Fig. 1.2). (A file is a collection of related data records; it will be discussed at length in Chapter 4.)

Thus, the ENVIRONMENT DIVISION may have two sections: the CONFIGURATION SECTION, which identifies the source and object computers, and the INPUT-OUTPUT SECTION, which assigns data files to input–output devices.

DATA DIVISION

The DATA DIVISION provides a detailed description of all input–output data files that are to be processed in the program. In essence, all input–output files named in the ENVIRONMENT DIVISION must be defined and described there (see Fig. 1.3).

```
IDENTIFICATION DIVISION.
PROGRAM-ID. 'PAYROLL'
AUTHOR. HENRY CHAI.
REMARKS. THIS PROGRAM PREPARES WEEKLY PAYROLL
         REPORT FOR MARCINKO-CHAI ASSOC.
DATE-WRITTEN. OCTOBER, 1973.
```

Fig. 1.1 Example of IDENTIFICATION DIVISION.

```
SEQUENCE   A   B
           ENVIRONMENT DIVISION.
           CONFIGURATION SECTION.
           SOURCE-COMPUTER.    IBM-370.
           OBJECT-COMPUTER.    IBM-370.
           INPUT-OUTPUT SECTION.
           FILE-CONTROL.
               SELECT CARD-IN
                   ASSIGN TO UR-2540R-S-INFILE.
               SELECT PRINT-OUT
                   ASSIGN TO UR-1403-S-PROUT.
```

Fig. 1.2 Example of ENVIRONMENT DIVISION.

```
SEQUENCE   A   B
           DATA DIVISION.
           FILE SECTION.
           FD  CARD-IN
               LABEL RECORD ARE OMITTED,
               DATA RECORD IS PAYROLL-CARD-REC.
           01  PAYROLL-CARD-REC.
               05 EMPLOYEE-NAME    PICTURE X(30).
               05 HOURLY-RATE      PICTURE 999V99.
               05 HOURS-WORKED     PICTURE 999V99.
               05 FILLER           PICTURE X(40).
           FD  PRINT-FILE
               LABEL RECORDS ARE OMITTED,
               DATA RECORDS IS PRINT-AREA.
           01  PRINT-AREA          PICTURE X(133).
           WORKING-STORAGE SECTION.
           77  CARD-COUNT          PICTURE 999 VALUE ZEROS.
```

Fig. 1.3 Example of DATA DIVISION.

In addition to file descriptions of input/output data, work areas for storing intermediate results and constants that will be used in the program also must be defined and described in the WORKING-STORAGE SECTION of this division.

PROCEDURE DIVISION

The PROCEDURE DIVISION contains commands and instructions that are required to solve a particular set of problems. The division is written much like ordinary English composition and usually consists of several paragraphs. (These are identified by the paragraph name, which is supplied by the programmer.) Each paragraph contains several sentences.

The names of the data fields defined in the DATA DIVISION are used to write sentences. The "verbs" of these sentences are selected from a special collection of COBOL reserved program verbs (see Appendix C). These program verbs form commands to direct the computer's activity. (In Fig. 1.4 they are OPEN, MOVE, and READ.)

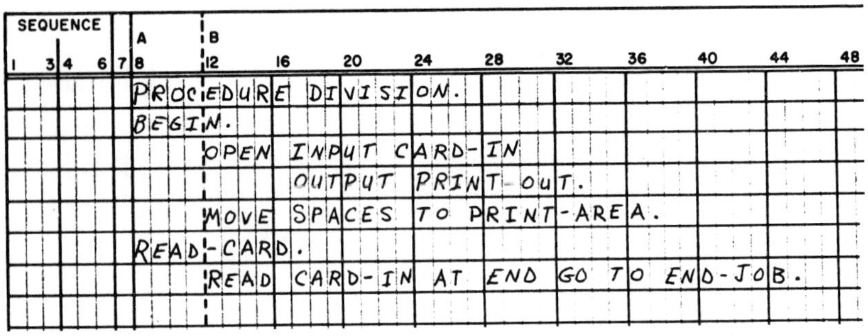

```
SEQUENCE   A   B
1  3 4  6 7 8   12  16  20  24  28  32  36  40  44  48
       PROCEDURE DIVISION.
       BEGIN.
           OPEN INPUT CARD-IN
                OUTPUT PRINT-OUT.
           MOVE SPACES TO PRINT-AREA.
       READ-CARD.
           READ CARD-IN AT END GO TO END-JOB.
```

Fig. 1.4 Example of PROCEDURE DIVISION.

1.4 COBOL CODING SHEET

The COBOL coding sheet (Fig. 1.5) provides the programmer with a standard method of writing COBOL source programs. The coding sheet is designed in such a way that each line of the coding sheet is used to record information that can be readily keypunched into a standard 80-column card. However, the format is not limited to cards. One can also key in the coded information directly to magnetic tape or paper tape if such devices are available.

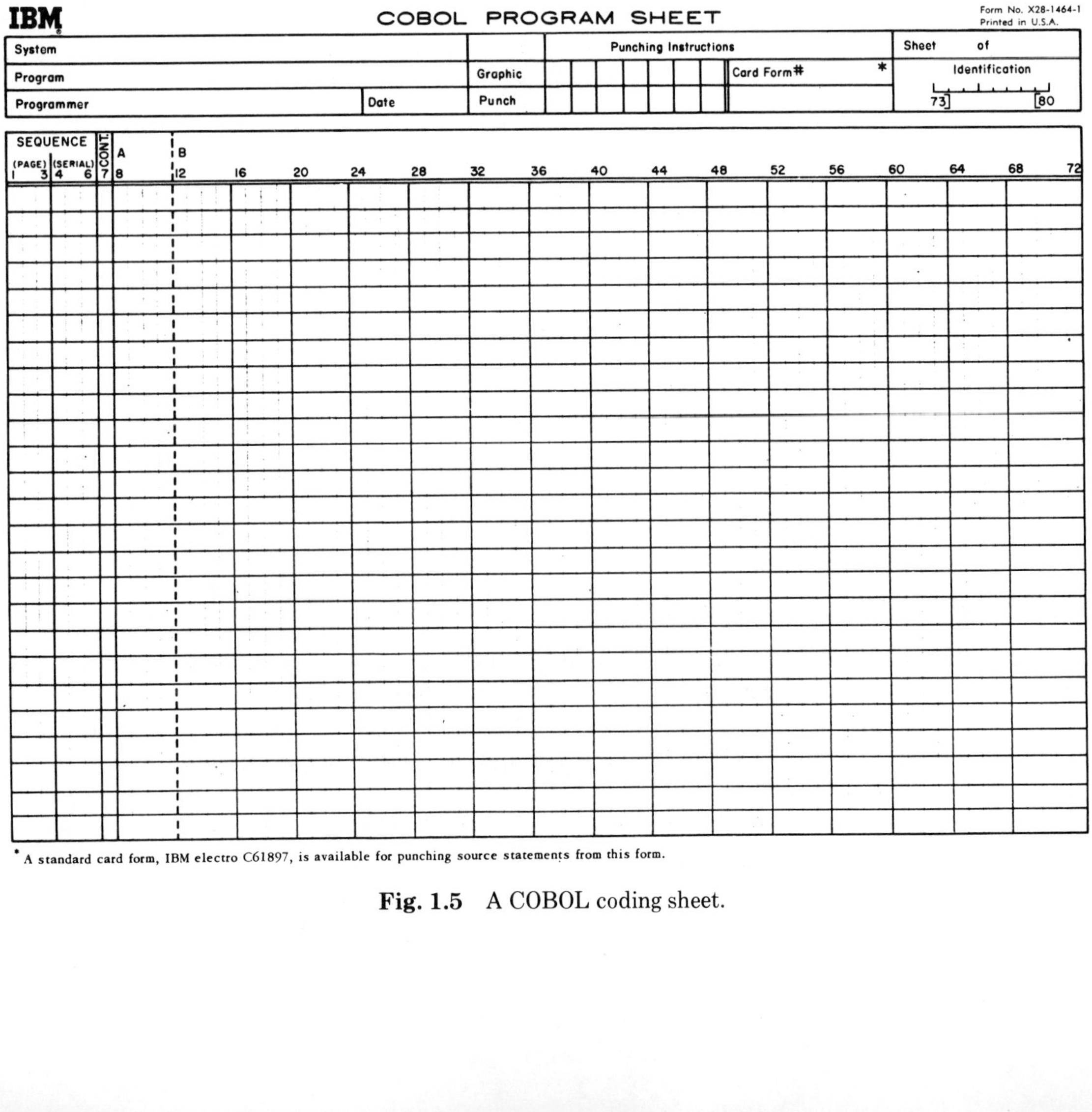

IBM COBOL PROGRAM SHEET Form No. X28-1464-1 Printed in U.S.A.

System | Punching Instructions | Sheet of
Program | Graphic | Card Form # * | Identification
Programmer | Date | Punch | 73 80

SEQUENCE (PAGE) (SERIAL) 1 3 4 6 | CONT. 7 | A 8 | B 12 16 20 24 28 32 36 40 44 48 52 56 60 64 68 72

* A standard card form, IBM electro C61897, is available for punching source statements from this form.

Fig. 1.5 A COBOL coding sheet.

Sequence Number (1–6)

The sequence number is written in columns 1 through 6 of the card. It is used to identify the relative position of each card in the source program. The use of the sequence number is optional, but if sequence numbers are present, they must be arranged in ascending order since, in this case, the compiler will perform a sequence check and indicate any error if the sequence is out of order. However, no sequence check will be performed if the field is left blank.

Continuation Indicator (7)

If two lines are needed to record literal (numeric and nonnumeric) information, a hyphen must be placed in column 7 of the continuation line. (A literal is an actual value used somewhere in a COBOL program. Literals are discussed fully in Chapter 4.)

Program Statement (8–72)

Columns 8 through 72 are used for writing the COBOL source statements. These columns are grouped into the A-margin (columns 8–11) and B-margin (columns 12–72).

There are some definite rules for margin entries. These rules will be presented later. However, if an entry must begin in A-margin, it may overflow into B-margin. If an entry is to be coded in B-margin, it may begin anywhere after column 11, within columns 12–72.

Identification Code (73–80)

Columns 73 through 80 are reserved for the program identification code. This code is assigned by the programmer to identify cards as belonging to a particular program. The identification code has no effect on the program.

Comment Line

Comments can be written anywhere in the source program. They are identified by writing an asterisk (*) in column 7 of the coding sheet.

1.5 A SIMPLE COBOL PROGRAM (SAMPLE PROGRAM 1A)

Before discussing the details of the COBOL language, we will illustrate how a COBOL program is written by presenting a simple program. This program will read a deck of cards and list each data card on the printer. At the end of the last data card it will print out the total number of cards that have been processed. The program logic, source listing, and sample output for this sample program follow.

Program Logic

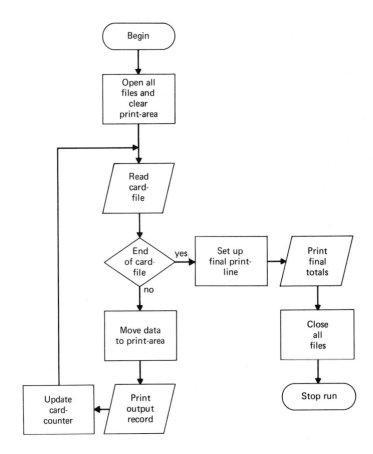

Source Listing

```
00001           IDENTIFICATION DIVISION.
00002           PROGRAM-ID.  'SAMPL1A'
00003           AUTHOR.   W.A.CHAI.
00004           REMARKS.  THIS PROGRAM READS A DECK OF CARDS,
00005                     THEN LISTS EACH DATA CARD ON PRINTER.
00006           DATE-WRITTEN.   NOV. 1973.
00007      ****************************************************************
00008           ENVIRONMENT DIVISION.
00009           CONFIGURATION SECTION.
00010           SOURCE-COMPUTER.  IBM-370.
00011           OBJECT-COMPUTER.  IBM-370.
00012           INPUT-OUTPUT SECTION.
00013           FILE-CONTROL.
00014               SELECT CARD-FILE  ASSIGN TO UR-2501-S-CARDIN.
00015               SELECT PRINT-FILE ASSIGN TO UR-1403-S-PRINT.
00016      ****************************************************************
00017           DATA DIVISION.
00018           FILE SECTION.
00019           FD  CARD-FILE
00020               LABEL RECORDS ARE OMITTED,
00021               DATA RECORD IS CARD-REC.
00022           01  CARD-REC      PICTURE  X(80).
00023           FD  PRINT-FILE
00024               LABEL RECORDS ARE OMITTED,
00025               DATA RECORDS IS PRINT-AREA.
00026           01  PRINT-AREA.
00027               05  FILLER    PICTURE  X(21).
00028               05  CARD-PRINT    PICTURE  X(80).
00029           WORKING-STORAGE SECTION.
00030           77  CARD-COUNTER PICTURE 9999 VALUE ZEROS.
00031           01  FINAL-PRINT-LINE.
00032               05 FILLER PICTURE X(10) VALUE SPACES.
00033               05 MESSAGE   PICTURE X(25) VALUE 'TOTAL NUMBER OF CARDS IS'.
00034               05 FILLER   PICTURE X(5) VALUE SPACES.
00035               05 COUNTER-P  PICTURE ZZZ9.
00036      ****************************************************************
```

1.5 A Simple COBOL Program (Sample Program 1A)

```
00037          PROCEDURE DIVISION.
00038          BEGIN.
00039              OPEN INPUT CARD-FILE, OUTPUT PRINT-FILE.
00040              MOVE SPACES TO PRINT-AREA.
00041          READ-CARDS.
00042              READ CARD-FILE AT END GO TO END-JOB.
00043              MOVE CARD-REC  TO CARD-PRINT.
00044              WRITE PRINT-AREA AFTER ADVANCING 1 LINES.
00045              ADD 1 TO CARD-COUNTER.
00046              GO TO READ-CARDS.
00047          END-JOB.
00048              MOVE SPACES TO PRINT-AREA.
00049              MOVE CARD-COUNTER TO COUNTER-P.
00050              MOVE FINAL-PRINT-LINE TO PRINT-AREA.
00051              WRITE PRINT-AREA AFTER ADVANCING 3 LINES.
00052              CLOSE CARD-FILE PRINT-FILE.
00053              STOP RUN.
```

Sample Output

```
BROWN, CHARLIE       99 LOSER STREET       KEARNY, N.J. 37352       2500  11/11/75
MARCINKO, GEORGE    125 OAK STREET         NEWTON,N.Y. 10014        3496  10/11/75
CHAI W A            121 LAKE STREET        MONTCLAIR NJ 07043       1468  12/31/75
CASH, JOHN K         69 WEB PLACE          BRONX,N.Y. 10052         1112  12/13/75
```
} blank cards

```
     IF YOU ARE READING THESE WORDS THAT MEANS THAT YOUR PROGRAM RAN.
     AT THIS POINT I AM VERY GLAD TO SEE THAT I AM FINISHED WITH IT.
THIS IS THE 9TH TIME I HAVE HANDED IT IN.

TOTAL NUMBER OF CARDS IS          10
```

Step 1: IDENTIFICATION DIVISION

The first step is to complete the program identification and description. This can be accomplished in the following manner:

```
        IDENTIFICATION DIVISION.
        PROGRAM-ID. 'SAMPL1A'
        AUTHOR. W. A. CHAI.
        REMARKS. THIS PROGRAM READS A DECK OF CARDS,
                 THEN LISTS EACH DATA CARD ON PRINTER.
        DATE-WRITTEN. NOV. 1973.
```

Here we observe that in this division we give a name to the program (that is, 'SAMPL1A'), the name of the programmer, the date the program was written, and other information that documents the program (that is, under REMARKS.) Words such as PROGRAM-ID, AUTHOR, REMARKS, and DATE-WRITTEN are COBOL reserved, whereas the rest of the words are supplied by the programmer.

Step 2: ENVIRONMENT DIVISION

First we describe the type of computer that will be used to translate and execute the program:

```
        ENVIRONMENT DIVISION.
        CONFIGURATION SECTION.
        SOURCE-COMPUTER. IBM-370.
        OBJECT-COMPUTER. IBM-370.
```

Next, we identify the data files to be used in our program and assign them to specific input/output devices:

```
           INPUT-OUTPUT SECTION.
           FILE CONTROL.
               SELECT CARD-FILE ASSIGN TO UR-2501-S-CARDIN.
               SELECT PRINT-FILE ASSIGN TO UR-1403-S-PRINT.
```

The above set of statements informs the COBOL compiler that a data file identified as CARD-FILE will be read by the IBM 2501 card reader, and an output file identified as PRINT-FILE will be printed out on the IBM 1403 printer.

Step 3: DATA DIVISION

In this division, the programmer must give a detailed description of the data file to be read or written during the execution of the program:

```
       DATA DIVISION.
       FILE SECTION.
       FD  CARD-FILE
           LABEL RECORDS ARE OMITTED,
           DATA RECORD IS CARD-REC.
       01  CARD-REC     PICTURE X(80).
       FD  PRINT-FILE.
           LABEL RECORDS ARE OMITTED
           DATA RECORDS IS PRINT-AREA.
           PRINT-AREA.
           05  FILLER      PICTURE X(21).
           05  CARD-PRINT  PICTURE X(80).
```

The FD (that is, file description) paragraph spells out the nature of the entire data file. The individual record descriptions begin with entry 01, followed by data names such as CARD-REC and PRINT-AREA. (These names are supplied by the programmer.) The PICTURE clauses describe the contents of the data records. For instance, X(80) specifies that the data record is 80 characters in length.

Next, the programmer must specify areas of storages where literal constants and intermediate results are stored during the program execution time:

```
       WORKING-STORAGE SECTION.
       77  CARD-COUNTER PICTURE 9999 VALUE ZEROS.
       01  FINAL-PRINT-LINE.
           05 FILLER    PICTURE X(10) VALUE SPACES.
           05 MESSAGE   PICTURE X(25) VALUE 'TOTAL NUMBER OF CARDS IS'.
           05 FILLER    PICTURE X(5)  VALUE SPACES.
           05 COUNTER-P PICTURE ZZZ9.
```

The above WORKING-STORAGE SECTION coding informs the computer to set aside four positions (bytes) of core memory for the CARD-COUNTER and 44 positions for the FINAL-PRINT-LINE. In addition, the value clauses in the coding "initialize" the storage area as specified. Words such as ZEROS and SPACES are COBOL reserved words to indicate that a particular working area should be set to zeros or blanks before execution of the program instruction.

Step 4: PROCEDURE DIVISION

This division, as we said earlier, contains the actual program commands and instructions that are required to complete our objective. The first step here is to prepare the input/output devices for processing. This is accomplished by utilizing the program verb OPEN. Following this statement, we usually clear our output area (or any other areas set aside for special use). This process is called initialization, which is accomplished by the MOVE statement as shown below:

```
        PROCEDURE DIVISION.
        BEGIN.
            OPEN INPUT CARD-FILE, OUTPUT PRINT-FILE.
            MOVE SPACES TO PRINT-AREA.
```

Once initialization is completed, we are ready to read data cards, move the information to the print area, and print it. However, before we go back to read more data cards, we increase the card-count by 1, so that we can keep track of the number of cards being processed. We identify this part of the routine under the paragraph name READ-CARDS:

```
        READ-CARDS.
            READ CARD-FILE AT END GO TO END-JOB.
            MOVE CARD-REC TO CARD-PRINT.
            WRITE PRINT-AREA AFTER ADVANCING 1 LINES.
            ADD 1 TO CARD-COUNTER.
            GO TO READ-CARDS.
```

Finally after reading and printing each record in the input file, we direct the program to go to END-JOB, where we must print out the final total and count before terminating the operation of the program:

```
        END-JOB.
            MOVE SPACES TO PRINT-AREA.
            MOVE CARD-COUNTER TO COUNTER-P.
            MOVE FINAL-PRINT-LINE TO PRINT-AREA.
            WRITE PRINT-AREA AFTER ADVANCING 3 LINES.
            CLOSE CARD-FILE PRINT FILE.
            STOP RUN.
```

In the above coding, note that the files that we opened in the beginning of the program are closed, and the final statement STOP RUN is given.

1.6 SUMMARY OF RULES FOR WRITING COBOL PROGRAM

1. The four divisions always appear in the given order. The name of the division must be followed by a space and then the word DIVISION. The division header always appears on a line by itself and must begin at the A-margin (column 8).
2. The ENVIRONMENT DIVISION and DATA DIVISION always contain sections with fixed names. However, sections are not found in the IDENTIFICATION DIVISION and are optional in the PROCEDURE DIVISION. In the PROCEDURE DIVISION, section names are created and supplied by the programmer as needed.

3. The section header must begin at the A-margin on a line by itself. The name of the section must be followed by a space and then the word SECTION.
4. All the divisions except the DATA DIVISION contain paragraphs. In the PROCEDURE DIVISION, paragraph names are supplied by the programmer (such as BEGIN, READ-CARDS, END-JOB). In the IDENTIFICATION DIVISION and ENVIRONMENT DIVISION, these names are fixed by the COBOL language.
5. Program commands and instructions are given solely in the PROCEDURE DIVISION. Words such as OPEN, CLOSE, MOVE, and GO TO are program verbs. They are employed to direct the action of the computer.
6. The COBOL program executes its instructions sequentially as they appear in the PROCEDURE DIVISION. However, the program can be altered by conditional statements. (A conditional statement causes the computer to test certain conditions with the path of the program determined by the results of the test.)
7. Every COBOL program must be terminated by the STOP RUN command. This command does not have to be the last statement of the program. It could appear anywhere in the PROCEDURE DIVISION as desired.

1.7 SAMPLE PROGRAM 1B: ADDRESS LABELS†

Note to the reader: The best way to develop an understanding of how a COBOL program is structured and functions is to keypunch a simple program and run (that is, execute) it on a computer. The sooner you do it, the quicker you can grasp the concept of computer programming.

In the following, we present another complete example of a COBOL program with an explanation of the program on a line-by-line basis. The reader is urged to study this program, keypunch it, and run it on a computer at his earliest convenience. (The program reads address cards and prints the address labels.)

Input Description

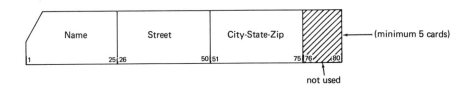

Sample Input

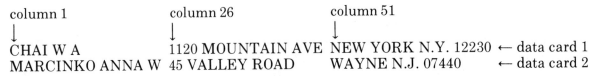

† See Exercise 4, page 28.

1.7   Sample Program 1B: Address Labels   25

Program Logic

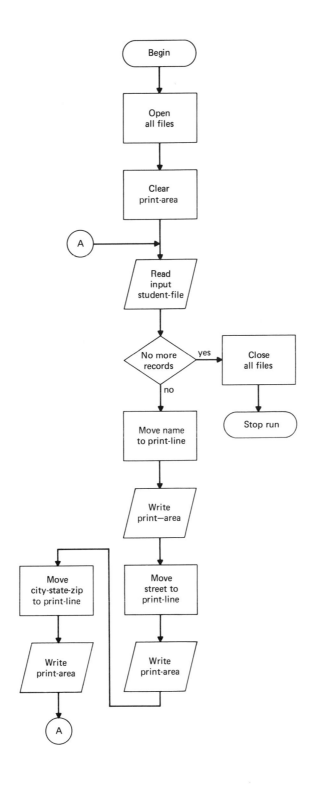

Source Listing

```
0CC01            IDENTIFICATION DIVISION.
0C002            PROGRAM-ID.  'SAMPL1B'.
CC003            AUTHOR.  CHAI
CC004            ****************************************************************
CC005            ENVIRONMENT DIVISION.
0C006            CONFIGURATION SECTION.
CC007            SOURCE-COMPUTER.  IBM-370.
0C008            OBJECT-COMPUTER.  IBM-370.
0C009            INPUT-OUTPUT SECTION.
0C010            FILE-CONTROL.
0C011                SELECT STUDENT-FILE ASSIGN TO UR-2540R-S-CARDIN.
CC012                SELECT PRINT-FILE ASSIGN TO  UR-1403-S-PROUT.
CC013            ****************************************************************
0C014            DATA DIVISION.
CC015            FILE SECTION.
CC016            FD   STUDENT-FILE
CC017                 LABEL RECORDS ARE OMITTED.
CC018            01   STUDENT-REC.
CC019                 04 NAME PICTURE   X(25).
0C020                 04 STREET PICTURE X(25).         } descriptions of
CC021                 04 CITY-STATE-ZIP PICTURE X(25). } input data cards
00022                 04 FILLER PICTURE X(5).
CC023            FD   PRINT-FILE
CC024                 LABEL RECORDS ARE OMITTED.
CC025            01   PRINT-AREA.
CC026                 04 FILLER   PICTURE X.           } output area
CC027                 04 PRINT-LINE PICTURE X(119).
CC028            ****************************************************************
CC029            PROCEDURE DIVISION.
CC030            BEGIN.
CC031                OPEN INPUT STUDENT-FILE, OUTPUT PRINT-FILE.   ← open all files
0C032                MOVE SPACES TO PRINT-AREA.
0C033            READ-PRINT.
CC034                READ STUDENT-FILE AT END GO TO END-JOB.    ← read input
00035                MOVE NAME TO PRINT-LINE.
CC036                WRITE PRINT-AREA AFTER ADVANCING 3 LINES.   } Print name,
CC037                MOVE STREET TO PRINT-LINE.                    street address,
CC038                 WRITE PRINT-AREA AFTER ADVANCING 1 LINES.    city, state, and zip code
0C039                MOVE CITY-STATE-ZIP TO PRINT-LINE.
0C040                 WRITE PRINT-AREA AFTER ADVANCING 1 LINES.
0C041                GO TO READ-PRINT.
0C042            END-JOB.
CC043                CLOSE STUDENT-FILE, PRINT-FILE. STOP RUN.    ← end of program
```

Sample Output

```
CHAI  W A
1120    MOUNTAIN AVE
NEW YORK   N.Y.   12230

MARCINKO   ANNA W
45 VALLEY ROAD
WAYNE  N.J   07440
```

Line-By-Line Explanations

00001	Division header: identifies the beginning of the IDENTIFICATION DIVISION.
00002	The name SAMPL1B, which has been assigned to the program by the programmer.
00003	Identifies the programmer.
00004	Asterisks used to separate each division of the COBOL program; they are treated as comments by the computer; there must be an asterisk in column 7 of the coding sheet.
00005	Specifies the beginning of the ENVIRONMENT DIVISION.
00006	Specifies the beginning of the CONFIGURATION SECTION.
00007	Indicates that the source program is to be compiled on an IBM System/370 computer.

00008	Indicates that the program (that is, the object program) is to be executed on an IBM System/370 computer.
00009	Specifies the beginning of the INPUT-OUTPUT SECTION (which is the second section of the ENVIRONMENT DIVISION).
00010	FILE-CONTROL is a paragraph-name; in this paragraph one must identify all the data files that are to be used in the program and assign them to specific input/output devices.
00011	Informs the computer that a data file identified as STUDENT-FILE will be read by the IBM 2540R card reader.†
00012	Specifies that a data file identified as PRINT-FILE is assigned to the IBM 1403 printer.†
00013	The same as 00004.
00014	Indicates the beginning of the DATA DIVISION.
00015	Specifies that the first section of the DATA DIVISION is the FILE SECTION.
00016–00017	FD stands for file description; STUDENT-FILE is the name of the file as specified in the ENVIRONMENT DIVISION; Files may be identified by internal labels, but there are no internal labels for a punched card file.
00018	01 is a level number used to indicate data records; in this statement, the name of the data record is STUDENT-REC.
00019–00021	The 04 level number specifies that data fields called NAME, STREET, CITY-STATE-ZIP are subparts of the record STUDENT-REC (01 level); each of these fields consists of 25 positions of alphanumeric characters [X(25)].
00022	FILLER is a special COBOL reserved name to specify parts of the storage areas not referred to by the program; in this case, it specifies that there are 5 spaces in the STUDENT-REC that are unused.
00023–00024	Specify the file description (FD) of the PRINT-FILE and indicate that internal labels of this file are omitted.
00025	Identifies that the data record for PRINT-FILE is PRINT-AREA (01 level).
00026	Specifies that the first position of the PRINT-AREA will not be used by the program (this first position is usually reserved for controlling vertical spacing on the printer).
00027	Specifies that the PRINT-LINE is a subfield of the record PRINT-AREA; PRINT-LINE contains up to 119 positions of alphanumeric characters [X(119)].
00028	The same as 00004 and 00013.
00029	Identifies the beginning of the PROCEDURE DIVISION.
00030	BEGIN is the first paragraph in the PROCEDURE DIVISION (the word BEGIN is a programmer-supplied-name).
00031	The OPEN statement specifies that the STUDENT-FILE is an input file and PRINT-AREA an output file; the statement makes these files available to the program.
00032	The MOVE statement here is to clear the output PRINT-AREA.

† *Note:* Names of system hardware units (for example, UR-2540R-S-CARDIN and UR-1403-S-PROUT) vary among different computers and operating systems. The reader is urged to consult his own installation format to obtain the correct coding.

00033	READ-PRINT is the name of the second paragraph.
00034	The READ statement instructs the computer to read the next record of the STUDENT-FILE; if there are no more records, it transfers the program control to END-JOB.
00035	Instructs the computer to move the contents of the NAME field to the output area PRINT-LINE.
00036	Instructs the computer to print the output area after skipping three lines.
00037	Instructs the computer to move the contents of STREET to the output area PRINT-LINE.
00038	Instructs the computer to print out the output PRINT-AREA after advancing one line (that is, single spacing).
00039	Instructs the computer to move the contents of CITY-STATE-ZIP to PRINT-LINE.
00040	Instructs the computer to print out the PRINT-AREA.
00041	Instructs the computer to execute the instructions given in the beginning of the READ-PRINT paragraph (that is, the READ statement).
00042	The beginning of the END-JOB paragraph will be automatically executed when all the input data cards are processed.
00043	All files are closed and the program is terminated.

EXERCISES

1. Define the following terms:

   source program   A-margin
   object program   B-margin
   compiler   ANS COBOL

2. Briefly explain the function of each of the divisions of a COBOL program.

3. True or false:
   (a) A program written in COBOL is known as an object program.
   (b) Every source program must first be compiled or translated into machine language before it can be executed.
   (c) Every COBOL program must contain four divisions. The order of the appearance of each division is not important.
   (d) A COBOL program is written much like ordinary English. It is relatively machine independent.
   (e) The A-margin begins in column 8.
   (f) The division-header must always begin at the A-margin and terminate with a period.
   (g) Comments can be written anywhere in the source program. They are identified by writing an asterisk (*) in column 7 of the coding sheet.

4. The COBOL source program listing for Sample Program 1B is given on page 24. The program reads address cards and prints the address labels. (The program logic is also shown on page 25. A line-by-line explanation is shown on pages 26-28.)
   (a) Keypunch the entire program.

(b) Prepare the data cards according to the input description for the program.
(c) Compile and execute.

Note: In order to get your program compiled and executed, you will undoubtedly have to set up certain job control cards.† For the IBM 360/370 OS system the job setup is presented below. However, you are urged to consult the local reference manual for possible variations of these job control cards, since there is no absolute standard.

column 1
↓

```
// JOB CARD
//*PASSWORD CARD
// EXEC COBUCG,PARM=APOST
//COB.SYSIN DD *
{Place your COBOL source program here}

/*
//GO.PROUT DD SYSOUT=A
//GO.CARDIN DD *
    {Place your data cards here}
/*
//
```

† A detailed description of job control statements is presented in Appendix B.

2
Elements of COBOL Language

In Chapter 1, the basic structure of the COBOL program was presented. The reader undoubtedly has noticed that COBOL is very similar to English, as both languages consist of symbols, words, sentences, and paragraphs. However, because COBOL is a computer language, its structure is more precise than English. Thus, in order to write COBOL programs correctly, the reader must familiarize himself with the basic rules of the COBOL language. In this chapter we discuss some basic elements that compose the COBOL language and learn the rules that govern them.

2.1 BASIC ELEMENTS

The COBOL language is made up of the following six language elements:

reserved words,
programmer-supplied names,
literals,
symbols,
level numbers,
pictures.

Each language element has a specific meaning and the use of each element is governed by exact rules. For instance, reserved words, symbols, and level numbers are provided in fixed sets by the COBOL compiler. They cannot be altered or invented. On the other hand, programmer-supplied names, literals, and pictures can be composed by the programmer according to certain rules. Figure 2.1 shows a COBOL statement using all six elements.

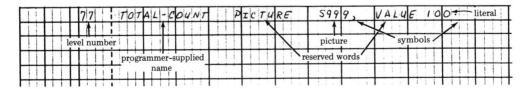

Fig. 2.1 Sample COBOL program entry.

2.2 RESERVED WORDS

Every COBOL statement must contain at least one reserved word, which conveys the meaning of the statement. Reserved words have preassigned meaning to the COBOL compiler. Such words must not be altered, misspelled, or used as programmer-supplied names. A list of more than 350 reserved words is given in Appendix C. The reader is urged to refer to this list whenever it is necessary.

Most reserved words are self-explanatory. However, every such word has syntax rules that govern its usage. For instance, in the following statements

```
        READ INFILE.
        MOVE IN-RECORD TO OUT-RECORD.
        WRITE OUT-RECORD.
```

READ, MOVE, TO, and WRITE are reserved words. The syntax rules for READ are not the same for WRITE. (In COBOL, we must READ a *file* and WRITE a *record*.) The reserved word MOVE has a still different set of syntax rules. Detailed descriptions of syntax rules are presented later whenever reserved words are used.

2.3 PROGRAMMER-SUPPLIED NAMES

Programmer-supplied names are words provided by the programmer and used to identify data (including working areas) and procedures. There are definite rules related to the formation of programmer-supplied names:

(1) A name cannot exceed 30 characters. It may contain letters (A through Z), digits (0 through 9), and hyphens (-). No other symbols should be used.
(2) No names can begin or end with a hyphen, but a hyphen can be used anywhere else in a name.

Programmer-supplied names	Status
WKLY-WAGE	valid
HOURLY RATE	invalid, space not allowed
S.O.S.	invalid, illegal character (.)
12345	valid procedure name only, invalid as data name
STATE-$-TAX	invalid, illegal character ($)
EMPIRE-STATE-BUILDING-IN-NEW-YORK	invalid, exceeds 30 characters
TAX-RETN-	invalid, ends in hyphen

Fig. 2.2 Programmer-supplied names.

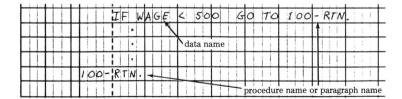

Fig. 2.3 Data name and procedure name.

(3) Blank spaces cannot appear anywhere in a name.
(4) Reserved words must not be used as programmer-supplied names.
(5) Names of data items (including working areas) must contain at least one letter, but names of procedures may be composed entirely of digits.

Examples of valid and invalid programmer supplied names are given in Fig. 2.2. Study them carefully. The list provides examples of frequent errors in the formation of programmer-supplied names. (Figure 2.3 illustrates the use of procedure name and data name.)

2.4 SYMBOLS

Symbols are special characters that have specific meaning in a COBOL program. COBOL symbols are divided into three groups: arithmetic symbols, conditional symbols, and punctuation symbols.

Arithmetic and Conditional Symbols

Arithmetic and conditional symbols (Fig. 2.4) are used to write formulas and mathematical notations. Detailed descriptions of these symbols will be presented in Chapter 7 when methods of computation are discussed.

Arithmetic symbols	Meaning	Conditional symbols	Meaning
+	plus sign, addition	=	equal
−	minus sign, subtraction	>	greater than
*	multiplication	<	less than
/	division		
**	exponentiation		

Fig. 2.4 Arithmetic and conditional symbols.

Punctuation Symbols

Some of the punctuation symbols in COBOL (Fig. 2.5) are used to improve the readability of the program, and so omission of punctuation does not necessarily result in an error.

Punctuation symbols	Meaning
.	period, marks end of statement or entry
,	comma, separates operands or clauses in a series
;	semicolon, separates clauses in a series
" " or ' '	quotation marks, enclose literals of nonnumeric type
( )	parentheses, enclose subscripts or expressions

Fig. 2.5 Punctuation symbols.

However, certain rules must be carefully observed. For instance, a period, comma, or semicolon must not be preceded by a space, but must be followed by a space. Other rules governing the use of punctuation symbols are presented in detail in later chapters. Examples of valid and invalid uses of symbols follow. The reader is urged to study them carefully.

Example 1

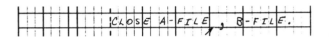

Incorrect, space cannot precede comma.

Example 2

Incorrect, space must follow comma.

Example 3

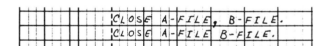

Both statements are correct.

Example 4

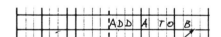

Incorrect, every COBOL entry must be terminated by a period.

2.5 SUMMARY

Three of the six basic elements of the COBOL language have been briefly discussed in this chapter. The remaining three elements—literals, level numbers, and pictures—are discussed in Chapter 4 when the need for such elements arises.

The presentation in this chapter has been made deliberately brief. By taking this approach, the authors hope it will enable the reader to start writing COBOL programs sooner. Spending additional effort on the details and idiosyncracies of language elements at this point would only burden the reader with too many rules and facts that might not only be too much to digest, but might also be terribly boring.

2.6 STANDARD NOTATION FOR FORMAT DESCRIPTION

In the next chapter, we begin to describe the structure of a COBOL program. We shall make use of what is called the format. The format will show the correct structure and allowable combinations of words and symbols in a COBOL statement.

In presenting these formats, we have used a standard format notation. This standard format notation is not only used in this particular text, but also in most COBOL reference manuals. The reader is urged to familiarize himself with the notation, which follows:

(1) All reserved words are printed entirely in capital letters (for example, SOURCE-COMPUTER, INPUT-OUTPUT).

(2) Reserved words required in the format are underlined. These underlined words may be omitted only if the portion of the format containing them is itself optional (for example, the reserved words IDENTIFICATION DIVISION are required).

(3) Optional reserved words are not underlined. These words are used only for the sake of readability (for example, the statement ADD data-1 TO data-2. shows that ADD is the required reserved word whereas TO is an optional reserved word that may be omitted by the programmer).

(4) Programmer-supplied information is always represented in the format by words printed entirely in lowercase letters. Such information is defined in the accompanying text.

(5) Optional portions of the format are enclosed in brackets ([ ]). Such portions of the format may be used or omitted depending on the requirements of the particular program (for example, the format [DATE-WRITTEN. [comment-entry] ...] is optional; the programmer may omit it from his program).

(6) Braces ({ }) enclosing vertically stacked items indicate that only one of the enclosed items is obligatory, for example

$$\begin{Bmatrix} ELSE \\ OTHERWISE \end{Bmatrix}.$$

(7) Three dots (..., that is, ellipsis) are used to indicate that the immediately preceding portions of the format may be repeated any number of times.

(8) Special symbols such as ., +, −, >, <, =, although not underlined, are required when such formats are used.

Some of these notations are illustrated in Fig. 2-6.

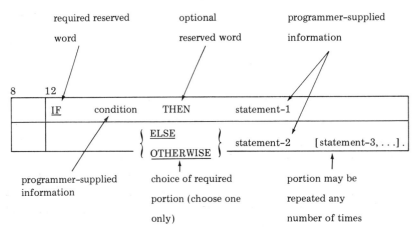

Fig. 2.6 An example of an entry format.

Note to the reader: At this point you may proceed with Chapters 3 and 4, which will provide you with a thorough background on COBOL programming before starting to write programs. However, if you want to start writing COBOL programs now, you can skip Chapters 3 and 4 and go directly to Chapter 5. (You can always read Chapters 3 and 4 as reference material whenever the need arises.)

Chapter 5 contains three completed programs as sample programs. These sample programs are designed specifically to help you understand COBOL programming. Make sure you go over these samples carefully.

There is a total of 32 sample programs with documentation, flowcharts, and sample printouts in this text. One of the quickest ways to learn how to write a COBOL program is to study these sample programs and run them on the computer yourself.

EXERCISES

1. List the six elements of the COBOL language.

2. In the following list of programmer-supplied names, identify errors if any:
   - (a) WEEKLY-WAGE
   - (b) BROADWAY JOE
   - (c) MONTCLAIR.STATE
   - (d) X281
   - (e) 1800
   - (f) $MONEY
   - (g) MARCINKO-CHAI-.

3. True or false:
   - (a) Every COBOL statement must contain at least one reserved word.
   - (b) Data names cannot begin with a number.
   - (c) Every programmer-supplied name must contain at least one letter. It cannot be all digits.
   - (d) The procedure name must contain at least one alphabetic character.
   - (e) The programmer-supplied name is defined by the programmer and may be formed from any alphabetic and special characters.
   - (f) Blank spaces are permitted within a name.
   - (g) COBOL statements must always be separated by either a comma or period. Omission of these punctuation marks would result in errors.
   - (h) A period, comma, or semicolon must not be preceded by a space, but must be followed by a space.
   - (i) The rules for creating procedure names are the same as the rules for creating data names. Both are programmer-supplied names.

3
IDENTIFICATION and ENVIRONMENT DIVISIONS

3.1 IDENTIFICATION DIVISION

The IDENTIFICATION DIVISION is the first of the four divisions required in a COBOL program. It is used by the programmer to identify the program and to provide other documentation about the program. The division has no effect on the execution of the program. The basic format of the IDENTIFICATION DIVISION is given in Fig. 3.1.

From the format, we can see that the division consists of a division-header and seven paragraph entries. The division-header IDENTIFICATION DIVISION must begin at A-margin. However, only three entries—the division-header, a PROGRAM-ID paragraph name (both are underlined in the format), and a program-name—are required. These minimum required entries are illustrated in Fig. 3.2.

The program-name entry of the PROGRAM-ID paragraph identifies the COBOL program. The rules for formation of a program-name are the same as for the procedure-

<u>IDENTIFICATION DIVISION.</u>
<u>PROGRAM-ID.</u> program-name.
[<u>AUTHOR.</u> [comment-entry] ...]
[<u>INSTALLATION.</u> [comment-entry] ...]
[<u>DATE-WRITTEN.</u> [comment-entry] ...]
[<u>DATE-COMPILED.</u> [comment-entry] ...]
[<u>SECURITY.</u> [comment-entry] ...]
[<u>REMARKS.</u> [comment-entry] ...]

Fig. 3.1 Format of IDENTIFICATION DIVISION.

```
IDENTIFICATION DIVISION.
PROGRAM-ID. 'SAMPL1A'.
```

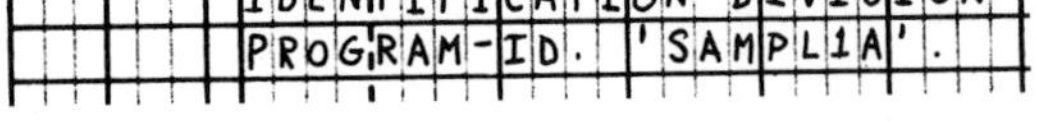

Fig. 3.2 Minimum required entries in IDENTIFICATION DIVISION.

```
001010  IDENTIFICATION DIVISION.
001020  PROGRAM-ID. SAMPLE-PROGRAM.
001030  AUTHOR. A-CHAI.
001040  INSTALLATION. MONTCLAIR STATE COLLEGE.
001050  DATE-WRITTEN. NOV. 12, 1973
001060  DATE-COMPILED. SUPPLIED BY THE COMPILER
001070  REMARKS. THIS PROGRAM READS A DECK OF CARDS
001080          AND LISTS EACH CARD ON THE PRINTER.
001090  ************************************************
```

Fig. 3.3 Expanded IDENTIFICATION DIVISION.

```
00001   001010   IDENTIFICATION DIVISION.
00002   001020   PROGRAM-ID. SAMPLE-PROGRAM.
00003   001030   AUTHOR. A-CHAI.
00004   001040   INSTALLATION. MONTCLAIR STATE COLLEGE.
00005   001050   DATE-WRITTEN. NOV. 12, 1973
00006   001060   DATE-COMPILED. NOV. 27, 1973
00007   001070   REMARKS. THIS PROGRAM READS A DECK OF CARDS
00008   001080-          AND LISTS EACH CARD ON THE PRINTER.
00009   001090   * * * * * * * * * * * * * * * * * * * * * * * * * * * * * * * * * * * *
```

Fig. 3.4 IDENTIFICATION DIVISION (compiled).

name. (Read Chapter 2 again if you do not remember!) However, only the first eight characters of the name are used to identify each program and these characters should therefore be unique as a program-name.

The other six paragraphs shown in Fig. 3.1—AUTHOR, INSTALLATION, DATE-WRITTEN, DATE-COMPILED, SECURITY, and REMARKS—are optional. The programmer is free to include any number of these paragraphs in his program as shown in Fig. 3.3. The use of these paragraphs generally provides useful documentation about the program. For instance, the DATE-COMPILED paragraph provides the compilation date of the source program listing. If it is included, the COBOL compiler automatically inserts the current date during program compilation. Figure 3.4 illustrates the action of the compiler.

3.2 ENVIRONMENT DIVISION†

The ENVIRONMENT DIVISION is the most computer-dependent division of the program. It has two specific functions:

(1) It identifies the computers to be used for compiling the source program and for running the object program.
(2) It relates the program data files to specific input/output units.

A general format for the ENVIRONMENT DIVISION is given in Fig. 3.5 and a typical entry is shown in Fig. 3.6.

† ENVIRONMENT DIVISION entries for Burroughs, Control Data, Honeywell, IBM, UNIVAC, XDS, and RCA Spectra 70 are shown in Appendix A.

ENVIRONMENT DIVISION.
CONFIGURATION SECTION.
SOURCE-COMPUTER paragraph
OBJECT-COMPUTER paragraph
[SPECIAL-NAMES paragraph]
[INPUT-OUTPUT SECTION.
FILE-CONTROL paragraph
[I-O-CONTROL paragraph]]

Fig. 3.5 Format of ENVIRONMENT DIVISION.

```
ENVIRONMENT DIVISION.
CONFIGURATION SECTION.
SOURCE-COMPUTER.   IBM-370.
OBJECT-COMPUTER.   IBM-370.
INPUT-OUTPUT SECTION.
FILE-CONTROL.
    SELECT CARD-FILE
        ASSIGN TO UR-2540R-S-INPUT.
    SELECT PRINT-FILE
        ASSIGN TO UR-1403-S-PROUT.
```

Fig. 3.6 Example of ENVIRONMENT DIVISION.

From Fig. 3.6 we see that this division is divided into two sections: the CONFIGURATION SECTION and the INPUT-OUTPUT SECTION.

CONFIGURATION SECTION

The configuration section deals with the overall specification of computers. It contains three paragraphs:

(1) SOURCE-COMPUTER identifies the computer upon which the program is to be compiled.
(2) OBJECT-COMPUTER specifies the computer upon which the program is to be executed.
(3) SPECIAL-NAMES relates function names to programmer-specified symbolic names. (The use of this paragraph is discussed in Chapter 5.)

The general format for source-computer and object-computer entries varies from one computer to another. For the IBM System 360/370 computers, these entries can take the form

SOURCE-COMPUTER.   computer-name.
OBJECT-COMPUTER.   computer-name.

where the computer-name may be specified as

IBM-370[-model-number]   or   IBM-360[-model-number]

The model-number entry (enclosed by brackets) is optional and can be omitted. Model numbers are usually represented by a letter followed by a number. For instance, H58 would indicate a model 158 computer with 262K bytes of storage. Examples of the CONFIGURATION SECTION are illustrated in Figs. 3.7 and 3.8.

```
        ENVIRONMENT  DIVISION.
        CONFIGURATION  SECTION.
        SOURCE-COMPUTER.    IBM-370-H55.
        OBJECT-COMPUTER.    IBM-370-K65.
```

Fig. 3.7 CONFIGURATION SECTION, using two different computers.

```
        ENVIRONMENT  DIVISION.
        CONFIGURATION  SECTION.
        SOURCE-COMPUTER.    UNIVAC-1108.
        OBJECT-COMPUTER.    UNIVAC-1108.
```

Fig. 3.8 CONFIGURATION SECTION, using a UNIVAC computer.

INPUT-OUTPUT SECTION

The INPUT-OUTPUT SECTION is used to relate program data files with input/output units. Although this section is an optional portion of the ENVIRONMENT DIVISION, it must be included in the program whenever input or output files are used, and since most of the programs process some sort of data files, this section is almost always present.

The INPUT-OUTPUT SECTION contains two paragraphs: the FILE-CONTROL paragraph, which is required whenever the INPUT-OUTPUT SECTION is written, and the I-O CONTROL paragraph, which may be omitted if no special techniques are to be defined.

The basic format for the FILE-CONTROL paragraph is

>   FILE-CONTROL.
>   SELECT file name
>   ASSIGN system-hardware-unit

The file name in the SELECT clause is a programmer-supplied name that identifies a data file in the program. (This data file must be defined in the DATA DIVISION.) The system-hardware-unit in the ASSIGN clause is a name for a particular class of devices recognized by the compiler. Both SELECT and ASSIGN clauses begin at B-margin, whereas the FILE-CONTROL paragraph begins at A-margin.

Names of system-hardware-units vary among different computers and operating systems. The reader is urged to consult his own installation format to obtain the correct coding. For the IBM System 360/370 computers under OS (operating system), system-hardware-units have the structure

>   class[-device]-organization-ddname

and under DOS (disk operating system), the system-hardware-unit becomes

>   SYSnnn-class-device-organization [-ddname]

where

nnn is a 3-digit number between 000 and 399. It represents the symbol unit to which the file is assigned.

class is a 2-character code that specifies the device class. Class codes are

DA: direct-access devices, such as magnetic disk,
UT: utility devices—including magnetic tape unit,
UR: unit-record devices, such as card reader, card punch, and line printer.

device is used to identify a particular input/output unit within a device class. It can be a 4- or 6-character field. The allowable system devices are

DA: 2301, 2302, 2303, 2311, 2314, 3330, 3340;
UT: 2301, 2302, 2311, 2314, 2400, 3330, 3340, 3410, 3420;
UR: 1403, 1404, 1442R, 1442P, 1443, 1445, 2501, 2520R, 2540R, 2540P (P indicates card punch, R indicates card reader).

organization is a 1-character code that specifies the file organization. The two most frequently used code numbers are

S: for file with standard sequential organization such as cards, printed reports, and tapes,
D: for file with direct organization, such as disk files.

ddname is a 1- to 8-character field specifying the external data definition name (such a name must correspond to the ddname in the job control statement). ddname is used to identify the file for the operating system, but it is optional.

The following examples are given in order to illustrate how SELECT and ASSIGN clauses are written for various data files.

Example 1: Operating System Is DOS (Fig. 3.9)

Data files are

Input: a punched-data-card file, 2540 card reader.
Output: a printed report, 1403 printer.

```
       INPUT-OUTPUT SECTION.
       FILE-CONTROL.
           SELECT CARD-FILE
               ASSIGN TO SYS005-UR-2540R-S.
           SELECT PRINT-FILE
               ASSIGN TO SYS003-UR-1403-S.
```

Fig. 3.9 INPUT-OUTPUT SECTION under DOS.

Example 2: Operating System Is OS (Fig. 3.10)

Input: (1) a punched-data-card file, 2540 card reader,
      (2) a magnetic-tape file, 2400 tape drive.
Output: (1) a printed report, 1403 printer,
      (2) a punched-card file, 2540 card punch,
      (3) a magnetic-tape file, 2400 tape drive.

```
         INPUT-OUTPUT SECTION.
         FILE-CONTROL.
             SELECT CARD-FILE
                 ASSIGN TO UR-2540R-S-INFILE.
             SELECT TAPEIN
                 ASSIGN TO UT-2400-S-TPFILE.
             SELECT PRINT-FILE
                 ASSIGN TO UR-1403-S-PROUT.
             SELECT PUNCH-CARD-FILE
                 ASSIGN TO UR-2540P-PCHOUT.
             SELECT TPOUT-FILE
                 ASSIGN TO UR-2400-S-TPOUT.
```

Fig. 3.10 INPUT-OUTPUT SECTION under OS.

EXERCISES

1. What are the functions of the IDENTIFICATION and ENVIRONMENT DIVISIONS?

2. How many different entries (that is, paragraphs) are there in the IDENTIFICATION DIVISION? What are the minimum required entries?

3. Briefly explain the function of the following terms:
   source computer
   object computer
   SELECT clause
   ASSIGN clause

4. Write the SELECT and ASSIGN clauses for the following files:
   punched-card file, named DATA-FILE
   printed-file, named WKLY-REPORT
   magnetic-tape file, named TAPE-IN

5. Write the IDENTIFICATION and ENVIRONMENT DIVISION entries for the files described in the system flowchart shown in Fig. 3.11.

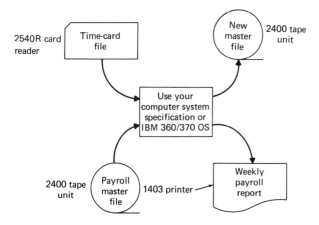

Fig. 3.11

6 True or false:
  (a) Division headers can begin at B-margin.
  (b) The ENVIRONMENT DIVISION is the most computer-dependent division of the program.
  (c) The CONFIGURATION SECTION contains only two paragraphs, SOURCE-COMPUTER and OBJECT-COMPUTER.
  (d) The INPUT-OUTPUT SECTION relates program data files to input/output units.
  (e) The FILE-CONTROL paragraph must begin at B-margin.
  (f) All input/output files are assigned to individual hardware devices by the ASSIGN clause.
  (g) The file name used in the SELECT clause must be a COBOL reserved name, and such a name cannot be altered by the programmer.
  (h) The INPUT-OUTPUT SECTION must appear in every COBOL program.

4
DATA DIVISION

The objective of the DATA DIVISION in a COBOL program is to provide the detailed specifications for all the files and data items required in the program. Of the four divisions of the COBOL program, this one is perhaps the most complex and the most difficult to understand. However, most of the entries in the DATA DIVISION are very similar in nature and tend to be repeated again and again. Thus, once the reader has a basic understanding of how the data are organized and structured, his work in the DATA DIVISION certainly will be simpler.

4.1 CONTENTS AND BASIC FORMAT

The DATA DIVISION may contain five sections:

The FILE SECTION, which describes the external data files and their records.
The WORKING-STORAGE SECTION, which describes the working area and constants utilized by the program.
The LINKAGE SECTION, which contains information that is passed from one program to another.
The COMMUNICATION SECTION, which contains information about the interface between the user-written telecommunication message (TCAM) and the COBOL teleprocessing program.
The REPORT SECTION, which describes the content and format of all reports that are to be generated by the report writer feature.

The FILE SECTION and WORKING-STORAGE SECTION are the most commonly used sections and are discussed in detail in this chapter. The LINKAGE SECTION is discussed in Chapter 16 and the REPORT SECTION in Chapter 15. The COMMUNICATION SECTION is very specialized and is not discussed in this book.

A basic format of the DATA DIVISION containing both the FILE SECTION and the WORKING-STORAGE SECTION is shown in Fig. 4.1 and a typical example is presented in Fig. 4.2.

DATA DIVISION.
[FILE SECTION.
{file-description-entry
{record-description-entry}...}...]
[WORKING-STORAGE SECTION.
 [independent-storage-entry]...
 [record-description-entry]...]

Fig. 4.1 DATA DIVISION format.

```
       DATA DIVISION.
       FILE SECTION.
       FD  ACCT-FILE
           LABEL RECORDS ARE OMITTED
           DATA RECORD IS CUSTOMER-REC.
       01  CUSTOMER-REC.
           03 NAME       PICTURE X(20).
           03 ADDRESS    PICTURE X(20).
           03 STATE-ZIP  PICTURE X(20).
           03 FILLER     PICTURE X(20).
       FD  PRINT-FILE
           LABEL RECORDS ARE OMITTED.
       01  PRINT-AREA PICTURE X(121).
       WORKING-STORAGE SECTION.
       77  CARD-KOUNTER  PICTURE 999 VALUE ZEROS.
       01  HEADING-1.
           05 FILLER  PICTURE X(20) VALUE SPACES.
           05 FILLER  PICTURE X(36)
               VALUE 'CUSTOMER ADDRESS LISTING'.
```

Fig. 4.2 A sample of DATA DIVISION.

4.2 FILE CONCEPTS

In a COBOL program, the data are organized as files, records, and data items.

The broadest data category is undoubtedly the file. A file may contain many records, which are moved into or out of core storage via an external input/output unit such as the card reader, printer, magnetic tape unit, or magnetic disk unit.

Within a file, records can be viewed as logical records or physical records. A logical record contains a group of related data items, whereas a physical record can consist of one or more logical records and is treated as one entity when put into or fetched out of core storage. The number of logical records contained in the physical record is called the blocking factor. A file is said to be unblocked if each physical record of the file contains one logical record (that is, blocking factor is one). Card files and printers are always unblocked, whereas tape files and disk files may contain block records to save storage spaces. Blocked record files are explained in Chapter 11.

4.3 FILE SECTION: THE FILE DESCRIPTION ENTRIES

All input/output files defined in the ENVIRONMENT DIVISION by the SELECT clause must be described in the FILE SECTION before the file can be processed by a COBOL program. If there is no input/output file being processed, then the FILE SECTION is not needed in the program.

The FILE SECTION header must always begin at A-margin. It contains both file description and record description entries. The former describe the physical structures of the file, whereas the latter are concerned with the data contents of each logical record. Each file description entry must be followed by the corresponding record description entries as shown in Fig. 4.1.

The general format of the file-description entry is shown in Fig. 4.3.

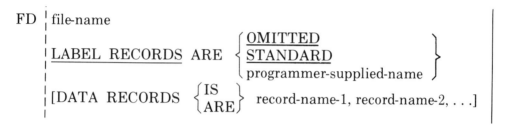

Fig. 4.3 General format of file-description entries.

The file-description entry is identified by the level indicator FD, which must be written in A-margin. The file-name is a programmer-supplied name and must be the same file-name used in the SELECT clause.

The file-description entry may contain up to seven clauses. (Figure 4.3 shows LABEL RECORDS and DATA RECORDS clauses.) There are four other clauses, namely, BLOCK CONTAINS, RECORDING MODE, RECORD CONTAINS, and VALUE OF, which are not shown. (They will be discussed later.) These clauses may appear in any order. However, the last clause in the format must be followed by a period.

The LABEL RECORDS clause is the only required entry. It has a special meaning for the tape and the disk files, which will be discussed in Chapters 11 and 14. For punched card or printer files, LABEL RECORDS ARE OMITTED should always be specified.

The DATA RECORD clause identifies each type of logical record within a file. It serves as documentation but is never required. Record-name-1, record-name-2, etc., are the names of the logical records. They are programmer-supplied names. The order in which the record-names are listed is not important.

Example

```
      FD  CUSTOMER-FILE
          LABEL RECORDS ARE OMITTED
          DATA RECORDS ARE CUSTOMER-REC.
```

In this example, the FD entry identifies the file-name as CUSTOMER-FILE, which is assumed to be the same file-name used in the SELECT clause. It contains both the LABEL RECORDS and DATA RECORDS clauses and there is only one period at the end of the entire entry. Since these clauses may appear in any order and only the LABEL RECORDS clause is required, the above FD entry is equivalent to the following:

```
       FD  CUSTOMER-FILE
           DATA RECORDS ARE CUSTOMER-REC
           LABEL RECORDS ARE OMITTED.
       FD  CUSTOMER-FILE LABEL RECORDS ARE OMITTED.
```

However, it would be incorrect to have

```
       FD  CUSTOMER-FILE
           DATA RECORDS ARE CUSTOMER-REC.
```

Since the LABEL RECORDS clause is always required, it cannot be omitted.

4.4 RECORD CONTENTS: GROUP AND ELEMENTARY DATA ITEMS

Earlier in this chapter, we said that logical records are usually made up of a collection of related data items. In COBOL, a data item can be viewed as a group item (field) or an elementary item. If a data item can be subdivided and contain other data items, then the data item is a group item; otherwise it is an elementary item. As an example, let us consider a logical weekly-time-card record format as shown in Fig. 4.4.

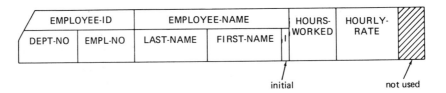

Fig. 4.4 Weekly-time-card record format.

This record format shows that the record is subdivided into four main groups, two of them containing subgroups:

$$\text{WEEKLY-TIME-CARD} \begin{cases} \text{EMPLOYEE-ID} \begin{cases} \text{DEPT-NO} \\ \text{EMPL-NO} \end{cases} \\ \text{EMPLOYEE-NAME} \begin{cases} \text{LAST-NAME} \\ \text{FIRST-NAME} \\ \text{INITIAL} \end{cases} \\ \text{HOURS-WORKED} \\ \text{HOURLY-RATE} \end{cases}$$

Obviously, in the above record, EMPLOYEE-ID and EMPLOYEE-NAME are group items, whereas LAST-NAME, FIRST-NAME, INITIAL, HOURS-WORKED, and HOURLY-RATE are elementary items (since they contain no subfields themselves).

4.5 LEVEL NUMBERS

In a COBOL program, a special set of code numbers is used to describe the relationship of data items in a record. These numbers are 01 through 49, 66, 77, and 88. They are known as level numbers. For the weekly-time-card record in Fig. 4.4, we might describe the numbers as shown in Fig. 4.5.

Observe that the levels are indicated by ascending values, but they need not be consecutive (that is, 01, 02, 03). In fact, the programmer has great flexibility in assigning level numbers. He may choose to use 01, 03, 05, 08, ..., or 01, 05, 010, ..., and so on.

```
01   WEEKLY-TIME-CARD.
     04   EMPLOYEE-ID.
          06   DEPT-NO  ⎫
          06   EMPL-NO  ⎬ (entries to follow)
     04   EMPLOYEE-NAME.
          06   LAST-NAME   ⎫
          06   FIRST-NAME  ⎬ (entries to follow)
          06   INITIAL     ⎭
     04   HOURS-WORKED ⎫
     04   HOURLY-RATE  ⎬ (entries to follow)
```

Fig. 4.5 Record description—level numbers.

The rules for using level numbers are

(1) 01 is used for a single logic record.
(2) 02 through 49 are used for a subfield of the 01 data record.
(3) 66 is used for a regrouping of data items.†
(4) 77 is reserved for a single independent elementary item in the WORKING-STORAGE SECTION.
(5) 88 is used to denote conditional values.†
(6) The data-name must always be preceded by a level number. If no programmer-supplied name is used, the COBOL reserved word FILLER must be used after the level number, for example,

$$05 \text{ FILLER} \quad \text{(entry to follow)}$$

However, FILLER must not be written at the 01 or 77 levels.

In the beginning, the reader may find it difficult to visualize and describe the structure of a logical record in terms of level numbers. To this end, more illustrated examples are presented at the end of the next section.

4.6 RECORD OR DATA DESCRIPTION FORMAT: PICTURE CLAUSE

The general format of a record or data description entry takes the form shown in Fig. 4.6.

† These will be discussed in later chapters as the need arises.

level number $\begin{cases}\text{data-name}\\ \underline{\text{FILLER}}\end{cases}$
[PICTURE clause]
[JUSTIFIED clause]
[USAGE clause]
[BLANK WHEN ZERO clause]
[OCCURS clause]
[SYNCHRONIZED clause]
[VALUE clause]

Fig. 4.6 General format of data description entries.

In this chapter, only PICTURE and VALUE clauses are discussed. Other clauses will be discussed in later chapters.

Picture clauses are used to describe the contents of an elementary data item. They reveal the size of the data field and the character of the data (that is, alphabetic, numeric, mixed, or edited).

The basic format of the PICTURE clause is

$$\begin{Bmatrix}\underline{\text{PICTURE}}\\ \underline{\text{PIC}}\end{Bmatrix} \text{ IS character string}$$

In COBOL, the character of data is indicated by the picture character symbols. There are 17 such symbols and they can be grouped into three categories: data character symbols, operational symbols, and edited symbols.

Data Character Symbols: A, X, 9

Data character symbols are used to indicate whether or not an elementary item is alphabetic (identified by the symbol A), numeric (identified by 9), or alphanumeric (identified by X).

For example, the statement

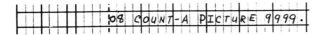

describes the elementary item COUNT-A as a 4-digit positive number. Alternatively, we can write

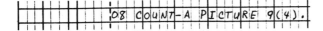

The digit 4 within parentheses indicates that the symbol 9 occurs four times in a sequence. In fact, this type of description can be applied to all picture character symbols. For example, the following two statements are equivalent:

```
        06 CODE-A PICTURE X(6).

        06 CODE-A PICTURE XXXXXX.
```

Both statements identify CODE-A as an elementary data item that contains six alphanumeric characters. We may also note that one can describe alphanumeric items by combining the symbols A, 9, and X. Such a representation can be used to stress the structure of certain data. If we write

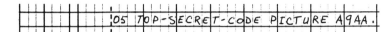

we specify that TOP-SECRET-CODE begins with a letter and is followed by one digit and two letters.

Operational Symbols: S, V, P

The operational symbols S, V, and P are used to indicate the operational sign and the assumed decimal point or position within a numeric field. Operational symbols should not be included in the size of the data item.

The symbol S is used to indicate that an elementary item has a plus or minus sign, and it must appear as the first character in the picture clause. For instance, the statement

```
77  COUNT-B  PICTURE  S999.
```

identifies COUNT-B as a 3-digit number that can store numbers between −999 and +999.

To illustrate how signed numeric numbers are processed in a COBOL program, consider numeric numbers punched in the card as shown in Fig. 4.7. Note that columns 1 through 3 of the card contain the value +135, where the positive sign (+) carries a 12-zone punch. Columns 11 through 13 contain the value −135, where the negative sign (−) carries an 11-zone punch. Columns 21 through 23 contain the value 135, which is unsigned. Unsigned numeric values are considered positive and do not carry any zone punches.

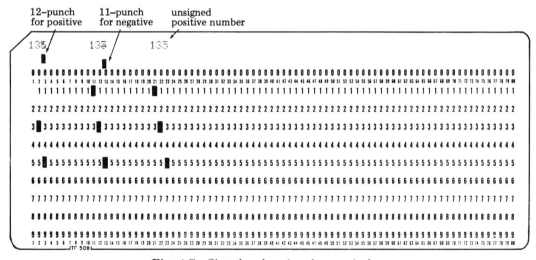

Fig. 4.7 Signed and unsigned numeric data.

The symbol V is used to indicate the position of an assumed decimal point and must not appear more than once in a picture clause. In the statement

```
10  HOURLY-RATE  PICTURE  9V99.
```

50 4 DATA DIVISION

HOURLY-RATE is described as a 3-digit elementary item with one integer digit and two decimals. Thus, if the contents of HOURLY-RATE is 655, it represents 6.55.

The symbol P is used to indicate an assumed position containing the value zero, but it does not occupy any physical position. Hence in the statements

```
04 A PICTURE 99PPP.
04 B PICTURE 9PPP9.
```

if the contents are 15, then A and B would represent the values 15,000 and 10,005, respectively.

As one can see, the symbol P represents a scaling position and is not included in the size of the data items.

In order to clarify the meaning of different picture symbols and their uses, additional examples are presented in Figs. 4.8 through 4.10. The reader is urged to examine them carefully.

Picture	Category	Core storage size	Actual contents	Actual meaning
999	numeric	3	123	123
99V9	numeric	3	123	12.3
9VPP99	numeric	3	123	1.0023
9P(3)V99	numeric	3	123	1000.23
A(5)	alphabetic	5	ABCDE	ABCDE
A9(4)	mixed	5	12AB	12AB
AV99	invalid			
X(10)	alphanumeric	10	12ABCD	12ABCD
9(3)P(3)V9	numeric	4	1234	123000.4

Fig. 4.8 Examples of picture symbols.

Example

Write a complete record description entry for the data-card

record-name: CUSTOMER-REC

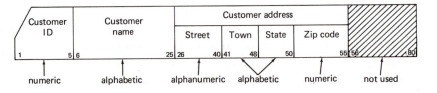

Fig. 4.9 CUSTOMER-REC format.

4.6 Record or Data Description Format: PICTURE Clause

Solution

```
        01  CUSTOMER-REC.
            05  CUSTOMER-ID       PICTURE  9(5).
            05  CUSTOMER-NAME     PICTURE  X(20).
            05  CUSTOMER-ADDRESS.
                10  STREET        PICTURE  X(15).
                10  TOWN          PICTURE  A(8).
                10  STATE         PICTURE  AA.
                10  ZIP-CODE      PICTURE  9(5).
            05  FILLER            PICTURE  X(25).
```

Fig. 4.10 Record-description entries.

Editing Symbols: $, +, −, DB, CR, *, Z, 0, B, ., ,

Editing symbols are used strictly to improve the readability of the output reports. They are not suitable for computation. For instance, the statement

```
            05  WAGE-P      PICTURE     $$$99.
```

defines WAGE-P as an edit field that accepts numeric data. If a number 650 is moved to WAGE-P, the edited result after printout will be $650. A detailed description of editing symbols will be presented in Chapter 6.

Finally, we may add that in the PICTURE clause, the word PICTURE can be replaced by PIC to shorten some of the writing, as shown in the following:

```
            06  NAME-1      PIC     A(8).
            06  CODE-1      PIC     X(5).
```

Example

An inventory file is stored on punched cards. The file contains both master records and sales records. Formats of these records are shown in Figs. 4.11 and 4.12, and a file/record description is given in Fig. 4.13.

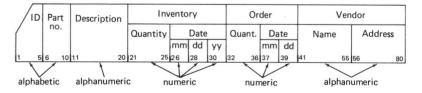

Fig. 4.11 Master record format.

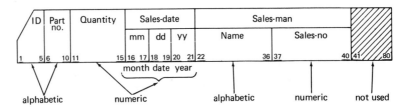

Fig. 4.12 Sales record format.

```
        FILE-CONTROL.
            SELECT INVTRY-FILE
                ASSIGN TO UR-2501-S-INPUT.
        DATA DIVISION.
        FILE SECTION.
        FD  INVTRY-FILE
            LABEL RECORDS ARE OMITTED
            DATA RECORDS ARE MASTER-REC SALES-REC.
        01  MASTER-REC.
            05  ID-M                PICTURE A(5).
            05  PART-NO-M           PICTURE A(5).
            05  DESCRIPTION         PICTURE X(10).
            05  INVENTORY.
                10  QUANTITY        PICTURE S9(5).
                10  DATE.
                    12  MM          PICTURE 99.
                    12  DD          PICTURE 99.
                    12  YY          PICTURE 99.
            05  ORDER.
                10  QUANT           PICTURE S9(5).
                10  DATE.
                    12  MM-O        PICTURE 99.
                    12  DD-O        PICTURE 99.
            05  VENDOR.
                10  NAME            PICTURE X(15).
                10  ADDRESS         PICTURE X(25).
        01  SALES-REC.
            05  ID-S                PICTURE A(5).
            05  PART-NO-S           PICTURE A(5).
            05  QUANTITY-S          PICTURE S9(5).
            05  SALES-DATE.
                10  MM-S            PICTURE 99.
                10  DD-S            PICTURE 99.
                10  YY-S            PICTURE 99.
            05  SALES-MAN.
                10  NAME-S          PICTURE A(15).
                10  SALES-NO-S      PICTURE 9(14).
            05  FILLER              PICTURE X(40).
```

Fig. 4.13 File/record description entries corresponding to Figs. 4.11 and 4.12.

4.7 WORKING-STORAGE SECTION: DESCRIPTION

The WORKING-STORAGE SECTION describes the work areas for storing intermediate results and constants that are utilized by the program. It has the general format

WORKING-STORAGE SECTION.
[independent-storage-item description entry] ...
[record-item description entry] ...

The independent-storage-item description entries contain all data entries that are independent and have no hierarchical relationship to one another. Such entries must begin with the special level number 77 and must precede any record description entries.

A typical WORKING-STORAGE SECTION is shown in Fig. 4.14.

```
       WORKING-STORAGE SECTION.
       77  CARD-COUNTER         PICTURE 99 VALUE ZEROS.
       77  TOTAL AMOUNT         PICTURE S9(5)V99 VALUE ZEROS.
       01  JOB-HEADING.
           05  FILLER           PICTURE X(20) VALUE SPACES.
           05  LITERAL-1        PICTURE X(11) VALUE 'VENDOR NAME'.
           05  FILLER           PICTURE X(15) VALUE SPACES.
           05  LITERAL-2        PICTURE X(6) VALUE 'AMOUNT'.
```

Fig. 4.14 Example of WORKING-STORAGE SECTION.

4.8 VALUE CLAUSE: LITERALS

The VALUE clause is used to define a constant or initial value of a working-storage item. For instance, in the statement

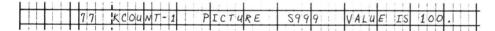

```
       77  KCOUNT-1    PICTURE  S999   VALUE IS 100.
```

the VALUE clause VALUE IS 100 would require the compiler to set KCOUNT-1 to 100 before executing any program statement. In general, the VALUE clause takes the form

VALUE IS literal

A literal is an actual value used somewhere in a COBOL program and supplied by the programmer whenever needed. There are three types of literals: numeric, nonnumeric, and figurative.

Numeric Literals

The basic rules of forming numeric literals are

(a) A numeric literal may contain up to 18 digits.
(b) A positive (+) or negative (−) sign and a decimal point (.) may be included with the literal.
(c) If there is a sign, it must appear as the leftmost character of the literal (that is, +200, −150). An unsigned numeric literal is assumed to be positive.

Numeric literals	Status
−0.01	valid
.508	valid
$50	invalid, dollar sign not permitted
−1/2	invalid, illegal character (slash)
55.	invalid, decimal point as rightmost character
123456789012346789	invalid, exceeds 18 digits
156 78	invalid, embedded blank space

Fig. 4.15 Valid and invalid numeric literals.

(d) A decimal point (.) may be used anywhere in the numeric literal except as the rightmost character. If the decimal point is desired, one can write the number with an extra zero in the form X.0.

Examples of valid and invalid numeric literals are presented in Fig. 4.15.

Nonnumeric Literals

Nonnumeric literals are used for display purposes either on the printer or on the console. They are indispensable in providing messages or headings on output reports. In the statement

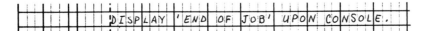

the END OF JOB message will be displayed on the operator's console. The END OF JOB message is a nonnumeric literal since it is enclosed in quotation marks.

The rules for nonnumeric literals are

(a) Nonnumeric literals may contain up to 120 characters.
(b) Any character in the available character set with the exception of the quotation mark may be used as a member of the literal.
(c) Nonnumeric literals must always be enclosed by quotation marks. The quotation marks are not part of the literal.
(d) Blank spaces are treated as valid characters in a nonnumeric literal.

Some valid and invalid nonnumeric literals are given in Fig. 4.16.

Figurative Constants

Figurative constants are special COBOL reserved words that have preassigned value. These figurative constants act as literals. There are six figurative constants (plus their plurals) in COBOL:

(1) ZERO (ZEROS): represents one or more zeros.
(2) SPACE (SPACES): represents one or more blanks.
(3) HIGH-VALUE (HIGH-VALUES): represents the highest values that can be placed in a storage location.
(4) LOW-VALUE (LOW-VALUES): represents the lowest values that can be placed in a storage location.

4.8 VALUE Clause: Literals

Nonnumeric literals	Status
'START REWIND'	valid
'OCTOBER 1, 1974'	valid
'12345'	valid
'ENTER STUDENT'S NAME'	invalid, imbedded quotation mark
'JOB ABORT.	invalid, missing a rightmost quotation mark
'IDENTIFICATION DIVISION'	valid

Fig. 4.16 Valid and invalid nonnumeric literals.

(5) ALL 'CHARACTER': generates a sequence of characters specified by any nonnumeric literal.

(6) QUOTE (QUOTES): represents one or more quotation marks.

The programmer can use these figurative constants as literals whenever the need is there. For example, the statement

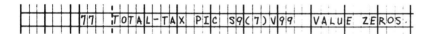

would initialize the data item TOTAL-TAX to zeros, whereas the statement

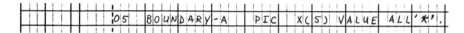

would have the same effect as

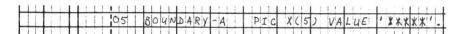

which describes the data item BOUNDARY-A as a 5-storage-position item containing five asterisks (*).

Example

Write the following data item description entries in the WORKING-STORAGE SECTION:

(1) a 2-digit line-counter, initialized to 1, and
(2) a record description entry for the heading

record-name: HEADING-1

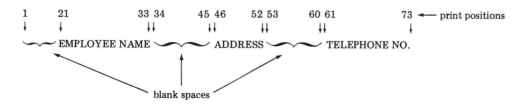

Fig. 4.17

56   4 DATA DIVISION

Solution

```
        WORKING-STORAGE SECTION.
   77   LINE-COUNTER    PIC  99      VALUE 1.
   01   HEADING-1.
        05 FILLER       PIC  X(20)   VALUE SPACES.
        05 NAME-H       PIC  X(13)   VALUE 'EMPLOYEE NAME'.
        05 FILLER       PIC  X(12)   VALUE SPACES.
        05 ADD-H        PIC  X(7)    VALUE 'ADDRESS'.
        05 FILLER       PIC  X(8)    VALUE SPACES.
        05 TELE-NO-H    PIC  X(13)   VALUE 'TELEPHONE NO.'
```

Fig. 4.18 WORKING-STORAGE SECTION entries.

4.9 SAMPLE PROGRAM 4A: OVERDUE PAYMENT NOTICE

To illustrate the complete structure of a COBOL program, a sample program with detailed division-by-division description is now presented. The reader is urged to study this program, keypunch it, and run it on the computer.

This program reads the payment record from the CUSTOMER-FILE and produces the overdue payment notices. Note that the spacing of the output is designed so that the customer's name and address will show in a window envelope, thus eliminating the need for separate addressing of the envelope.

Input Description: PAYMENT-REC

Sample input Data: PUNCHED CARDS†

```
1                      21                  41                        66    71   78
↓                      ↓                   ↓                         ↓     ↓    ↓
MARCINKO, GEORGE       125 OAK STREET      NEWTON,N.Y. 10014         34960 10/11/75
CHAI W A               121 LAKE STREET     MONTCLAIR NJ 07043        14680 12/31/75
CASH, JOHN K           69 WEB PLACE        BRONX,N.Y. 10052          11120 12/13/75
```

† Numbers (1, 21, and so on) indicate column positions.

4.9 Sample Program 4A: Overdue Payment Notice   57

Program Logic

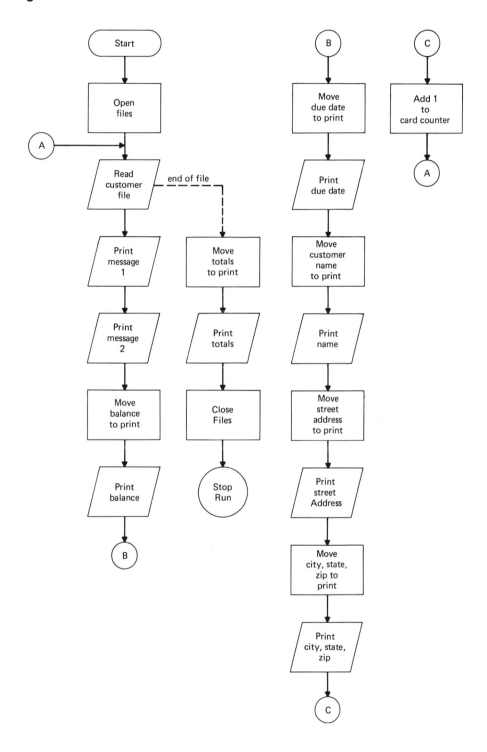

58   4 DATA DIVISION

Source Listing

```
0C001           IDENTIFICATION DIVISION.
0C002           PROGRAM-ID. 'SAMPL4A'
0C003           AUTHOR.  CHAI
0C004           REMARKS.  THIS PROGRAM READS CUSTOMER FILE AND PRODUCES AN
0C005                    OVERDUE PAYMENT NOTICES.
0C006           ENVIRONMENT DIVISION.
0C007           INPUT-OUTPUT SECTION.
0C008           FILE-CONTROL.
0C009               SELECT CUSTOMER-FILE ASSIGN TO UR-2501-S-SYSIN.
0C010               SELECT PRINT-FILE ASSIGN TO UR-1403-S-SYSOUT.
0C011      *******************************************************************
0C012           DATA DIVISION.
0C013           FILE SECTION.
0C014           FD CUSTOMER-FILE
0C015               LABEL RECORDS ARE OMITTED,
0C016               DATA RECORD IS PAYMENT-REC.
0C017           01 PAYMENT-REC.
0C018               05 NAME PIC A(20).
0C019               05 STREET-ADDRESS PIC X(20).
0C020               05 CITY-STATE-ZIP PIC X(20).          ⎫
0C021               05 FILLER PIC X(5).                   ⎬ input description
0C022               05 BALANCE PIC 999V99.                ⎪
0C023               05 DUE-DATE PIC X(8).                 ⎪
0C024               05 FILLER PIC X(2).                   ⎭
0C025           FD PRINT-FILE
0C026               LABEL RECORDS ARE OMITTED
0C027               DATA RECORDS IS PRINT-AREA.
0C028           01 PRINT-AREA.                            ⎫
0C029               05 FILLER PIC X(16).                  ⎬ output area
0C030               05 PRINT-LINE PIC X(100).             ⎭
0C031           WORKING-STORAGE SECTION.
0C032           77 CARD-KOUNTER PIC 9999 VALUE ZEROS.
0C033           01 LINE-1.
0C034               05 FILLER PIC X(16) VALUE SPACES.
0C035               05 FILLER PIC X(39) VALUE       'HAVE YOU OVERLOOKED YOUR PAYM
0C036         -     'ENT....'.
0C037           01 LINE-1A.
0C038               05 FILLER PIC X(16) VALUE SPACES.                           ⎫
0C039               05 FILLER PIC X(50) VALUE 'IF ALREADY PAID PLEASE DISREGARD  ⎪ line-by-line
0C040         -     'THIS NOTICE.'.                                              ⎬ output descriptions
0C041           01 LINE-2.                                                       ⎪
0C042               05 FILLER PIC X(16) VALUE SPACES.                            ⎪
0C043               05 FILLER PIC X(13) VALUE 'PAYMENT DUE    '.                 ⎪
0C044               05 BALANCE-P PIC $$$9.99.                                    ⎪
0C045           01 LINE-3.                                                       ⎪
0C046               05 FILLER PIC X(16) VALUE SPACES.                            ⎪
0C047               05 FILLER PIC X(10) VALUE 'DUE-DATE'.                        ⎪
0C048               05 DUE-DATE-P PIC X(8).                                      ⎭
0C049           01 FINAL-PRINT-LINE.                                             ⎫
0C050               05 FILLER PIC X(10) VALUE SPACES.                            ⎪
0C051               05 MSSAGE PIC X(35) VALUE 'TOTAL NUMBER OF CARDS IS'.        ⎬ final print line
0C052               05 FILLER PIC X(5) VALUE SPACES.                             ⎪
0C053               05 KOUNTER-P PIC Z9.                                         ⎭
0C054      *******************************************************************
0C055           PROCEDURE DIVISION.
0C056           BEGIN.
0C057               OPEN INPUT CUSTOMER-FILE, OUTPUT PRINT-FILE.      ← open all files
0C058           READ-CARDS.
0C059               READ CUSTOMER-FILE AT END GO TO EOJ.              ← read input
0C060               WRITE PRINT-AREA FROM LINE-1 AFTER ADVANCING 10 LINES.    ⎫
0C061               WRITE PRINT-AREA FROM LINE-1A AFTER ADVANCING 1 LINES.    ⎪
0C062               MOVE BALANCE TO BALANCE-P.                                ⎪
0C063               WRITE PRINT-AREA FROM LINE-2 AFTER ADVANCING 4 LINES.     ⎪ print output
0C064               MOVE DUE-DATE TO DUE-DATE-P.                              ⎬ (one line at a time, a total
0C065               WRITE PRINT-AREA FROM LINE-3 AFTER ADVANCING 2 LINES.     ⎪ of 7 lines per input card)
0C066               MOVE NAME TO PRINT-LINE.                                  ⎪
0C067               WRITE PRINT-AREA AFTER ADVANCING 6 LINES.                 ⎪
0C068               MOVE STREET-ADDRESS TO PRINT-LINE.                        ⎪
0C069               WRITE PRINT-AREA AFTER ADVANCING 1 LINES.                 ⎪
0C070               MOVE CITY-STATE-ZIP TO PRINT-LINE.                        ⎪
0C071               WRITE PRINT-AREA AFTER ADVANCING 1 LINES.                 ⎪
0C072               ADD 1 TO CARD-KOUNTER.                                    ⎪
0C073               GO TO READ-CARDS.                                         ⎭
0C074           EOJ.
0C075               MOVE CARD-KOUNTER TO KOUNTER-P.                     ⎫
0C076               MOVE FINAL-PRINT-LINE TO PRINT-AREA.                ⎪
0C077               WRITE PRINT-AREA AFTER ADVANCING 4 LINES.           ⎬ end of program
0C078               CLOSE CUSTOMER-FILE, PRINT-FILE.                    ⎪
0C079               STOP RUN.                                           ⎭
```

4.9 Sample Program 4A: Overdue Payment Notice

Sample Output

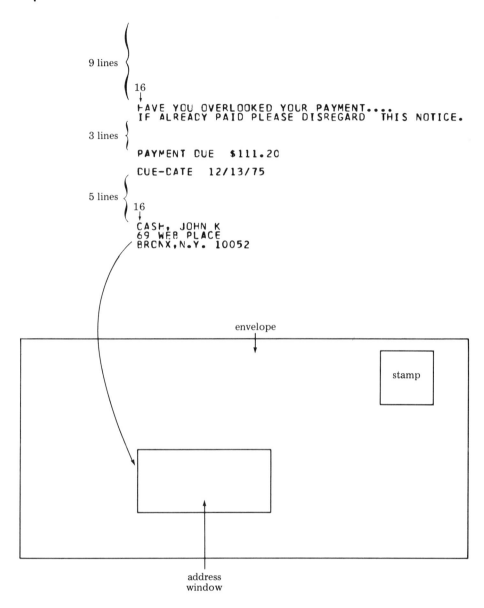

Programming Notes: Division-by-Division Explanation

(1) 00001–00005: IDENTIFICATION DIVISION. These statements identify the program as 'SAMPL4A', name the programmer, and give a brief description of the program (under REMARKS).

(2) 00006–00010: ENVIRONMENT DIVISION. These statements identify the data files as CUSTOMER-FILE and PRINT-FILE and assign these files to specific input/output devices (an IBM 2501 card reader and 1403 line printer). (The ASSIGN clause is usually machine dependent. The reader should consult the local COBOL manual for proper device names.)

(3) 00011: Asterisks are used to improve the readability of the program. (They are used to separate each division of the COBOL program.) These asterisks are treated as comments and must be preceded by an asterisk in column 7.

(4) 00012-00053: DATA DIVISION. These statements describe data files and working-storage areas utilized by the program. The division contains two sections: the FILE SECTION and the WORKING-STORAGE SECTION.

    A. 00013-00030: FILE SECTION. The FILE SECTION provides a detailed description of the CUSTOMER-FILE and PRINT-FILE. Note that each file description begins with an FD and is followed by the LABEL clause and the DATA RECORD clause. The record description entries follow immediately after each file description entry. These entries are identified by the 01 level number (sequence 00018 and 00019). The 05 level numbers specify the individual data fields of each record. Sequence 00017-00024 shows the data record PAYMENT-REC containing 7 data fields. Sequence 00028-00030 indicates the PRINT-AREA, which contains two data fields; one is identified as FILLER (00029), which is a special COBOL reserved name to indicate part of the storage areas that are not affected by the program instructions. The other field is the PRINT-LINE, which contains one-hundred positions of alphanumeric characters.

    B. 00031-00053: WORKING-STORAGE SECTION. This section describes the working area and the constants that are utilized by the program. It contains one independent-storage item CARD-KOUNTER and four group items LINE-1, LINE-1A, LINE-2, and LINE-3. Note that the independent item CARD-KOUNTER is identified by the level number 77, while the group items all have an 01 level number. Group items must follow all the 77 level numbers in the WORKING-STORAGE SECTION. Some individual highlights of these entries are presented below.

      (i) 00032: The CARD-KOUNTER is a four-digit field. The VALUE ZEROS clause is used to set the field with initial value zeros.

      (ii) 00033-00036: LINE-1 is a group item that is a composite of two data items identified as FILLER. The first data item (00034) reserves 16 blank spaces. The second defines a nonnumeric literal 'HAVE YOU OVERLOOKED YOUR PAYMENT . . .'. Such literals must be enclosed by quotation marks. Also note that two lines are needed to specify the literal information. Thus, a hyphen is placed in column 7 of the continuation line (00036). Note that the same hyphen is also found in 00040.

      (iii) 00044, 00053: These lines contain the special editing symbols $ and Z in the PICTURE clause. These symbols will be discussed in detail in Chapter 6.

(5) 00055-00079: PROCEDURE DIVISION. These statements specify the required program instructions as outlined in the program flowchart (page 57). They consist of three paragraphs (also known as procedures), namely, BEGIN, READ-CARDS, and EOJ.

The BEGIN paragraph contains only one instruction, namely, the OPEN statement, which in effect prepares the input/output device for processing.

The READ-CARDS paragraph contains fifteen statements, which direct the computer to read input data from the CUSTOMER-FILE and to print out the overdue payment notice. Note that there is a WRITE statement for each line of printout and all data must be "moved" to the output record area (that is, PRINT-AREA) before printing out.

The EOJ paragraph prints out the final total and closes all files before terminating the program execution via the statement STOP RUN. This paragraph will be executed only if all input records from the CUSTOMER-FILE have been processed.

EXERCISES

1. What is the function of the DATA DIVISION?

2. Define the following terms:
   file   logical record
   record   level indicator
   data item   filler
   elementary item

3. Briefly explain the function of the following terms:
   FILE SECTION   LABEL RECORD clause
   WORKING-STORAGE SECTION   PICTURE clause
   BLOCK CONTAINS clause   VALUE clause

4. True or false:
   (a) A file may not contain more than one type of record.
   (b) An elementary item may be divided into smaller data fields.
   (c) Each data item must contain a level indicator when appearing in the DATA DIVISION.
   (d) Every file description entry begins with the level indicator FD.
   (e) If the ENVIRONMENT DIVISION of a program contains three SELECT entries, then there must be three FD entries in the DATA DIVISION.
   (f) The LABEL RECORD clause is the only required clause in the file description entry for each file named.
   (g) The number of level numbers must be consecutive in the description of data items.
   (h) The 02 level indicates that the data item is a record.
   (i) The statement

   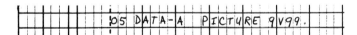

   reserves four positions in core for DATA-A.

5. An inventory file containing stock records that are key punched on data cards has the following format:

   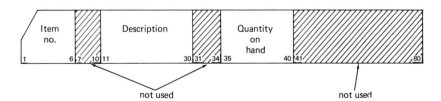

   Write a complete file and record descriptions for this file.

62   4   DATA DIVISION

6   Fill in the appropriate information for the following problems:

(a)

Actual data in core	Meaning	Picture
123	1.23	
13579	135.79	
25	0.0025	
25	25000.00	
15	1000.05	

(b)

Actual data in core	Meaning	Picture
456		9(3)V.
456		VP(3)999.
456		9P(3)V99.

(c)

Actual data in core	Field size	Picture
MARCINKO-CHAI ASSOC.	19	
123 Duncan St.	14	
123 456	7	
123	3	
5%	1	
TR3-2812	8	

7   Write record-description entries for the following record:

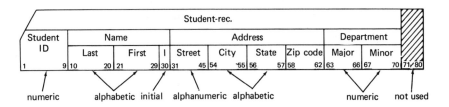

8   Which of the following items represent valid numeric or nonnumeric literals? (Otherwise, identify errors.)

    (a)   +1,412   (e)   '1974'
    (b)   861.   (f)   'DATA DIVISION'
    (c)   −416   (g) $180.50
    (d)   'It won't work'   (h)   75.55

9   Write the following data item description entries in the WORKING-STORAGE SECTION.

    (1)   A 5-position BONUS-A, initialized to 275.50.
    (2)   A record-description entry for the following heading:

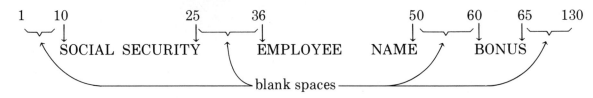

5
PROCEDURE DIVISION

The PROCEDURE DIVISION specifies the commands and instructions that the computer is to follow. It is written much like ordinary English and usually consists of a series of paragraphs that may be grouped into sections. Paragraphs are identified by programmer-supplied names. These names, known as procedure names, must begin at the A-margin of the coding form and are used to refer to the procedure. In the example shown in Fig. 5.1, the PROCEDURE DIVISION contains three paragraphs, BEGIN, READ-CARD, and END-JOB. Each paragraph normally contains a series of sentences that are composed of one or more statements. Most of the statements begin with a "verb"—a COBOL reserved word that specifies the action to be taken by the computer. In Fig. 5.1, words such as OPEN, READ, MOVE, GO TO, CLOSE, and STOP are COBOL verbs. Statements must begin at the B-margin of the coding form.

COBOL statements follow certain specific formats. Before they can write successful programs, beginning programmers must learn the functions of each of these statements. In this chapter some of the most commonly used statements are discussed. These statements are

    OPEN   ACCEPT
    CLOSE   DISPLAY
    MOVE   GO TO
    READ   STOP
    WRITE   PERFORM

5.1 OPEN STATEMENT

Every input/output file defined in the COBOL program must be "opened" before it can be processed and must be "closed" after the processing of that file is completed.

The OPEN statement is used to initiate the processing of files. The purpose of the statement is to activate each file and to ensure that each file has been properly set (for example, mounted on a tape drive).

5 PROCEDURE DIVISION

```
            PROCEDURE DIVISION.
        BEGIN.
            OPEN INPUT CARD-FILE OUTPUT PRINT-FILE.
            MOVE SPACES TO PRINT-AREA.
        READ-CARD.
            READ CARD-FILE AT END GO TO END-JOB.
            MOVE CARD-REC TO PRINT-AREA.
            WRITE PRINT-AREA.
            GO TO READ-CARD.
        END-JOB.
            CLOSE CARD-FILE, PRINT-FILE.
            STOP RUN.
```

Fig. 5.1 Example of PROCEDURE DIVISION.

The simplest form of the OPEN statement is

$$\text{OPEN} \left\{ \begin{array}{l} \underline{\text{INPUT}} \\ \underline{\text{OUTPUT}} \\ \underline{\text{I-O}} \end{array} \right\} \text{file-name-1 [, file-name-2, \ldots]}$$

Notice in the format that the word INPUT must be used for a file that may be read only (for example, input data card file), the word OUTPUT must be used for a file that may be written only (for example, printed report file), and the word I–O is used for a file that may be read from or written on (for example, update files). The following examples illustrate how the OPEN statement can be properly coded.

Example 1

The above statement would cause both of the files CARDFILE AND TPFILE to be opened as input files. But it would be incorrect to have written

The key word INPUT must appear only once in an OPEN statement. However, one may open two input files with separate OPEN statements:

```
            OPEN INPUT CARDFILE.
            OPEN INPUT TPFILE.
```

(The above comments apply as well to OUTPUT and I–O files.)

Example 2

```
            OPEN INPUT CARDFILE
                 OUTPUT PRINTFILE
                 I-O UPDATE-FILE.
```

Example 3

```
OPEN INPUT CARDFILE.
OPEN I-O UPDATE-FILE.
OPEN OUTPUT PRINTFILE.
```

Both of the above examples are valid. Example 2 shows that one may use a single OPEN statement to open files of different kinds. In fact, the order of the files that are to be opened is not important so long as files have been opened prior to any other input/output statement, such as READ or WRITE.

5.2 CLOSE STATEMENT

The CLOSE Statement is used to deactivate a file from the program. Once a file is closed, it can not be processed by the program again unless it is opened again. Thus, no files should be closed unless all processing has been completed on that file.

The simplest form of the CLOSE statement is

$$\text{CLOSE file-name-1, file-name-2, ...}$$

Note that more than one file can be closed with a single CLOSE statement. For example the statement

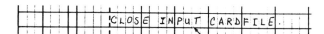

would cause the two files CARDFILE and PRINTFILE to be closed. Note also that the type of files (INPUT, OUTPUT, or I-O) being closed should not be specified. In fact, the statement

```
CLOSE INPUT CARDFILE.
```

is incorrect (file type INPUT is not allowed in the CLOSE statement) and would cause a syntax error during the COBOL program compilation.

5.3 MOVE STATEMENT

The MOVE statement is used to move the contents of one data area in the main storage to another area. The MOVE statement has the following format:

$$\text{MOVE} \begin{Bmatrix} \text{identifier-1} \\ \text{literal} \end{Bmatrix} \text{TO identifier-2 [, identifier-3, ...]}$$

In the format, identifier-1 and literal represent the sending (source) field; identifier-2 [, identifier-3, ...] represents the receiving field. The data designated by identifier-1 or literal are moved to identifier-2, then to identifier-3 (if specified), and so on. The contents of the sending field are unchanged after the MOVE statement.

Some examples of the MOVE statement are given below.

Example 1

Example 2

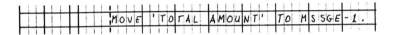

Example 3

In Example 1, the contents of X would be moved to the data areas named Y, Z, and W. In Example 2, the literal 'TOTAL AMOUNT' is the source field that would be moved to the data area identified by MSSGE-1. In Example 3, a figurative constant SPACES is used to clear the area identified by PRINT-LINE by blank spaces. There are many rules governing the MOVE statements. A detailed description of these rules will be presented in the next chapter.

5.4 READ STATEMENT

The purpose of the READ statement is to make available the next logical record from an input or I–O file. In files such as data cards and magnetic tapes (that is, sequential files), the READ statement must contain an AT END clause, which prescribes the action that is to be taken after the last record of the file has been processed. The READ statement for the sequential file takes the form

<u>READ</u> file-name RECORD <u>INTO</u> data-record AT <u>END</u> imperative-statement.

In the READ statement, the file-name must be defined by a file description (FD) entry in the DATA DIVISION. When a READ statement is executed, the next logical record in the named file is transferred from the input unit and stored in the area defined in the DATA DIVISION.

The AT END clause is required for files such as cards and tapes. The 'imperative-statement' is executed when an end-of-data condition is detected for the input file. For example, the statement

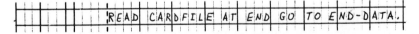

would direct the computer to execute the first instruction following the procedure name END-DATA when the end-of-data condition is detected. (The statement GO TO END-DATA is an example of an imperative statement.)

A READ statement with the INTO identifier option will, in effect, not only store the input record at its usual input area as specified in the file description entry, but move it to a new storage area as identified by the identifier. The identifier must be the name of a working-storage entry or an output record of a previously opened file. For instance, the statement

```
        READ SALES-FILE INTO WORK-RECORD
            AT END GO TO END-JOB.
```

would cause the next logical record from SALES-FILE to be placed in the input area as well as in the area specified by WORK-RECORD.

The use of the READ statement as it applies to random-access files and tape files is discussed in Chapters 11 and 14.

5.5 WRITE STATEMENT

The WRITE statement is used to transfer data from internal storage to a file on an external unit. The WRITE statement as applied to a printer or card punched unit takes the form

$$\underline{\text{WRITE}} \text{ record-name} \left[\underline{\text{FROM}} \text{ identifier-1}\right]$$
$$\left[\begin{Bmatrix}\underline{\text{BEFORE}}\\\underline{\text{AFTER}}\end{Bmatrix} \underline{\text{ADVANCING}} \begin{Bmatrix}\text{identifier-2 LINES}\\\text{integer LINES}\\\text{mnemonic-name}\end{Bmatrix}\right]$$

Note that in the WRITE format we use the record-name, whereas in the READ format the file-name is used. That is, in COBOL, we *READ* a file and *WRITE* a record.

The record-name in the WRITE statement is the name of a logical record in the FILE SECTION of the DATA DIVISION, while identifier-1, if used, must refer to an area in the WORKING-STORAGE SECTION or in another FD.

The FROM option is an often used feature. If it is specified, contents stored in identifier-1 are moved to the output area, after which the writing is accomplished. That is, the statement

WRITE record-name FROM identifier-1.

is equivalent to the statement

MOVE identifier-1 TO record-name.

followed by the statement

WRITE record-name.

Printed Report†

In case a printer is used for output, each output record occupies one printed line and lines advance automatically either *before* or *after* the writing, depending on the ADVANCING option.

† The WRITE statement for the magnetic tape and disk files is discussed in Chapters 11 and 14, respectively.

5 PROCEDURE DIVISION

The effect of an ADVANCING option is obvious: If BEFORE is used, the writing is performed before the line is advanced. Otherwise, writing occurs after the line is advanced. If the ADVANCING option is not used, single spacing will automatically occur (before printing) each time the WRITE statement is executed.

Example 1

The statement

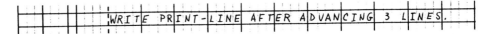

would automatically advance the page 3 lines before printing the data.

Example 2

The statement

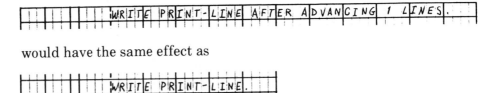

would have the same effect as

Example 3

The statement

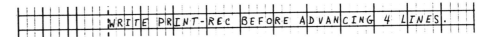

would first print the data then advance the page 4 lines. Since the word LINES is optional, this statement would have the same effect as

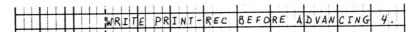

If identifier-2 is used in the ADVANCING option, the printer page would advance the specified number of lines according to the contents of identifier-2. Identifier-2 must be the name of a nonnegative elementary item containing an integer whose value is less than 100. For example, if in the WORKING-STORAGE SECTION, we have

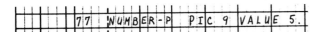

then the statement

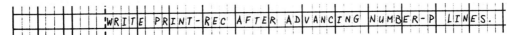

would advance the page 5 lines before printing.

Note: In certain COBOL compilers, when 0 (zero) is specified in the integer LINES option, it may result in a "page eject" (that is, skipping to the top of a new page). For example, the statements

```
        WRITE PRINT-AREA AFTER 0 LINES.
        WRITE PRINT-AREA AFTER 0.
        WRITE PRINT-AREA POSITION 0.
```

could all cause the printer to print out the contents of PRINT-AREA after skipping to the top of a new page.

Mnemonic-Name Option for Printing

The mnemonic-name option is used to monitor the carriage-control mechanism of the printer for performing spacing and skipping. When the mnemonic named is used, it must be defined in the SPECIAL-NAMES paragraph of the ENVIRONMENT DIVISION. For example, in the statement

```
        WRITE PRINT-REC AFTER ADVANCING CHANNEL-1.
```

CHANNEL-1 is a mnemonic name (why?) that must be defined in the ENVIRONMENT DIVISION. These entries might appear as follows:

```
        ENVIRONMENT DIVISION.
        SOURCE-COMPUTER. IBM-370.
        OBJECT-COMPUTER. IBM-370.
        SPECIAL-NAMES.
            C01 IS CHANNEL-1.
```

where C01 is a functional name that would cause the carriage-control tape to skip to CHANNEL-1 (that is, go to the top of a new page). Other functional names and their meanings pertinent to the IBM 360/370 system computers are

CSP: suppress spacing,
C01 through C12: skip to CHANNEL-1 through CHANNEL-12, respectively.

Mnemonic names are machine dependent. The reader is urged to consult the local COBOL manual for further information before using them.

5.6 ACCEPT STATEMENT

READ and WRITE statements are used to transfer large amounts of data records between external units and the internal storages. These records must be organized as files. However, for small amounts of data that are not suitably organized as files (for example, communication between console operator and the program), the ACCEPT and DISPLAY statements are employed.

The ACCEPT statement is often used to receive data from an on-line typewriter or low-volume data from the card reader. The statement takes the form

ACCEPT identifier <u>FROM</u> mnemonic name.

Identifier may be either a fixed-length group item or an elementary item, which must be defined in the WORKING-STORAGE SECTION of the DATA DIVISION. The mnemonic name may assume either the meaning SYSIN (that is, card reader) or CONSOLE, and it must be specified in the SPECIAL-NAMES paragraph of the ENVIRONMENT DIVISION. Some examples of ACCEPT statements are shown below.

Example 1

Example 2

Example 3

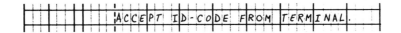

In Example 1, since the FROM option is not specified, input would come from SYSIN. In this case, an input record size of 80 characters or a multiple of 80 is assumed.

In Examples 2 and 3, TERMINAL and CARD-READER are mnemonic names that must be defined in the SPECIAL-NAMES paragraph of the ENVIRONMENT DIVISION. These entries might appear as follows:

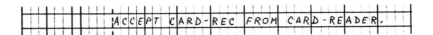

When the ACCEPT statement is encountered, in some systems the computer will suspend the execution of the program and display the message AWAITING REPLY. The program would resume its normal operations after the appropriate data are entered through the ACCEPT statement.

5.7 DISPLAY STATEMENT

The DISPLAY statement is often used to print brief messages on the console typewriter to the operator concerning program status or error conditions that might occur during the execution of a program. The DISPLAY statement takes the form

$$\underline{\text{DISPLAY}} \begin{Bmatrix} \text{identifier-1} \\ \text{literal-1} \end{Bmatrix} \begin{bmatrix} \begin{Bmatrix} \text{identifier-2} \\ \text{literal-2} \end{Bmatrix} \end{bmatrix} [\underline{\text{UPON}} \text{ mnemonic-name}].$$

The mnemonic name must be specified in the SPECIAL-NAMES paragraph of the ENVIRONMENT DIVISION. Such names may be associated only with reserved functional names CONSOLE, SYSPUNCH (that is, card punch), and SYSOUT (line printer). When the UPON option is omitted, the SYSOUT device is assumed.

Some examples of DISPLAY statements are presented below.

Example 1

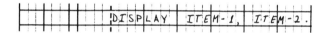

Example 2

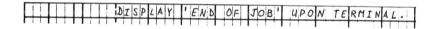

Example 3

Example 4

In Examples 1 and 2, since the UPON option is not given, output would be from the printer (SYSOUT). For SYSOUT, the maximum logical record size is 120 characters. In Examples 3 and 4, TERMINAL and LINE-PRINTER are mnemonics that must be defined in the SPECIAL-NAMES paragraph of the ENVIRONMENT DIVISION. These entries might appear as

Also note that in Example 4, a literal message "NUMBER OF RECORDS ARE" followed by the contents of RECORD-COUNT would be printed on the system line-printer. The RECORD-COUNT is an identifier that must be defined in the WORKING-STORAGE SECTION of the DATA DIVISION.

5.8 GO TO STATEMENT

In a COBOL program, statements are usually executed sequentially. However, there are times when it is necessary to alter the sequence and cause the program to transfer its control to another portion of the program. Such a transfer is accomplished by a branching statement. The simplest branching statement is the GO TO statement, which has the form

<u>GO TO</u> procedure-name.

Procedure-name must be the name of a paragraph or section defined in the PROCEDURE DIVISION. When the GO TO statement is executed, the program is unconditionally branched to the paragraph or section specified. Then the normal flow of control of the program would be assumed at the start of the paragraph or section. For example, the statement

```
            GO TO READ-MORE.
```

would cause the program to branch to a procedure (that is, paragraph) called READ-MORE.

Other types of branching statements are discussed in later chapters.

5.9 STOP STATEMENT

Every COBOL program must have a STOP statement of the form

```
            STOP RUN.
```

Such a statement signifies the end of the program execution and switches the control of the computer back to the operating system. The STOP RUN statement need not be the last statement in the program physically, but it must be the last statement to be executed by the program. All input/output files definitely must be closed before a STOP RUN statement is issued.

There is another form of the STOP statement, namely,

<u>STOP</u> literal.

Literal may be a numeric, nonnumeric, or figurative constant. For example, the statement

would cause the operator console to display the appropriate message and would halt the execution until restarted by the operator.

5.10 PERFORM STATEMENT

The PERFORM statement is often recognized as one of the most powerful statements in COBOL. It provides a convenient way to transfer the program control to and from a procedure (that is, paragraph or routine) written elsewhere in a program. Thus, it enables the programmer to divide a complicated and massive program into a collection of small

5.10 PERFORM Statement 73

and fairly straightforward routines (that is, procedures). There are four different formats for the PERFORM statement. The simplest PERFORM statement has the format

<u>PERFORM</u> procedure-name-1

Procedure-name-1 may be either a paragraph or section name. In this format, the statement would cause the computer to execute the first statement in procedure-name-1. After the execution of the entire collection of instructions in procedure-name-1, the program would automatically return to execute the statement immediately following the PERFORM command.

Example 1

In the coding

```
            PERFORM SUM-ROUTINE.
            WRITE PRINT-REC.
transfer to
            .
            .                                   return to
            .
    SUM-ROUTINE.
            ADD SALES-AMT TO SUM.
            ADD 1 TO KOUNTER.
            MOVE SUM-REC TO PRINT-REC.
    PROC-X
```

the PERFORM statement would cause the program to branch to the procedure named SUM-ROUTINE. After all the statements in SUM-ROUTINE are executed (in this case, there are three statements), the program would automatically return the control to the statement immediately following the PERFORM command, that is,

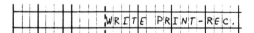

Thus, the use of the PERFORM statement enables the program to branch out to a procedure (paragraph, or section) and then return to the statement immediately following the branching point. However, if a GO TO statement or a conditional statement appears within the procedure named, the program control might not return to its proper place, as shown in the following example.

Example 2

In this example, upon the execution of the PERFORM command, the program would branch to PARA-X. The program first executes the READ B-REC statement and then branches to PARA-W if B-CODE is equal to 'W'. Thus, in this case, the program would not return to the statement following the PERFORM command.

74   5 PROCEDURE DIVISION

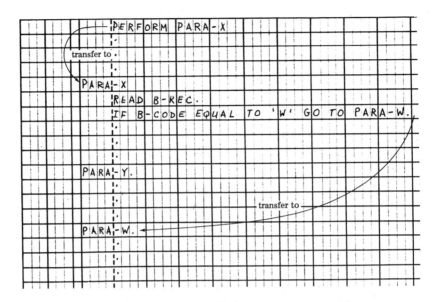

Other types of PERFORM statements will be discussed in Chapter 10.

5.11 SAMPLE PROGRAM 5A: CUSTOMER ADDRESS LISTING

In order to illustrate the complete structure of a COBOL program, a sample program that produces a customer name and address listing from a file of data cards is presented here. The complete documentation for this problem, including the input/output formats, flowchart, and COBOL program source listing are illustrated.

Input Description

Each card contains customer number, name, and address. The format of the card is illustrated below:

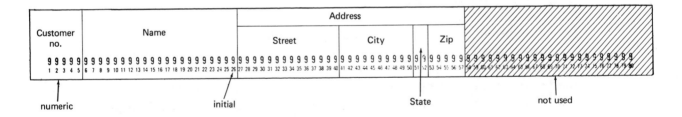

Sample Input

```
12345 SMITH BOOK STORE      123 VALLY RD MONTCLAIR NJ 07043   ← card #1
12479 MARCINKO-CHAI ASSOC  1245 BROADWAY NEW YORK NY 10024   ← card #2
```

Output Description

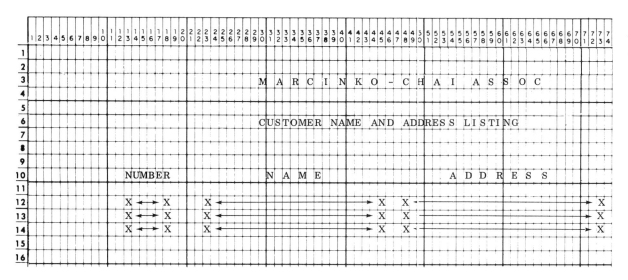

Program Logic

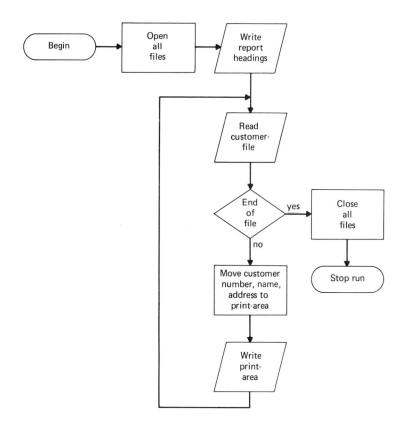

Source Listing

```
00001              IDENTIFICATION DIVISION.
00002              PROGRAM-ID.  'SAMPL5A'
00003         ***************************************
00004              ENVIRONMENT DIVISION.
00005              CONFIGURATION SECTION.
00006              SOURCE-COMPUTER.    IBM-370.
00007              OBJECT-COMPUTER.    IBM-370.
00008              INPUT-OUTPUT SECTION.
00009              FILE-CONTROL.
00010                  SELECT  CUSTOMER-FILE
00011                      ASSIGN TO UR-2501-S-CARDIN.
00012                  SELECT PRINT-FILE
00013                      ASSIGN TO UR-1403-S-PROUT.
00014         ***************************************
00015              DATA DIVISION.
00016              FILE SECTION.
00017              FD  CUSTOMER-FILE
00018                  LABEL RECORDS ARE OMITTED
00019                  DATA RECORDS ARE CUSTOMER-REC.
00020              01  CUSTOMER-REC.
00021                  05  CUSTOMER-NO     PIC   X(5).
00022                  05  CUSTOMER-NAME   PIC   X(21).
00023                  05  CUSTOMER-ADDRESS.
00024                      08  STREET  PIC   X(14).
00025                      08  CITY    PIC   X(10).
00026                      08  STATE   PIC   AA.
00027                      08  FILLER  PIC   XX.
00028                      08  ZIP     PIC   9(5).
00029                  05  FILLER      PIC   X(21).
00030              FD  PRINT-FILE
00031                  LABEL RECORDS ARE OMITTED
00032                  DATA RECORDS ARE PRINT-AREA.
00033              01  PRINT-AREA PIC X(133).
00034              WORKING-STORAGE SECTION.
00035              01  HEADING-1.
00036                  05  FILLER  PIC  X(21) VALUE SPACES.
00037                  05  FILLER  PIC  X(45) JUST RIGHT
00038                      VALUE 'M A R C I N K O - C H A I  A S S O C'.
00039              01  HEADING-2.
00040                  05  FILLER  PIC  X(30) VALUE SPACES.
00041                  05  FILLER  PIC  X(40)
00042                      VALUE 'CUSTOMER NAME AND ADDRESS LISTING'.
00043              01  HEADING-3.
00044                  05  FILLER PIC X(19)  JUST RIGHT
00045                      VALUE 'NUMBER'.
00046                  05  FILLER  PIC X(17)  JUST RIGHT
00047                      VALUE 'N A M E'.
00048                  05  FILLER  PIC  X(31)  JUST RIGHT
00049                      VALUE 'A D D R E S S'.
00050              01  PRINT-LINE.
00051                  05  FILLER  PIC X(13)  VALUE SPACES.
00052                  05  CUSTOMER-NO-P  PIC 9(5).
00053                  05  FILLER  PIC X(5)  VALUE SPACES.
00054                  05  NAME-P  PIC  X(26).
00055                  05  ADDRESS-P PIC  X(35).
00056         ***************************************
00057              PROCEDURE DIVISION.
00058              BEGIN.
00059                  OPEN  INPUT CUSTOMER-FILE  OUTPUT PRINT-FILE.
00060                  WRITE PRINT-AREA FROM HEADING-1 AFTER ADVANCING 1 LINES.
00061                  WRITE PRINT-AREA FROM HEADING-2 AFTER ADVANCING 3 LINES.
00062                  WRITE PRINT-AREA FROM HEADING-3 AFTER ADVANCING 4 LINES.
00063              READ-PRINT.
00064                  READ CUSTOMER-FILE AT END GO TO END-JOB.
00065                  MOVE CUSTOMER-NO  TO  CUSTOMER-NO-P.
00066                  MOVE CUSTOMER-NAME  TO NAME-P.
00067                  MOVE CUSTOMER-ADDRESS TO ADDRESS-P.
00068                  WRITE PRINT-AREA FROM PRINT-LINE AFTER ADVANCING 2 LINES.
00069                  GO TO READ-PRINT.
00070              END-JOB.
00071                  CLOSE CUSTOMER-FILE, PRINT-FILE.
00072                  STOP RUN.
```

Annotations:
- Lines 00020–00029: input descriptions
- Line 00033: output area
- Lines 00035–00038: report heading (first line)
- Lines 00039–00042: report heading (second line)
- Lines 00043–00049: subheading
- Lines 00050–00055: detail print line (one input card per print line)
- Lines 00060–00062: print headings
- Lines 00064–00068: print input data
- Lines 00070–00072: end of program

5.12 Sample Program 5B: 80/80 Card Listing (ACCEPT and DISPLAY Statements)

Sample Output

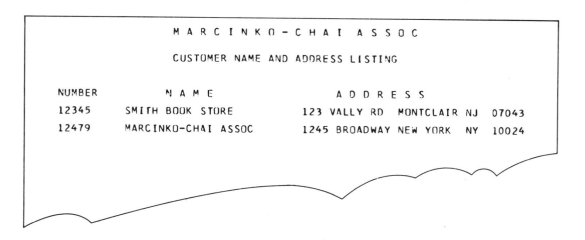

Programming Notes

(1) 00033: 01 PRINT-AREA PIC X(133).

The IBM 1403 printer allows up to 132 printed positions per line. However, 133 printed positions are specified here. The reason for the extra position is that with IBM equipment the first position of the printed record is always reserved for the printer to control the positioning of the printed line. This position is known as the carriage-control character, which is never printed. The WRITE statement in COBOL would automatically cause an appropriate character to be inserted in this position. However, it is the responsibility of the programmer to reserve this position, as done here.

(2) 00037: 05 FILLER PIC X(45) JUST RIGHT
      00038:   VALUE 'MARCINKO-CHAI ASSOC.'

The JUST RIGHT clause causes the computer to override the convention of left-justifying. Thus, values are stored from right to left as shown below (a detailed discussion of the JUSTIFIED clause is given in Chapter 6):

```
| 1 3|4  6|7|8    |12    16    20    24    28    32    36    40    44    48
|    |    | |  M  A  R  C  I  N  K  O  -  C  H  A  I     A  S  S  O  C  .  .
```

5.12 SAMPLE PROGRAM 5B: 80/80 CARD LISTING (ACCEPT AND DISPLAY STATEMENTS)

COBOL programs tend to be wordy and are unusually long especially for the beginner, who must often keypunch his own source program. The following program is perhaps one of the shortest COBOL programs that can be written. The program reads data cards and lists each card on the printer. To circumvent some of the coding, ACCEPT and DISPLAY statements are employed. (These statements do not require file organizations as explained in the text.) The program also omits any CONFIGURATION SECTION entries in the ENVIRONMENT DIVISION. (Only the ENVIRONMENT DIVISION header appears.)

78   5   PROCEDURE DIVISION

Such omissions are entirely acceptable for IBM 360/370 systems. However, these omissions may cause problems with other computer systems. (In this case, you must include all the required CONFIGURATION SECTION entries.)

Sample Input

HENRY LIPSHITZ   555 JACKSON AVE   NEW YORK, NY 10019   1116749505044545
GARY SCARCELLA   MEADOW LANE   ANDOVER, NJ 07821   1029742304914050

Note: A blank card must be inserted to signify the end of data.

Program Logic

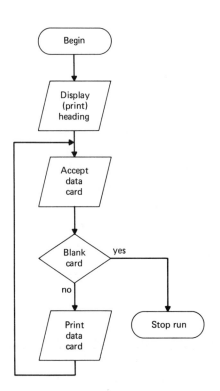

Source Listing

```
0C001            IDENTIFICATION DIVISION.
0C002            PROGRAM-ID.  'SAMPL5B'.
0C003            ENVIRONMENT DIVISION.
0C004            DATA DIVISION.
0C005            WORKING-STORAGE SECTION.
0C006            01  CARD-REC  PIC  X(80).
0C007            PROCEDURE DIVISION.
0C008            BEGIN.
0C009                DISPLAY '*******80/80 CARD LISTING******************'.
0C010                DISPLAY '  '.
0C011            READ-PRINT.
0C012                ACCEPT  CARD-REC.
0C013                IF CARD-REC IS EQUAL TO SPACES STOP RUN.
0C014                DISPLAY  CARD-REC.
0C015                GO TO READ-PRINT.
```

Sample Output

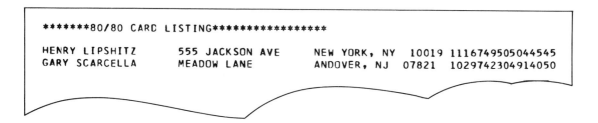

Job Control Statement Setup for IBM 360/370 Systems

```
//JOB
//*PASSWORD
// EXEC COBUCG,PARM=(APOST)
//COB.SYSIN DD *
   place source program here
/*
//GO.SYSOUT DD SYSOUT=A  ← specifies output class for DISPLAY command
//GO.SYSIN DD *  ← DD statement for ACCEPT statement
   place data cards here
/*
//
```

5.13 SAMPLE PROGRAM 5C: PAGE HEADING, CURRENT DATE, AND PAGE NUMBER

This sample program is a slight modification of the program on page 24. It illustrates

(1) skipping to a new page on a report after a predetermined number of lines have been printed, and
(2) printing current date in mm/dd/yy format as part of a report heading.

Input Description

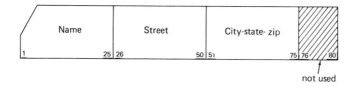

Sample Input

```
SMITH JOE.              22 CHURCH ST.        SHOETOWN. NJ 07750.
KENNEDY KATHY.          1 SEASIDE BLVD.      CAPE COD MASS. 03210.
```

80 5 PROCEDURE DIVISION

Program Logic

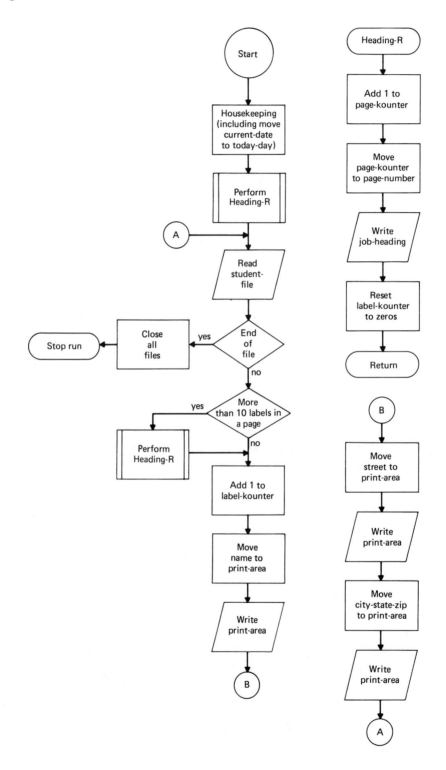

5.13 Sample Program 5C: Page Heading, Current Date, and Page Number 81

Output Description

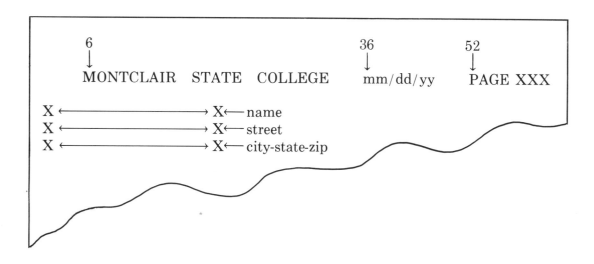

Source Listing

```
00001              IDENTIFICATION DIVISION.
00002              PROGRAM-ID.  'SAMPL5C'
00003              AUTHOR.  CHAI
00004         ****************************************************************
00005              ENVIRONMENT DIVISION.
00006              CONFIGURATION SECTION.
00007              SOURCE-COMPUTER.  IBM-370.
00008              OBJECT-COMPUTER.  IBM-370.
00009              SPECIAL-NAMES.
00010                  C01 IS TOP-OF-PAGE.        ← C01 is an IBM function-name for
00011              INPUT-OUTPUT SECTION.              skipping to top of new page
00012              FILE-CONTROL.
00013                  SELECT STUDENT-FILE
00014                      ASSIGN TO UR-2540R-S-CARDIN.
00015                  SELECT PRINT-FILE
00016                      ASSIGN TO UR-1403-S-PROUT.
00017         ****************************************************************
00018              DATA DIVISION.
00019              FILE SECTION.
00020              FD   STUDENT-FILE
00021                   LABEL RECORDS ARE OMITTED.
00022              01   STUDENT-REC.
00023                   04 NAME PICTURE     X(25).     ⎫
00024                   04 STREET PICTURE   X(25).     ⎬ input data card
00025                   04 CITY-STATE-ZIP PICTURE X(25). ⎭  descriptions
00026                   04 FILLER PICTURE   X(5).
00027              FD   PRINT-FILE
00028                   LABEL RECORDS ARE OMITTED.
00029              01   PRINT-AREA.
00030                   04 FILLER     PICTURE X.       ⎫ output print-area
00031                   04 PRINT-LINE PICTURE X(119).  ⎭
00032              WORKING-STORAGE SECTION.
00033              77   LABEL-KOUNTER PIC 99 VALUE ZEROS.   ⎫ counters to keep track of page
00034              77   PAGE-KOUNTER  PIC 999 VALUE ZEROS.  ⎬ number, card number, etc.
00035              77   CARD-KOUNTER  PIC 9999 VALUE ZEROS. ⎭
00036              01   JOB-HEADING.
00037                   05 FILLER PIC X(6) VALUE SPACES.                    ⎫
00038                   05 FILLER PIC X(30) VALUE 'MONTCLAIR STATE COLLEGE'. ⎪
00039                   05 TODAY-DAY PIC X(8).                              ⎬ report heading
00040                   05 FILLER PIC X(12) VALUE 'PAGE' JUST RIGHT.        ⎪
00041                   05 FILLER PIC X(5) VALUE SPACES.                    ⎪
00042                   05 PAGE-NUMBER PIC ZZ9.                             ⎭
00043         ****************************************************************
00044              PROCEDURE DIVISION.
00045              BEGIN.
00046                  OPEN INPUT STUDENT-FILE, OUTPUT PRINT-FILE.
00047                  MOVE SPACES TO PRINT-AREA.
00048                  MOVE CURRENT-DATE TO TODAY-DAY.   ← obtain current date from system
00049                  PERFORM HEADING-R.
00050              READ-PRINT.
00051                  READ STUDENT-FILE AT END GO TO END-JOB.
00052                  IF LABEL-KOUNTER > 10 PERFORM HEADING-R. ← allow 10 labels per printed page
00053                  ADD 1 TO LABEL-KOUNTER.
00054                  MOVE NAME TO PRINT-LINE.
```

82 5 PROCEDURE DIVISION

```
00055              WRITE PRINT-AREA AFTER ADVANCING 3 LINES.  ⎫
00056              MOVE STREET TO PRINT-LINE.                 ⎪
00057              WRITE PRINT-AREA AFTER ADVANCING 1 LINES.   ⎬  print name, street address,
00058              MOVE CITY-STATE-ZIP TO PRINT-LINE.          ⎪  and city, state, zip
00059              WRITE PRINT-AREA AFTER ADVANCING 1 LINES.  ⎪
00060              GO TO READ-PRINT.                           ⎭
00061          END-JOB.
00062              CLOSE STUDENT-FILE, PRINT-FILE. STOP RUN. ←── end of program
00063          HEADING-R.
00064              ADD 1 TO PAGE-KOUNTER.                     ⎫
00065              MOVE PAGE-KOUNTER TO PAGE-NUMBER.           ⎪
00066              WRITE PRINT-AREA FROM JOB-HEADING            ⎬ skip to top of new page
00067                 AFTER ADVANCING TOP-OF-PAGE.             ⎪ and print report heading.
00068              MOVE ZEROS TO LABEL-KOUNTER.                ⎭
```

Sample Output

```
              SMITH JOE.              ⎫
              22 CHURCH ST.           ⎪
              SHOETOWN. NJ 07750.     ⎬
                                      ⎪  10 labels/page
              KENNEDY KATHY.          ⎪
              1 SEASIDE BLVD.         ⎪
              CAPE COD MASS. 03210.   ⎭
```

Job Control Statements

// JOB CARD
//*PASSWORD
// EXEC COBUCG,PARM='APOST,BUF=6K'
//COB.SYSIN DD *
   place source program here
/*
//GO.PROUT DD SYSOUT=A
//GO.CARDIN DD *
   place data cards here
/*
//

Programming Notes

In this program there are several statements that are either employed for the first time or have special meaning. Thus, their use requires some clarification, and they are briefly discussed below.

  (1A)   00009:   SPECIAL-NAMES.
            00010:   C01 IS TOP-OF-PAGE.

The SPECIAL-NAMES paragraph defines C01 as TOP-OF-PAGE (which is a programmer-supplied name). The C01 is an IBM 360/370 system name for the skipping-to-next-page function. Other computer systems have different system names for such functions. The reader should consult the local computer system manual (for example, "System Programmer's Guide") for the correct name.

  (1B)   00066:   WRITE PRINT-AREA FROM JOB-HEADING
            00067:   AFTER ADVANCING TOP-OF-PAGE.

TOP-OF-PAGE is a programmer-supplied name as defined in the SPECIAL-NAMES paragraph. The WRITE statement causes the printer to skip to next page before printing out the contents of JOB-HEADING.

(2)   00033:   77   LABEL-KOUNTER PIC 99 VALUE ZEROS.
       00034:   77   PAGE-KOUNTER PIC 999 VALUE ZEROS.

The data item LABEL-KOUNTER is set up to keep track of the number of labels being printed per page, and the data item PAGE-KOUNTER to keep track of the number of pages being printed. However, it is the programmer's responsibility to increment these counters. Such a task is accomplished by the use of ADD statements, that is,

       00053:   ADD 1 TO LABEL-KOUNTER.
       00064:   ADD 1 TO PAGE-KOUNTER.

(The VALUE clauses in 00033 and 00034 initialize both KOUNTERS to zero.)

(3)   00042:   05 PAGE-NUMBER PIC ZZ9.

The picture symbol Z is an editing symbol that causes the printer to replace leading zeros by blank spaces (for example, 019 will be displayed as 19). A detailed discussion of the editing symbols will be given in Chapter 6.

(4)   00048:   MOVE CURRENT-DATE TO TODAY-DAY.

CURRENT-DATE is a specially defined data name (that is, register) for the IBM 360/370 computers. CURRENT-DATE is valid only as the sending field in a MOVE command. This field contains the current date in mm/dd/yy format (for example, October 12, 1974 would be represented as 10/12/74). The MOVE statement here causes the program to accept the current date from the system and store it in TODAY-DAY, which is a programmer-supplied name.

Most computer systems do not have CURRENT-DATE as a register. However, they usually have a special system data field DATE, which contains the current data in yymmdd format; for example, July 4, 1974 would be expressed as 740704 in DATE.

(5)   00049:   PERFORM HEADING-R.

The PERFORM statement directs the program to branch to the paragraph named HEADING-R. After all the statements in HEADING-R are executed (cards 00063 through 00068) the program would return the control to the statement immediately following the PERFORM command, that is, the READ statement. (A detailed discussion of the PERFORM statement is presented in Chapter 9.)

(6)   00052:   IF LABEL-KOUNTER > 10 PERFORM HEADING-R.

The IF statement is a conditional statement (see Chapter 8) that causes the computer to PERFORM HEADING-R if the contents of LABEL-KOUNTER exceed 10; otherwise the computer would execute the next sequential statement, that is,

       00053:   ADD 1 TO LABEL-KOUNTER.

EXERCISES

1   Briefly explain the function of the PROCEDURE DIVISION.

84   5   PROCEDURE DIVISION

2   Describe each of the following terms:

    statement   paragraph (procedure)
    sentence   section

3   In the following coding, correct errors (if any).
    It is assumed that

    A-FILE is the name of an input file.
    A-REC is the name of the data record in A-FILE.
    B-FILE is the name of an output file.
    B-REC is the name of the data record in B-FILE.

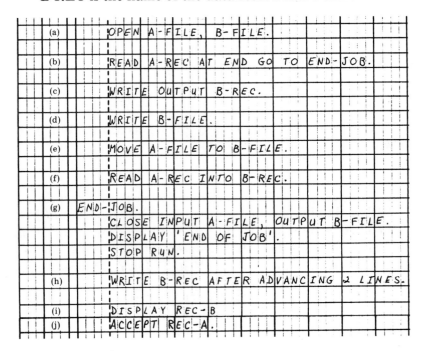

4   Briefly explain the functions of
    (a)   ACCEPT statement.
    (b)   Display statement.
    (c)   STOP RUN statement.

5   Write the COBOL program to produce a listing of the students of a college.

Input Description: Student Name and Address Cards

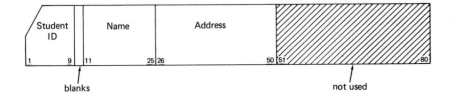

Output Description: Student listing

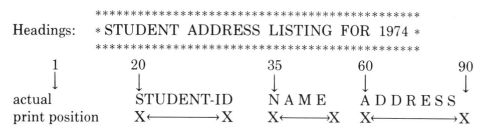

6. Modify Sample Program 4A (page 58) to print the following overdue payment notice:

DID YOU FORGET ... YOUR PAYMENT WAS DUE FIVE DAYS AGO.
} 2 lines
IF IT IS NOT ALREADY ON THE WAY, PLEASE SEND IT TODAY.
THANK YOU.
} 2 lines
CUSTOMER INQUIRIES 201-893-4700
} 2 lines
PAYMENT DUE $XXX.XX
} 2 lines
DUE DATE mm/dd/yy
} 10 lines
X⟵⟶X⟵ name
X⟵⟶X⟵ address
X⟵⟶X⟵ city state zip

7. Write a COBOL program to produce a printed report as specified in the following:

Input Description: Salesman Record

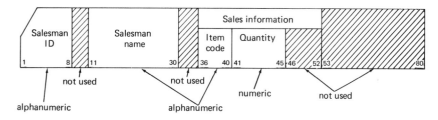

Output Description: Salesman Report

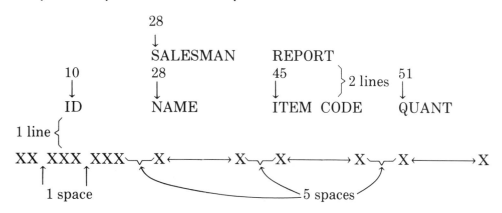

6
Editing and Data Manipulations

6.1 EDITING CHARACTERS

One of the most important considerations in business data processing is not only that data should be correctly processed, but a readable and properly edited report must be produced when the processing is completed. In COBOL, editing in most cases can be accomplished by moving the source field to a receiving field whose PICTURE clause contains appropriate editing characters. For instance, the statement

```
       06  TOTAL-AMOUNT-P   PIC  $9,999.99.
```

defines TOTAL-AMOUNT-P as an edited field (that is, receiving field) that accepts numeric data. If a source field containing 785680 is moved to TOTAL-AMOUNT-P, the edited result printed out would be $7856.80 as shown below:

Source field	Receiving (edited) field
Picture: 9999V99	Picture: $9999.99
Value: 785680	Result: $7856.80

There are eleven editing character symbols. These symbols together with their meanings are listed in Fig. 6.1. Each editing character represents a symbol in the edited field and must be counted in the size of the item. Editing can only be performed in the elementary item. The PICTURE clause of an edit item (that is, receiving item) cannot contain the character symbol S. A detailed description of the editing character symbols is given in the following sections.

Symbol	Category of source item	Meaning
.	numeric	actual decimal point
Z	numeric	zero suppress
*	numeric	check protect
$	numeric	currency sign
+	numeric	plus
−	numeric	minus
,	numeric	comma
CR	numeric	credit sign
DB	numeric	debit sign
0	numeric and alphanumeric	zero
B	all	blank

Fig. 6.1 Editing characters.

6.2 NUMERIC EDITING

There are essentially two ways that editing can be properly performed in a numeric field. One is by insertion of characters and the other is by suppression and replacement.

Insertion of Decimal Point

The editing symbol period (.) is often used in a PICTURE clause to insert an actual decimal point in a numeric item. However, a PICTURE must not contain more than one period and the period must not appear in the same PICTURE as the character V. Some examples of decimal point insertions are shown in Fig. 6.2.

Source item		Receiving item	
Picture	Content	Picture	Edited result
9(4)V99	654321	9(4).99	6543.21
9(4)V99	054321	9(4).99	0543.21
99	54	99.99	54.00
999V999	000546	999.99	00.54
9999V99	500000	999.99	000.00
9V99	567	99V.99	invalid (symbol V not allowed)
9V99	567	S99.99	invalid (symbol S not allowed)

Fig. 6.2 Insertion of decimal points.

Suppression of Leading Zeros by Blank Spaces: Z's

In business data processing, in order to produce a readable printout, leading zeros in a numeric item are often replaced by blanks. In COBOL, such a task can be accomplished by the editing symbol Z.

The symbol Z, if used, must precede any character symbol 9. In addition, if Z's are used only to the left of a decimal point, then every leading zero corresponding to Z in the edited field would be replaced by a blank. Examples are shown in Fig. 6.3.

Source item		Receiving item	
Picture	Content	Picture	Edited result
9999	0805	ZZZ9	805
999V99	00102	ZZZ.99	1.02
999V	102	ZZZ.99	102.00
9(4)V99	001234	Z(4).ZZ	12.34
9(3)V99	00000	Z(3).ZZ	(blanks)
9(3)V99	00001	Z(3).ZZ	.01
9(3)V99	00001	9ZZ.ZZ	invalid (symbol 9 cannot precede Z's)

Fig. 6.3 Suppression of leading zeros.

Suppression of Leading Zeros by Asterisks: *

In a business report, it is often desirable to replace the leading zeros by asterisks (*) for protection purposes (for example, printing the amount of money on checks and other payment documents). For such purposes the editing symbol * may be used. The rule governing the use of * is the same as for the symbol Z.

Asterisks and Z's cannot be used together in the same PICTURE clause. Figure 6.4 presents examples of asterisk insertions.

Source field		Receiving field	
Picture	Content	Picture	Edited result
9(6)	012345	***999	*12345
9(6)	000123	***999	***123
9(6)	000012	***999	***012
9(5)V99	0012345	*(5).99	**123.45
9(5)V99	0012345	9**.99	invalid (9 cannot precede *)
9(5)V99	0012345	**ZZZ.99	invalid (* and Z cannot appear together)

Fig. 6.4 Insertion of asterisks.

Insertion of Commas, Spaces, or Zeros

To insert a comma, space, or zero in an edited field, one can write a comma, B, or zero (0) wherever a comma, space, or zero, respectively, is desired. Unlike the symbols Z, *, and actual decimal point, these insertion characters may appear in any combination, as shown in Fig. 6.5.

Insertion of a Fixed Currency Sign: $

To obtain a fixed currency sign $ in an edited field, one inserts a single $ sign as the leftmost character in the PICTURE clause of the receiving field.

The symbol $ can be used together with other editing symbols such as Z, ., or *. Examples of the use of $ are shown in Fig. 6.6.

6.2 Numeric Editing

Source item		Receiving item	
Picture	Content	Picture	Edited result
9(7)	1234567	9,999,999	1,234,567
999	123	9BB99	1 23
999	123	90099	10023
9999	1234	9,009,990	1,002,340
9(3)V99	12345	9,990,000.00	1,230,000.45
9(3)	123	9B00B990	1 00 230

Fig. 6.5 Insertions of commas, spaces, and zeros.

Source field		Receiving field	
Picture	Content	Picture	Content
9999	0123	$9999	$0123
9999	0123	$Z999	$ 123
9999	0123	$*999	$*123
9(5)V99	0012345	$*****.99	$**123.45
9(5)V99	0123456	$**,***.99	$*1,234.56
9(4)	0123	$Z**9	invalid (Z and * cannot appear together)
9(5)	00123	ZZ$999	invalid (Z cannot precede $ sign)

Fig. 6.6 Insertion of fixed $ sign.

Source field		Receiving field	
Picture	Content	Picture	Edited result
S999	−123	+999	−123
S999	+456	999+	456+
S999	+628	−999	+628
S999V99	−12345	999.99DB	123.45DB
S999V99	+15768	999.99DB	157.68
S9(3)V99	+57950	+$999.99	$579.50
S9(3)V99	−65125	+$999.99	−$651.25
S9(3)V99	−18200	$999.99CR	$182.00CR
S999	−246	+999CR	invalid (only one sign indicator can appear)

Fig. 6.7 Insertion of indicator for sign value.

Source field		Receiving field	
Picture	Content	Picture	Edited result
9(5)V99	000450	$$$$$$.99	$4.50
999V99	−00515	++++.99	−5.15
999V99	00000	++++.++	(blanks)
9(5)V99	0475682	$$$,$$$.99	$4,756.82
999	−475	−$$$	invalid ($, +, and − cannot appear together in floating string)

Fig. 6.8 Floating sign insertions.

Insertion of the Indicator for the Sign Value of the Edited Field: +, −, CR, DB

There are four symbols that can be used to indicate the sign value of the edited field: +, −, DB, and CR. However, only one of these symbols can appear in a PICTURE clause.

+ (plus) and − (minus) signs. If either the + or − sign is used, it must appear as the right- or leftmost character in the PICTURE clause.

CR and DB symbols. CR (credit) and DB (debit) symbols can also be used to indicate negative data values. These symbols must appear as the rightmost characters of a PICTURE clause. CR and DB occupy two positions each when used.

When either CR or DB is used, the edited result will contain the symbol indicator (CR or DB) if the value of the source item is negative. Otherwise, the symbol will be replaced by blank spaces.

Examples of the sign value indicators are given in Fig. 6.7.

Floating Sign Insertions and Floating Strings

The symbols $, +, and − can be used as floating signs, which can be inserted up to the leftmost digit of a numeric field. At the same time, these floating indicators can replace the leading nonsignificant zeros by blank spaces.

The symbols $, +, and − are mutually exclusive when used as floating insertion symbols. However, other simple insertion symbols such as comma, B (blank), and 0 (zero) can be used within a floating string. Examples of insertions are presented in Fig. 6.8.

6.3 ALPHANUMERIC EDITING

There is only one type of editing available for an alphanumeric field: simple insertion using the symbols 0 (zero) and B (blank). Some examples of alphanumeric editing are shown in Fig. 6.9.

Source field		Receiving field	
Picture	Content	Picture	Edited result
X(6)	AD1005	XXBBX(4)	AD 1005
AA999	ZP123	ZPB90099	ZP 10023
A(4)	NAME	ABABABA	N A M E
X(5)	CODE5	XXXXBX000	CODE 5000

Fig. 6.9 Alphanumeric editing.

6.4 PERMISSIBLE MOVES: THE MOVE STATEMENT

Perhaps one of the most frequently used statements in COBOL is the MOVE statement. On the surface, as seen in Chapter 5, the MOVE statement looks quite simple to code. The statement

```
          MOVE  ITEM-1  TO  ITEM-2.
```

6.5 Numeric Moves

	Receiving field				
Source field	GR	AL	AN	NU	NE
Group (GR)	Y	Y	Y	Y	Y
Alphabetic (AL)	Y	Y	Y	N	N
Alphanumeric (AN)	Y	Y	Y	Y[a]	Y[a]
Numeric (NU)	Y[b]	N	Y[c]	Y	Y
Numeric edited (NE)	Y	N	Y	N	N

[a] Permissible, but result is unpredictable.
[b] Move without conversion (like AN to AN).
[c] If the decimal point is at the right of the least significant digit, then it is permissible.

Fig. 6.10 Table of permissible and nonpermissible moves.

is a typical MOVE statement. When such a statement is executed, the contents of ITEM-2 are replaced by the contents of ITEM-1. The contents of ITEM-1 are unchanged here.

However, there are certain restrictions on the movement of data due to the difference between the structure and class of sending (that is, source) and receiving fields. Figure 6.10 presents a table of permissible (Y) and nonpermissible (N) moves.

With the exception of the first row and the first column, Fig. 6.10 indicates the permissible types of moves when both source field (that is, sending field) and receiving field are elementary items. (Such moves are called elementary moves.) The letter Y is used when a move is permissible, whereas N is used to indicate that a move is not allowed. For instance, the table shows that an alphabetic field cannot be moved into a numeric field. The reason is that the numeric field can only contain digits, whereas an alphabetic field may contain letters or spaces.

In COBOL, the numeric field can take on a number of internal storage formats such as external decimal, binary, packed decimal, or floating point. These internal data structures are generally machine dependent. The reader is urged to consult appropriate hardware manufacturers' manuals for descriptions.

6.5 NUMERIC MOVES

The numeric move is one in which both source and receiving fields are numeric items. In such a move, alignment by decimal point (if present) and necessary zero filling of unused positions would take place. The following examples illustrate how numerical move statements are used.

Example 1

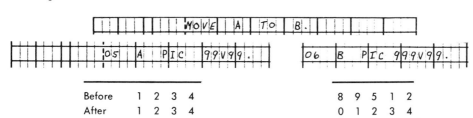

Example 2

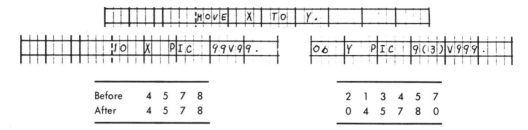

Before	4	5	7	8	2	1	3	4 5 7
After	4	5	7	8	0	4	5	7 8 0

Example 3

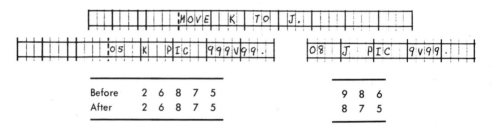

Before	2	6	8	7	5	9	8	6
After	2	6	8	7	5	8	7	5

Notice that in Examples 1 and 2, since the receiving fields (B and Y) were longer than the sending fields A and X, zero filling occurred on one or both ends of the receiving fields. In Example 3, however, the receiving field J is shorter than the source field K. Therefore, the leftmost digits and the rightmost digit were both truncated.

When numeric data are moved to an edited field, the data are edited according to the editing characters specified in the receiving field. The following examples illustrate the operation of the edited move.

Example 4

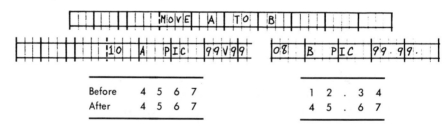

Before	4	5	6	7	1	2	.	3	4
After	4	5	6	7	4	5	.	6	7

Example 5

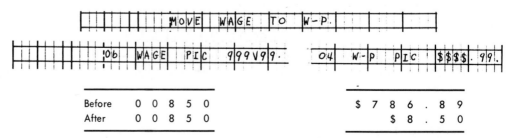

Before	0	0	8	5	0	$	7	8	6 . 8 9
After	0	0	8	5	0		$	8	. 5 0

Example 6

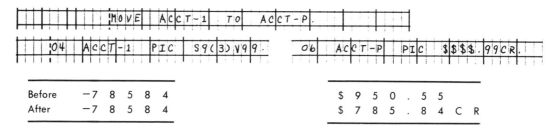

6.6 ALPHANUMERIC MOVES

If in a MOVE statement the receiving field is an alphanumeric, alphabetic, or group item, then such a move is classified as an alphanumeric move.

In general, in an alphanumeric move, the movement of the data from the sending field is aligned at the leftmost position of the receiving field. A number of examples are presented below to illustrate the alphanumeric move.

Example 1

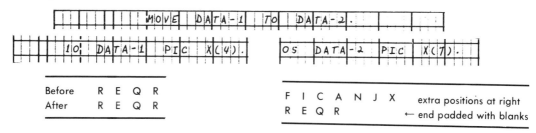

Example 2

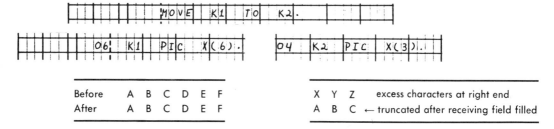

In Example 1, the receiving field is larger than the source field (that is, sending field), and so the extra positions at the right end of the receiving field are padded with blank spaces. (These spaces are generated by the computer.)

In Example 2, the receiving field is shorter than the sending field. Thus the excess characters are truncated after the receiving field is filled.

JUSTIFIED RIGHT Clause

In general, the alphanumeric move statement would automatically be left-justified, that is, would position the data into the receiving field from left to right. However, such a process can be reversed by specifying the JUSTIFIED RIGHT clause in the data description entry of the receiving field. This clause causes information to be moved from right to left and any unfilled positions at the left in the receiving field are automatically padded with blank spaces. However, it should be noted that this clause can only be used for alphanumeric or alphabetic fields.

Example 3

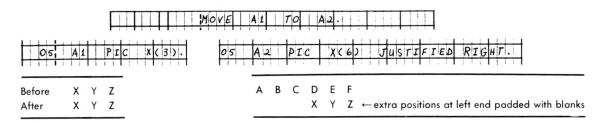

Example 4

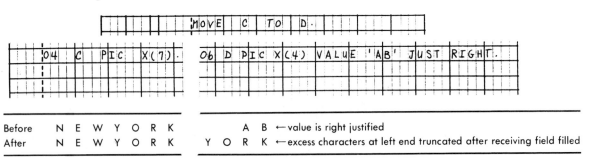

Notice that the JUSTIFIED (JUST) clause can be used to initialize the value of the data item as shown in Example 4.

6.7 GROUP MOVE

A group move is one in which either source or receiving field or both is a group item. A group move is always permissible and is treated as though it were an alphanumeric elementary move. However, in a group move, there is no conversion of data from one form of internal representation to another. The receiving field essentially is filled without any consideration for the individual elementary items (characteristics) contained in the receiving area. For example, in the following entries, RECORD-1 and RECORD-2 are group items:

```
01  RECORD-1.
    05  NAME         PIC  X(15).
    05  RATE         PIC  S99V99.
    05  HOUR         PIC  99.

01  RECORD-2.
    04  ID-NO.       PIC  9(6).
    04  DESCRIPTION  PIC  X(20).
```

These two records certainly are dissimilar. However, the MOVE statement

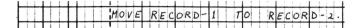

is permissible. Upon the execution of this statement, the contents of RECORD-1 would be transferred to RECORD-2. The following shows the contents of these two record areas before and after the MOVE operation:

Before

RECORD-1

| M | A | R | C | I | N | K | O | - | C | H | A | I | | | 0 | 8 | 5 | 0 | 3 | 5 |

RECORD-2

| 5 | 2 | 3 | 4 | 1 | 7 | I | N | V | E | N | T | O | R | Y | P | A | R | T | X | Y | Z | W | | |

After

RECORD-1

| M | A | R | C | I | N | K | O | - | C | H | A | I | | | 0 | 8 | 5 | 0 | 3 | 5 |

RECORD-2

| M | A | R | C | I | N | K | O | - | C | H | A | I | | | 0 | 8 | 5 | 0 | 3 | 5 | | | | |

Notice that the extra positions at the right end of RECORD-2 are padded with blank spaces after the execution of the MOVE statement.

6.8 SAMPLE PROGRAM 6A: WEEKLY CHARGE ACCOUNT SUMMARY REPORT

This sample program is developed to illustrate the use of edited and printed reports. The program reads a punched-data-card file named ACCT-FILE and prints each record on the printer file. Note that in the output printout the check protection symbol * is used to replace the leading zeros.

Input Description

Sample Input

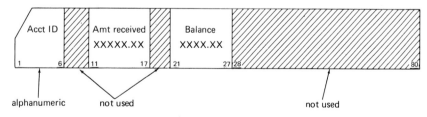

Program Logic

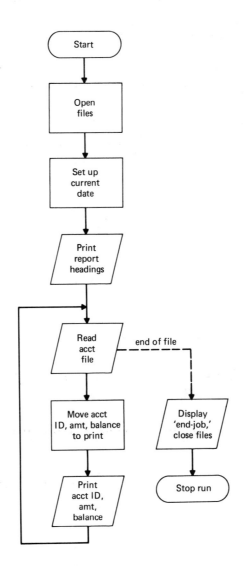

Source Listing

```
0C001          IDENTIFICATION DIVISION.
0C002          PROGRAM-ID.  'SAMP6A'.
0C003          DATE-WRITTEN. NOV.27,1973
00004      ************************************************************
0C005          ENVIRONMENT DIVISION.
0C006          CONFIGURATION SECTION.
0C007          SOURCE-COMPUTER.  IBM-370.
0C008          OBJECT-COMPUTER.  IBM-370.
0C009          SPECIAL-NAMES.
0C010              C01 IS NU-PAGE.         ← C01 is IBM function name for
0C011          INPUT-OUTPUT SECTION.            skipping to top of new page
0C012          FILE-CONTROL.
0C013              SELECT ACCT-FILE
0C014                  ASSIGN TO UR-2501-S-CARDIN.
0C015              SELECT  ACCT-REPORT
0C016                  ASSIGN TO UR-1403-S-PROUT.
0C017      ************************************************************
```

6.8 Sample Program 6A: Weekly Charge Account Summary Report

```
00018       DATA DIVISION.
00019       FILE SECTION.
00020       FD  ACCT-FILE
00021           LABEL RECORDS ARE OMITTED,
00022           DATA RECORDS ARE ACCT-REC.
00023       01  ACCT-REC.
00024           04  ACCT-ID   PIC  X(6).
00025           04  FILLER    PIC  X(4).
00026           04  AMT-REC   PIC  S9(5)V99.           ⎫
00027           04  FILLER    PIC  X(3).               ⎬  input descriptions
00028           04  BALANCE   PIC  S9(5)V99.           ⎪
00029           04  FILLER    PIC  X(53).              ⎭
00030       FD  ACCT-REPORT
00031           LABEL RECORDS ARE OMITTED
00032           DATA RECORDS ARE PRINT-AREA.
00033       01  PRINT-AREA   PIC  X(133).   ←——— output area
00034       WORKING-STORAGE SECTION.
00035       01  REPORT-HEADING.
00036           04  FILLER    PIC  X(39)  JUST RIGHT   ⎫
00037               VALUE 'WEEKLY CHARGE ACCOUNT REPORT AS OF '.
00038           04  TODAY-DATE PIC X(8).               ⎭
00039       01  HEADING-1.
00040           04  FILLER    PIC  X(5)   VALUE SPACES.
00041           04  FILLER    PIC  X(13)  VALUE 'ACCOUNT ID'.    ⎫
00042           04  FILLER    PIC  X(15)  VALUE 'AMOUNT RECEIVED'. ⎬ report heading and subheadings
00043           04  FILLER    PIC  X(17)  JUST RIGHT    ⎪
00044               VALUE 'BALANCE'.                   ⎭
00045       01  SUB-1.
00046           04  FILLER    PIC  X(5)   VALUE SPACES.
00047           04  FILLER    PIC  X(48)  VALUE ALL '-'.
00048       01  LINE-1.
00049           04  ACCT-ID-P PIC  X(14)  JUST RIGHT.   ⎫
00050           04  FILLER    PIC  X(7)   VALUE SPACES. ⎬ detail line (one printed
00051           04  AMT-REC-P PIC  $ZZ,ZZ9.99.          ⎪  line per data card)
00052           04  FILLER    PIC  X(10)  VALUE SPACES. ⎪
00053           04  BALANCE-P PIC  $**,**9.99CR.        ⎭
00054      *******************************************************
00055       PROCEDURE DIVISION.
00056       OPEN-1.
00057           OPEN INPUT ACCT-FILE  OUTPUT ACCT-REPORT.
00058           MOVE CURRENT-DATE TO TODAY-DATE.   ←——— obtains current date from system
00059           WRITE PRINT-AREA FROM REPORT-HEADING           ⎫
00060               AFTER ADVANCING NU-PAGE.                   ⎬ print heading and subheadings
00061           WRITE PRINT-AREA FROM HEADING-1 AFTER ADVANCING 3 LINES. ⎪
00062           WRITE PRINT-AREA FROM SUB-1 AFTER ADVANCING 1 LINES.    ⎭
00063       READ-PRINT.
00064           READ ACCT-FILE AT END GO TO END-JOB.  ⎫
00065           MOVE ACCT-ID TO ACCT-ID-P.            ⎪
00066           MOVE AMT-REC TO AMT-REC-P.            ⎬ print one line for
00067           MOVE BALANCE TO BALANCE-P.            ⎪  each data card
00068           WRITE PRINT-AREA FROM LINE-1          ⎪
00069               AFTER ADVANCING 2 LINES.          ⎪
00070           GO TO READ-PRINT.                     ⎭
00071       END-JOB.
00072           DISPLAY 'END-JOB' UPON CONSOLE.     ⎫
00073           CLOSE ACCT-FILE, ACCT-REPORT.       ⎬ end of program
00074           STOP RUN.                           ⎭
```

Sample Output

```
                                                   current date in mm/dd/yy
                                                         ↓
         WEEKLY CHARGE ACCOUNT REPORT AS OF 06/02/75
1 line ⎰
       ⎱ ACCOUNT ID     AMOUNT RECEIVED         BALANCE
         -----------------------------------------------

            123455      $    123.45         $***157.50
            587428      $      1.50         $***123.54CR
            45621       $  4,000.00         $*6,500.00CR
            S45678      $    234.55         $12,345.67
            G33312      $    123.50         $***124.42CR  ←——— CR indicates negative number
                                                ↑
                                    check protection symbols
```

6.9 SAMPLE PROGRAM 6B: MINIMUM PAYMENT NOTICE

This sample program is a slight modification of Sample Program 4A. It reads the customer file and produces a minimum payment notice. The spacing of the output is designed to fit the customer's name and address to a window envelope, thus eliminating the need for separate addresssing of envelopes.

Input Description

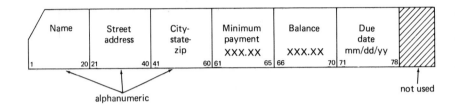

Sample Input

MARCINKO, GEORGE 125 OAK STREET NEWTON, N.Y. 10014 12575 3496010/11/75

Sample Output

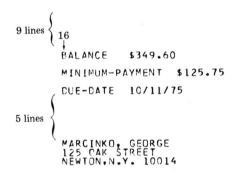

6.9 Sample Program 6B: Minimum Payment Notice

Program Logic

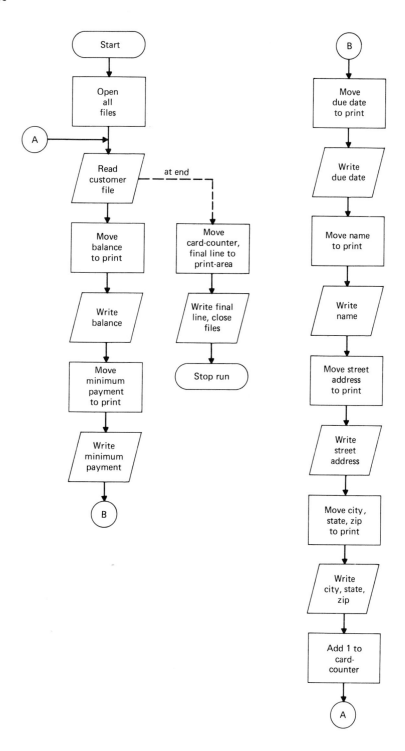

Source Listing

```
00001            IDENTIFICATION DIVISION.
00002            PROGRAM-ID. 'SAMPL6B'
00003            AUTHOR.  CHAI
00004            DATE-WRITTEN. 3/2/75.
00005            REMARKS.  THIS PROGRAM READS CUSTOMER FILE AND
00006                 PRODUCES MINIMUM PAYMENT NOTICES.
00007            ****************************************************
00008            ENVIRONMENT DIVISION.
00009            INPUT-OUTPUT SECTION.
00010            FILE-CONTROL.
00011                 SELECT CUSTOMER-FILE ASSIGN TO UR-2501-S-SYSIN.
00012                 SELECT PRINT-FILE ASSIGN TO UR-1403-S-SYSOUT.
00013            ****************************************************
00014            DATA DIVISION.
00015            FILE SECTION.
00016            FD  CUSTOMER-FILE
00017                LABEL RECORDS ARE OMITTED, DATA RECORD IS PAYMENT-REC.
00018            01  PAYMENT-REC.
00019                05  NAME PIC A(20).
00020                05  STREET-ADDRESS PIC X(20).
00021                05  CITY-STATE-ZIP PIC X(20).          } input descriptions
00022                05  MINIMUM-PAYMENT PIC    999V99.
00023                05  BALANCE PIC  999V99.
00024                05  DUE-DATE PIC X(8).
00025                05  FILLER PIC X(2).
00026            FD  PRINT-FILE
00027                LABEL RECORDS ARE OMITTED, DATA RECORD IS PRINT-AREA.
00028            01  PRINT-AREA.
00029                05  FILLER PIC X(16).                  } output area
00030                05  PRINT-LINE PIC X(80).
00031            WORKING-STORAGE SECTION.
00032            77  CARD-COUNTER PIC 9999 VALUE ZEROS.
00033            01  LINE-1.
00034                05  FILLER PIC X(16) VALUE SPACES.
00035                05  FILLER PIC X(10) VALUE 'BALANCE'.
00036                05  BALANCE-P PIC $$$9.99.
00037            01  LINE-2.
00038                05  FILLER PIC X(16) VALUE SPACES.
00039                05  FILLER PIC X(17) VALUE 'MINIMUM-PAYMENT'.
00040                05  MINIMUM-PAYMENT-P PIC $$$9.99.     } output line-by-line
00041            01  LINE-3.                                  descriptions
00042                05  FILLER PIC X(16) VALUE SPACES.
00043                05  FILLER PIC X(10) VALUE 'DUE-DATE'.
00044                05  DUE-DATE-P PIC X(8).
00045            01  FINAL-PRINT-LINE.
00046                05  FILLER PIC X(10) VALUE SPACES.
00047                05  MSSAG PIC X(28) VALUE 'TOTAL NUMBER OF CARDS IS'.
00048                05  FILLER PIC X(5) VALUE SPACES.
00049                05  COUNTER-P PIC Z9.
00050            ****************************************************
00051            PROCEDURE DIVISION.
00052            BEGIN.
00053                OPEN INPUT CUSTOMER-FILE.
00054                OPEN OUTPUT PRINT-FILE.
00055            READ-CARDS.
00056                READ CUSTOMER-FILE AT END GO TO END-JOB.
00057                MOVE BALANCE TO BALANCE-P.
00058                WRITE PRINT-AREA FROM LINE-1 AFTER ADVANCING 10 LINES.
00059                MOVE MINIMUM-PAYMENT TO MINIMUM-PAYMENT-P.
00060                WRITE PRINT-AREA FROM LINE-2 AFTER ADVANCING 2 LINES.
00061                MOVE DUE-DATE TO DUE-DATE-P.
00062                WRITE PRINT-AREA FROM LINE-3 AFTER ADVANCING 2 LINES.
00063                MOVE NAME TO PRINT-LINE.                } print output
00064                WRITE PRINT-AREA AFTER ADVANCING 6 LINES.
00065                MOVE STREET-ADDRESS TO PRINT-LINE.
00066                WRITE PRINT-AREA AFTER ADVANCING 1 LINES.
00067                MOVE CITY-STATE-ZIP TO PRINT-LINE.
00068                WRITE PRINT-AREA AFTER ADVANCING 1 LINES.
00069                ADD 1 TO CARD-COUNTER.
00070                GO TO READ-CARDS.
00071            END-JOB.
00072                MOVE CARD-COUNTER TO COUNTER-P.
00073                MOVE FINAL-PRINT-LINE TO PRINT-AREA.    } end of program
00074                WRITE PRINT-AREA AFTER ADVANCING 4 LINES.
00075                CLOSE CUSTOMER-FILE PRINT-FILE.
00076                STOP RUN.
```

EXERCISES

1 Fill in the last column in the following tables:

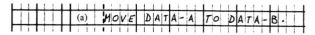

(a) MOVE DATA-A TO DATA-B.

DATA-A Picture	DATA-A Contents	DATA-B Picture	DATA-B Contents
99V99	1234	99.99	12.34
99V99	0123	99.99	01.23
99	46	99.99	46.00
999V99	12345	99.99	23.45
999V99	80000	99.99	00.00
S9V99	123	S9.99	1.23

(b) MOVE A-FIELD TO B-FIELD.

A-FIELD Picture	A-FIELD Contents	B-FIELD Picture	B-FIELD Contents
999	0706	ZZZ9	` 706`
999V99	00150	ZZZ.99	`  1.50`
99V99	1234	ZZ.ZZ	`12.34`
99V99	0000	ZZ.ZZ	`     `
99V99	0004	ZZ.ZZ	`  .04`
99V99	0004	9ZZZ	`0   `

(c) MOVE DATA-1 TO EDITED-1.

DATA-1 Picture	DATA-1 Contents	EDITED-1 Picture	EDITED-1 Contents
999V99	01234	***.99	`*12.34`
99999	00012	**999	`**012`
99999	00012	****9	`***12`
99999	00000	****9	`****0`
99999	00000	*(5)	`*****`
99999	12345	9****	`12345`
99999	12345	**Z99	`12345`

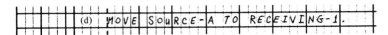

(d) MOVE SOURCE-A TO RECEIVING-1.

SOURCE-A		RECEIVING-1	
Picture	Contents	Picture	Contents
9(7)	1234567	9,999,999	
9999	1234	9B9B99	
9999	1234	9009099	
9(8)	12345678	99BB9(5)	

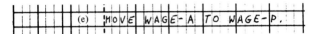

(e) MOVE WAGE-A TO WAGE-P.

WAGE-A		WAGE-P	
Picture	Contents	Picture	Contents
9999	0012	$9999	
9999	0012	$$$$9	
9999	0012	$Z999	
9999	0012	$**99	
9(5)V99	1234567	$**,***.99	
9(4)	1234	$Z**9	
9(4)	0123	Z$99	

(f) MOVE ACCOUNT-A TO ACCOUNT-P.

ACCOUNT-A		ACCOUNT-P	
Picture	Contents	Picture	Contents
S9999	−1234	+$9999	
S9(4)	−1234	$9999DB	
S9(4)	+1234	$9999CR	
S9(4)V99	−123456	$*,***.99DB	
S9(4)	−1234	$$,$$$.99+	
S9999	−1234	−9999CR	

```
            (g) |  MOVE AAAA TO BBBB.
```

AAAA		BBBB	
Picture	Contents	Picture	Contents
9(3)	123	99	
9(3)	123	9(5)	
X(3)	ABC	XX	
X(3)	ABC	X(5)	
9(3)V99	12345	9(2)V99	
9(3)V99	12345	9(6)V99	
A(3)	ABC	A(7) JUST RIGHT	
A(3)	ABC	999	

2 Consider the following entries:

```
            06  DATA-A     PIC X(4).
        77  COUNT-A    PIC X(5) VALUE 'TOTAL'.
```

What would be the contents of DATA-A after each of the following statements is executed?

(a) MOVE ZEROS TO DATA-A.
(b) MOVE 'ZEROS' TO DATA-A.
(c) MOVE COUNT-A TO DATA-A.
(d) MOVE 'TOTAL VALUE' TO DATA-A.

3 Consider the following entries:

```
            06 A   PIC 9(5).
            06 B   PIC X(5).
            06 C   PIC A(5).
```

Which of the following MOVE statements are invalid and why?

(a) MOVE A TO B.
(b) MOVE B TO A.
(c) MOVE A TO C.
(d) MOVE C TO A.
(e) MOVE B TO C.
(f) MOVE C TO B.
(g) MOVE A TO A.
(h) MOVE A TO 9999.

104 6 Editing and Data Manipulations

PROGRAMMING EXERCISES

4 Write the COBOL program to produce the following printed report:

Input Description: Salesman Record

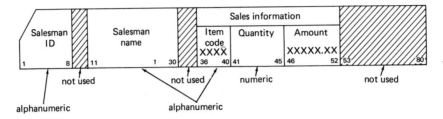

Output Description: Salesman Report

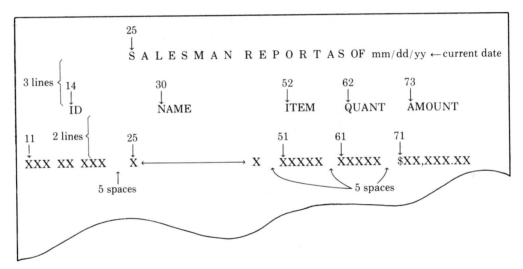

5 Write the COBOL program to produce the following printed report:

Input Description: Customer Purchase Record

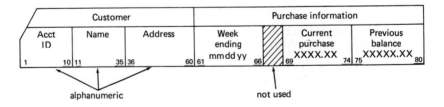

Output Description: Customer Purchase Report

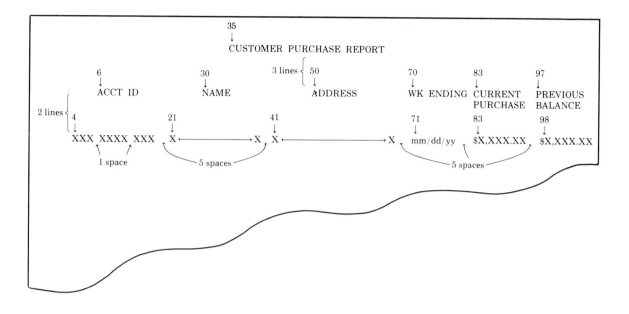

7
Calculations

Simple numerical calculations such as addition, subtraction, multiplication, and division are essential to many business applications. In COBOL, these arithmetic operations can be carried out by using the verbs ADD, SUBTRACT, MULTIPLY, and DIVIDE. However, if a more complicated expression has to be evaluated, a more general verb COMPUTE can be utilized. Some examples of the use of these verbs are given below:

```
ADD 1 TO COUNTER-A.
ADD A, B, C GIVING D.
SUBTRACT A FROM B GIVING C.
MULTIPLY RATE BY HOURS-WORKED GIVING-PAY ROUNDED.
DIVIDE WKLY-PAY BY 5 GIVING AVG-DAILY-RATE.
COMPUTE TAX-A = 50.0 + 0.10 * (WAGE - 100.0)
```

This chapter essentially discusses the various ways to perform the necessary calculations in COBOL.

7.1 ADD STATEMENT

The ADD statement causes two or more numeric data items to be added and the results stored. There are two basic ways to specify the ADD command:

Format 1

$$\underline{\text{ADD}} \left\{ \begin{matrix} \text{identifier-1} \\ \text{literal-1} \end{matrix} \right\} \left[\begin{matrix} \text{, identifier-2, ...} \\ \text{, literal-2, ...} \end{matrix} \right] \underline{\text{TO}} \text{ identifier-m } [\underline{\text{ROUNDED}}]$$

[, identifier-n [<u>ROUNDED</u>] ...]

[ON <u>SIZE</u> <u>ERROR</u> imperative statement]

7.1 ADD Statement 107

Format 2

$$\underline{\text{ADD}} \left\{ \begin{matrix} \text{identifier-1} \\ \text{literal-1} \end{matrix} \right\}, \left\{ \begin{matrix} \text{identifier-2} \\ \text{literal-2} \end{matrix} \right\} \left[\begin{matrix} , \text{identifier-3}, \ldots \\ , \text{literal-3}, \ldots \end{matrix} \right]$$

$\underline{\text{GIVING}}$ identifier-m [$\underline{\text{ROUNDED}}$] [, identifier-n [$\underline{\text{ROUNDED}}$] ...]

[; ON $\underline{\text{SIZE}}$ $\underline{\text{ERROR}}$ imperative-statement]

In Format 1, the word TO is used, and there can be more than one identifier (that is, operand) prior to the word TO. In this format, the values of all data name items prior to the word TO are added, and this sum is then added to each data item coming after TO. For example, the statement

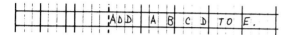

would cause the values of A, B, C, D, and E to be added and their sum stored in E. We present some specific examples.

Example 1

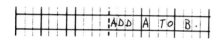

	A	B
Before	5	10
After	5	15

Note that A is added to B. The answer is stored in B and the contents of A remain unchanged.

Example 2

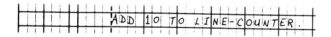

Note that a numerical literal may be used prior to the TO option. However, a numeric literal may not be used after the word TO. For instance, the statement

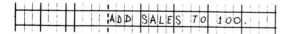

would be incorrect.

Example 3

ADD K1, K2 TO L1, L2.

	K1	K2	L1	L2
Before	10	20	−5	5
After	10	20	25	35

In this example, the sum of K1 and K2 would be added to both L1 and L2. The sum of K1, K2, and L1 would be stored in L1, and the sum of K1, K2, and L2 would be stored in L2.

GIVING Option

When Format 2 is used, the values of all data items and literals prior to GIVING are to be added and the result is to be stored in the area identified by data-name-m, data-name-n, and so on. For example, the statement

```
ADD D1, D2 GIVING D3.
```

would cause the values of D1 and D2 to be added and this sum stored in D3. A specific case is

	D1	D2	D3
Before	10	15	34
After	10	15	25

Note that the previous value of D3 does not enter the calculation. More examples of ADD statements are shown in Fig. 7.1. However, it should be stressed that using both TO and GIVING in the same ADD statement is not allowed.

7.2 ROUNDED OPTION

If a computed result has more decimals than are available in the stored area, the excess digits would simply be truncated. For example, if TAX-1 and TAX-2 are defined as

```
05 TAX-1   PIC 99V999.
05 TAX-2   PIC 99V99.
```

in the DATA DIVISION, and the contents of TAX-1 and TAX-2 are assumed to be

TAX-1: 0 4 5 6 8
TAX-2: 1 2 3 1

then the execution of the statement

```
ADD TAX-1 TO TAX-2
```

would yield

$$\text{TAX-2:} \quad 1\ 6\ 8\ 7$$

The true result of the addition is 16.878, but since TAX-2 can only accommodate two decimals the last digit disappears when the number is stored. Since in most cases simple truncation is unacceptable, the computation result should be rounded before it is stored. In COBOL, every computation statement has a ROUNDED option. Suppose the above statement was written

```
        ADD TAX-1 TO TAX-2 ROUNDED.
```

Then the result stored in TAX-2 would be 1688, which is the rounded version of 16.878. Figures 7.1 and 7.2 provide some additional examples of the effect of the ROUNDED option.

Calculation results	Picture	Value without rounding	Value after rounding
11.39	99V9	11.3	11.4
9.746	9V9	9.7	9.8
6.434	9V9	6.4	6.4
0.078	9V9	0.0	0.1

Fig. 7.1 Effects of the ROUNDED option.

7.3 ON SIZE ERROR OPTION

Every computation statement has the ON SIZE ERROR option to check an undetected computation error. Such errors often occur when the programmer is not careful in assigning the area that is to be reserved for a computation result. For instance, if DATA1 is defined as a 4-digit area and has the value 78.50, that is,

```
        06 DATA1 PIC 99V99.
```

then the statement

would give a value 108.50, which is too large to be stored in the area DATA1. If such a statement is executed, the contents of DATA1 would be undefined. To detect such an error, the programmer can rewrite the above ADD statement as

```
        ADD 30 TO DATA1
            ON SIZE ERROR GO TO DATA1-TOO-LARGE.
```

Upon the execution of the above statement, the program would branch to the routine

110   7   Calculations

Variable	A	B	C	D
Picture	9V	99V99	99V9	999V9
Value before execution	8.	5.65	95.8	128.6
Value after execution:				
ADD A, B GIVING C.	8.	5.65	13.6	—
ADD A, B GIVING C ROUNDED.	8.	5.65	13.7	—
ADD A, C GIVING B ON SIZE ERROR				
MOVE 99.99 TO B.	8	99.99	95.8	—
ADD A TO B GIVING C.	invalid, TO and GIVING cannot appear in same ADD statement			

Fig. 7.2 Some examples of ADD statements.

called DATA1-TOO-LARGE and leave the contents of DATA1 unchanged. If DATA1 is big enough to accommodate the computation result, the normal calculation would take place as if the ON SIZE ERROR option had not been specified. More examples are presented in Fig. 7.2.

7.4 SUBTRACT STATEMENT

The SUBTRACT statement is used to subtract one data item or a sum of two or more data items from one or more items. The SUBTRACT statement has two basic formats:

Format 1

$$\underline{\text{SUBTRACT}} \left\{ \begin{array}{l} \text{identifier-1} \\ \text{literal-1} \end{array} \right\} \left[\begin{array}{l} \text{, identifier-2, } \ldots \\ \text{, literal-2, } \ldots \end{array} \right] \underline{\text{FROM}} \ \text{identifier-m} \ [\underline{\text{ROUNDED}}]$$

$$[\text{, identifier-n } [\underline{\text{ROUNDED}}] \ldots] \ [; \text{ON } \underline{\text{SIZE}} \ \underline{\text{ERROR}} \ \text{imperative-statement}]$$

Format 2

$$\underline{\text{SUBTRACT}} \left\{ \begin{array}{l} \text{identifier-1} \\ \text{literal-1} \end{array} \right\} \left[\begin{array}{l} \text{, identifier-2, } \ldots \\ \text{, literal-2, } \ldots \end{array} \right] \underline{\text{FROM}} \left\{ \begin{array}{l} \text{identifier-m} \\ \text{literal-m} \end{array} \right\}$$

$$\underline{\text{GIVING}} \ \text{identifier-n} \ [\underline{\text{ROUNDED}}] \ [\text{, identifier-o} \ [\underline{\text{ROUNDED}}] \ldots]$$

$$[; \text{ON } \underline{\text{SIZE}} \ \underline{\text{ERROR}} \ \text{imperative-statement}]$$

If Format 1 is used, the values of all the operands that come before FROM are added and then the sum is subtracted from the value of identifier-m, identifier-n, and so on. All decimal points are automatically aligned during computation.

Example 1

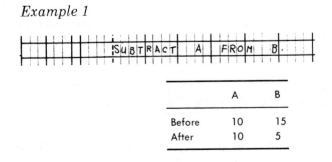

	A	B
Before	10	15
After	10	5

Example 2

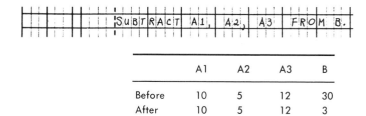

	A1	A2	A3	B
Before	10	5	12	30
After	10	5	12	3

Example 3

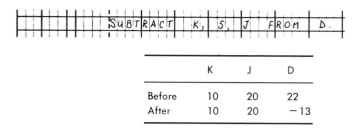

	K	J	D
Before	10	20	22
After	10	20	−13

Example 4

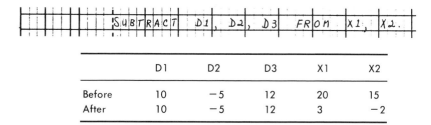

	D1	D2	D3	X1	X2
Before	10	−5	12	20	15
After	10	−5	12	3	−2

Example 5

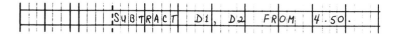

This statement is invalid, because the operand following FROM must be a data name.

GIVING Option

If Format 2 is used, the values of the operands before FROM are added, the sum is then subtracted from identifier-m or literal-m, and the result is stored in identifier-n, identifier-o, and so on.

Example 6

SUBTRACT A FROM B GIVING C.

	A	B	C
Before	10	25	−10
After	10	25	15

Example 7

	TAX	FICA	INSURANCE	GROSS	NET
Before	25.50	10.0	4.50	125.0	190.0
After	25.50	10.0	4.50	125.0	85.0

Example 8

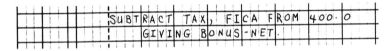

	TAX	FICA	BONUS-NET
Before	100.0	25.0	150.0
After	100.0	25.0	275.0

The main point to remember is that in a GIVING option (that is, Format 2), the data name that follows the GIVING option is not used in the computation and may contain editing symbols if such a data name is not used in additional computation, for example, in the statement

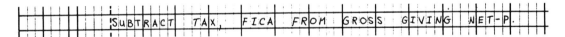

where NET-P is a numeric edited field defined as

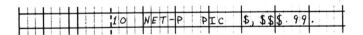

The ROUNDED and SIZE ERROR options are used in the same manner as described in the ADD statement.

7.5 MULTIPLY STATEMENT

The MULTIPLY statement is used to multiply two numeric data items. It also has two formats:

Format 1

$$\underline{\text{MULTIPLY}} \begin{Bmatrix} \text{identifier-1} \\ \text{literal-1} \end{Bmatrix} \underline{\text{BY}} \text{ identifier-2 } [\underline{\text{ROUNDED}}]$$

$$[, \text{identifier-3 } [\underline{\text{ROUNDED}}] \ldots]$$

$$[; \text{ON } \underline{\text{SIZE}} \underline{\text{ERROR}} \text{ imperative-statement}]$$

Format 2

$$\underline{\text{MULTIPLY}} \begin{Bmatrix} \text{identifier-1} \\ \text{literal-1} \end{Bmatrix} \underline{\text{BY}} \begin{Bmatrix} \text{identifier-2} \\ \text{literal-2} \end{Bmatrix}$$

$$\underline{\text{GIVING}} \text{ identifier-3 } [\underline{\text{ROUNDED}}]$$

$$[\text{ON } \underline{\text{SIZE}} \underline{\text{ERROR}} \text{ imperative-statement}]$$

With Format 1, the value of identifier-1 or literal-1 is multiplied by the value of identifier-2 and the result is stored in identifier-2. In Format 2, the multiplication result is stored in a new location identified as identifier-3.

Example 1

	X1	X2
Before	10	020
After	10	200

Example 2

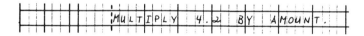

	AMOUNT
Before	020.0
After	084.0

Example 3

MULTIPLY WAGE BY .0585 GIVING FICA.

7 Calculations

	WAGE	FICA
Before	200.0	105.60
After	200.0	011.70

Example 4 (Invalid statement)

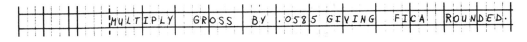

MULTIPLY AMOUNT BY 6.0.

Example 5

MULTIPLY GROSS BY .0585 GIVING FICA ROUNDED.

	GROSS	FICA
Before	101.00	28.67
After	101.00	05.91

The ROUNDED and SIZE options are used in the same manner as described in the ADD statement.

7.6 DIVIDE STATEMENT

The DIVIDE statement is used to perform the division operation of two numeric items. There are two formats:

Format 1

$$\underline{\text{DIVIDE}} \left\{ \begin{array}{l} \text{identifier-1} \\ \text{literal-1} \end{array} \right\} \underline{\text{INTO}} \text{ identifier-2 } [\underline{\text{ROUNDED}}]$$

$$[\text{ON } \underline{\text{SIZE}} \underline{\text{ERROR}} \text{ imperative statement}]$$

Format 2

$$\underline{\text{DIVIDE}} \left\{ \begin{array}{l} \text{identifier-1} \\ \text{literal-1} \end{array} \right\} \left\{ \begin{array}{l} \underline{\text{INTO}} \\ \underline{\text{BY}} \end{array} \right\}$$

$$\left\{ \begin{array}{l} \text{identifier-2} \\ \text{literal-2} \end{array} \right\} \underline{\text{GIVING}} \text{ identifier-3 } [\underline{\text{ROUNDED}}]$$

$$[\underline{\text{REMAINDER}} \text{ identifier-4}] [\text{ON } \underline{\text{SIZE}} \underline{\text{ERROR}} \text{ imperative-statement}]$$

In Format 1, the first operand (identifier-1 or literal-1) is the divisor and identifier-2 the dividend. Upon execution of this statement, the value of identifier-1 or literal-1 is divided into the value of identifier-2 and the result (that is, the quotient) is stored in identifier-2. The original contents of identifier-2 are destroyed.

Example 1

	A	B
Before	10	150.0
After	10	15.0

Example 2

	GRADE
Before	33.0
After	2.20

Example 3

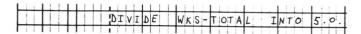

This statement is invalid, because the second operand must be a data name.

In Format 2, the programmer can use either DIVIDE INTO or DIVIDE BY and obtain the remainder in a separate data item, namely, identifier-4.

Example 4

Example 5

7   Calculations

Example 6

```
          DIVIDE PART-NO BY 5 GIVING GROUP-NO ROUNDED
                 REMAINDER DEPT-NO.
```

	PART-NO	GROUP-NO (not rounded)	GROUP-NO (rounded)	DEPT-NO (remainder)
Before	29	9	—	7.2
After	29	5	6	4.0

In this example, the ROUNDED option is specified. Thus, the quotient (in this case, GROUP-NO) is rounded after the remainder is determined.

7.7   COMPUTE STATEMENT

The COMPUTE statement is usually used to perform complicated calculation when the simple arithmetic statements become unwieldy. The format of the COMPUTE statement is

$$\underline{\text{COMPUTE}}\ \text{identifier-1}\ [\underline{\text{ROUNDED}}] = \begin{Bmatrix} \text{identifier-2} \\ \text{literal-1} \\ \text{arithmetic} \\ \text{expression} \end{Bmatrix}$$

$$[\underline{\text{ON}}\ \underline{\text{SIZE}}\ \underline{\text{ERROR}}\ \text{imperative-statement}]$$

The COMPUTE statement essentially provides an alternative way of coding arithmetic expressions. The statement often allows one to code in a single statement what may require several other statements using ADD, SUBTRACT, MULTIPLY, or DIVIDE. For example, the statement

```
          COMPUTE GROSS = RATE * (HOURS + 1.5 * OVERTIME).
```

would calculate the gross pay according to the formula

$$\text{gross pay} = \text{rate} \times (\text{regular hours} + 1.5 \times \text{overtime}).$$

Such a formula would normally require at least three statements involving ADD and MULTIPLY.

Also note that the COBOL COMPUTE statement looks almost exactly like the desired equation, with the one exception that the symbol * is used as the multiplication operator. In fact, in COBOL every arithmetic expression is written in much the same way as in ordinary mathematics by the use of arithmetic operators, variables, and parentheses. The symbols for the different arithmetic operators are given in the following table:

7.7 COMPUTE Statement

Operator	Meaning
+	addition
−	subtraction
*	multiplication
/	division
**	exponentiation (for example, A**2 means a^2)

Some standard arithmetic expressions and their corresponding COMPUTE statements are given in the next table:

Arithmetic expression	COMPUTE statements
$c = a + b$	COMPUTE C = A + B.
$d = a - b$	COMPUTE D = A − B.
$p = a \times b$	COMPUTE P = A * B.
$q = \dfrac{a}{b}$	COMPUTE Q = A / B.
$c = a^2 + b^2$	COMPUTE C = A ** 2 + B ** 2.
$k = \dfrac{a + b - c}{4}$	COMPUTE K = (A + B − C) / 4.
$a = 5.601$	COMPUTE A = 5.601.
$w = \sqrt{z}$	COMPUTE W = Z ** .5.
$e = \dfrac{(a + b)}{c} + d$	COMPUTE E = (A + B) / C + D.
$z = \dfrac{x^2 + y}{w + 5}$	COMPUTE Z = (X ** 2 + Y) / (W + 5).

In a COMPUTE statement, the value to the left of the equal sign will be replaced by the value resulting from the calculation specified to the right. The calculation to the right of the equal sign is evaluated from left to right. However, operations within parentheses are always executed first, and then exponentiation, multiplication, or division. Addition and subtraction have the lowest priority. These two operations will always be evaluated last from left to right if present.

Example 1

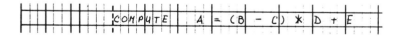

In this statement, the subtraction is performed first (because it is within the parentheses), then the multiplication, and finally the addition.

Example 2

If the statement in Example 1 had been mistakenly written as

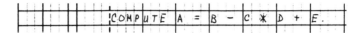

then the multiplication would have been performed first (that is, only C is multiplied by D), then the subtraction, and finally the addition, in that order (from left to right).

It should further be noted that every arithmetic operator must be preceded and followed by at least one blank space when appearing in a COMPUTE statement. However, a blank must not follow a left nor precede a right parenthesis.

Example 3

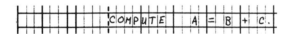

There must be at least one space before and after an operational sign.

Example 4

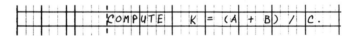

There must not be a space immediately after a left or before a right parenthesis.

7.8 SAMPLE PROGRAM 7A: DAILY SALES REPORT

This program reads the DAILY-SALES-FILE, computes the total and average daily sales, and produces a printed report. The program also uses the END-OF-PAGE option to skip to the top of a new page when an end of page condition is sensed. (See the programming notes for a more detailed explanation.)

Input Description: SALES-REC

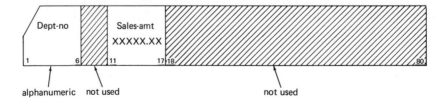

7.8 Sample Program 7A: Daily Sales Report

Sample Input

```
1     6      11
↓     ↓      ↓
A0001R       0098550
A0101R       0214575
B1123R       0069515
B2175R       0081000
B1712R       0021575
C1234W       0410500
D1021R       0097515
E7111R       0110751
E8123W       0212685
F9110R       0099550
F9112R       0012550
G1761R       0123450
X7470W       0912345
```

Program Logic

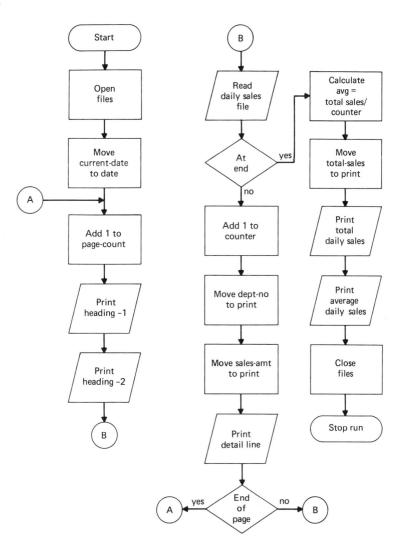

Source Listing

```
00001       IDENTIFICATION DIVISION.
00002       PROGRAM-ID. SAMPL7A
00003       AUTHOR. CHAI
00004       INSTALLATION. MONTCLAIR STATE COLLEGE.
00005       DATE-WRITTEN. NOV 27, 1975.
00006       REMARKS. THIS PROGRAM READ THE DAILY-SALES-FILE,
00007                OF ITS RETAIL DEPARTMENTS
00008                COMPUTES THE TOTAL AND AVERAGE-SALES,
00009                THEN PRODUCES THE DAILY-SALES-REPORT.
00010      ****************************************************************
00011       ENVIRONMENT DIVISION.
00012       CONFIGURATION SECTION.
00013       SOURCE-COMPUTER. IBM-370.
00014       OBJECT-COMPUTER. IBM-370.
00015       SPECIAL-NAMES.
00016           C01 IS TOP-OF-PAGE.
00017       INPUT-OUTPUT SECTION.
00018       FILE-CONTROL.
00019           SELECT DAILY-SALES-FILE ASSIGN TO UR-2540R-S-INPUT.
00020           SELECT REPORT-FILE      ASSIGN TO UR-1403-S-PROUT.
00021      ****************************************************************
00022       DATA DIVISION.
00023       FILE SECTION.
00024       FD  DAILY-SALES-FILE
00025           LABEL RECORDS ARE OMITTED
00026           DATA RECORD IS SALES-REC.
00027       01  SALES-REC.
00028           03  DEPT-NO     PIC  X(6).
00029           03  FILLER      PIC  X(4).
00030           03  SALES-AMT   PIC  S9(5)V99.
00031           03  FILLER      PIC  X(63).
00032       FD  REPORT-FILE
00033           LABEL RECORDS ARE OMITTED
00034           DATA RECORD IS PRINT-AREA.
00035       01  PRINT-AREA  PICTURE  X(132).
00036       WORKING-STORAGE SECTION.
00037       77  TOTAL-SALES  PIC   S9(7)V99 VALUE ZEROS.
00038       77  KOUNT        PIC   999 VALUE ZEROS.
00039       77  PAGE-KOUNT   PIC   999 VALUE ZEROS.
00040       01  HEADING-1.
00041           03  FILLER    PIC   X(5)  VALUE SPACES.
00042           03  FILLER    PIC   X(33)
00043                        VALUE 'DAILY-SALES REPORT (RETAILS ONLY)'
00044           03  FILLER    PIC   X(10) VALUE SPACES.
00045           03  DATE-P    PIC   X(8).
00046           03  FILLER    PIC   X(5)  VALUE SPACES.
00047           03  FILLER    PIC   X(4)  VALUE 'PAGE'.
00048           03  FILLER    PIC   X(2)  VALUE SPACES.
00049           03  PAGE-NO   PIC   ZZ9.
00050       01  HEADING-2.
00051           03  FILLER    PIC   X(18)  VALUE SPACES.
00052           03  FILLER    PIC   X(10) VALUE 'DEPARTMENT'.
00053           03  FILLER    PIC X(14) VALUE 'SALES' JUST RIGHT.
00054       01  PRINT-LINE.
00055           03  FILLER    PIC   X(20) VALUE SPACES.
00056           03  DEPT-NO-P PIC   X(6).
00057           03  FILLER    PIC   X(7)  VALUE SPACES.
00058           03  SALES-P   PIC   $ZZ,ZZ9.99.
00059       01  LINE-2.
00060           03  FILLER    PIC   X(10) VALUE SPACES.
00061           03  FILLER    PIC   X(20) VALUE 'TOTAL DAILY SALES '.
00062           03  TOTAL-P   PIC   $Z,ZZZ,ZZ9.99.
00063       01  LINE-3.
00064           03  FILLER    PIC   X(10) VALUE SPACES.
00065           03  FILLER    PIC   X(23) VALUE 'AVERAGE DAILY SALES '.
00066           03  AVERAGE-P PIC   $ZZ,ZZ9.99.
00067      ****************************************************************
00068       PROCEDURE DIVISION.
00069       INITIALIZATION-ROUTINE.
00070           OPEN INPUT DAILY-SALES-FILE
00071                OUTPUT REPORT-FILE.
00072           MOVE CURRENT-DATE TO DATE-P.
00073       TOP-PAGE-ROUTINE
00074           ADD 1 TO PAGE-KOUNT.
00075           MOVE PAGE-KOUNT TO PAGE-NO.
00076           WRITE PRINT-AREA FROM HEADING-1 AFTER ADVANCING TOP-OF-PAGE.
00077           WRITE PRINT-AREA FROM HEADING-2 AFTER ADVANCING 3 LINES.
00078           MOVE SPACES TO PRINT-AREA.
00079           WRITE PRINT-AREA AFTER ADVANCING 2 LINES.
00080       READ-A.
00081           READ DAILY-SALES-FILE AT END GO TO EOJ.
00082           ADD 1 TO KOUNT.
00083           MOVE DEPT-NO  TO DEPT-NO-P
00084           MOVE SALES-AMT TO SALES-P.
00085           ADD SALES-AMT TO TOTAL-SALES.
00086           WRITE PRINT-AREA FROM PRINT-LINE AFTER ADVANCING 2 LINES
00087               AT END-OF-PAGE GO TO TOP-PAGE-ROUTINE.
00088           GO TO READ-A.
00089       EOJ.
00090           DIVIDE KOUNT INTO TOTAL-SALES GIVING AVERAGE-P ROUNDED.
00091           MOVE TOTAL-SALES TO TOTAL-P.
00092           WRITE PRINT-AREA FROM LINE-2 AFTER ADVANCING 3 LINES.
00093           WRITE PRINT-AREA FROM LINE-3 AFTER ADVANCING 2 LINES.
00094           CLOSE DAILY-SALES-FILE,  REPORT-FILE.
00095           STOP RUN.
```

- lines 00027–00031: input description
- lines 00040–00053: report heading and subheading
- lines 00054–00058: detail line (one print line per data card)
- lines 00059–00066: (final lines) report footing
- lines 00076–00077: print heading and subheading
- lines 00086–00087: print detail lines
- lines 00092–00093: print final lines

Sample Output

```
            DAILY-SALES REPORT (RETAILS ONLY)          05/27/75      PAGE    1

                    DEPARTMENT            SALES

                       A0001R         $     985.50
                       A0101R         $   2,145.75
                       B1123R         $     695.15
                       B2175R         $     810.00
                       B1712R         $     215.75
                       C1234W         $   4,105.00
                       D1021R         $     975.15
                       E7111R         $   1,107.51
                       E8123W         $   2,126.85
                       F9110R         $     995.50
                       F9112R         $     125.50
                       G1761R         $   1,234.50
                       X7470W         $   9,123.45

            TOTAL DAILY SALES     $    24,645.61
            AVERAGE DAILY SALES   $     1,895.82
```

Programming Notes

1. CURRENT-DATE

```
00072        MOVE CURRENT-DATE TO DATE-P.
```

CURRENT-DATE is a special IBM COBOL register that contains the current date in dd/mm/yy. (See Sample Program 5C for more detailed information.)

2. END-OF-PAGE

```
00086        WRITE PRINT-AREA FROM PRINT-LINE AFTER ADVANCING 2 LINES
00087          AT END-OF-PAGE GO TO TOP-PAGE-ROUTINE.
```

END-OF-PAGE is a standard COBOL reserved word used to test whether the printed line has reached the bottom of the page. In some computer systems (for example, IBM 360/370 systems) this end of page condition exists whenever a "channel 12 punch" on the carriage control tape is sensed by the on-line printer. If so, the program will branch to TOP-PAGE-ROUTINE after the execution of the WRITE statement. Otherwise, the computer will execute the next sequential statement, that is,

```
00088        GO TO READ-A.
```

7.9 SAMPLE PROGRAM 7B: WEEKLY PAYROLL REPORT

This is a simplified payroll program that reads weekly time cards. (We call these cards EMPLOYEE-CARD-REC.) Each card contains the employee's name, social security number, hourly rate, hours worked, and amount of deduction as shown in the input description. The program then computes the following:

$$\text{wage (gross)} = \text{hourly rate} \times \text{hours worked}$$
$$\text{FICA} = 5.85\% \text{ of wage (rounded)}$$
$$\text{tax} = 10\% \text{ of wage (rounded)}$$
$$\text{net} = \text{wage} - \text{FICA} - \text{tax} - \text{deduction}$$

The program also computes the total amounts for these items.

Input Description

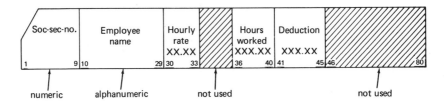

Sample Input

SOC-SEC-NO	NAME	HRLY RATE	HOURS WKED	DEDUCTIONS†
1	10	30	36	41
123456789	FRAN WAGNER	0520	04000	00050
234567894	KEN SMITH	0430	03500	0004K ←
146853417	MARGARET CHAI	1040	04500	0010− ←
157483446	ANNA MARCINKO	0822	08000	00022
346546131	PETER JONESN	0250	01200	00010
343656451	ALVIN WARGA	0310	02200	0012N ←
345678413	JIM SCOTT	1120	03600	00075

† Arrows on right indicate negative numbers, which cause credit symbol CR to appear at right of printout.

7.9 Sample Program 7B: Weekly Payroll Report

Program Logic

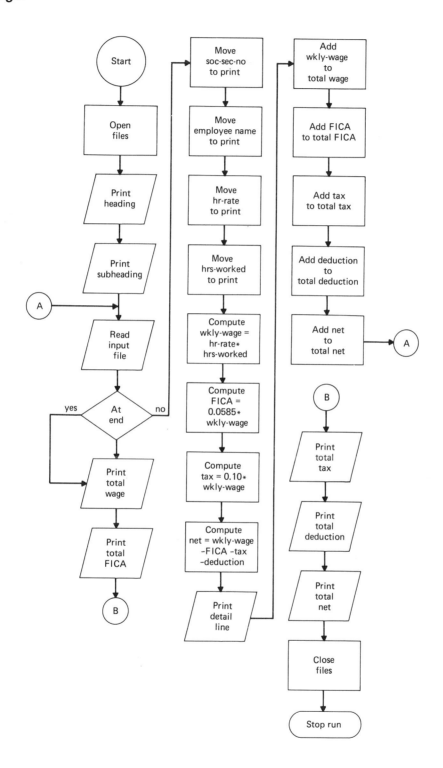

124   7   Calculations

Source Listing

```
00001              IDENTIFICATION DIVISION.
00002              PROGRAM-ID. 'SAMPL7B'
00003              DATE-WRITTEN. OCTOBER 9, 1974
00004              REMARKS. THIS PROGRAM READS A DECK OF PAYROLL CARDS AND COMPUTES WAGE.
00005          ***************************************
00006              ENVIRONMENT DIVISION.
00007              CONFIGURATION SECTION.
00008              SOURCE-COMPUTER. IBM-370.
00009              OBJECT-COMPUTER. IBM-370.
00010              INPUT-OUTPUT SECTION.
00011              FILE-CONTROL.
00012                  SELECT INPUT-FILE ASSIGN TO UR-2501-S-CARDIN.
00013                  SELECT OUTPUT-FILE ASSIGN TO UR-1403-S-PROUT.
00014          ***************************************
00015              DATA DIVISION.
00016              FILE SECTION.
00017              FD  INPUT-FILE
00018                  LABEL RECORDS ARE OMITTED
00019                  DATA RECORD IS EMPLOYEE-CARD-REC.
00020              01  EMPLOYEE-CARD-REC.
00021                  05  SOC-SEC-NO PIC X(9).
00022                  05  EMPLOYEE-NAME PIC A(20).
00023                  05  HOURLY-RATE PIC 99V99.
00024                  05  FILLER PIC XX.
00025                  05  HOURS-WORKED PIC 999V99.
00026                  05  DEDUCTION PIC 999V99.
00027                  05  FILLER PIC X(35).
00028              FD  OUTPUT-FILE
00029                  LABEL RECORDS ARE OMITTED
00030                  DATA RECORD IS PRINT-AREA.
00031              01  PRINT-AREA PIC X(133).
00032              WORKING-STORAGE SECTION.
00033              77  WEEKLY-WAGE PIC S9(4)V99 VALUE ZEROS.
00034              77  FICA PIC S9(3)V99 VALUE ZEROS.
00035              77  TAX PIC S9(4)V99 VALUE ZEROS.
00036              77  NET PIC S9(4)V99 VALUE ZEROS.
00037              77  KOUNTER-W PIC S9(5)V99 VALUE ZEROS.
00038              77  KOUNTER-F PIC S9(4)V99 VALUE ZEROS.
00039              77  KOUNTER-T PIC S9(5)V99 VALUE ZEROS.
00040              77  KOUNTER-D PIC S9(4)V99 VALUE ZEROS.
00041              77  KOUNTER-N PIC S9(5)V99 VALUE ZEROS.
00042              01  HEADING-1.
00043                  05  FILLER PIC X(30) VALUE SPACES.
00044                  05  FILLER PIC X(21) VALUE 'WEEKLY PAYROLL REPORT'.
00045              01  HEADING-A.
00046                  05  FILLER PIC X(45) VALUE SPACES.
00047                  05  TOTAL-A PIC X(20).
00048                  05  TOTAL-B PIC $ZZZZ.99.
00049              01  SUB-HEADING.
00050                  05  FILLER PIC X(4) VALUE SPACES.
00051                  05  FILLER PIC X(23) VALUE 'SOC-SEC-NO'.
00052                  05  FILLER PIC X(15) VALUE 'NAME'.
00053                  05  FILLER PIC X(12) VALUE 'HOURLY-RATE'.
00054                  05  FILLER PIC X(16) VALUE 'HOURS-WORKED'.
00055                  05  FILLER PIC X(13) VALUE 'WAGE'.
00056                  05  FILLER PIC X(12) VALUE 'FICA'.
00057                  05  FILLER PIC X(13) VALUE 'TAX'.
00058                  05  FILLER PIC X(14) VALUE 'DEDUCTION'.
00059                  05  FILLER PIC X(3) VALUE 'NET'.
00060              01  PRINT-LINE.
00061                  05  FILLER PIC X(5) VALUE SPACES.
00062                  05  SOC-SEC-NO-P PIC 9(9).
00063                  05  FILLER PIC X(5) VALUE SPACES.
00064                  05  EMPLOYEE-NAME-P PIC X(20).
00065                  05  FILLER PIC X(5) VALUE SPACES.
00066                  05  HOURLY-RATE-P PIC $ZZ.99.
00067                  05  FILLER PIC X(8) VALUE SPACES.
00068                  05  HOURS-WORKED-P PIC ZZZ.99.
00069                  05  FILLER PIC X(4) VALUE SPACES.
00070                  05  WEEKLY-WAGE-P PIC $ZZZZ.99.
00071                  05  FILLER PIC X(4) VALUE SPACES.
00072                  05  FICA-P PIC $ZZZ.99.
00073                  05  FILLER PIC X(6) VALUE SPACES.
00074                  05  TAX-P PIC $ZZZZ.99.
00075                  05  FILLER PIC X(5) VALUE SPACES.
00076                  05  DEDUCTION-P PIC   $ZZZ.99CR.
00077                  05  FILLER PIC X(5) VALUE SPACES.
00078                  05  NET-P PIC $ZZZZ.99.
00079          ***************************************
00080              PROCEDURE DIVISION.
00081              TASK-1.
00082                  OPEN INPUT INPUT-FILE, OUTPUT OUTPUT-FILE.
00083                  MOVE HEADING-1 TO PRINT-AREA.
00084                  WRITE PRINT-AREA BEFORE ADVANCING 1 LINES.
00085                  WRITE PRINT-AREA FROM SUB-HEADING AFTER ADVANCING 4 LINES.
```

} input description (lines 0020–0027)

} report heading and subheading (lines 0042–0059)

} detail line (one print line per data card) (lines 0060–0078)

} print heading and subheading (lines 0084–0085)

7.9 Sample Program 7B: Weekly Payroll Report

```
00086        TASK-2.
00087            READ INPUT-FILE AT END GO TO TASK-4.
00088            MOVE SOC-SEC-NO TO SOC-SEC-NO-P.
00089            MOVE EMPLOYEE-NAME TO EMPLOYEE-NAME-P.
00090            MOVE HOURLY-RATE TO HOURLY-RATE-P.
00091            MOVE HOURS-WORKED TO HOURS-WORKED-P.
00092        TASK-3.
00093            COMPUTE WEEKLY-WAGE ROUNDED = HOURLY-RATE * HOURS-WORKED.  ⎫
00094            MULTIPLY .0585 BY WEEKLY-WAGE GIVING FICA ROUNDED.         ⎬ perform
00095            MULTIPLY 0.10 BY WEEKLY-WAGE GIVING TAX ROUNDED.           ⎪ computation
00096            SUBTRACT FICA TAX DEDUCTION FROM WEEKLY-WAGE GIVING NET.   ⎭
00097            MOVE WEEKLY-WAGE TO WEEKLY-WAGE-P.
00098            MOVE FICA TO FICA-P.
00099            MOVE TAX TO TAX-P.
00100            MOVE DEDUCTION TO DEDUCTION-P.
00101            MOVE NET TO NET-P.
00102            MOVE PRINT-LINE TO PRINT-AREA.
00103            WRITE PRINT-AREA AFTER ADVANCING 2 LINES.       ⟵ print detail lines
00104            ADD WEEKLY-WAGE TO KOUNTER-W.                   ⎫
00105            ADD FICA TO KOUNTER-F.                          ⎪
00106            ADD TAX TO KOUNTER-T.                           ⎬ update all totals
00107            ADD DEDUCTION TO KOUNTER-D.                     ⎪
00108            ADD NET TO KOUNTER-N.                           ⎭
00109            GO TO TASK-2.
00110        TASK-4.
00111            MOVE 'TOTAL WEEKLY-WAGE' TO TOTAL-A.                       ⎫
00112            MOVE KOUNTER-W TO TOTAL-B.                                 ⎪
00113            WRITE PRINT-AREA FROM HEADING-A AFTER ADVANCING 4 LINES.   ⎪
00114            MOVE 'TOTAL FICA' TO TOTAL-A.                              ⎪
00115            MOVE KOUNTER-F TO TOTAL-B.                                 ⎪
00116            WRITE PRINT-AREA FROM HEADING-A AFTER ADVANCING 4 LINES.   ⎪
00117            MOVE 'TOTAL TAX' TO TOTAL-A.                               ⎬ print final totals
00118            MOVE KOUNTER-T TO TOTAL-B.                                 ⎪
00119            WRITE PRINT-AREA FROM HEADING-A AFTER ADVANCING 4 LINES.   ⎪
00120            MOVE 'TOTAL DEDUCTION' TO TOTAL-A.                         ⎪
00121            MOVE KOUNTER-D TO TOTAL-B.                                 ⎪
00122            WRITE PRINT-AREA FROM HEADING-A AFTER ADVANCING 4 LINES.   ⎪
00123            MOVE 'TOTAL NET' TO TOTAL-A.                               ⎪
00124            MOVE KOUNTER-N TO TOTAL-B.                                 ⎪
00125            WRITE PRINT-AREA FROM HEADING-A AFTER ADVANCING 4 LINES.   ⎭
00126        END-JOB.
00127            CLOSE INPUT-FILE, OUTPUT-FILE. STOP RUN.
```

Sample Output

WEEKLY PAYROLL REPORT

SOC-SEC-NO	NAME	HOURLY-RATE	HOURS-WORKED	WAGE	FICA	TAX	DEDUCTION	NET
123456789	FRAN WAGNER	$ 5.20	40.00	$ 208.00	$ 12.17	$ 20.80	$ .50	$ 174.53
234567894	KEN SMITH	$ 4.30	35.00	$ 150.50	$ 8.80	$ 15.05	$ .42CR	$ 127.07
146853147	MARGARET CHAI	$10.40	45.00	$ 468.00	$ 27.38	$ 46.80	$ 1.00CR	$ 394.82
157483446	ANNA MARCINKO	$ 8.22	80.00	$ 657.60	$ 38.47	$ 65.76	$ .22	$ 553.15
346546131	PETER JONESN	$ 2.50	12.00	$ 30.00	$ 1.76	$ 3.00	$ .10	$ 25.14
343656451	ALVIN WARGA	$ 3.10	22.00	$ 68.20	$ 3.99	$ 6.82	$ 1.25CR	$ 58.64
345678413	JIM SCOTT	$11.20	36.00	$ 403.20	$ 23.59	$ 40.32	$ .75	$ 338.54

```
              TOTAL WEEKLY-WAGE    $1985.50

              TOTAL FICA           $ 116.16

              TOTAL TAX            $ 198.55

              TOTAL DEDUCTION      $   1.10

              TOTAL NET            $1671.89
```

7.10 SAMPLE PROGRAM 7C: CHECKING ACCOUNT REPORT

This sample program produces a simple checking account report for a bank. It reads a depositor file containing individual account records. Each record contains the depositor's name, account number, number of checks written, and dollar amount of checks written as specified in the input description. The computational requirements of this program are

(1) average amount per check written for each depositor (rounded), and
(2) total number of checks written, total amount of checks written, and average amount of checks written by all depositors (rounded).

Input Description: ACCOUNTS RECORD

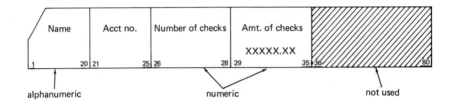

Sample Input

```
                        21   26  29
                        ↓    ↓   ↓
MARCINKO A J            004770100080000
WARGA M K               012490070035075
CHAI WA                 027630090051403
SMITH R J               071740130131015
JONES W K               092730200074795
GOODRICH D K            116870050116672
```

7.10 Sample Program 7C: Checking Account Report

Program Logic

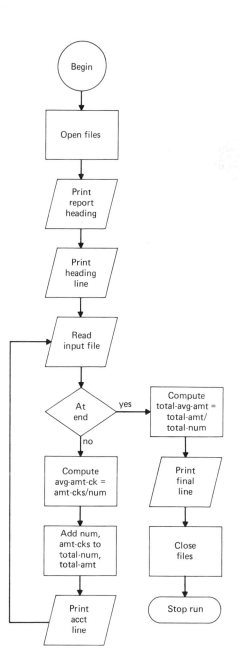

Source Listing

```
00001              ID DIVISION.
00002              PROGRAM-ID. SAMPL7C.
00003              ENVIRONMENT DIVISION.
00004              INPUT-OUTPUT SECTION.
00005              FILE-CONTROL.
00006                  SELECT INPUT-FILE ASSIGN TO UR-2501-S-SYSIN.
00007                  SELECT OUTPUT-FILE ASSIGN TO UR-1403-S-SYSOUT.
00008         **********************************************************
00009              DATA DIVISION.
00010              FILE SECTION.
00011              FD  INPUT-FILE LABEL RECORDS ARE OMITTED.
00012              01  ACCOUNTS-RECORD.
00013                  02 NAME            PIC A(20).
00014                  02 ACC-NUM         PIC 9(5).
00015                  02 NUM-CHECKS      PIC 9(3).
00016                  02 AMT-CHECKS      PIC 9(5)V99.
00017                  02 FILLER          PIC X(45).
```
} input description

128   7 Calculations

```
00019              FD  OUTPUT-FILE LABEL RECORDS ARE OMITTED.
00019              01  PRINT-LINE       PIC X(121).
00020          WORKING-STORAGE SECTION.
00021          77  WS-TOT-AMT-CHECKS PIC 9(6)V99 VALUE ZEROS.
00022          77  WS-TOT-NUM-CHECKS PIC 9(3) VALUE ZEROS.
00023          77  WS-TOT-AVG-AMT-CHECKS   PIC 9(5)V99 VALUE ZEROS.
00024          01  REPORT-HEADING PIC X(50) VALUE 'CHECKING ACCOUNT REPORT'
00025              JUST RIGHT.
00026          01  HEADING-LINE PIC X(80) VALUE '      DEPOSITOR           ACC NO
00027         -    ' CHECKS    AMOUNT       AVERAGE '.
00028          01  ACCOUNT-LINE.
00029              02  FILLER           PIC X(1).
00030              02  NAME-OUT         PIC A(20).
00031              02  FILLER           PIC X(3).
00032              02  ACC-NUM-OUT      PIC 9(5).
00033              02  FILLER           PIC X(3).
00034              02  NUM-CHECKS-OUT   PIC Z(3).
00035              02  FILLER           PIC X(3).
00036              02  AMT-CHECKS-OUT   PIC $$,$$9.99.
00037              02  FILLER           PIC X(3).
00038              02  AVG-AMT-CHECK    PIC $$,$$9.99.
00039          01  FINAL-LINE.
00040              02  FILLER    PIC X(22) VALUE SPACES.
00041              02  FILLER    PIC X(10) VALUE 'TOTAL '.
00042              02  TOT-NUM-CHECKS PIC ZZ9.
00043              02  FILLER PIC XX   VALUE SPACES.
00044              02  TOT-AMT-CHECKS PIC $$$,$$9.99.
00045              02  FILLER PIC XXX VALUE SPACES.
00046              02  TOT-AVG-AMT-CHECKS     PIC $$,$$9.99.
00047          ****************************************************************
00048          PROCEDURE DIVISION.
00049          OPEN-R.
00050              OPEN INPUT INPUT-FILE OUTPUT OUTPUT-FILE.
00051              WRITE PRINT-LINE FROM REPORT-HEADING AFTER 0.
00052              WRITE PRINT-LINE FROM HEADING-LINE AFTER 3.
00053              MOVE SPACES TO ACCOUNT-LINE.
00054          READ-DATA.
00055              READ INPUT-FILE AT END GO TO LAST-LINE.
00056              DIVIDE AMT-CHECKS BY NUM-CHECKS GIVING AVG-AMT-CHECK ROUNDED.
00057              ADD NUM-CHECKS TO WS-TOT-NUM-CHECKS, ADD AMT-CHECKS
00058              TO WS-TOT-AMT-CHECKS.
00059              MOVE WS-TOT-AMT-CHECKS TO TOT-AMT-CHECKS.
00060              MOVE WS-TOT-NUM-CHECKS TO TOT-NUM-CHECKS.
00061              MOVE NAME TO NAME-OUT.
00062              MOVE ACC-NUM TO ACC-NUM-OUT.
00063              MOVE NUM-CHECKS TO NUM-CHECKS-OUT.
00064              MOVE AMT-CHECKS TO AMT-CHECKS-OUT.
00065              WRITE PRINT-LINE FROM ACCOUNT-LINE AFTER 2.
00066              GO TO READ-DATA.
00067          LAST-LINE.
00068              DIVIDE WS-TOT-AMT-CHECKS BY WS-TOT-NUM-CHECKS GIVING
00069              WS-TOT-AVG-AMT-CHECKS ROUNDED.
00070              MOVE WS-TOT-AVG-AMT-CHECKS TO TOT-AVG-AMT-CHECKS.
00071              WRITE PRINT-LINE FROM FINAL-LINE AFTER 3.
00072              CLOSE INPUT-FILE OUTPUT-FILE.
00073              STOP RUN.
```

Lines 00028–00038: detail line (one print line per data card)

Lines 00039–00046: print final totals

Sample Output

```
                         CHECKING ACCOUNT REPORT

         DEPOSITOR       ACC NO   CHECKS    AMOUNT      AVERAGE

      MARCINKO A J        00477     10       $800.00      $80.00

      WARGA   M K         01249      7       $350.75      $50.11

      CHAI    WA          02763      9       $514.03      $57.11

      SMITH     R J       07174     13     $1,310.15     $100.78

      JONES   W K         09273     20       $747.95      $37.40

      GOODRICH  D K       11687      5     $1,166.72     $233.34

                          TOTAL    64     $4,889.60      $76.40
```

EXERCISES

1 In the table below, find the values of the data-names after the execution of the statements:

	A	B	C
PICTURE	S9V	S9V9	S99V99
Value before execution	6.	2.0	9.78
Value after execution			
(a) ADD A, B GIVING C.			
(b) ADD B TO A ROUNDED.			
(c) SUBTRACT A FROM C.			
(d) SUBTRACT A FROM B GIVING C.			
(e) MULTIPLY A BY B GIVING C.			
(f) MULTIPLY A BY B ON SIZE ERROR MOVE 9.9 TO B.			
(g) DIVIDE B INTO A.			
(h) DIVIDE A INTO B GIVING C.			
(i) DIVIDE A BY 4.0 GIVING B REMAINDER C.			
(j) COMPUTE C = (A + B) / B.			
(k) COMPUTE A = (C + B) ON SIZE ERROR MOVE 1 TO A.			

2 Convert the following formulas into COMPUTE statements:
  (a) $B = P(1 + r)^n$.
  (b) FICA = 5.85% of NET-INCOME.
  (c) $a = 150 + 2.5q^2 + 6s$.
  (d) $t = \dfrac{a + b + s^2}{w}$
  (e) $C = \dfrac{p + q}{r + s} + w$.
  (f) $d = (x - y)^2 + (z - w)^2$.
  (g) $z = \sqrt{\dfrac{p + q}{r}}$
  (h) $p = 5x^3 + 6x^2 - 3x + 1 - \dfrac{2}{1 + x + x^2}$.

3 Modify programming exercise 6-4 so that the program will produce a summary at the end of the report containing the total sales amount, total number of salesmen, and average sales per salesman.

4 Write a COBOL program according to the following specification:

Input Description: CUSTOMER-PURCHASE-RECORD

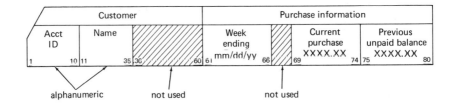

Processing

(a) For each customer, calculate

finance charge = 1.5% of previous unpaid balance,

new balance = previous unpaid balance + finance charge + current purchase.

(b) Calculate total amount for current purchase, finance charge, new balance, and number of accounts.

Output Description: CUSTOMER PURCHASE REPORT

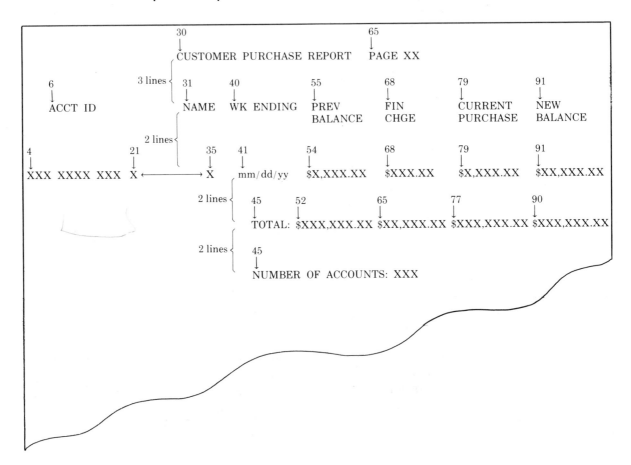

8
Conditional Statements: The IF Statement

8.1 INTRODUCTION

There are basically two types of executable statements in COBOL. One is the imperative statement, which gives the computer a direct command to be executed. For instance, the statements

```
ADD A TO B.
WRITE RECORD-A.
OPEN INPUT CARDFILE.
MOVE SPACES TO PRINT-AREA.
GO TO NEXT-ROUTINE.
```

are imperative statements, giving the computer unconditional directions.

The other type of statement is the conditional statement. Such statements direct the computer to perform specific operations only if certain conditions occur. For example, the statement

```
IF GROSS-PAY IS GREATER THAN 1000.0
    GO TO EXCEED-1000.
ADD 1 TO COUNTER.
```

directs the computer to branch its control to the procedure (paragraph) named EXCEED-1000 only if the value of GROSS-PAY exceeds 1000.0; otherwise the program executes the sequential instruction, namely,

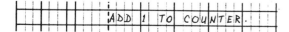

There are many forms of conditional statements, some of which might even appear to be imperative statements. Consider the statement

```
        ADD A TO B ON SIZE ERROR
          GO TO SIZE-ERROR-ROUTINE.
```

which is a conditional statement since the contents of A are added to B if and only if their sum is not too large to be stored in B. If the sum is too large, no addition takes place and the program branches to SIZE-ERROR-ROUTINE.

There are a number of COBOL verbs that can be used in both imperative and conditional statements. Figure 8-1 presents a list of COBOL verbs that can play such dual roles.

Imperative	Conditional	Discussion
ADD SUBTRACT MULTIPLY DIVIDE COMPUTE	ON SIZE ERROR	Chapter 7
GO TO	DEPENDING ON	Chapter 16
READ WRITE	AT END AT END-OF-PAGE	Chapter 5
READ WRITE	INVALID TEST	Chapter 14
PERFORM	UNTIL	Chapter 10

Fig. 8.1 COBOL verbs used as both imperative and conditional statements.

The IF statement is always a conditional statement regardless of its form. This chapter discusses how to code various IF statements including the relation test, the sign test, the class test, the conditional name test, and the compound test.

8.2 GENERAL DISCUSSION OF THE IF STATEMENT

The exact form of the IF statement is

$$\text{IF condition} \begin{Bmatrix} \text{statement-1} \\ \underline{\text{NEXT SENTENCE}} \end{Bmatrix} \begin{Bmatrix} \text{ELSE statement-2} \\ \text{ELSE NEXT SENTENCE} \end{Bmatrix}$$

The IF statement is executed by first evaluating the condition that follows the IF. If the condition is fulfilled (true), the statement immediately following the condition (for example, statement-1) is executed. If the condition is true and NEXT SENTENCE is written, the program passes its control to the next sentence after the IF statement.

If the condition is false, either the statement following the ELSE (statement-2) is executed or the next sentence is executed.

8.2 General Discussion of the IF Statement

Example 1: Program Flow and Coding with the ELSE Clause

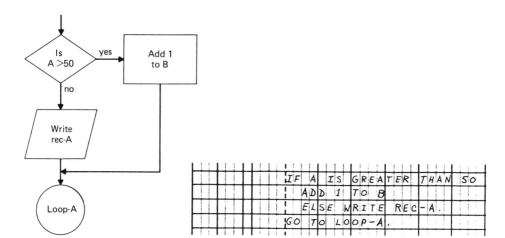

In this example, if the value of A exceeds 50, the statement ADD 1 TO B would be executed. After the execution, the program would skip the WRITE statement and execute GO TO LOOP-A.

On the other hand, if the value of A does exceed 50, the ADD statement would be bypassed, and instead the statement WRITE REC-A would be executed. In both cases, the statement after the IF statement, that is, GO TO LOOP-A, would always be executed next, as illustrated in the flowchart.

Example 2: IF Statement without ELSE Option

If the reserved word ELSE is omitted in the last example, the WRITE REC-A statement would be executed by the program regardless of whether the condition A IS GREATER THAN 50 is true or false. This is illustrated in the following flowchart and coding:

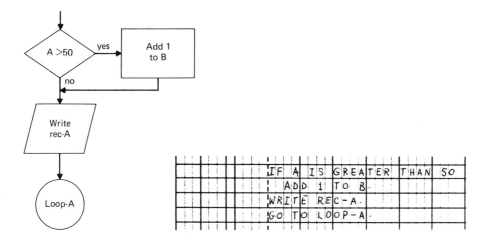

Example 3

The conditional part of the IF statement may contain any number of imperative statements. This is illustrated in the coding

```
    IF HOURS IS GREATER THAN 40.0
   ( ADD 1 TO COUNTER-A,
(a)  SUBTRACT 40.0 FROM HOURS GIVING OVERTIME,
   ( COMPUTE GROSS = RATE * (HOURS + 1.5 * OVERTIME).
    GO TO PRINT-ROUTINE.
```

In this example, the value of the data item HOURS is tested to see if it exceeds 40.0; if so, the statements indicated in (a) are executed, and then the program passes its control to the next statement after the IF, namely, GO TO PRINT-ROUTINE. Statements in (a) would not be executed if HOURS is not greater than 40.0.

The program flowchart of these statements is

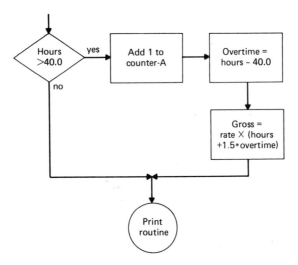

Example 4

The punctuation symbol period (.) plays a very important role in the execution of the conditional statement. For instance, if we alter the IF statement in Example 3 slightly by adding a period at the end of each statement in (a), as shown in the following,

```
    IF HOURS IS GREATER THAN 40.0
   (  ADD 1 TO COUNTER-A.
(a) SUBTRACT 40.0 FROM HOURS GIVING OVERTIME.
   ( COMPUTE GROSS = RATE * (HOURS + 1.5 * OVERTIME).
    GO TO PRINT-ROUTINE.
```

then the program would execute the last two statements in (a) regardless of whether HOURS IS GREATER THAN 40.0 is true or false. A program flowchart for this example is

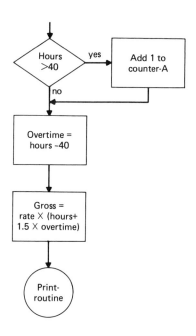

Example 5: NEXT SENTENCE Option

The NEXT SENTENCE option in the IF statement can be used to improve readability and circumvent unnecessary fragmentation of the coding. For example, the coding

```
       IF A IS EQUAL TO B GO TO PRINT-A.
       ELSE
           ADD 1 TO B, MOVE C TO D.
       PRINT-A.
           WRITE REC-A.
```

has the same effect as

```
       IF A IS EQUAL TO B NEXT SENTENCE,
       ELSE
           ADD 1 TO B, MOVE C TO D.
           WRITE REC-A.
```

which is less fragmented.

8.3 RELATION TEST

The relation test is perhaps the most frequently used test in an IF statement. It causes a comparison of two operands (that is, two data items) as indicated in the following format:

$$\left\{\begin{array}{l}\text{identifier-1}\\ \text{literal-1}\\ \text{arithmetic-}\\ \text{expression-1}\end{array}\right\} \text{relation-operator} \left\{\begin{array}{l}\text{identifier-2}\\ \text{literal-2}\\ \text{arithmetic-}\\ \text{expression-2}\end{array}\right\}$$

The relation-operator in the test may be any one of the following:

$$\text{IS [\underline{NOT}]} \left\{\begin{array}{l}\underline{\text{GREATER}}\text{ THAN}\\ \underline{\text{LESS}}\text{ THAN}\\ \underline{\text{EQUAL}}\text{ TO}\end{array}\right\}$$

The relation-operator must be preceded by and followed by at least one blank space. Following are some examples of valid and invalid IF statements involving the relation test.†

Example 1

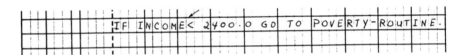

Invalid, a space must precede the relation-operator.

Example 2

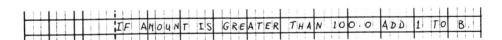

Example 3

Example 4

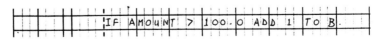

Examples 2, 3, and 4 are equivalent and valid.

† The symbols > and < mean "greater than" and "less than," respectively.

Example 5

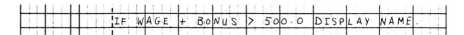

This is a valid statement, since an arithmetic expression can be used as an operand.

Example 6

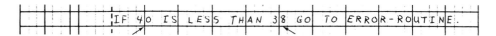

Invalid, two literals may not be used in the relation test.

Example 7

```
         IF COLLEGE-NAME IS NOT = 'MONTCLAIR'
            GO TO OTHER-COLLEGE-ROUTINE.
```

A valid statement.

There are definite rules and restrictions in the use of the relation test. Certain data items, due to their internal data structures, are not allowed in a relation test. However, internal data structures are machine dependent, and so the interested reader should consult the local manual for further details.

Comparison of Numeric Operands

For operands whose class is numeric, a comparison is made with respect to the algebraic value of the operands. The length of the data item or literal, in terms of number of digits represented, is not significant. Unsigned numeric operands are considered positive for purposes of comparison, and zero is considered as a unique value, regardless of sign. Examples of numeric comparison are given in Figs. 8.2 and 8.3.

Operands				
A		B		Relationship
Picture	Content	Picture	Content	of A to B
999V99	15561	999V99	10098	A > B
9V99	875	99V99	0186	A > B
S9V99	+176	9V99	176	A = B
S9	+0	S9V99	−000	A = B
S999	−747	9V99	001	A < B
999	511	999V99	51100	A = B

Fig. 8.2 Examples of numeric comparison.

138   8 Conditional Statements: The IF Statement

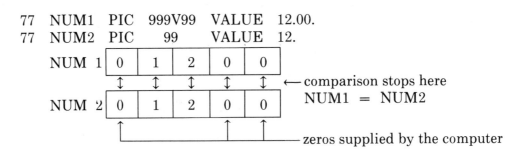

Fig. 8.3 An example of how a numeric comparison is performed.

Nonnumeric Comparison

When one or both operands in a relation test are nonnumeric, a comparison is made with respect to the collating sequence of the characters for that computer system. For IBM 360/370 systems, the collating sequence of characters in ascending order is the EBCDIC (Extended Binary Coded Decimal Interchange Code), set as shown in the following:

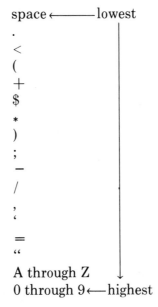

In a nonnumeric comparison, values are compared from left to right, character by character, until either two characters are found not equal, or the ends of items are reached. If operands of unequal size are compared, comparison proceeds as though the shorter operand were extended on the right by sufficient spaces to make two operands of equal size. Some examples follow that illustrate how this comparison process is performed.

Example 1

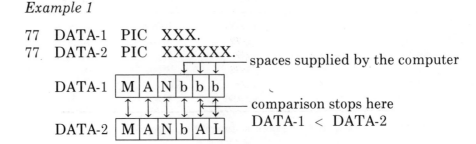

Example 2

```
77  A-FIELD  PIC  XXXXX  VALUE  'ABCbb'.
77  B-FIELD  PIC  XXX    VALUE  'ABC'.
```

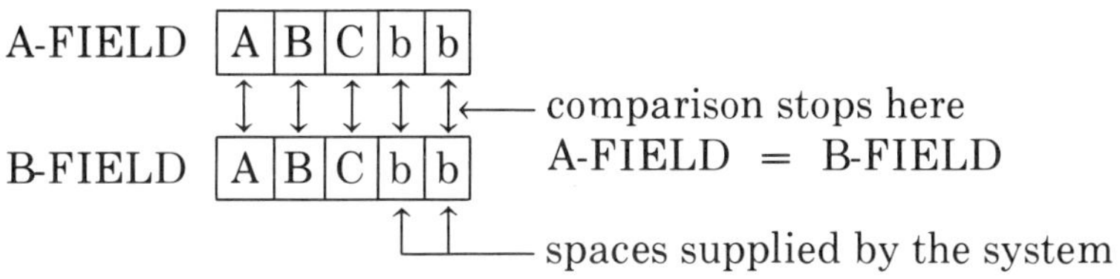

A-FIELD │A│B│C│b│b│
                      ← comparison stops here
B-FIELD │A│B│C│b│b│   A-FIELD = B-FIELD
              └─┴─ spaces supplied by the system

Example 3

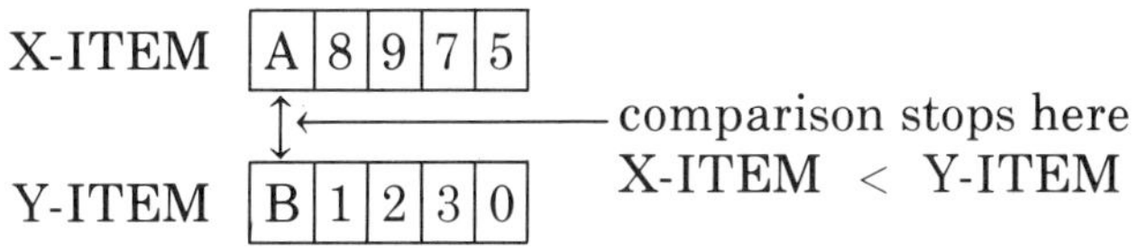

X-ITEM │A│8│9│7│5│
         ←── comparison stops here
Y-ITEM │B│1│2│3│0│   X-ITEM < Y-ITEM

More examples of nonnumeric comparisons are given in Fig. 8.4.

Operands				
A		B		Relationship
Picture	Content	Picture	Content	of A to B
XXX	MAN	XXX	Z12	A < B
XXX	MAN	XXX	12Z	A < B
XXX	MAN	X(5)	12ABC	A < B
XXX	MAN	X(5)	MANbb	A = B
XXX	MAN	X(5)	bMANb	A > B
AAA	ABC	XXX	A12	A < B
999	123	AAA	TWO	A > B
999	123	A(5)	bTWOb	A > B
XXX	bb1	999	001	A < B

Fig. 8.4 Examples of nonnumeric comparison.

8.4 SIGN TEST

A sign test can be used to determine whether or not the value of a numeric operand or arithmetic expression is less than, greater than, or equal to zero. The general format for a sign condition is

$$\left\{ \begin{array}{l} \text{identifier} \\ \text{arithmetic-expression} \end{array} \right\} \text{IS [\underline{NOT}]} \left\{ \begin{array}{l} \underline{\text{POSITIVE}} \\ \underline{\text{NEGATIVE}} \\ \underline{\text{ZERO}} \end{array} \right\}$$

An operand is positive if its value is greater than zero and is negative if it is less than zero. Several examples of a sign test follow.

140 8 Conditional Statements: The IF Statement

Example 1

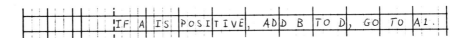

Example 2

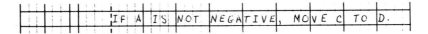

It should be noted here that the condition A IS POSITIVE is not equivalent to the condition A IS NOT NEGATIVE, since the latter condition could also be interpreted as A IS EITHER POSITIVE OR ZERO.

Example 3

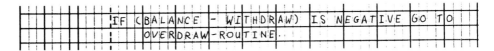

In this example, the program would subtract the value of WITHDRAW from the value of BALANCE (the contents of both items are undisturbed) and see if the result is negative. The statement is identical to

Example 4

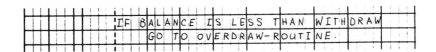

8.5 CLASS TEST

The class test may be used to determine whether or not a data item is alphabetic or numeric. The test is often used to detect input data errors (for example, in keypunching) and to ensure that correct data are being processed. The format of class test is

$$\text{identifier IS } \underline{\text{NOT}} \left\{ \frac{\text{NUMERIC}}{\text{ALPHABETIC}} \right\}$$

In COBOL, a data item is said to be numeric if it contains only numerical digits 0 through 9 with or without an operational sign. It is an alphabetic item if it contains one or more alphabetic letters or blank spaces. Some examples of the class tests are

```
        IF ZIP-CODE IS NOT NUMERIC GO TO DATA-ERROR-ROUTINE.
        IF NAME IS NOT ALPHABETIC GO TO NAME-ERROR-ROUTINE.
```

Type of data	Valid form of the class tests	
Alphabetic Picture (A)	alphabetic	not alphabetic
Alphanumeric Picture (X) or group stems	alphabetic numeric	not alphabetic not numeric
Numeric Picture (9)	numeric	not numeric

Fig. 8.5 Valid form of the class tests.

There are definite rules governing the use of class tests. For example, the alphabetic test cannot be applied to data items whose PICTURE clause describes them as numeric (that is, all 9s). The table in Fig. 8.5 shows the valid form of the various class tests.

It should be stressed that in order for data items whose contents are signed numbers (that is, +5, −700, +0, and so forth) to be properly evaluated as numeric in a class test, the data item PICTURE clause must have the symbol S. For example, in the coding

```
        05 X PICTURE S9 VALUE +5.
        05 Y PICTURE 9 VALUE +5.
```

the statement IF X IS NUMERIC ... would be evaluated as true, whereas the statement IF Y IS NUMERIC ... would be interpreted as false. However, if Y contains an unsigned number, say Y = 10, then IF Y IS NUMERIC ... would be evaluated as true.

8.6 CONDITION-NAME TEST

The condition-name test causes a conditional variable to be evaluated. The test is often used to improve the documentation and readability of the coding and facilitate modification. Its use is perhaps best illustrated by examples.

Suppose a college has a computer program to process students' registration. In this program, each student is identified by a one-position numeric field called class-code. The class-codes are 0 for freshmen, 1 for sophomores, 2 for juniors, 3 for seniors, and 4 for transfers. Suppose, based on the value of class-code, the program will branch to one of five different procedures. This could be accomplished as follows:

```
        IF CLASS-CODE = 0 GO TO ROUTINE-1.
        IF CLASS-CODE = 1 GO TO ROUTINE-2.
        IF CLASS-CODE = 2 GO TO ROUTINE-3.
        IF CLASS-CODE = 3 GO TO ROUTINE-4.
        IF CLASS-CODE = 4 GO TO ROUTINE-5.
        GO TO CLASS-CODE-ERROR-ROUTINE.
```

There is nothing wrong with the above coding. However, looking at the program, it is not obvious what the class-code of 0, 1, 2, 3, or 4 means.

An alternative approach would be to apply the condition-name to the class-code. A condition-name is defined by the level number 88. Such an entry must only be associated with the elementary item in the DATA DIVISION. It has the following format:

$$88 \text{ condition-name} \left\{ \begin{array}{c} \underline{\text{VALUE IS}} \\ \underline{\text{VALUES ARE}} \end{array} \right\} \text{literal-1 [\underline{THRU} literal-2]}$$
$$[\text{literal-3 \underline{THRU} literal 4}, \ldots]$$

In our previous example, if the following entries are coded in the DATA DIVISION,

```
    05  CLASS-CODE PIC 9.
        88  FRESHMAN VALUE 0.
        88  SOPHOMORE VALUE 1.
        88  JUNIOR VALUE 2.
        88  SENIOR VALUE 3.
        88  TRANSFER VALUE 4.
```

then the corresponding PROCEDURE DIVISION entries could be coded

```
        IF FRESHMAN GO TO ROUTINE-1.
        IF SOPHOMORE GO TO ROUTINE-2.
        IF JUNIOR GO TO ROUTINE-3.
        IF SENIOR GO TO ROUTINE-4.
        IF TRANSFER GO TO ROUTINE-5.
        GO TO CLASS-CODE-ERROR-ROUTINE.
```

which, as one can see, is more readable.

It is possible to have a condition-name represent a range of values. This can be accomplished by using the THRU option. For example, the following data description entries show that the condition variable STUDENT-GRADE can have values from 0.00 through 4.00:

```
    04  STUDENT-GRADE PIC 9V99.
        88  PROBATION VALUE 0 THRU 1.99.
        88  AVERAGE VALUE 2.00 THRU 2.99.
        88  DEAN-LIST VALUE 3.00 THRU 3.49.
        88  HONOR-ROLL VALUE 3.50 THRU 4.00.
```

Thus, the statement IF PROBATION GO TO PRINT-NAME-ROUTINE would instruct the computer to check whether or not the value of STUDENT-GRADE is between 0.00 and 1.99. If so, the program would branch to the PRINT-NAME-ROUTINE.

8.7 COMPOUND TEST

Compound tests are used to combine two or more simple tests in a single IF statement. This is accomplished by using the logical operators OR and AND. (These logical operators are also known as logical connectives.)

Logical Operator OR

OR is used to mean either or both. For example, the statements in Fig. 8.6 would direct the computer to execute GO TO BONUS-ROUTINE if either of the conditions SALES-AMT > 2000.0 or NUMBER-OF-SALES > 10 is true. If both of these conditions are false, the next sequential statement, GO TO READ-ROUTINE, would be executed.

A program flowchart for this example is also shown in Fig. 8.6. Note that if OR is not used, then the IF statement would require two separate IF statements:

```
IF SALES-AMT > 2000 GO TO BONUS-ROUTINE.
IF NUMBER-OF-SALES > 10 GO TO BONUS-ROUTINE.
GO TO READ-ROUTINE.
```

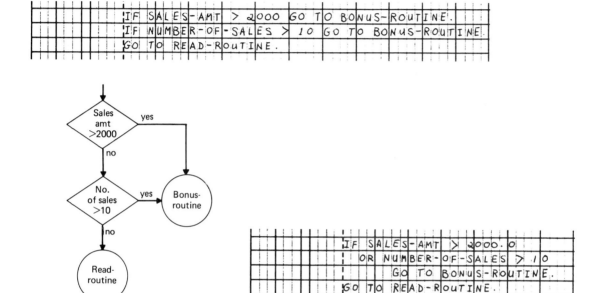

Fig. 8.6 Program flowchart and coding for OR operator.

Logical Operator AND

The word AND, as might be expected, means both. For example, if we had replaced the word OR by AND in the previous example, it would appear as

```
IF SALES-AMT > 200
   AND NUMBER-OF-SALE > 10
   GO TO BONUS-ROUTINE.
GO TO READ-ROUTINE.
```

The statement GO TO BONUS-ROUTINE would be executed only if both conditions were fulfilled. If either one of the conditions is false, the program would execute the next statement after the IF statement, namely, GO TO READ-ROUTINE. The program flowchart is depicted in Fig. 8.7.

The logical operators OR and AND can also be used to combine three or more conditions. However, if more than two simple conditions are combined, parentheses must be used to specify the order in which conditions are evaluated. The computer will always begin its evaluation with the innermost pair of parentheses and proceed to the outermost. To demonstrate this rule, consider the following example.

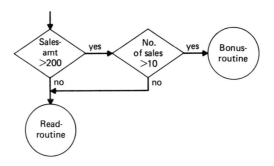

Fig. 8.7 Program flowchart for AND operator.

Example

```
IF (A > 5 AND (B < 10 AND C > 15))
         ADD 1 TO A-COUNT
    ELSE ADD 1 TO B-COUNT
GO TO PRINT-ROUTINE
```

In this example, evaluation begins with conditions specified within the innermost parentheses. Thus, the conditions (B < 10 AND C > 15) would be evaluated first. The evaluation would determine the truth value, say X (X is either true or false). Next, the condition (A > 5 and X) is evaluated, giving the final truth value. If this condition is true, the program would execute the statement ADD 1 TO A-COUNT. Otherwise, ADD 1 TO B-COUNT would be executed. The flowchart indicating the logical flow of this example is as follows:

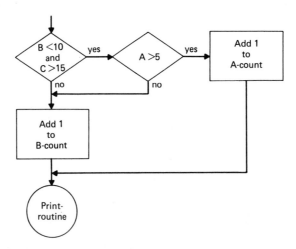

If parentheses are not used, the conditions are evaluated in the following order:

1. Arithmetic expression.
2. Relation-operators.
3. NOT condition.
4. AND and its surrounding conditions, starting from left to right.
5. OR and its surrounding conditions, starting from left to right.

Consider the expression

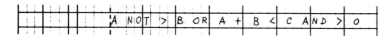

This would be evaluated (A NOT > B) OR ((A+B = C) AND D > 0). Thus the order of evaluation is

1. (A+B) is evaluated, giving some intermediate result, say X.
2. (X = C) is evaluated giving some intermediate truth value, say X_1.
3. (D > 0) is evaluated, giving truth value X_2.
4. (X_1 and X_2) are evaluated, giving truth value Y.
5. (A NOT > B) is evaluated, giving truth value Z.
6. (Z OR Y) is evaluated, giving the final truth value and the result of the expression.

Note to the reader: Although writing compound conditions often shortens a certain amount of coding, in most instances, it is rather complicated and provides a fertile ground for logic errors. For this reason, the reader should perhaps avoid using compound condition statements at first.

8.8 SAMPLE PROGRAM 8A: WEEKLY PAYROLL WITH TAX ROUTINE

This program is a slight modification of Sample Program 7B. It calculates wage, FICA, and net as in Sample Program 7B. However, the tax is computed according to the following formula:

$$\begin{aligned}
\text{tax} &= 0 & \text{if} \quad \text{wage} &\leq \$50, \\
&= 10\% \text{ of (wage over \$50)} & \text{if} \quad \$50 < \text{wage} &\leq \$100, \\
&= \$5 + 20\% \text{ of (wage over \$100)} & \text{if} \quad \text{wage} &> \$100.
\end{aligned}$$

The program logic for tax computation is shown below:

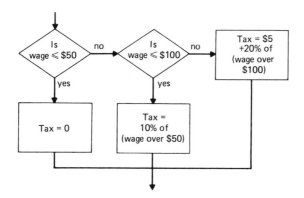

In addition, the numeric test is used to ensure that both the hourly rate and hours worked are keypunched with numeric data. The input and output formats of this program are the same as in Sample Program 7B. The source listings for the two programs differ only in their IDENTIFICATION DIVISION and PROCEDURE DIVISION.

Source Listing

```
00001          IDENTIFICATION DIVISION.
00002          PROGRAM-ID. 'SAMPL8A'
00003          DATE-WRITTEN. OCTOBER 9, 1974
00004          REMARKS. THIS PROGRAM READS A DECK OF PAYROLL CARDS AND COMPUTES WAGE.
00005      ***********************************
00006          ENVIRONMENT DIVISION.
00007          CONFIGURATION SECTION.
00008          SOURCE-COMPUTER. IBM-370.
00009          OBJECT-COMPUTER. IBM-370.
00010          INPUT-OUTPUT SECTION.
00011          FILE-CONTROL.
00012              SELECT INPUT-FILE ASSIGN TO UR-2501-S-CARDIN.
00013              SELECT OUTPUT-FILE ASSIGN TO UR-1403-S-PROUT.
00014      ***********************************
00015          DATA DIVISION.
00016          FILE SECTION.
00017          FD  INPUT-FILE
00018              LABEL RECORDS ARE OMITTED
00019              DATA RECORD IS EMPLOYEE-CARD-REC.
00020          01  EMPLOYEE-CARD-REC.
00021              05  SOC-SEC-NO PIC X(9).
00022              05  EMPLOYEE-NAME PIC A(20).
00023              05  HOURLY-RATE PIC 99V99.
00024              05  FILLER PIC XX.
00025              05  HOURS-WORKED PIC 999V99.
00026              05  DEDUCTION PIC 999V99.
00027              05  FILLER PIC X(35).
00028          FD  OUTPUT-FILE
00029              LABEL RECORDS ARE OMITTED
00030              DATA RECORD IS PRINT-AREA.
00031          01  PRINT-AREA PIC X(133).
00032          WORKING-STORAGE SECTION.
00033          77  WEEKLY-WAGE PIC S9(4)V99 VALUE ZEROS.
00034          77  FICA PIC S9(3)V99 VALUE ZEROS.
00035          77  TAX PIC S9(4)V99 VALUE ZEROS.
00036          77  NET PIC S9(4)V99 VALUE ZEROS.
00037          77  KOUNTER-W PIC S9(5)V99 VALUE ZEROS.
00038          77  KOUNTER-F PIC S9(5)V99 VALUE ZEROS.
00039          77  KOUNTER-T PIC S9(5)V99 VALUE ZEROS.
00040          77  KOUNTER-D PIC S9(5)V99 VALUE ZEROS.
00041          77  KOUNTER-N PIC S9(5)V99 VALUE ZEROS.
00042          01  HEADING-1.
00043              05  FILLER PIC X(30) VALUE SPACES.
00044              05  FILLER PIC X(21) VALUE 'WEEKLY PAYROLL REPORT'.
00045          01  HEADING-A.
00046              05  FILLER PIC X(45) VALUE SPACES.
00047              05  TOTAL-A PIC X(20).
00048              05  TOTAL-B PIC $ZZZZ.99.
00049          01  SUB-HEADING.
00050              05  FILLER PIC X(4) VALUE SPACES.
00051              05  FILLER PIC X(23) VALUE 'SOC-SEC-NO'.
00052              05  FILLER PIC X(15) VALUE 'NAME'.
00053              05  FILLER PIC X(12) VALUE 'HOURLY-RATE'.
00054              05  FILLER PIC X(16) VALUE 'HOURS-WORKED'.
00055              05  FILLER PIC X(13) VALUE 'WAGE'.
00056              05  FILLER PIC X(12) VALUE 'FICA'.
00057              05  FILLER PIC X(13) VALUE 'TAX'.
00058              05  FILLER PIC X(14) VALUE 'DEDUCTION'.
00059              05  FILLER PIC X(3) VALUE 'NET'.
00060          01  PRINT-LINE.
00061              05  FILLER PIC X(5) VALUE SPACES.
00062              05  SOC-SEC-NO-P PIC 9(9).
00063              05  FILLER PIC X(5) VALUE SPACES.
00064              05  EMPLOYEE-NAME-P PIC X(20).
00065              05  FILLER PIC X(5) VALUE SPACES.
00066              05  HOURLY-RATE-P PIC $ZZ.99.
00067              05  FILLER PIC X(8) VALUE SPACES.
00068              05  HOURS-WORKED-P PIC ZZZ.99.
00069              05  FILLER PIC X(4) VALUE SPACES.
00070              05  WEEKLY-WAGE-P PIC $ZZZZ.99.
00071              05  FILLER PIC X(4) VALUE SPACES.
00072              05  FICA-P PIC $ZZZ.99.
00073              05  FILLER PIC X(6) VALUE SPACES.
00074              05  TAX-P PIC $ZZZZ.99.
00075              05  FILLER PIC X(5) VALUE SPACES.
00076              05  DEDUCTION-P  PIC    $ZZZ.99CR.
00077              05  FILLER PIC X(5) VALUE SPACES.
00078              05  NET-P PIC $ZZZZ.99.
00079      ***********************************
00080          PROCEDURE DIVISION.
00081          TASK-1.
00082              OPEN INPUT INPUT-FILE, OUTPUT OUTPUT-FILE.
00083              MOVE HEADING-1 TO PRINT-AREA.
00084              WRITE PRINT-AREA BEFORE ADVANCING 1 LINES.
00085              WRITE PRINT-AREA FROM SUB-HEADING AFTER ADVANCING 4 LINES.
00086          TASK-2.
00087              READ INPUT-FILE AT END GO TO TASK-4.
00088      ***********************************
00089      *   NOTE  VALIDATE INPUT DATA.
00090      ***********************************
```

8.8 Sample Program 8A: Weekly Payroll with Tax Routine

```
00091               IF HOURLY-RATE NOT NUMERIC      ⎫
00092                   GO TO DATA-ERROR-R.         ⎬ validate input data
00093               IF HOURS-WORKED NOT NUMERIC     ⎪
00094                   GO TO DATA-ERROR-R.         ⎭
00095          ***********************************************************
00096               MOVE SOC-SEC-NO TO SOC-SEC-NO-P.
00097               MOVE EMPLOYEE-NAME TO EMPLOYEE-NAME-P.
00098               MOVE HOURLY-RATE TO HOURLY-RATE-P.
00099               MOVE HOURS-WORKED TO HOURS-WORKED-P.
00100           TASK-3.
00101               COMPUTE WEEKLY-WAGE ROUNDED = HOURLY-RATE * HOURS-WORKED.
00102          ***********************************************************
00103          *    NOTE   COMPUTE TAX HERE.
00104          ***********************************************************
00105               IF WEEKLY-WAGE LESS THAN 50           ⎫
00106                   MOVE ZEROS TO TAX                 ⎪
00107               ELSE IF WEEKLY-WAGE LESS THAN 100     ⎬ compute tax
00108                   COMPUTE TAX ROUNDED = 0.10 * (WEEKLY-WAGE - 50.0)  ⎪
00109                   ELSE COMPUTE TAX ROUNDED =        ⎪
00110                     5.0 + 0.20 * (WEEKLY-WAGE - 100).  ⎭
00111          ***********************************************************
00112               MULTIPLY .0585 BY WEEKLY-WAGE GIVING FICA ROUNDED.
00113               SUBTRACT FICA TAX DEDUCTION FROM WEEKLY-WAGE GIVING NET.
00114               MOVE WEEKLY-WAGE TO WEEKLY-WAGE-P.
00115               MOVE FICA TO FICA-P.
00116               MOVE TAX TO TAX-P.
00117               MOVE DEDUCTION TO DEDUCTION-P.
00118               MOVE NET TO NET-P.
00119               MOVE PRINT-LINE TO PRINT-AREA.
00120               WRITE PRINT-AREA AFTER ADVANCING 2 LINES.     ← print detail line
00121               ADD WEEKLY-WAGE TO KOUNTER-W.         ⎫
00122               ADD FICA TO KOUNTER-F.                ⎪
00123               ADD TAX TO KOUNTER-T.                 ⎬ update all totals
00124               ADD DEDUCTION TO KOUNTER-D.           ⎪
00125               ADD NET TO KOUNTER-N.                 ⎭
00126               GO TO TASK-2.
00127           TASK-4.
00128               MOVE 'TOTAL WEEKLY-WAGE' TO TOTAL-A.
00129               MOVE KOUNTER-W TO TOTAL-B.
00130               WRITE PRINT-AREA FROM HEADING-A AFTER ADVANCING 4 LINES.  ⎫
00131               MOVE 'TOTAL FICA' TO TOTAL-A.         ⎪
00132               MOVE KOUNTER-F TO TOTAL-B.            ⎪
00133               WRITE PRINT-AREA FROM HEADING-A AFTER ADVANCING 4 LINES.  ⎪
00134               MOVE 'TOTAL TAX' TO TOTAL-A.          ⎪
00135               MOVE KOUNTER-T TO TOTAL-B.            ⎬ print final totals
00136               WRITE PRINT-AREA FROM HEADING-A AFTER ADVANCING 4 LINES.  ⎪
00137               MOVE 'TOTAL DEDUCTION' TO TOTAL-A.    ⎪
00138               MOVE KOUNTER-D TO TOTAL-B.            ⎪
00139               WRITE PRINT-AREA FROM HEADING-A AFTER ADVANCING 4 LINES.  ⎪
00140               MOVE 'TOTAL NET' TO TOTAL-A.          ⎪
00141               MOVE KOUNTER-N TO TOTAL-B.            ⎪
00142               WRITE PRINT-AREA FROM HEADING-A AFTER ADVANCING 4 LINES.  ⎭
00143           END-JOB.
00144               CLOSE INPUT-FILE, OUTPUT-FILE. STOP RUN.
00145          ***********************************************************
00146          *    INPUT DATA-ERROR ROUTINE.
00147          ***********************************************************
00148           DATA-ERROR-R.
00149               DISPLAY 'DATA ERROR ' EMPLOYEE-CARD-REC UPON SYSOUT
00150               GO TO TASK-2.
00151          ***********************************************************
```

Sample Output

SOC-SEC-NO	NAME	HOURLY-RATE	HOURS-WORKED	WAGE	FICA	TAX	DEDUCTION	NET
123456789	FRAN WAGNER	$ 5.20	40.00	$ 208.00	$ 12.17	$ 26.60	$ .50	$ 168.73
234567894	KEN SMITH	$ 4.30	35.00	$ 150.50	$ 8.80	$ 15.10	$ .42CR	$ 127.02
146853147	MARGARET CHAI	$10.40	45.00	$ 468.00	$ 27.38	$ 78.60	$ 1.00CR	$ 363.02
157483446	ANNA MARCINKO	$ 8.22	80.00	$ 657.60	$ 38.47	$ 116.52	$ .22	$ 502.39
346546131	PETER JONESN	$ 2.50	12.00	$ 30.00	$ 1.76	$ .00	$ .10	$ 28.14
343656451	ALVIN WARGA	$ 3.10	22.00	$ 68.20	$ 3.99	$ 1.82	$ 1.25CR	$ 63.64
345678413	JIM SCOTT	$11.20	36.00	$ 403.20	$ 23.59	$ 65.64	$ .75	$ 313.22

```
              TOTAL WEEKLY-WAGE    $1985.50

              TOTAL FICA           $ 116.16

              TOTAL TAX            $ 304.28

              TOTAL DEDUCTION      $   1.10

              TOTAL NET            $1566.16
```

8.9 SAMPLE PROGRAM 8B: SALESMAN COMMISSION COMPUTATION

Most salesmen work on a commission basis; that is, their earnings are determined by the number of items they sell. Suppose that there are two types of items to be sold: major items and minor items. If a salesman sells more than 3000 units of the major items, he will receive an additional 1% commission. If he sells less than 3000 such units, ½ of 1% will be deducted from his base rate. Also, if a salesman sells between 500 and 2000 units of minor items, he will receive an additional $50 bonus.

The base commission rate for each salesman is dependent on the number of years he is with the company. This is determined according to the following table:

Years in service	Base commission rate (%)
1	3
2	5
3	6
4–6	8
7–9	9
10 or more	10

This program reads the salesmen's records and computes each salesman's earnings by multiplying the sum of major and minor items sold by the commission rate as described above.

Input Description: Salesman-Record (INREC)

Column	Content
1–20	salesman's name
21–22	years in service XX
23–27	major items sold XXXXX
28–32	minor items sold XXXXX

Sample Input

```
1                    21
↓                    ↓
henry brown          050400000600
james melvill        030200000300
della street         100600000700
debra who            010450000800
robin egg            070800002100
harold byeme         080210004500
jay classless        040960003100
may spitz            020880004500
```

8.9 Sample Program 8B: Salesman Commission Computation

Program Logic

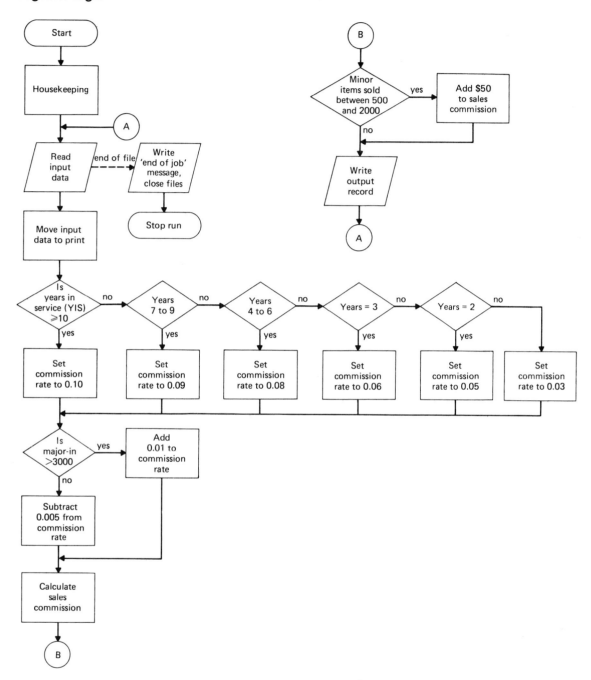

Source Listing

```
00001           IDENTIFICATION DIVISION.
00002           PROGRAM-ID. SAMPL8B.
00003      ***********************************************
00004           ENVIRONMENT DIVISION.
00005           CONFIGURATION SECTION.
00006           SOURCE-COMPUTER. IBM-370.
00007           OBJECT-COMPUTER. IBM-370.
00008           INPUT-OUTPUT SECTION.
00009           FILE-CONTROL.
00010               SELECT INFILE ASSIGN TO UR-2540R-S-IN.
00011               SELECT OUTFILE ASSIGN TO UR-1403-S-OUT.
00012      ***********************************************
```

8 Conditional Statements: The IF Statement

```
CC013            DATA DIVISION.
0C014            FILE SECTION.
0C015            FD  INFILE
CC016                LABEL RECORDS OMITTED.
0C017            01  INREC.
00018                02  NAME-IN PIC X(20).
CC019                02  YEARS PIC 99.
0C020                    88  TEN-UP VALUE 10 THRU 99.
0C021                    88  SEVEN-TO-NINE VALUE 7 THRU 9.
CC022                    88  FOUR-TO-SIX VALUE 4 THRU 6.     } condition-names
CC023                    88  THREE VALUE 3.
0C024                    88  TWO VALUE 2.
00025                    88  ONE VALUE 1.
00026                02  MAJOR-IN PIC 9(5).
CC027                02  MINOR-IN PIC 9(5).
0C028                    88  MINOR-IN-VALUE VALUE 500 THRU 2000.
0C029                02  FILLER PIC X(48).
0C030            FD  OUTFILE
CC031                LABEL RECORDS OMITTED.
0C032            01  OUTREC PIC X(132).
0C033            WORKING-STORAGE SECTION.
0C034            77  PERC PIC 99V999.
0C035            77  COMM PIC 9(6)V99.
0C036            01  OUTRECORD.
0C037                02  FILLER PIC X(5) VALUE SPACES.
00038                02  NAME-OUT PIC X(20) VALUE SPACES.
00039                02  FILLER PIC X(5) VALUE SPACES.
0C040                02  YEARS-EMPLOYED PIC 99 VALUE ZEROS.
00041                02  FILLER PIC X(10) VALUE SPACES.
00042                02  NET-COMMISSION PIC $ZZ,ZZ9.99.
0C043                02  FILLER PIC X(10) VALUE SPACES.
0C044                02  COMMISSION-RATE PIC Z9.9.
CC045                02  PERSIGN PIC X VALUE ' '.
00046                02  FILLER PIC X(10) VALUE SPACES.
0C047                02  MAJOR-ITEMS-SOLD PIC $ZZZZ9 VALUE ZEROS.
00048                02  FILLER PIC X(15) VALUE SPACES.
0C049                02  MINOR-ITEMS-SOLD PIC $ZZZZ9 VALUE ZEROS.
0C050            01  HEADER.
00051                02  FILLER PIC X(5) VALUE SPACES.
00052                02  FILLER PIC X(25) VALUE 'NAME'.
00053                02  FILLER PIC X(12) VALUE 'YRS.EMPL.'.
00054                02  FILLER PIC X(19) VALUE 'NET COMMISSION'.
00055                02  FILLER PIC X(15) VALUE 'COMM.RATE'.
00056                02  FILLER PIC X(20) VALUE 'MAJOR ITEMS SOLD'.
0C057                02  FILLER PIC X(36) VALUE 'MINOR ITEMS SOLD'.
0C058           ***************************************************
CC059            PROCEDURE DIVISION.
00060            OPEN-UP.
00061                OPEN INPUT INFILE, OUTPUT OUTFILE.
00062                MOVE SPACES TO OUTREC.
00063                MOVE ' COMMISSION DETERMINATION' TO OUTREC.
00064                WRITE OUTREC AFTER ADVANCING 5 LINES.
00065                WRITE OUTREC FROM HEADER AFTER ADVANCING 5 LINES.
00066            READ-IT.
00067                READ INFILE AT END GO TO END-IT.
CC068                MOVE NAME-IN TO NAME-OUT.
00069                MOVE YEARS TO YEARS-EMPLOYED.
00070                MOVE MAJOR-IN TO MAJOR-ITEMS-SOLD.
0C071                MOVE MINOR-IN TO MINOR-ITEMS-SOLD.
0C072            FIGURE-IT.
00073                IF TEN-UP  MOVE .10 TO PERC
0C074                    ELSE IF SEVEN-TO-NINE MOVE .09 TO PERC
00075                        ELSE IF FOUR-TO-SIX MOVE .08 TO PERC     } use condition-name tests
0C076                            ELSE IF THREE MOVE .06 TO PERC
0C077                                ELSE IF TWO MOVE .05 TO PERC
0C078                                    ELSE IF ONE MOVE .03 TO PERC.
0C079                IF MAJOR-IN IS GREATER THAN 3000
0C080                    ADD .01 TO PERC
0C081                    ELSE SUBTRACT .005 FROM PERC.
00082                COMPUTE COMM ROUNDED = PERC * (MAJOR-IN + MINOR-IN).
0C083                IF MINOR-IN-VALUE  ADD 50 TO COMM.
0C084                MULTIPLY PERC BY 100 GIVING COMMISSION-RATE.
00085                MOVE COMM TO NET-COMMISSION.
00086                WRITE OUTREC FROM OUTRECORD AFTER ADVANCING 1 LINES.
0C087                GO TO READ-IT.
00088            END-IT.
00089                MOVE ' END OF JOB' TO OUTREC.
CC090                WRITE OUTREC AFTER ADVANCING 10 LINES.
00091                CLOSE INFILE, OUTFILE.
00092                STOP RUN.
```

Sample Output

COMMISSION DETERMINATION

NAME	YRS.EMPL.	NET COMMISSION	COMM.RATE	MAJOR ITEMS SOLD	MINOR ITEMS SOLD
HENRY BROWN	05	$ 464.00	9.0	$ 4000	$ 600
JAMES MELVILL	03	$ 126.50	5.5	$ 2000	$ 300
DELLA STREET	10	$ 787.00	11.0	$ 6000	$ 700
DEBRA WHO	01	$ 262.00	4.0	$ 4500	$ 800
ROBIN EGG	07	$ 1,010.00	10.0	$ 8000	$ 2100
HAROLD BYEME	08	$ 561.00	8.5	$ 2100	$ 4500
JAY CLASSLESS	04	$ 1,143.00	9.0	$ 9600	$ 3100
MAY SPITZ	02	$ 798.00	6.0	$ 8800	$ 4500

8.10 DUPLICATE DATA NAMES

COBOL permits the programmer to define two or more items with identical names. However, each time such a name is referenced, the programmer must qualify the name so that there is no confusion about which data area is being referred to. For example, suppose REC-1 and REC-2 both contain A-FIELD:

```
01  REC-1.
    05  A-FIELD PIC X(5).
01  REC-2.
    05  A-FIELD PIC X(5).
```

Then any reference to the A-FIELD must have the name of the record (or group), such as

```
MOVE A-FIELD OF REC-1 TO SAVE-1.
MOVE A-FIELD OF REC-2 TO SAVE-2.
```

The general format for qualification is

$$\text{identifier-1} \left\{ \begin{array}{c} \text{OF} \\ \text{ON} \end{array} \right\} \text{identifier-2}$$

where identifier-2 must be a group name to which identifier-1 belongs.

CORRESPONDING Option

There are some definite advantages to using duplicate data names (there are many disadvantages too!). However, such advantages can only be realized by using the CORRESPONDING option; for example, if CUSTOMER-REC and PRINT-REC are group items with the following entries:

```
01  CUSTOMER-REC.
    04  CUSTOMER-ID     PIC X(5).
    04  NAME            PIC X(25).
    04  STREET          PIC X(25).
    04  CITY-STATE-ZIP  PIC X(25).

01  PRINT-REC.
    04  FILLER          PIC X(5).
    04  NAME            PIC X(25).
    04  FILLER          PIC X(5).
    04  STREET          PIC X(25).
    04  FILLER          PIC X(5).
    04  CITY-STATE-ZIP  PIC X(25).
```

To move NAME, STREET, CITY-STATE-ZIP from CUSTOMER-REC to PRINT-REC, it suffices to specify

```
MOVE CORRESPONDING CUSTOMER-REC TO PRINT-REC.
```

This one statement has the same effect as

```
            MOVE NAME OF CUSTOMER-REC TO NAME OF PRINT-REC.
            MOVE STREET OF CUSTOMER-REC TO STREET OF PRINT-REC.
            MOVE CITY-STATE-ZIP OF CUSTOMER TO CITY-STATE-ZIP
                OF PRINT-REC.
```

Thus, by utilizing the CORRESPONDING option with duplicate names, one can combine many statements into a single one.

The CORRESPONDING option is also available on both ADD and SUBTRACT statements. The general format of these statements is

$$\text{MOVE} \left\{ \begin{array}{l} \underline{\text{CORRESPONDING}} \\ \underline{\text{CORR}} \end{array} \right\} \text{identifier-1 TO identifier-2}$$

$$\text{ADD} \left\{ \begin{array}{l} \underline{\text{CORRESPONDING}} \\ \underline{\text{CORR}} \end{array} \right\} \text{identifier-1 TO identifier-2}$$
$$[\underline{\text{ROUNDED}}]$$
$$[\text{ON } \underline{\text{SIZE ERROR}} \ldots]$$

$$\text{SUBTRACT} \left\{ \begin{array}{l} \underline{\text{CORRESPONDING}} \\ \underline{\text{CORR}} \end{array} \right\} \text{identifier-1 FROM identifier-2}$$
$$[\underline{\text{ROUNDED}}]$$
$$[\text{ON } \underline{\text{SIZE ERROR}} \ldots]$$

where identifier-1 and identifier-2 must be group names.

Example

```
00072       MOVE CURRENT-DATE TO DATE-P.
```

where

```
        01 UPDATE-REC.
            05 ID PIC X(8).
            05 FILLER PIC X(2).
            05 SALES-AMT PIC S9(5)V99.
            05 FILLER PIC X(3).
            05 RET-AMT PIC S9(5)V99.
            05 FILLER PIC X(3).
            05 BACK-ORDER PIC S9(5)V99.
            05 FILLER PIC X(3).
        01 TOTAL-A.
            04 SALES-AMT PIC S9(5)V99.
            04 RET-AMT PIC S9(5)V99.
            04 BACK-ORDER PIC S9(5)V99.
            04 BALANCE PIC S9(5)V99.
```

Upon the execution of the ADD statement, the values of SALES-AMT, RET-AMT, and BACK-ORDER of UPDATE-REC will be added to the values of SALES-AMT, RET-AMT, and BACK-ORDER in TOTAL-A. There will be no change in the contents of BALANCE since it is not part of the UPDATE-REC.

8.11 SAMPLE PROGRAM 8C: PURCHASE ANALYSIS REPORT

This program produces a purchase analysis report for a business concern. It reads individual vendor records and computes the amount purchased by multiplying the quantity purchased with the unit price.

To detect any invalid data in the input punched card, the program applies the numeric test on the data fields that contain unit price and quantity purchased. Any data card that fails this test will be rejected with an error message printed through the DISPLAY command.

The program also uses the MOVE CORRESPONDING statement to circumvent some of the coding.

Input Description: Vendor Record

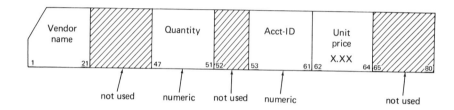

Sample Input

```
1                          47    53       62
↓                          ↓     ↓        ↓
MARCINKO-CHAI ASSOC       10500  025001010025
BUSINESS SUPPLIES         00725  123456789425
NEW YORK DATA INC         00500  245678101725
HENRY KEYIN SERVICES      80500  111145675008
```

Sample Output

```
           PURCHASE ANALYSIS REPORT BY VENDOR AS OF 07/08/75 PAGE  1
           ************************************************
    ACCT ID        VENDORS NAME         QUANTITY   UNIT PRICE      AMOUNT
    025 00 1010    MARCINKO-CHAI ASSOC    10500      $0.25       $*2,625.00
    123 45 6789    BUSINESS SUPPLIES        725      $4.25       $*3,081.25
    245 67 8101    NEW YORK DATA INC        500      $7.25       $*3,625.00
    111 14 5675    HENRY KEYIN SERVICES   80500      $0.08       $*6,440.00
```

154   8   Conditional Statements: The IF Statement

Program Logic

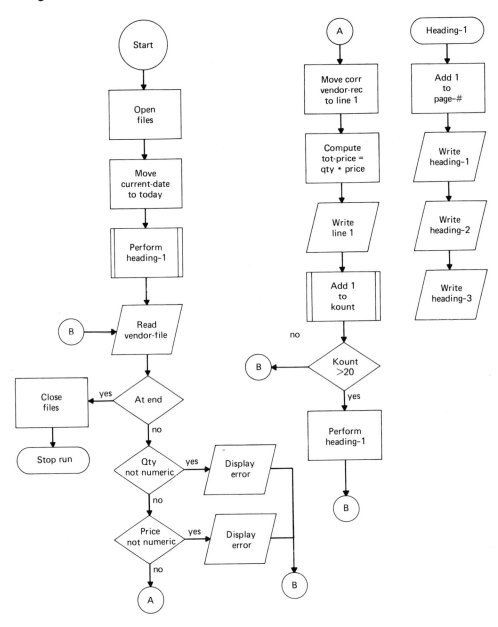

Source Listing

```
00001              IDENTIFICATION DIVISION.
00002              PROGRAM-ID. 'SAMPL8C'
00003              INSTALLATION.        MONTCLAIR STATE COLLEGE.
00004              REMARKS.             THIS PROGRAM TAKES CARD INPUT AND COMPUTES
00005                                   UNIT PRICE TIMES QUANTITY AND PRINTS OUT
00006                                   A PURCHASE ANALYSIS REPORT BY VENDOR.
00007             ***********************************************************
00008              ENVIRONMENT DIVISION.
00009              CONFIGURATION SECTION.
00010              SOURCE-COMPUTER.     IBM-370.
00011              OBJECT-COMPUTER.     IBM-370.
00012              SPECIAL-NAMES.
00013                  C01 IS NEW-PAGE.
00014              INPUT-OUTPUT SECTION.
00015              FILE-CONTROL.
00016                  SELECT VENDOR-FILE ASSIGN TO UR-2501-S-CARDIN.
00017                  SELECT PRINT-FILE ASSIGN TO UR-1403-S-PROUT.
00018             ***********************************************************
```

```
00019           DATA DIVISION.
00020           FILE SECTION.
00021           FD  VENDOR-FILE LABEL RECORDS ARE OMITTED.
00022           01  VENDOR-REC.
00023               04  VENDOR-NAME    PIC X(21).
00024               04  FILLER         PIC X(25).
00025               04  QUANTITY       PIC 9(5).
00026               04  FILLER         PIC X.
00027               04  ACCT-ID        PIC 9(9).
00028               04  UNIT-PRICE     PIC 9V99.
00029               04  FILLER         PIC X(16).
00030           FD  PRINT-FILE LABEL RECORDS ARE OMITTED.
00031           01  PRINT-AREA         PIC X(120).
00032           WORKING-STORAGE SECTION.
00033           77  PAGE-KOUNT         PIC 99 VALUE ZEROES.
00034           77  LINE-KOUNT         PIC 99 VALUE ZEROES.
00035           77  TOT-PRICE          PIC 9(5)V99 VALUE ZEROES USAGE COMP.
00036           01  JOB-HEADING1.
00037               04  FILLER         PIC X(48) VALUE IS '           PURCHASE ANALYSI
00038          -    'S REPORT BY VENDOR AS OF '.
00039               04  TODAY-DATE     PIC X(8).
00040               04  FILLER         PIC X(6) VALUE IS ' PAGE
00041               04  PAGE-NO        PIC Z9.
00042           01  JOB-HEADING2.
00043               04  FILLER         PIC X(7) VALUE SPACES.
00044               04  FILLER         PIC X(57) VALUE ALL '*'.
00045           01  JOB-HEADING3.
00046               04  FILLER         PIC X(69) VALUE IS '     ACCT ID       VEND
00047          -    'ORS NAME           QUANTITY  UNIT PRICE      AMOUNT'.
00048           01  LINE1.
00049               04  ACCT-ID        PIC B999B99B9999BBB.
00050               04  VENDOR-NAME    PIC X(21).
00051               04  QUANTITY       PIC B(5)Z(5)B(5).
00052               04  UNIT-PRICE     PIC $9.99.
00053               04  AMOUNT         PIC B(5)$**,***.99.
00054          ***************************************************************
00055           PROCEDURE DIVISION.
00056           BEGIN.
00057               OPEN INPUT VENDOR-FILE, OUTPUT PRINT-FILE.
00058               MOVE CURRENT-DATE TO TODAY-DATE.
00059               PERFORM HEADING-1.
00060           READ-PRINT.
00061               READ VENDOR-FILE AT END GO TO THE-END.
00062               IF QUANTITY OF VENDOR-REC NOT NUMERIC DISPLAY VENDOR-REC
00063                   UPON CONSOLE GO TO READ-PRINT.
00064               IF UNIT-PRICE OF VENDOR-REC NOT NUMERIC DISPLAY VENDOR-REC
00065                   UPON CONSOLE GO TO READ-PRINT.
00066               MOVE CORRESPONDING VENDOR-REC TO LINE1.
00067               MULTIPLY QUANTITY OF VENDOR-REC BY UNIT-PRICE OF VENDOR-REC
00068                   GIVING TOT-PRICE.
00069               MOVE TOT-PRICE TO AMOUNT.
00070               WRITE PRINT-AREA FROM LINE1 AFTER ADVANCING 2 LINES.
00071               ADD 1 TO LINE-KOUNT.
00072               IF LINE-KOUNT > 20 PERFORM HEADING-1.
00073               GO TO READ-PRINT.
00074           HEADING-1.
00075               ADD 1 TO PAGE-KOUNT.
00076               MOVE PAGE-KOUNT TO PAGE-NO.
00077               WRITE PRINT-AREA FROM JOB-HEADING1 AFTER ADVANCING NEW-PAGE.
00078               WRITE PRINT-AREA FROM JOB-HEADING2 AFTER ADVANCING 1 LINES.
00079               WRITE PRINT-AREA FROM JOB-HEADING3 AFTER ADVANCING 3 LINES.
00080               MOVE ZEROES TO LINE-KOUNT.
00081           THE-END.
00082               CLOSE VENDOR-FILE, PRINT-FILE.
00083               STOP RUN.
```

duplicate names are used here

qualified names are used

MOVE CORRESPONDING statement is used

EXERCISES

1 In the following problems correct the errors, if any.

(a) IF AMOUNT EQUAL TO '100' ADD AMOUNT TO TOT-A.

(b) IF A GREATER THAN B GO TO ROUTINE-A
    ADD A TO B
    ELSE ADD C TO D.

(c) 04 CLASS-CODE
    88 SENIOR VALUE 'S'.

156 8 Conditional Statements: The IF Statement

```
(d) 02 STATE-CODE PIC AA.
       88 NEW-JERSEY VALUE 'NJ'.

    IF NEW-JERSEY EQUAL TO 'NJ'
        GO TO JERSEY-R.

(e) IF A > B AND C > D GO TO P1.

(f) IF X > 100 OR X EQUAL TO '200' GO TO R1.
```

2 In the following table, state whether DATA-1 is equal to, greater than, or less than DATA-2:

DATA-1	DATA-2	Answer
11.0	11	
+22	22	
12X	123	
0123	123	
55.5	55.50	
ABC	5ABC	
XYZ	XYZ b (b, blank)	

3 Code the following routines according to the flowcharts.

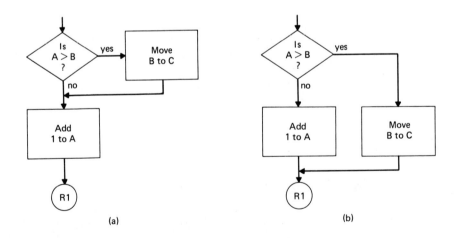

(a)   (b)

Exercises

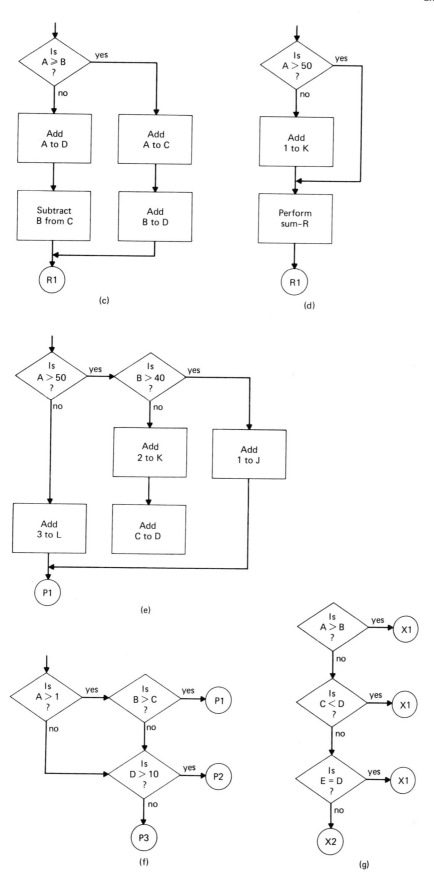

4 Write an IF statement that will cause the control to branch to a procedure called PARA-1 if DATA-1 is between 1000 and 2000.

5 Modify Sample Program 6B (page 98) so that the minimum payment is computed according to the following formula:

$$\text{minimum payment} = \begin{cases} \text{balance} & \text{if } \text{balance} \leq \$20, \\ \$20 + 10\% \text{ of (balance} - 20) & \\ & \text{if } \$20 < \text{balance} \leq \$100, \\ \$36 + 20\% \text{ of (balance} - \$100) & \\ & \text{if } \text{balance} > \$100. \end{cases}$$

6 Write a program to generate a student payment summary report according to the following specifications:

Input Description: Student cards

Column	Content
1–9	social security number
10–30	student name
31–32	semester hours
33–80	not used

Processing

For each student, compute the following:

$$\text{tuition} = \begin{cases} \text{semester hours} \times \$45 & \text{if semester hours} < 12, \\ \$540 & \text{otherwise,} \end{cases}$$

$$\text{fees} = \begin{cases} \$2.50 \times \text{semester hours} & \text{if semester hours} < 12, \\ \$30 & \text{otherwise,} \end{cases}$$

payment = tuition + fees.

Output Description

Print one line for each student with appropriate headers. Each line should contain the student's tuition, fees, and payment together with the input data. At the end of the report print the totals for the number of students, tuition, fees, and payments.

7 The following formulas are used by an appliance company to compute the sales' earnings:

Commission code	Salesman classification	
1	CLASS-A	$100 + 1% of (total sales − base)
2	CLASS-B	$50 + 2% of (total sales − base)
3	CLASS-C	10% of (total sales − base)
4	CLASS-D	20% of (total sales − base)

Write a COBOL program that will read each salesman's records, compute each salesman's earnings, and print one line for each salesman with the input information and the salesman's earnings. The data card has the following format:

Column	Content
1–5	salesman ID
6	commission code
7–10	not used
11–30	name
31–35	base amount XXXXX
36–43	total sales XXXXXX.XX
44–80	not used

Your program must perform numeric testing to ensure that both the base amount and the total sales are punched with numeric data. If any card fails this test, the message 'INVALID NUMERIC DATA FIELD' should be printed. Your program must also use the condition name to determine the salesman's classification.

8 A major discount store maintains its stock records on punched cards with the following format:

Column	Content
1–4	stock number (numeric)
5–10	not used
11–30	stock description
31–35	quantity on hand XXXXX
36–38	reorder point XXX
39–80	not used

When the quantity on hand is less than the reorder point, the stock clerk must place a new order. The order quantity is computed according to the following table:

Stock number	Type	Order quantity
00001–10000	A	2 × reorder point
10001–30000	B	3.5 × reorder point
30001–60000	C	6.5 × reorder point
Over 60000	D	10 × reorder point

Write a program to perform the following:

(a) Read the stock record.
(b) Use the numeric test to ensure that both quantity on hand and reorder point are punched with numeric data. If not, display error message and skip to read next record.

(c) Use the conditional-name test to determine stock type from the stock number.
(d) Compute the order quantity. (Set the order quantity to zero if no order is placed.)
(e) Print a line for each stock item processed with appropriate headers. Each line must contain all information from the data card and the computed order quantity.

9

Table Handling

9.1 TABLE CONSTRUCTION

In business data processing, it is often desirable to organize certain data in the form of a table. Such a table can be composed of any number of similar items, such as tax rates, pay classes, insurance premium rates, and sales commission rates.

In COBOL, one-, two-, or three-dimensional (that is, levels) tables can be constructed. Examples of one- and two-dimensional tables are shown in Figs. 9.1 and 9.2, respectively.

Pay-class	Pay-rate ($)
1	2.50
2	3.25
3	4.25
4	5.75
5	7.00

Fig. 9.1 A one-dimensional table.

Dept. no.	Products-sales (in $1000)			
	I	II	III	IV
1	10	5	2	16
2	8	16	5	6
3	16	5	7	2
4	5	6	8	4
5	11	10	16	18

Fig. 9.2 A two-dimensional table.

To construct a table, one must use the OCCURS clause and/or the REDEFINES clause in the data description entries. The format and use of these two clauses will now be discussed.

OCCURS Clause

The OCCURS clause specifies the number of times a field definition will be repeated in a table. The clause may be used to describe any data item provided it is not an 01, 66, 77, or 88 level. The format of the OCCURS clause is

OCCURS integer TIMES.

To set up the fields for the table in Fig. 9.1, the data description entries may contain the OCCURS clause as shown in the following:

```
01  PAY-RATE-TABLE.
    04 PAY-RATE PIC S9V99 OCCURS 5 TIMES.
```

By using the OCCURS clause as shown above, five fields are set up in storage, each with a PICTURE of S9V99. Each table entry is identified by an appropriate subscript, which indicates the order of appearance of the entry within the table. In fact, one may think of the storage layout of PAY-RATE-TABLE as

```
PAY-RATE (1)
PAY-RATE (2)
PAY-RATE (3)
PAY-RATE (4)
PAY-RATE (5)
```

Each time the name PAY-RATE is used in the PROCEDURE DIVISION, it must be properly subscripted. For example, the statement

```
MOVE PAY-RATE (4) TO RATE.
          ↳ at least one space
```

would cause the contents of the fourth table entry to be moved (that is, copied) to the data item RATE and the statement

```
MULTIPLY PAY-RATE (2) BY HOURS GIVING WAGE.
              ↳ at least one space
```

would multiply the contents of the second entry of the table by the contents of HOURS, and the result would be stored in WAGE.

The subscript may be either an integer constant (that is, numerical literal) or integer variable. These values must be positive or unsigned. They cannot be zero or negative.

Example 1

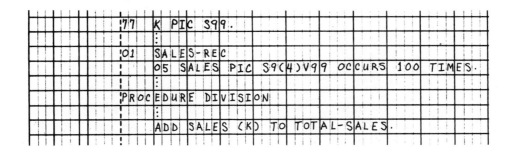

9.1 Table Construction 163

In the above coding, if K contains 8 at the time of execution, the statement in the PROCEDURE DIVISION would be identical to

```
            ADD SALES (8) TO TOTAL-SALES.
```

REDEFINES Clause

The REDEFINES clause is often used in conjunction with the OCCURS clause to initialize the value of the table. Such a procedure is necessary because in COBOL, VALUE and OCCURS clauses cannot appear together in a data description entry. Suppose, for example, the following data description entries were used to set up a table as shown in Fig. 9.1:

```
       01  PAY-RATE-VALUES.
           03  FILLER  PIC  S9V99  VALUE  2.50.
           03  FILLER  PIC  S9V99  VALUE  3.25.
           03  FILLER  PIC  S9V99  VALUE  4.25.
           03  FILLER  PIC  S9V99  VALUE  5.75.
           03  FILLER  PIC  S9V99  VALUE  7.00.
```

Notice that PAY-RATE-VALUES consist of five fields to convert PAY-RATE-VALUES into a table. We can now use the REDEFINES and the OCCURS clauses as follows:

```
       01  PAY-RATE-TABLE REDEFINES PAY-RATE-VALUES.
           04  PAY-RATE  PIC  S9V99  OCCURS  5  TIMES.
```

By using the REDEFINES clauses, PAY-RATE-TABLE and PAY-RATE-VALUES are simply two different names for the same storage area. Thus each field in PAY-RATE-VALUES is an entry in PAY-RATE-TABLE and may be referred to by the identifier PAY-RATE and a subscript. For example, PAY-RATE (2) refers to the value 3.25, which is the second entry in PAY-RATE-VALUES.

Example 2

Suppose it is required in a program to convert a numeric month code into the month name, that is, MONTH (1) = 'JAN', MONTH (2) = 'FEB', and so on. To accomplish this, we could set up the month name by using the VALUE clause in the WORKING-STORAGE SECTION of the DATA DIVISION:

```
       01  MONTH-VALUES.
           05  FILLER  PIC  A(3)  VALUE  'JAN'.
           05  FILLER  PIC  A(3)  VALUE  'FEB'.
           05  FILLER  PIC  A(3)  VALUE  'MAR'.
                  .
                  .
                  .
           05  FILLER  PIC  A(3)  VALUE  'DEC'.
```

In fact, to circumvent some of the coding, we could code MONTH-VALUES as

```
01  MONTH-NAMES  PIC A(36)
    VALUE 'JANFEBMARAPRMAYJUNJULAUGSEPOCTNOVDEC'.
```

Then the REDEFINES and OCCURS clauses could be used to convert MONTH-NAMES into a one-dimensional table:

```
01  MONTH-TABLES REDEFINES MONTH-NAMES.
    03 MONTH OCCURS 12 TIMES PIC A(3).
```

This coding would define a one-dimensional table with MONTH (1) corresponding to 'JAN', MONTH (2) to 'FEB', and so forth.

9.2 TWO- AND THREE-DIMENSIONAL TABLES

Two-dimensional tables deal with two variables, thus requiring two subscripts to locate an individual entry. In COBOL, these tables are handled in much the same way as one-dimensional tables. To illustrate, suppose the table in Fig. 9.3 were going to be used in a program. Its values would be coded in the WORKING-STORAGE SECTION of the DATA DIVISION as shown in Fig. 9.4.

	Premium rate ($)	
Age group	Class I	Class II
under 18 (I)	1.75	1.95
19–25 (II)	2.10	2.30
26–40 (III)	2.35	2.65
41–59 (IV)	2.45	2.95
60 or over (V)	2.90	3.15

Fig. 9.3 A two-dimensional table.

In order to convert the value entries in Fig. 9.4 into two-dimensional tables, the REDEFINES and OCCURS clauses would now be used. The coding is

```
01  PREMIUM-RATE-TABLE.
    03 AGE-GROUP OCCURS 5 TIMES.
       05 RATE PIC S9V99 OCCURS 2 TIMES.
```

The above coding would set up 10 data fields in storage and would have the following storage layout:

Premium-Rate Table

Age-group (1)		Age-group (2)		Age-group (5)	
Rate (1, 1)	Rate (1, 2)	Rate (2, 1)	Rate (2, 2)	Rate (5, 1)	Rate (5, 2)
1.75	1.95	2.10	2.30	2.90	3.15

```
            DATA DIVISION.
                    .
                    .
                    .
            WORKING-STORAGE SECTION.
                    .
                    .
                    .
            01  PREMIUM-RATE-VALUES.
                03  FILLER  PIC  S9V99  VALUE 1.75.
                03  FILLER  PIC  S9V99  VALUE 1.95.
                03  FILLER  PIC  S9V99  VALUE 2.10.
                03  FILLER  PIC  S9V99  VALUE 2.30.
                03  FILLER  PIC  S9V99  VALUE 2.35.
                03  FILLER  PIC  S9V99  VALUE 2.65.
                03  FILLER  PIC  S9V99  VALUE 2.45.
                03  FILLER  PIC  S9V99  VALUE 2.95.
                03  FILLER  PIC  S9V99  VALUE 2.90.
                03  FILLER  PIC  S9V99  VALUE 3.15.
```

Fig. 9.4 Value entries for the table in Fig. 9.3.

The first entry of the table is referred to as Rate (1, 1), which corresponds to Age-Group I (that is, under 18) and Rate Class I, and has contents of 1.75. The second entry is referred to as Rate (1, 2), which corresponds to Age-Group I and Rate Class II. The third entry is Rate (2, 1), which corresponds to Age-Group II and Rate Class I, and so on. It should be evident that the first subscript in RATE always represents Age-Group, whereas the second subscript denotes Rate-Class. For example, Rate (5, 2) would be the last entry on the table, corresponding to Age-Group V and Rate Class II.

Thus, for each of the age groups, there are two data fields corresponding to the two premium rate classes. This relationship is determined by the fact that in the coding, the level number 05 of RATE is lower than that of AGE-GROUP. If the level number of both items were equal, then the table would not be two dimensional.

Also notice that in the storage layout, not only have we constructed a two-dimensional table RATE, we have also constructed a one-dimensional table AGE-GROUP and a single field PREMIUM-RATE-TABLE. Thus the statement

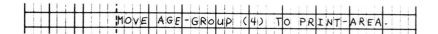
```
            MOVE AGE-GROUP (4) TO PRINT-AREA.
```

would cause the contents of RATE (4, 1) and RATE (4, 2) to be "copied" into PRINT-AREA, whereas the statement

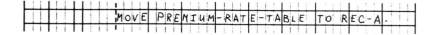
```
            MOVE PREMIUM-RATE-TABLE TO REC-A.
```

would "copy" the entire contents of the table to REC-A. Such flexibility in data manipulation again exemplifies the power of COBOL programming.

Example

Consider the following entries in the WORKING-STORAGE SECTION of the DATA DIVISION:

```
01  TABLE-AREA.
    03  A OCCURS 4 TIMES PIC 99.
    03  B OCCURS 3 TIMES.
        05  C OCCURS 2 TIMES PIC XXX.
        05  D OCCURS 2 TIMES PIC 99.
        05  E OCCURS 2 TIMES PIC 9.
    03  F.
        05  G OCCURS 4 TIMES PIC X.
        05  H OCCURS 5 TIMES PIC 99.
```

Here we have defined three different tables, namely:

(1) The first group A is a one-dimensional table with the following storage layout:

```
    A (1)
    A (2)
    A (3)
    A (4)
```

Each time the data name A was used, it would have to be subscripted. Thus it would be incorrect to write

```
    MOVE A TO A-AREA.
           ↑—invalid, A must be subscripted
```

(2) The second group B contains three elementary items: C, D, and E. The storage layout would be

```
         ⎧ C (1, 1)              ⎧ C (2, 1)              ⎧ C (3, 1)
         | C (1, 2)              | C (2, 2)              | C (3, 2)
         | D (1, 1)              | D (2, 1)              | D (3, 1)
  B (1) ⎨                 B (2) ⎨                 B (3) ⎨
         | D (1, 2)              | D (2, 2)              | D (3, 2)
         | E (1, 1)              | E (2, 1)              | E (3, 1)
         ⎩ E (1, 2)              ⎩ E (2, 2)              ⎩ E (3, 2)
```

Notice that data items C, D, and E each represent a two-dimensional table. They require the use of two subscripts whenever they are referred to.

(3) In the third group, the data item F does not contain an OCCURS clause, but its subordinated elementary items G and F do. The storage layout would be

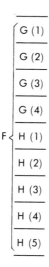

Here, all the elements of G precede all the elements of H and each element of G and H must be properly subscripted. However, since F does not contain an OCCURS clause itself, it cannot be subscripted. Thus, in essence, F contains two one-dimensional tables; the first one, G, consists of four elements and the second table, H, consists of five. Also note that the PICTURE codes of G and H do not have to be the same.

Three-Dimensional Table

The technique applied to constructing one- and two-dimensional tables can be readily used to define a three-dimensional table. For example, the following coding

```
01  SALES-TABLE.
    03  LOCATION OCCURS 2 TIMES.
        05  DEPARTMENT OCCURS 2 TIMES.
            07  SALES-BY-QTR OCCURS 4 TIMES
                PIC S9(5)V99.
```

would cause the computer to set up 16 (2 × 2 × 4) storage fields. Each of the fields has the picture code S9(5)V99. The storage layout may be viewed as follows:

$$
\text{Location (1)} \begin{cases} \text{DEPARTMENT (1, 1)} \begin{cases} \text{SALES-BY-QTR (1, 1, 1)} \\ \text{SALES-BY-QTR (1, 1, 2)} \\ \text{SALES-BY-QTR (1, 1, 3)} \\ \text{SALES-BY-QTR (1, 1, 4)} \end{cases} \\ \text{DEPARTMENT (1, 2)} \begin{cases} \text{SALES-BY-QTR (1, 2, 1)} \\ \text{SALES-BY-QTR (1, 2, 2)} \\ \text{SALES-BY-QTR (1, 2, 3)} \\ \text{SALES-BY-QTR (1, 2, 4)} \end{cases} \end{cases}
$$

Location (2) {
 DEPARTMENT (2, 1) { SALES-BY-QTR (2, 1, 1)
                     SALES-BY-QTR (2, 1, 2)
                     SALES-BY-QTR (2, 1, 3)
                     SALES-BY-QTR (2, 1, 4)

 DEPARTMENT (2, 2) { SALES-BY-QTR (2, 2, 1)
                     SALES-BY-QTR (2, 2, 2)
                     SALES-BY-QTR (2, 2, 3)
                     SALES-BY-QTR (2, 2, 4)

Thus SALES-BY-QTR (1, 2, 3) would represent the data located in the third position of the second department of location 1.

9.3 RULES FOR CODING SUBSCRIPTS

The coding of subscripts follows essentially the same rules that govern the coding of parentheses. That is:

(1) A blank space must not follow a left parenthesis nor is a blank space permitted to precede a right parenthesis:

(2) At least one blank space must be present between the name being subscripted and the left parenthesis.

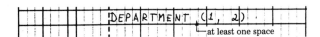

(3) A comma must be used to separate subscripts within a pair of parentheses. However, a space must follow each comma, but no space precedes the comma.

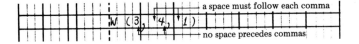

(4) The subscript can be represented by a numeric literal integer or by a data-name, which must be a numeric elementary item. Both the numeric literal and the data-name must represent a positive integer.

Example 1

MOVE X (-1, 2) TO A.
— invalid, subscript cannot be a negative integer

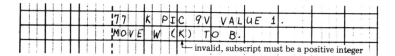

Example 2

```
77  K  PIC 9V VALUE 1.
MOVE W (K) TO B.
             ↑— invalid, subscript must be a positive integer
```

Example 3

```
77  I  PIC 9.
77  J  PIC 9.
77  K  PIC 9.
MOVE 1 TO I.
MOVE 2 TO J.
MOVE 3 TO K.
MOVE X(I, J, K) ← correct as shown
```

9.4 SAMPLE PROGRAM 9A: CREATING HOURLY RATE TABLE FROM PUNCHED CARDS

This program illustrates how an internal table can be created directly from punched cards without the use of the REDEFINES and the VALUE clauses. The table contains 12 entries:

Class	Rate ($)	Class	Rate ($)
01	2.00	07	5.50
02	2.25	08	7.00
03	2.50	09	8.50
04	3.00	10	10.50
05	3.50	11	12.50
06	4.50	12	15.00

Each input data card contains a class code (columns 1–2) and hourly rate (columns 6–9). These data cards can be entered in any order. The program will check each class code to ensure that it is within the range of the table size (that is, not greater than 12).

Sample Input

```
 1    6       1    6
 ↓    ↓       ↓    ↓
 02  0225    01  0200
 04  0300    03  0250
 06  0450    05  0350
 08  0700    07  0550
 10  1050    09  0850
 12  1500    11  1250
```

9 Table Handling

Source Listing

```
00001             IDENTIFICATION DIVISION.
00002             PROGRAM-ID. SAMPL9A.
00003      **************************************************
00004             ENVIRONMENT DIVISION.
00005             CONFIGURATION SECTION.
00006             SOURCE-COMPUTER. IBM-360.
00007             OBJECT-COMPUTER. IBM-360.
00008             INPUT-OUTPUT SECTION.
00009             FILE-CONTROL.
00010                 SELECT INFILE ASSIGN TO UR-2540R-S-IN.
00011                 SELECT OUTFILE ASSIGN TO UR-1403-S-OUT.
00012      **************************************************
00013             DATA DIVISION.
00014             FILE SECTION.
00015             FD  INFILE
00016                 LABEL RECORDS ARE OMITTED.
00017             01  INREC.
00018                 03  CLASS-CODE  PIC 99.
00019                     88  CLASS-CODE-VALUE VALUE 1 THRU 12.   ←── conditional name is used
00020                 03  FILLER PIC XXX.
00021                 03  RATE PIC 99V99.
00022                 03  FILLER PIC X(71).
00023             FD  OUTFILE
00024                 LABEL RECORDS OMITTED.
00025             01  OUTREC.
00026                 03  PRINTLINE PIC X(132).
00027             WORKING-STORAGE SECTION.
00028             77  SUBSCRIPT PIC 99 VALUE ZEROS.
00029             77  COUNT PIC 99 VALUE ZEROS.
00030             01  HEADING1.
00031                 03  FILLER PIC X(20) VALUE SPACES.
00032                 03  FILLER PIC X(17) VALUE 'HOURLY RATE TABLE'.
00033             01  HEADING2.
00034                 03  FILLER PIC X(20) VALUE SPACES.
00035                 03  FILLER PIC X(14) VALUE 'CLASS     RATE'.
00036             01  TABLE-TABLE.                                ←── defining a table
00037                 02  TABLE1 OCCURS 12 TIMES.                     with 12 entries
00038                     03  FILLER PIC X(20).
00039                     03  CLASS-CODE PIC 99.
00040                     03  FILLER PIC X(8).
00041                     03  RATE PIC $Z9.99.
00042      **************************************************
00043             PROCEDURE DIVISION.
00044                 OPEN INPUT INFILE, OUTPUT OUTFILE.
00045                 WRITE OUTREC FROM HEADING1 AFTER ADVANCING 0 LINES.
00046                 WRITE OUTREC FROM HEADING2 AFTER ADVANCING 2 LINES.
00047             PARA1.
00048                 READ INFILE AT END GO TO END-INFILE.
00049                 IF NOT CLASS-CODE-VALUE                     ←── use condition-name test
00050                     DISPLAY 'ERROR IN CLASS-CODE ', INREC UPON SYSOUT    to validate class-code
00051                 ELSE
00052                     MOVE CLASS-CODE OF INREC TO SUBSCRIPT.
00053                     MOVE SPACES TO TABLE1 (SUBSCRIPT).
00054                     MOVE CORR INREC TO TABLE1 (SUBSCRIPT).  ←── use subscript to locate entry in table
00055                 GO TO PARA1.
00056             END-INFILE.
00057                 ADD 1 TO COUNT.
00058                 WRITE OUTREC FROM TABLE1 (COUNT)
00059                     AFTER ADVANCING 1 LINES.
00060                 IF COUNT IS LESS THAN 12 GO TO END-INFILE.
00061                 CLOSE INFILE, OUTFILE.
00062                 STOP RUN.
```

Sample Output

```
                    HOURLY RATE TABLE
                    CLASS     RATE
                    01      $ 2.00
                    02      $ 2.25
                    03      $ 2.50
                    04      $ 3.00
                    05      $ 3.50
                    06      $ 4.50
                    07      $ 5.50
                    08      $ 7.00
                    09      $ 8.50
                    10      $10.50
                    11      $12.50
                    12      $15.00
```

9.5 SAMPLE PROGRAM 9B: SALESMAN COMMISSION COMPUTATION WITH RATE TABLE

This program is a modification of Sample Program 8B (page 148). It calculates salesmen's commissions based on the number of items sold, as described in Sample Program 8B.

However, to illustrate how the OCCURS and the REDEFINES clauses can be used, this program constructs an internal table called RATE-TABLE-2, which defines the base commission rate. This table contains ten entries as shown:

Years in service	Commission rate (%)
1	3.5
2	4.0
3	5.0
4	6.5
5	6.5
6	6.5
7	8.5
8	8.5
9	8.5
10 or more	10

The input/output descriptions and program logic of this program are basically the same as in Sample Program 8B (see pages 148–150).

Source Listing

```
00001              IDENTIFICATION DIVISION.
00002              PROGRAM-ID. SAMPL9B.
00003      **************************************
00004              ENVIRONMENT DIVISION.
00005              CONFIGURATION SECTION.
00006              SOURCE-COMPUTER. IBM-370.
00007              OBJECT-COMPUTER. IBM-370.
00008              INPUT-OUTPUT SECTION.
00009              FILE-CONTROL.
00010                  SELECT INFILE ASSIGN TO UR-2540R-S-IN.
00011                  SELECT OUTFILE ASSIGN TO UR-1403-S-OUT.
00012      **************************************
00013              DATA DIVISION.
00014              FILE SECTION.
00015              FD  INFILE
00016                  LABEL RECORDS OMITTED.
00017              01  INREC.
00018                  02 NAME-IN PIC X(20).
00019                  02 YEARS PIC 99.
00020                     88 OVER-TEN VALUE 11 THRU 99.
00021                  02 MAJOR-IN PIC 9(5).
00022                  02 MINOR-IN PIC 9(5).              ── condition-names are used
00023                     88 MINOR-IN-VALUE VALUE 500 THRU 2000.
00024                  02 FILLER PIC X(48).
00025              FD  OUTFILE
00026                  LABEL RECORDS OMITTED.
00027              01  OUTREC PIC X(132).
00028              WORKING-STORAGE SECTION.
00029              77  PERC PIC 99V999.
00030              77  COMM PIC 9(6)V99.
00031              01  RATE-TABLE.
00032                  02 ONE   PIC 9V999 VALUE 0.035.    ⎫
00033                  02 TWO   PIC 9V999 VALUE 0.040.    ⎪
00034                  02 THREE PIC 9V999 VALUE 0.050.    ⎪
00035                  02 FOUR  PIC 9V999 VALUE 0.065.    ⎬ specifies values of
00036                  02 FIVE  PIC 9V999 VALUE 0.065.    ⎪ commission rates
00037                  02 SIX   PIC 9V999 VALUE 0.065.    ⎪
00038                  02 SEVEN PIC 9V999 VALUE 0.085.    ⎪
00039                  02 EIGHT PIC 9V999 VALUE 0.085.    ⎪
00040                  02 NINE  PIC 9V999 VALUE 0.085.    ⎪
00041                  02 TEN   PIC 9V999 VALUE 0.100.    ⎭
```

9 Table Handling

```
00042          01  RATE-TABLE-2 REDEFINES RATE-TABLE.      } redefines RATE-TABLE
00043              02  COM-RATE PIC 9V999 OCCURS 10 TIMES.
00044          01  OUTRECORD.
00045              02  FILLER PIC X(5) VALUE SPACES.
00046              02  NAME-OUT PIC X(20) VALUE SPACES.
00047              02  FILLER PIC X(5) VALUE SPACES.
00048              02  YEARS-EMPLOYED PIC 99 VALUE ZEROS.
00049              02  FILLER PIC X(10) VALUE SPACES.
00050              02  NET-COMMISSION PIC $ZZ,ZZ9.99.
00051              02  FILLER PIC X(10) VALUE SPACES.
00052              02  COMMISSION-RATE PIC Z9.9.
00053              02  PERSIGN PIC X VALUE ' '.
00054              02  FILLER PIC X(10) VALUE SPACES.
00055              02  MAJOR-ITEMS-SOLD PIC $ZZZZ9 VALUE ZEROS.
00056              02  FILLER PIC X(15) VALUE SPACES.
00057              02  MINOR-ITEMS-SOLD PIC $ZZZZ9 VALUE ZEROS.
00058          01  HEADER.
00059              02  FILLER PIC X(5) VALUE SPACES.
00060              02  FILLER PIC X(25) VALUE 'NAME'.
00061              02  FILLER PIC X(12) VALUE 'YRS.EMPL.'.
00062              02  FILLER PIC X(19) VALUE 'NET COMMISSION'.
00063              02  FILLER PIC X(15) VALUE 'COMM.RATE'.
00064              02  FILLER PIC X(20) VALUE 'MAJOR ITEMS SOLD'.
00065              02  FILLER PIC X(36) VALUE 'MINOR ITEMS SOLD'.
00066          ***************************************************
00067          PROCEDURE DIVISION.
00068          OPEN-UP.
00069              OPEN INPUT INFILE, OUTPUT OUTFILE.
00070              MOVE SPACES TO OUTREC.
00071              MOVE ' COMMISSION DETERMINATION' TO OUTREC.
00072              WRITE OUTREC AFTER ADVANCING 5 LINES.
00073              WRITE OUTREC FROM HEADER AFTER ADVANCING 5 LINES.
00074          READ-IT.
00075              READ INFILE AT END GO TO END-IT.
00076              MOVE NAME-IN TO NAME-OUT.
00077              MOVE YEARS TO YEARS-EMPLOYED.
00078              MOVE MAJOR-IN TO MAJOR-ITEMS-SOLD.
00079              MOVE MINOR-IN TO MINOR-ITEMS-SOLD.
00080          FIGURE-IT.
00081              IF OVER-TEN  MOVE .10 TO PERC          <--- condition-name test
00082                 ELSE MOVE COM-RATE (YEARS) TO PERC. <--- use subscript to access
00083              IF MAJOR-IN IS GREATER THAN 3000            data from rate-table
00084                 ADD .01 TO PERC
00085                 ELSE SUBTRACT .005 FROM PERC.
00086              COMPUTE COMM ROUNDED = PERC * (MAJOR-IN + MINOR-IN).
00087              IF MINOR-IN-VALUE  ADD 50 TO COMM.
00088              MULTIPLY PERC BY 100 GIVING COMMISSION-RATE.
00089              MOVE COMM TO NET-COMMISSION.
00090              WRITE OUTREC FROM OUTRECORD AFTER ADVANCING 1 LINES.
00091              GO TO READ-IT.
00092          END-IT.
00093              MOVE ' END OF JOB' TO OUTREC.
00094              WRITE OUTREC AFTER ADVANCING 10 LINES.
00095              CLOSE INFILE, OUTFILE.
00096              STOP RUN.
```

Sample Output

```
COMMISSION DETERMINATION


 NAME                     YRS.EMPL.    NET COMMISSION    COMM.RATE    MAJOR ITEMS SOLD    MINOR ITEMS SOLD
 HENRY BROWN              05           $    395.00        7.5         $  4000             $   600
 JAMES MELVILL            03           $    103.50        4.5         $  2000             $   300
 DELLA STREET             10           $    787.00       11.0         $  6000             $   700
 DEBRA WHO                01           $    288.50        4.5         $  4500             $   800
 ROBIN EGG                07           $    959.50        9.5         $  8000             $  2100
 HAROLD BYEME             08           $    528.00        8.0         $  2100             $  4500
 JAY CLASSLESS            04           $    952.50        7.5         $  9600             $  3100
 MAY SPITZ                02           $    665.00        5.0         $  8800             $  4500
```

EXERCISES

1 In each of the following problems, correct the errors, if any.

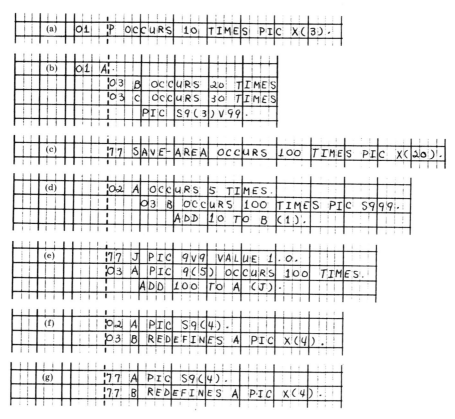

2 Describe the storage layout for the following entries in the DATA DIVISION (you may use diagrams):

3 Use the REDEFINES and the OCCURS clauses to define values for the following tables in core storage.

(a) SALES-COMMISSION-RATE

Commission class	Commission rate
1	0.010
2	0.035
3	0.070
4	0.105
5	0.12

(b) ACCOUNT-ID and PASSWORD TABLE

Class	ID	Password
1	M10001	NULLPASS
2	MAE101	SUPERCHK
3	MSC001	ALCHAI01
4	SC0001	OPSYS101
5	MARC01	MARCINKO
6	RANDXX	NEWACCT1

4 The XXX Company has an undetermined number of employees. At the end of the year, each employee is given an annual bonus. This bonus is computed by multiplying the annual earnings of the employee by an appropriate bonus rate. However, no employee will be getting more than a $2500 bonus. The bonus rate, depending on the number of years of service, is listed in the following table:

Years in service	Bonus rate
1–3	0.015
4–5	0.020
6–10	0.035
11–15	0.055
16–20	0.10
over 20	0.20

Write a program to compute the bonus and generate a printed report. Input to the program is the Employee-Payroll-Record as shown in the following:

Column	Content
1–20	employee name
21–22	years in service
23–25	not used
26–32	annual earnings XXXXX.XX
33–80	not used

Output should contain one line for each employee with appropriate editing. The bonus rate should be coded as an internal table.

5 Modify programming project 8-13 so that the base amount and salesman's commission rate will be defined as an internal table as shown in the following:

Commission code	Base amount ($)	Commission rate
1	5000	0.02
2	10,000	0.03
3	20,000	0.15
4	50,000	0.20

6 Modify programming project 8-14 so that both the reorder point and order quantity are specified internally according to the following table:

Stock number	Type	Reorder point	Order quantity
00001–10000	A	5000	10000
10001–30000	B	4000	14000
30001–60000	C	10000	65000
over 60000	D	3000	30000

10

The PERFORM Statement

The simplest type of PERFORM statement using the form

PERFORM procedure-name

has been discussed in Chapter 5. In this chapter we shall discuss four other formats associated with the use of the PERFORM statement.

10.1 PERFORM/THRU OPTION

The first type of PERFORM statement we shall discuss here has the format

PERFORM procedure-name-1 THRU procedure-name-2

Procedure-name-1 and procedure-name-2 may be either paragraph or section names. In this format, the PERFORM statement would cause the computer to execute a series of consecutive procedures and/or sections. The execution always begins with the first statement in procedure-name-1 and ends with the last statement in procedure-name-2. Any procedures between procedure-name-1 and procedure-name-2 are also executed. After this is done the computer returns to execute the statement immediately following the PERFORM statement, as in the following program.

10.2 EXIT Statement

Example 1

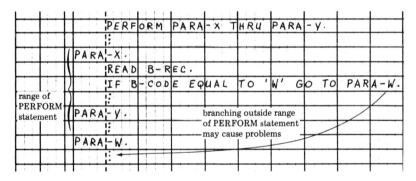

When the PERFORM command is executed, the program branches to the procedure PROC-A. After all the statements within PROC-A and PROC-E are executed (the last statement to be executed is MOVE A TO B) the program returns its control to the statement following the PERFORM statement ADD B TO SUM. However, if a branch or conditional statement is within the range of the PERFORM statement, the program control may not return to the statement following the PERFORM, as illustrated in Example 2.

Example 2

In this example, upon execution of the PERFORM command, the program would branch to PARA-X; first the program executes the READ B-REC statement, and then it branches to PARA-W if B-CODE is equal to 'W'. Thus, in this case the program would not return to the statement following the PERFORM command.

10.2 EXIT STATEMENT

The EXIT statement is used to provide a common endpoint for a series of procedures. Thus, it makes a transfer possible at the end of a procedure named in the PERFORM command. Its format is

procedure-name. <u>EXIT</u>

The EXIT statement must be preceded by a paragraph-name and must be the only statement in the paragraph.

To demonstrate how it works, consider Example (3).

Example

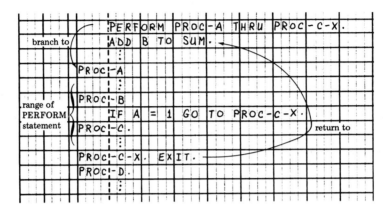

Notice that this example is very similar to Example 1, Section 10.1, with the exception that an EXIT paragraph is added and the PERFORM command is slightly modified. The EXIT command, for all practical purposes, serves as a dummy paragraph. It provides a common endpoint to which the program logic can branch. Remember that when the EXIT command is used, it must be preceded by a procedure-name and must be the only statement in that procedure as shown.

10.3 PERFORM/TIMES OPTION

The second format of the PERFORM statement is

PERFORM procedure-name-1 [THRU procedure-name-2]
$\begin{Bmatrix} \text{identifier-1} \\ \text{integer-1} \end{Bmatrix}$ TIMES.

In this format, the procedures named within the PERFORM range are executed as many times as specified.

Example 1

```
PERFORM ADD-ROUTINE 100 TIMES.
```

Example 2

```
PERFORM PROC-A THRU PROC-E 10 TIMES.
```

Example 3

```
            PERFORM LOOP-ROUTINE K TIME.
```

In Example 1, the PERFORM command causes the procedure named ADD-ROUTINE to be executed 100 times before returning to the statement following the PERFORM.

In Example 2, the THRU option is present. Thus, procedures within PROC-A and PROC-E (inclusive) will be executed 10 times before returning.

In Example 3, LOOP-ROUTINE will be executed depending on the value of K. The data name K must be an elementary numeric item with no decimal digits. If K is negative or zero, the PERFORM statement will be bypassed; consequently the next sentence following the PERFORM will be executed.

10.4 PERFORM/UNTIL OPTION

PERFORM procedure-name-1 [<u>THRU</u> procedure-name-2] <u>UNTIL</u> condition.

In this format, repetitive execution of the PERFORM command is carried out until the specified condition is fulfilled.

Example 1

```
            PERFORM PRINT-ROUTINE UNTIL N > 12.
```

Example 2

```
            PERFORM SEARCH-ROUTINE UNTIL NAME = 'CHAI'
              OR COUNTER > 1600.
```

Example 3

```
          PERFORM ROUTINE-A THRU ROUTINE-W
             UNTIL SUM > 9000.00.
```

When the UNTIL condition option is used, the procedures specified by the PERFORM command are executed until the specified condition is fulfilled. At such time the program returns its control to the statement following the PERFORM command. If the condition is already being fulfilled when the PERFORM command is first encountered, the program will bypass the PERFORM statement and execute the next sequential statement. For example, in Example 1, if the value of N is already greater than 12 when the statement is encountered, then PRINT-ROUTINE will not be executed and the control will automatically transfer to the next sequential sentence.

10.5 PERFORM/VARYING OPTIONS

The general format of the PERFORM/VARYING option is

PERFORM procedure-name-1 [THRU procedure-name-2]

VARYING identifier-1 FROM $\begin{Bmatrix} \text{literal-2} \\ \text{identifier-2} \end{Bmatrix}$

BY identifier-3 UNTIL condition-1

[AFTER identifier-4 FROM $\begin{Bmatrix} \text{literal-5} \\ \text{identifier-5} \end{Bmatrix}$

BY $\begin{Bmatrix} \text{literal-6} \\ \text{identifier-6} \end{Bmatrix}$ UNTIL condition-2

[AFTER identifier-7 FROM $\begin{Bmatrix} \text{literal-8} \\ \text{identifier-8} \end{Bmatrix}$

BY $\begin{Bmatrix} \text{literal-9} \\ \text{identifier-9} \end{Bmatrix}$ UNTIL condition-3]]

This format contains the most powerful version of the PERFORM statement. It may contain one to three varying identifiers. Its use is best explained by examples.

Example 1. VARYING Option Applied to One Identifier

```
        PERFORM SUM-ROUTINE VARYING K FROM 1 BY 1
            UNTIL K IS EQUAL TO 100.
    :
SUM-ROUTINE.
        ADD X (K) TO SUM.
```

When the PERFORM statement is encountered, the procedure SUM-ROUTINE is executed exactly 99 times. The sequence of events is shown in Fig. 10.1 and is explained as follows:

(1) K is set to 1 and SUM-ROUTINE is executed once.
(2) The value of K is automatically incremented by 1 at the end of the execution of SUM-ROUTINE.
(3) The condition K IS EQUAL TO 100 is evaluated. If the condition is not fulfilled, the specified procedure (SUM-ROUTINE) is again executed.
(4) Steps 2 and 3 are repeated until the condition K IS EQUAL TO 100 is fulfilled. When this happens, the program transfers the control to the statement following the PERFORM command.

Incidentally, the above statement would cause SUM-ROUTINE to be executed 99 times. When K is incremented to 100, the condition is satisfied and SUM-ROUTINE would not be executed again. If SUM-ROUTINE were to be executed 100 times, either of the following statements could be used:

```
        PERFORM SUM-ROUTINE VARYING K FROM 1 BY 1
            UNTIL K IS EQUAL TO 101.
```

10.5 PERFORM/VARYING Options 181

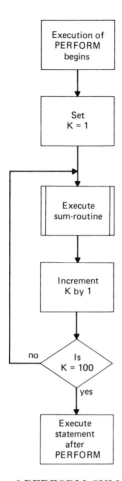

Fig. 10.1 Logical flow of PERFORM SUM-ROUTINE VARYING K FROM 1 BY 1 UNTIL K IS EQUAL TO 100.

```
        PERFORM SUM-ROUTINE VARYING K FROM 100 BY 1
            UNTIL K = 0.
```

Example 2. VARYING Option Applied to Two Identifiers

```
        PERFORM PROC-6 THRU PROC-8
            VARYING SUB1 FROM N1 BY 1
            UNTIL SUB1 IS GREATER THAN 100
            AFTER SUB2 FROM N2 BY KOUNT
            UNTIL SUB2 IS GREATER THAN 400.
```

The preceding statement applies the VARYING option to two identifiers, namely, SUB1 and SUB2. The statement is executed in the following way:

(1) SUB1 and SUB2 are set to their initial values, that is, SUB1 = N1, SUB2 = N2.
(2) Condition-1, SUB1 > 100, is evaluated; if true, control is passed to the next sequential statement after the PERFORM command. If not fulfilled, condition-2, SUB2 > 400, is evaluated.

(3) If condition-2 is not fulfilled, PROC-6 through PROC-8 (inclusive) is executed once.
(4) SUB2 is incremented by the value of KOUNT.
(5) Condition-2, SUB2 > 400, is checked again; if it is not fulfilled, steps 3 and 4 are repeated.
(6) If condition-2, SUB2 > 400, is fulfilled, SUB2 would be reset to its initial value, that is, SUB2 = N2.
(7) SUB1 is incremented by 1.
(8) Steps 2 through 7 are repeated until condition-1, SUB1 > 100, is fulfilled.

Figure 10.2 presents the program flowchart for these events. The program flow for the VARYING option applied to three identifiers is essentially the same as for two, and so we omit its discussion here.

Example 3

This example uses PERFORM to calculate the sum of 50 data items. We first assume the following partial COBOL coding:

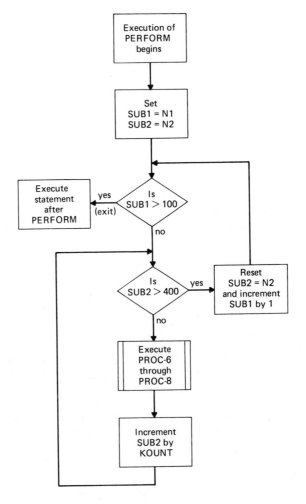

Fig. 10.2 Logical flow of the PERFORM statement in Example 2.

```
77  I  PIC 999 VALUE ZEROS.
77  TOTAL-X  PIC 9(7)V99.
01  X-TABLE.
    03 X OCCURS 50 TIMES 9(5)V99.
```

In order to calculate the sum of X (1), X (2), ..., X (100) and store the resulting sum in TOTAL-X, we may code the following statements in the PROCEDURE DIVISION:

```
        MOVE ZEROS TO TOTAL-X
        PERFORM SUM-X-R
            VARYING I FROM 1 BY 1
            UNTIL I = 51.
            :
SUM-X-R.
        ADD X (I) TO TOTAL-X.
```

When the PERFORM statement is encountered, the procedure SUM-X-R is executed exactly 50 times; each time, the subscript variable I would be automatically incremented by 1. Thus, the statement

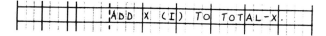

would add X (1), X (2), ..., X (50) to TOTAL-X as specified.

10.6 NESTED-LOOPS

When the THRU option is used in a PERFORM statement, it is entirely possible to execute one or more PERFORM commands within the range of procedure-name-1 and procedure-name-2. These PERFORM commands form a nested loop. However, due to the

```
            PERFORM P-1 THRU P-5.
    P-1.
        :
    P-2. PERFORM P-3 THRU P-4.
        :
    P-3.
        :
    P-4.
        :
    P-5.
        :
    P-6.
```

range of first PERFORM statement

range of second PERFORM statement

Fig. 10.3 (a) Permissible nested PERFORMS.

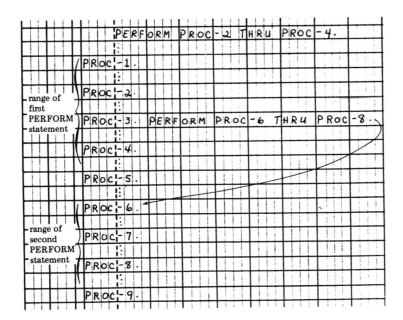

Fig. 10.3 (b) Permissible nested PERFORMS.

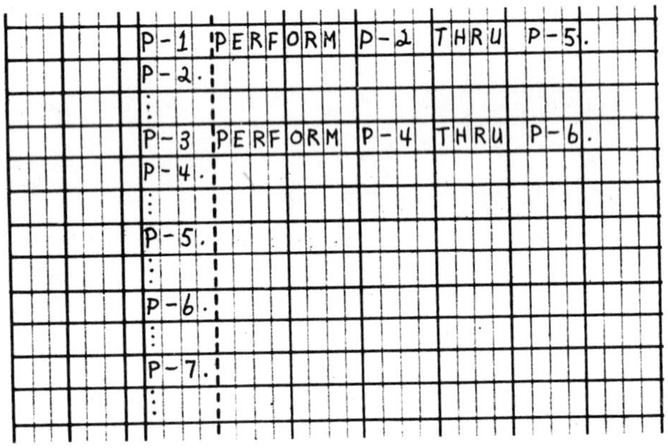

Fig. 10.4 Incorrect structure of the nested PERFORMS.

structure of the PERFORM statement, extreme care must be exercised to ensure the correctness of the program logic. Figures 10.3 and 10.4 illustrate both permissible and incorrect structures of the nested PERFORMS. The reader is urged to study them carefully.

10.7 SAMPLE PROGRAM 10A: DEPRECIATION SCHEDULES

This program computes depreciation schedules using the sum-of-digits method of depreciation, which is as follows: Suppose that one has an asset (an item of equivalent worth) of $7000, which depreciated over a 3-year period. After 3 years the item can be sold as scrap

10.7 Sample Program 10A: Depreciation Schedules

with a value of $1000. The accompanying table shows how the calculation is performed by using the sum-of-digits method, given the following data: original cost, $7000; scrap, $1000; total amount of depreciation (cost − scrap), $7000 − $1000 = $6000; useful life, 3 years.

Year	Depreciation rate	Depreciation
1	$\dfrac{3}{1+2+3} = \dfrac{3}{6}$	$6000 \times \dfrac{3}{6} = 3000$
2	$\dfrac{2}{1+2+3} = \dfrac{2}{6}$	$6000 \times \dfrac{2}{6} = 2000$
3	$\dfrac{1}{1+2+3} = \dfrac{1}{6}$	$6000 \times \dfrac{1}{6} = 1000$

Note that the depreciation rate changes from year to year. It consists of a denominator that is the sum of the digits from 1 up to the useful life of the item to be depreciated. Thus, if an item is to be depreciated in n years, then the depreciation rate for each year would be arrived at as follows: Since $1 + 2 + 3 + \cdots + n = n(n+1)/2$, the depreciation rate for each year, starting from the first year is simply

$$\frac{n}{n(n+1)/2}, \frac{(n-1)}{n(n+1)/2}, \frac{(n-2)}{n(n+1)/2}, \ldots, \frac{1}{n(n+1)/2}.$$

Input and output requirements of this program are as follows:

Input Description: Asset Punch Card File

Columns	Contents
1–6	asset identification
7–15	original cost of the asset, XXXXXXX.XX
16–23	scrap value, XXXXXX.XX
24–25	useful life (in years) XX
26–80	not used

Sample Input Data

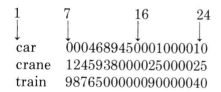

```
      1       7        16       24
      ↓       ↓         ↓        ↓
      car    000468945000100 0010
      crane  124593800002500 0025
      train  987650000009000 0040
```

186 10 The PERFORM Statement

Program Logic

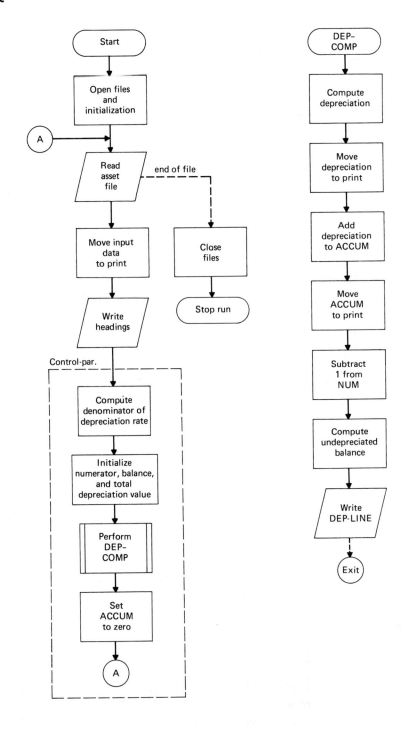

Source Listing

```
00001              IDENTIFICATION DIVISION.
00002              PROGRAM-ID. 'SAMPLE10A'.
00003              AUTHOR. LESTER THIERWECHTER.
00004      ****************************************************************************
00005              ENVIRONMENT DIVISION.
00006              CONFIGURATION SECTION.
00007              SOURCE-COMPUTER. IBM-370.
00008              OBJECT-COMPUTER. IBM-370.
00009              SPECIAL-NAMES.
00010                  C01 IS NU-PAGE.
00011              INPUT-OUTPUT SECTION.
00012              FILE-CONTROL.
00013                  SELECT ASSET-PCH ASSIGN TO UR-2501-S-CARDIN.
00014                  SELECT DEP-SCH ASSIGN TO UR-1403-S-PRINTOUT.
00015      ****************************************************************************
00016              DATA DIVISION.
00017              FILE SECTION.
00018              FD  ASSET-PCH
00019                  LABEL RECORDS ARE OMITTED
00020                  DATA RECORD IS ASSET-DATA.
00021              01  ASSET-DATA.
00022                  03   ASSET-ID    PIC X(6).
00023                  03   COST        PIC 9(7)V99.               ⎫
00024                  03   SCRAP       PIC 9(6)V99.               ⎬ input description
00025                  03   USE-LIFE    PIC 99.                    ⎭
00026                  03   FILLER      PIC X(55).
00027              FD  DEP-SCH
00028                  LABEL RECORD OMITTED
00029                  DATA RECORD IS DEP-LINE.
00030              01  DEP-LINE         PIC X(132).
00031              WORKING-STORAGE SECTION.
00032              77  NUM              PIC 99V9(8).
00033              77  DEN              PIC 9(4)V9(8).
00034              77  DEP              PIC 9(7)V99.
00035              77  ACCUM            PIC 9(7)V99    VALUE ZERO.
00036              77  BAL              PIC 9(7)V99.
00037              77  TOT-DEP          PIC S9(7)V99.
00038              01  OUT-LINE.
00039                  03   FILLER      PIC X(5).
00040                  03   YEAR        PIC 99.
00041                  03   FILLER      PIC X(5).                  ⎫
00042                  03   CUR-DEP     PIC $Z,ZZZ,ZZZ.99.         ⎪ detail line
00043                  03   FILLER      PIC X(5).                  ⎬ (one print-line
00044                  03   ACC-DEP     PIC $Z,ZZZ,ZZZ.99.         ⎪ per year)
00045                  03   FILLER      PIC X(5).                  ⎪
00046                  03   BALANCE     PIC $ZZ,ZZZ,ZZZ.99.        ⎭
00047                  03   FILLER      PIC X(71).
00048              01  HEAD-1.
00049                  03   FILLER      PIC X(4)       VALUE SPACE.        ⎫
00050                  03   YR          PIC A(4)       VALUE 'YEAR'.       ⎪
00051                  03   FILLER      PIC X(5)       VALUE SPACE.        ⎪
00052                  03   C-D         PIC X(12)      VALUE 'CUR. DEPREC.'. ⎬ report subheading
00053                  03   FILLER      PIC X(4)       VALUE SPACE.        ⎪
00054                  03   A-D         PIC X(14)      VALUE 'ACCUM. DEPREC.'. ⎪
00055                  03   U-D         PIC X(19)      VALUE '    UNDEPREC BALANCE'. ⎭
00056              01  REPORT-HEAD.
00057                  03   FILLER      PIC X(12)      VALUE ' ASSET-ID '.     ⎫
00058                  03   ASSET-ID-H  PIC X(10).                             ⎪
00059                  03   FILLER      PIC X(15)      VALUE 'ORIGINAL COST'.  ⎬ report heading
00060                  03   COST-H      PIC $Z,ZZZ,ZZ9.99.                     ⎪
00061                  03   FILLER      PIC X(18)      VALUE '    SCRAP VALUE'.⎪
00062                  03   SCRAP-H     PIC $ZZZ,ZZ9.99.                       ⎭
00063      ****************************************************************************
00064              PROCEDURE DIVISION.
00065              BEGIN.
00066                  OPEN INPUT ASSET-PCH, OUTPUT DEP-SCH.
00067                  MOVE SPACE TO OUT-LINE.
00068              READ-DATA.
00069                  READ ASSET-PCH AT END CLOSE ASSET-PCH, DEP-SCH, STOP RUN.
00070              WRITE-HEADING.
00071                  MOVE ASSET-ID TO ASSET-ID-H.
00072                  MOVE COST TO COST-H.
00073                  MOVE SCRAP TO SCRAP-H.
00074                  WRITE DEP-LINE FROM REPORT-HEAD
00075                      AFTER ADVANCING NU-PAGE.
00076                  WRITE DEP-LINE FROM HEAD-1
00077                      AFTER ADVANCING 3 LINES.
00078              CONTROL-PAR.
00079                  COMPUTE DEN = (USE-LIFE * (USE-LIFE + 1)) / 2.
00080                  MOVE USE-LIFE TO NUM.
00081                  MOVE COST TO BAL.
00082                  SUBTRACT SCRAP FROM COST GIVING TOT-DEP.
00083                      PERFORM DEP-COMP VARYING YEAR FROM 1 BY 1   ⎫ use PERFORM statement to branch
00084                          UNTIL YEAR > USE-LIFE.                  ⎭ to DEP-COMP routine
00085                  MOVE 0 TO ACCUM.
00086                  GO TO READ-DATA.
00087              DEP-COMP.
00088                  COMPUTE DEP ROUNDED = (NUM / DEN) * TOT-DEP.    ⎫
00089                  MOVE DEP TO CUR-DEP.                            ⎪
00090                  ADD DEP TO ACCUM.                               ⎬ compute
00091                  MOVE ACCUM TO ACC-DEP.                          ⎪ depreciation
00092                  SUBTRACT 1 FROM NUM.                            ⎬ schedule
00093                  SUBTRACT ACCUM FROM BAL GIVING BALANCE.         ⎪
00094                  WRITE DEP-LINE FROM OUT-LINE                    ⎪
00095                      AFTER ADVANCING 2 LINES.                    ⎭
```

Sample Output

```
            ASSET-ID   CAR       ORIGINAL COST   $   4,689.45      SCRAP VALUE   $   100.00

            YEAR     CUR. DEPREC.    ACCUM. DEPREC.    UNDEPREC BALANCE
            01     $     834.45    $      834.45    $     3,855.00
            02     $     751.00    $    1,585.45    $     3,104.00
            03     $     667.56    $    2,253.01    $     2,436.44
            04     $     584.11    $    2,837.12    $     1,852.33
            05     $     500.67    $    3,337.79    $     1,351.66
            06     $     417.22    $    3,755.01    $       934.44
            07     $     333.78    $    4,088.79    $       600.66
            08     $     250.33    $    4,339.12    $       350.33
            09     $     166.89    $    4,506.01    $       183.44
            10     $      83.44    $    4,589.45    $       100.00
```

10.8 USAGE CLAUSE

COBOL provides two different formats for storing numeric data items internally: DISPLAY and COMPUTATION. They may be specified by the programmer thru the USAGE clause of the form

$$\text{USAGE IS} \begin{Bmatrix} \underline{\text{DISPLAY}} \\ \underline{\text{COMPUTATIONAL}} \\ \underline{\text{COMP}} \end{Bmatrix}$$

The DISPLAY format must be used when numeric data are entered from a punched card or printed on a line printer. However to use this format there is really no need for the programmer to specify anything since the computer will automatically assume the numeric item is in the <u>DISPLAY</u> unless specified otherwise. For example, the statement

```
        04  A  PIC  S999  USAGE IS DISPLAY.
```

is equivalent to

```
        04  A  PIC  S999.
```

The COMPUTATIONAL (or COMP) format is used to permit internal arithmetic to be performed more efficiently. This is because in most computers a numeric item in the DISPLAY format must be first converted to the COMPUTATIONAL format before any arithmetic or COMPARE operation can be performed. For example, the statement

```
        ADD 1 TO TOTAL-A.
```

is executed much faster if TOTAL-A is specified as

```
        77  TOTAL-A  PIC  S9(4)  VALUE ZEROS  USAGE IS COMPUTATIONAL.
```

rather than

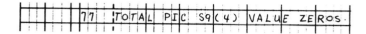

Also note that in the USAGE clause, the word COMPUTATIONAL can be replaced by COMP and USAGE IS can be omitted. For example, the following codings are all equivalent and declare that SUM-A is a computational field:

```
03  SUM-A  PIC  S9(4)V99  USAGE IS COMPUTATION.
03  SUM-A  PIC  S9(4)V99  USAGE IS COMP.
03  SUM-A  PIC  S9(4)V99  COMPUTATION.
03  SUM-A  PIC  S9(4)V99  COMP.
```

10.9 SAMPLE PROGRAM 10B: STUDENT TEST SCORES COMPUTATION

This program reads student test scores punched on data cards and determines the total scores and the averages. There is one test score per data card, and these can be entered in any order.

To facilitate computation, the program sets up an internal table that can process up to 100 different students. Each entry in the table contains the student's number, name, number of tests entered, and total scores.

When a punched card is read, the program will first search the table for the matching student number. If there is no match, the program will store the input data at the first available location in the table. If a matching student number is found, the program then compares the student names. If the names do not match, an error message will be printed. The test score will be added as long as the student numbers are the same, whether or not the names match.

After all the data cards are read, the program will compute the average score for the number of tests entered per student as well as the average score for maximum number of tests. (Note that it is quite possible a student may miss a test; therefore, the number of tests entered may be different from one student to another.)

Input: Student Test Card (CARD-IN)

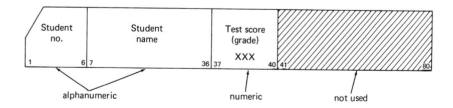

10 The PERFORM Statement

Sample Input

```
1      7                              37
↓      ↓                              ↓
       123456mark s. fistes           089
       907254moe d. lawn              065
       414960ted e. bare              086
       073335arthur ritus             063
       456978terry bull               045
       052124don e. brook             094
       334434ed cetera                100
       626803horace race              087
       625295sid e. slicker           077
       558452moe mentum               078
       123456mark s. fister           093
       485912lem n. juice             090
       161653bud n. genius            095
       829932warren peace             088
       534487max e. mum               100
       121736phil osophy              080
       019020fran tastik              025
       456978terry bull               011
       623375pat n. leather           084
       212831ann teek                 078
       123456mark s. fistes           100
       626803horace race              099
       626803horace race              085
       625295sid e. slicker           092
       625295sid e. slicker           092
       346069matt maddix              096
       346069matt maddix              096
       558452moe mentum               085
       558452moe mentum               087
       485912lem n. juice             090
       485912lem n. juice             092
       161653bud n. genius            097
       161653bud n. genius            093
       829932warren peace             100
       829932warren peace             100
       534487max e. mum               100
       534487max e. mum               100
       121736phil osophy              015
       121736phil osophy              045
       019020fran tastik              080
       212831ann teek                 099
       212831ann teek                 067
       019020fran tastik              075
```

10.9 Sample Program 10B: Student Test Score Computation

Program Logic

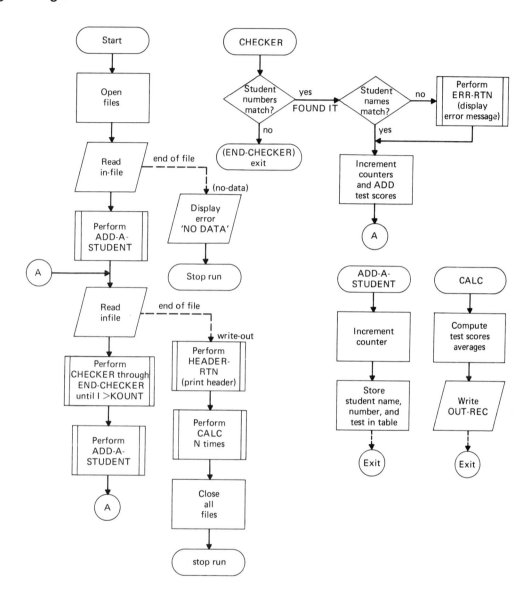

Source Listing

```
00001           IDENTIFICATION DIVISION.
00002           PROGRAM-ID. SAMPL10B.
00003       ****************************************
00004           ENVIRONMENT DIVISION.
00005           CONFIGURATION SECTION.
00006           SOURCE-COMPUTER. IBM-370.
00007           OBJECT-COMPUTER. IBM-370.
00008           SPECIAL-NAMES.
00009               C01 IS TOP-OF-PAGE.
00010           INPUT-OUTPUT SECTION.
00011           FILE-CONTROL.
00012               SELECT IN-FILE ASSIGN TO UR-2501-S-INPUT.
00013               SELECT OUT-FILE ASSIGN TO UR-1403-S-PROUT.
00014       ****************************************
```

```
00015           DATA DIVISION.
00016           FILE SECTION.
00017           FD  IN-FILE
00018               RECORDING MODE IS F
00019               LABEL RECORDS OMITTED
00020               DATA RECORD IS CARD-IN.
00021           01  CARD-IN.
00022               02  STUDENT-IN.
00023                   03  STUD-NO-IN PIC X(6).
00024                   03  STUD-NAME-IN PIC X(30).
00025                   03  GRADE-IN PIC 999.
00026               02  FILLER PIC X(41).
00027           FD  OUT-FILE
00028               RECORDING MODE F
00029               LABEL RECORDS OMITTED
00030               DATA RECORD IS OUT-LINE.
00031           01  OUT-LINE PIC X(133).
00032           WORKING-STORAGE SECTION.
00033           77  KOUNT PIC 999  VALUE ZEROS  COMP.   ⎫
00034           77  L PIC 99  VALUE ZEROS  COMP.        ⎬  USAGE IS COMPUTATIONAL
00035           77  I PIC 999  VALUE ZEROS  COMP.       ⎪  specified here (to obtain more
00036           77  MAX PIC 999  VALUE ZEROS  COMP.     ⎭  efficiency in program computation)
00037           01  STUDENT-LIST.
00038               02  STUDENT OCCURS 100 TIMES.       ⎫
00039                   03  STUD-NO PIC X(6).           ⎪
00040                   03  STUD-NAME PIC X(30).        ⎬  define table with 100 entries
00041                   03  TESTS PIC 999.              ⎪
00042                   03  POINTS PIC 9(5).            ⎭
00043           01  STUDENT-OUT.
00044               02  FILLER PIC X(8) VALUE SPACES.
00045               02  STUD-NO-OUT PIC X(6).
00046               02  FILLER PIC X(10) VALUE SPACES.
00047               02  STUD-NAME-OUT PIC X(30).
00048               02  FILLER PIC X(11) VALUE SPACES.
00049               02  TESTS-OUT PIC Z99.
00050               02  FILLER PIC X(11) VALUE SPACES
00051               02  POINTS-OUT PIC ZZ,ZZ9.
00052               02  FILLER PIC X(11) VALUE SPACES.
00053               02  AVE-OUT PIC ZZZ9.99.
00054               02  FILLER PIC X(7) VALUE SPACES.
00055               02  AVE-OUT-2 PIC ZZZ9.99.
00056           01  HEADER.
00057               02  FILLER PIC X(6) VALUE SPACES.
00058               02  FILLER PIC X(11) VALUE 'STUDENT NO.'.
00059               02  FILLER PIC X(18) VALUE SPACES.
00060               02  FILLER PIC X(7) VALUE 'N A M E'.
00061               02  FILLER PIC X(22) VALUE SPACES.
00062               02  FILLER PIC X(5) VALUE 'TESTS'.
00063               02  FILLER PIC X(9) VALUE SPACES.
00064               02  FILLER PIC X(10) VALUE 'TOTAL PTS.'.
00065               02  FILLER PIC X(9) VALUE SPACES.
00066               02  FILLER PIC X(7) VALUE 'AVERAGE'.
00067               02  FILLER PIC X(5) VALUE SPACES.
00068               02  FILLER PIC X(19) VALUE
00069                   'AVE. FOR MAX. TESTS'.
00070      ****************************************************
00071           PROCEDURE DIVISION.
00072           OPEN-UP. OPEN INPUT IN-FILE, OUTPUT OUT-FILE.
00073               READ IN-FILE AT END GO TO NO-DATA.
00074               PERFORM ADD-A-STUDENT.
00075           READ-CARD. READ IN-FILE AT END GO TO WRITE-OUT.
00076               PERFORM CHECKER THRU END-CHECKER VARYING
00077               I FROM 1 BY 1 UNTIL I > KOUNT.
00078               PERFORM ADD-A-STUDENT.
00079               GO TO READ-CARD.
00080           CHECKER. IF STUD-NO-IN EQUAL STUD-NO (I)
00081               GO TO FOUND-IT.
00082           END-CHECKER. EXIT.
00083           FOUND-IT. IF STUD-NAME-IN NOT EQUAL TO STUD-NAME (I) PERFORM
00084               ERR-RTN. ADD 1 TO TESTS (I). ADD GRADE-IN TO
00085               POINTS (I). IF MAX LESS THAN TESTS (I)
00086               MOVE TESTS (I) TO MAX. GO TO READ-CARD.
00087           ADD-A-STUDENT. ADD 1 TO KOUNT.
00088               MOVE STUD-NO-IN TO STUD-NO (KOUNT).
00089               MOVE STUD-NAME-IN TO STUD-NAME (KOUNT).
00090               MOVE 1 TO TESTS (KOUNT).
00091               MOVE GRADE-IN TO POINTS (KOUNT).
00092           NO-DATA. DISPLAY '***ERROR*** NO DATA, RUN ABORTED'
00093               UPON SYSOUT.
00094               STOP RUN.
00095           ERR-RTN. DISPLAY
00096               '***ERROR*** STUDENT NUMBERS MATCH BUT NAMES DO NOT...',
00097               STUD-NO-IN UPON SYSOUT. DISPLAY
00098               'FIRST NAME ASSUMED... ', STUD-NAME (I) UPON SYSOUT.
00099               DISPLAY ', TEST SCORE IS ', GRADE-IN UPON SYSOUT.
00100               MOVE STUD-NAME (I) TO STUD-NAME-IN.
00101           WRITE-OUT. PERFORM HEADER-RTN.
00102               PERFORM CALC VARYING I FROM 1 BY 1 UNTIL I > KOUNT.
00103               CLOSE IN-FILE, OUT-FILE. STOP RUN.
00104           CALC. COMPUTE AVE-OUT ROUNDED = POINTS (I) / TESTS (I).
00105               COMPUTE AVE-OUT-2 ROUNDED = POINTS (I) / MAX.
00106               MOVE STUD-NAME (I) TO STUD-NAME-OUT.
00107               MOVE STUD-NO (I) TO STUD-NO-OUT.
00108               MOVE TESTS (I) TO TESTS-OUT.
00109               MOVE POINTS (I) TO POINTS-OUT.
00110               ADD 1 TO L. IF L NOT LESS THAN 20 PERFORM HEADER-RTN.
00111               WRITE OUT-LINE FROM STUDENT-OUT AFTER ADVANCING 2.
00112           HEADER-RTN. MOVE 0 TO L.
00113               WRITE OUT-LINE FROM HEADER AFTER ADVANCING TOP-OF-PAGE.
```

10.9 Sample Program 10B: Student Test Score Computation

Sample Output

STUDENT NO.	NAME	TESTS	TOTAL PTS.	AVERAGE	AVE. FOR MAX. TESTS
123456	MARK S. FISTES	03	282	94.00	94.00
907254	MOE D. LAWN	02	142	71.00	47.33
414960	TED E. BARE	03	271	90.33	90.33
073335	ARTHUR RITUS	01	63	63.00	21.00
456978	TERRY BULL	03	116	38.67	38.67
052124	DON E. BROOK	03	259	86.33	86.33
334434	ED CETERA	03	284	94.67	94.67
626803	HORACE RACE	03	271	90.33	90.33
625295	SID E. SLICKER	03	261	87.00	87.00
346069	MATT MADDIX	03	288	96.00	96.00
558452	MOE MENTUM	03	250	83.33	83.33
485912	LEM N. JUICE	03	272	90.67	90.67
161653	BUD N. GENIUS	03	285	95.00	95.00
829932	WARREN PEACE	03	288	96.00	96.00
534487	MAX E. MUM	03	300	100.00	100.00
121736	PHIL OSOPHY	03	140	46.67	46.67
019020	FRAN TASTIK	03	180	60.00	60.00
623375	PAT N. LEATHER	01	84	84.00	28.00
212831	ANN TEEK	03	244	81.33	81.33

EXERCISES

1 How many times will the procedure named ADD-R be executed by the following PERFORM statement?

```
(a)  PERFORM ADD-R VARYING K FROM 1 BY 1 UNTIL K = 100.
(b)  PERFORM ADD-R VARYING K FROM 1 BY 1 UNTIL K > 100.
(c)  PERFORM ADD-R K TIMES.   (where K has the value 0)
```

2 In the following coding correct the errors, if any.

```
        (a) PERFORM R1 10 TIMES.
            STOP RUN.
        R1. IF X = Y GO TO R2.
            ADD 5 TO X.
        R2. ADD 10 TO Y.
```

10 The PERFORM Statement

```
         (b)  PERFORM P1 N TIMES
         ...
     P1       MOVE A TO B
              ADD 1 TO N.
```

Given the following partial coding in the DATA DIVISION,

```
     77  N       PIC S999.
     77  J       PIC S999.
     77  K       PIC S999.
     77  SUM-X   PIC S9(6)V99.
     77  SUM-XZ  PIC S9(6)V99.
     77  X-MAX   PIC S9(3)V99.

     02  X OCCURS 100 TIMES PIC S9(3)V99.
     02  Y OCCURS 50 TIMES.
         03  Z OCCURS 100 TIMES PIC S9(3)V99.
     02  SUM-XY OCCURS 50 TIMES PIC S9(6)V99.
```

write a routine by using the PERFORM statement to accomplish the following tasks:

3 Find the maximum element of X's and store the value in X-MAX.

4 Calculate $SUM - X = X(1) + X(2) + \cdots + X(N)$, where $N \leq 100$.

5 Calculate $SUM - XZ = X(1)Z(1) + X(2)Z(2) + \cdots + X(N)Z(N)$.

6 Calculate for each I, $SUM - XY(I) = Y(I,1)X(1) + Y(I,2)X(2) + \cdots + Y(I,N)X(N)$, where $N \leq 100$.

7 Modify Sample Program 2B (page 00) by using the PERFORM statement so that the program will print four (that is, across the page) address labels per row.

8 Write a program to produce customer overdue payment reports as follows:

Input Description: **CUSTOMER-RECORD**

Column	Content
1–20	customer name
21–26	acct. ID
27–40	customer address
41	number of overdue payments (1 through 6)
42–77	six overdue payments fields
42–47	current overdue payment XXX.XX
48–53	payment that is one month but not two months overdue
.	
.	
.	
72–77	payment that is at least five months overdue
78–80	not used

Output Description

Print the information from each card and total overdue payment on one line at the end of the report. Print the grand total for all overdue payments with appropriate column headings.

Part II
Advanced Topics

11
Magnetic Tape Processing

Magnetic tape has been used by many installations as a faster means of input/output than punched cards. It is relatively inexpensive, has high storage capacity, and is less cumbersome than cards. Thus, magnetic tape files are used most often and especially when a large volume of data is involved in processing.

11.1 MAGNETIC TAPE CHARACTERISTICS

A typical magnetic tape is 2400 feet long and ½ inch wide (see Fig. 11.1a). However, there are other types of tapes that have lengths of 1200, 600, or 250 feet. Data are recorded on the tape by magnetizing a certain spot on its surface.

There are basically two different types of tape for coding: 9-track and 7-track. Figure 11.1b illustrates coding on a 9-track tape. In this tape, a magnetized spot contains 9 vertical positions, called bits. Each bit may or may not be activated (that is, turned on or recorded). Different combinations of "on" and "off" bits are used to record different characters on the tape. In Fig. 11.1b, the on-bits are represented by a "1" in a bit position, the off-bits by a space.

Notice in Fig. 11.1b that there is always an odd number of activated spots to represent a character. This is accomplished by coding each character with 8 bits and using the last bit as a parity or check bit. A parity bit is used to ensure the accuracy of the tape operation. As a tape is read or written, each character is checked for its corrected parity. If the parity does not match the tape unit it will report the parity error. However, it is up to the individual program to handle such error occurrences. In most cases, parity errors are caused by dust on the tape. Rereading that portion of the tape would remove the dust and thus correct the error.

Fig. 11.1a A typical tape reel.

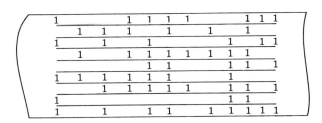

Fig. 11.1b Nine-track tape.

11.2 TAPE DENSITY AND ACCESS RATE

The number of characters that can be recorded on a tape depends on the density of the tape. Density is commonly expressed in terms of bytes per inch (bpi). A byte is a set of bits that can be entered in a single column of tape. Some common densities are 200, 556, 800, 1600, and 6250 bpi. On a tape with 800 bpi, one can record 800 columns of data in one inch of tape. Thus, it is possible to record the contents of 288,000 cards on one 2400-foot reel of 800 bpi tape [2400 (feet) × 12 (inches/foot) × 10 (cards/inch)].

Access rate depends on the tape density and the speed of the tape drive. A typical tape drive can have speeds of 75, 125, and 200 inches per second. Thus, at 800 bpi, the maximum access rate is somewhere below 160,000 (800 × 200) characters per second. However, the average access rate is lower and depends on how the data are recorded, which will be discussed in the next section.

11.3 TAPE RECORDS, BLOCKS, AND INTERBLOCK RECORD GAP

Unlike punched cards, information recorded on a magnetic tape is not restricted to any fixed record size. It can be organized in the form of blocks with various formats. Each block of data in a tape may contain one or many logical records. However, blocks of records are physically separated on tape by a length of blank tape, averaging about 0.6 or 0.75 inches. This gap is called the interblock gap (IBG), which is automatically produced at the time of writing. It provides the necessary time for starting and stopping during the processing of writing or reading. Examples of interblock gaps are shown in Figs. 11.2 and 11.3.

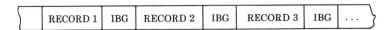

Fig. 11.2 Unblocked tape records.

| IBG | RECORD 1 | RECORD 2 | RECORD 3 | RECORD 4 | RECORD 5 | IBG |

Fig. 11.3 Blocked tape records.

Blocks

The use of blocks has an important effect on the storage capacity of the tape reel. To illustrate this, suppose that it is necessary to store 24,000 card records in a magnetic tape with a density of 800 bpi. If we "write" these records as one record per block as shown in Fig. 11.2, the total tape required would be 1700 feet, which is computed as follows:

$$(\underbrace{80 \times \frac{1}{800}}_{\text{length of each block (1 record per block)}} + \underbrace{0.75}_{\text{IBG}})/\underbrace{12}_{\text{12 inches/foot}} \times \underbrace{24,000}_{\text{number of blocks}} = 1700 \text{ feet.}$$

Note that because of the interblock gap (IBG) only 200 feet ($80/800 \times 1/12 \times 24,000$) out of the entire 1700 feet are actually used for storing data. The rest of the 1500 feet are "wasted" by the presence of IBG.

To improve the overall utilization of tape reels, consider that five records are grouped together into one physical block on a tape as shown in Fig. 11.3. The total tape required to record the entire file would be

$$(5 \times 80 \times \frac{1}{800} + 0.75)/12 \times \frac{24,000}{5} = 1.25 \times 400 = 500 \text{ feet.}$$

Thus we could have saved a considerable amount of tape by grouping five records together in one block (that is, $1700 - 500 = 1200$ feet of tape on reel).

Blocking records on a tape can also increase the processing efficiency. A tape file with 24,000 unblocked records would require a total of 24,000 start-go-stop actions to process the entire file. The same file with five records per block would require only 4800 (that is, 24,000/5) such I/O actions. Thus, considerable processing time can be saved as a result.

It should be noted that there is a drawback to blocking records since the program must provide enough core storage to contain the entire block of records for processing. Thus, if a tape file is blocked with 100 80-character records per block, it would require a minimum of 8000 bytes (characters) of core storage for the file. Such an amount of space might not be available. If this is indeed the case, the programmer must decrease the block size to fulfill the storage requirements.

Tape Labels

Tape labels are used to ensure that a correct tape file is being processed and not being inadvertently "scratched." These labels appear as the first and last pieces of data in the file. (Labels appearing in the beginning are called volume labels or leader labels, whereas those appearing in the end are known as the trailer labels, as shown in Fig. 11.4.)

Each installation usually has its own standard for creating and processing tape labels. In general, these labels typically contain information such as

file identifier,
creation date,
retention date,
security (password),
volume sequence indicator,
end-of-file indicator.

| HEADER LABELS | TM | TAPE FILE (records) | TM | TRAILER LABELS | TM |

Fig. 11.4 Tape labels.

For the IBM 360/370 systems, standard tape labels are automatically processed through the use of the job control language. The reader is urged to consult the local system manual for further information.

Load-Point, End-of-Reel Markers, and Tape Markers

Every tape reel has a load-point and end-of-reel marker to signify the beginning and end of the reel. These markers are aluminum strips located about 10 feet from each end, thus providing enough tape to allow threading or dismounting of the reels by the operator. When a tape reel is mounted, photoelectric cells in the tape unit automatically sense these markers as either the load-point marker (where reading or writing is to begin) or the end-of-reel marker. However, for reading, the tape unit recognizes only another special symbol, namely, tape mark (TM) as the end of file or reel (see Fig. 11.5). This tape mark is a unique character that marks the end of a file of information. The tape mark is generated automatically by the computer on the tape following the last record of the file when the file is created.

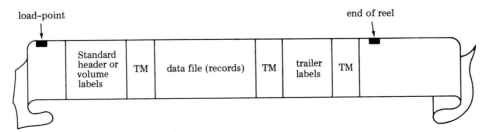

Fig. 11.5 TM symbol.

11.4 COBOL INSTRUCTIONS FOR PROCESSING TAPE FILES

COBOL program instructions for tape files are very similar to those of punched cards or printer files. These files are organized in a sequential manner, that is, records must be processed in the order in which they appear. In COBOL, there are several instructions that have special meaning for the processing of tape files. We will present these instructions here according to the program division. We begin with the ENVIRONMENT DIVISION, since there are no special instructions involved in the IDENTIFICATION DIVISION.

ENVIRONMENT DIVISION

SELECT and ASSIGN clause

The general format for the SELECT and ASSIGN clause is

$$\text{SELECT file-name}$$
$$\text{ASSIGN TO integer-1 system-name-1 [system-name-2]} \ldots$$
$$\left[\text{FOR } \underline{\text{MULTIPLE}} \left\{\begin{array}{c}\underline{\text{REEL}}\\ \underline{\text{UNIT}}\end{array}\right\}\right]$$

11.4 COBOL Instructions for Processing Tape Files

The SELECT and ASSIGN clauses for tape files are almost identical to the clauses for a card or printer file. The only essential difference is the system-name-1 specified for the I/O device. For the IBM 360/370 Systems, it may be specified as

(1) *Under OS*

```
       SELECT TAPE-FILE
              ASSIGN TO UT-2400-S-TAPEIN.
```

(2) *Under DOS*

```
       SELECT TAPE-FILE
              ASSIGN TO SYS010-UT-2400-S.
```

The initial UT stands for "utility," which is used to represent a tape file.

System-name-1 for other manufacturers' tape units is presented in Appendix A. For example, on a UNIVAC 1108 computer, it may be specified as

```
       SELECT TAPE-FILE
              ASSIGN TO UNISERVO.
```

MULTIPLE $\left\{\begin{array}{l}\underline{\text{REEL}}\\ \underline{\text{UNIT}}\end{array}\right\}$ option

In cases where a file consists of more than one reel, several tape units may be assigned for the file. For example, the statement

```
       SELECT MASTER-FILE
              ASSIGN TO UT-2400-S-TAPE1, UT-2400-S-TAPE2,
              UT-2400-S-TAPE3
              FOR MULTIPLE UNIT.
```

would inform the computer system (that is, the operating system) that there are three tape reels, namely, TAPE1, TAPE2, and TAPE3, for the MASTER-FILE. When the end of the reel at the first unit is reached (that is, TAPE1), the computer system would automatically switch to the second unit TAPE2 and start processing there. In most computers, the MULTIPLE REEL/UNIT clause is optional. It is there for the purpose of documentation and would thus be treated as a comment when specified.

RESERVE clause

The RESERVE clause permits the user to modify the number of input/output buffer areas allocated for the file processing:

$$\text{RESERVE}\left\{\begin{array}{l}\underline{\text{NO}}\\ \text{integer-1}\end{array}\right\}\text{ALTERNATE}\left[\begin{array}{l}\text{AREA}\\ \text{AREAS}\end{array}\right]$$

If the RESERVE clause is specified, the number of input/output buffer areas allocated is equal to the value of integer-1. For example, the statements

```
           SELECT A-FILE
               ASSIGN TO UT-2400-S-MASTER
               RESERVE 2 ALTERNATE AREAS.
```

would direct the computer to reserve two main memory areas for processing the A-FILE. If the RESERVE clause is omitted, the number of input/output areas allocated would depend on a particular computer system. For most of the computer systems, two alternate I/O areas are automatically reserved to make I/O overlap possible, thus speeding the execution time. Beginning programmers seldom use the RESERVE clause unless it is programmed for a very small computer with limited core storage.

I-O-CONTROL paragraph

The I-O-CONTROl is an optional paragraph that defines certain special techniques to be used in the program. The interested reader should consult the local manual for further description.

DATA DIVISION

We discussed the coding of the DATA DIVISION in Chapter 4. However, there are several entries that have some special meanings in processing the tape file. These entries are part of the file descriptions (FD):

BLOCK CONTAINS clause,
RECORDING MODE clause,
RECORD CONTAINS clause,
LABEL RECORDS clause,
VALUE clause.

BLOCK CONTAINS clause

The BLOCK CONTAINS clause is used to indicate the size of a physical record and takes the form

$$\underline{\text{BLOCK}} \text{ CONTAINS}[\text{integer-1 } \underline{\text{TO}} \text{ integer-2}] \left\{ \begin{array}{l} \text{RECORDS} \\ \text{CHARACTERS} \end{array} \right\}$$

where integer-1 and integer-2 are unsigned integers.

The BLOCK CONTAINS clause is required only when the physical record contains more than one logical record. Otherwise, this clause is not needed.

Example 1

A tape file has 40 records per block and each record is 80 characters long. In this case, the BLOCK CONTAINS clause is required and it may be any one of the following:

11.4 COBOL Instructions for Processing Tape Files

```
BLOCK CONTAINS 40 RECORDS
BLOCK CONTAINS 3200 CHARACTERS
BLOCK CONTAINS 3200
BLOCK 3200
```

Notice that in this example, unless the word RECORDS is specified, CHARACTERS is assumed.

Example 2

A magnetic tape file has 1 to 6 records per block. Each record contains 80 characters. The BLOCK CONTAINS clause is required here. Any one of the following statements is acceptable:

```
BLOCK CONTAINS 1 TO 6 RECORDS
BLOCK CONTAINS 80 TO 480 CHARACTERS
BLOCK CONTAINS 80 TO 480
BLOCK 80 TO 480
```

RECORDING MODE clause

The RECORDING MODE clause is used to indicate the format of the logical records within a file. If this clause is not included in the program, the COBOL compiler scans each record-description entry to determine the recording mode for the file. Thus the RECORDING MODE clause is never required. It is usually included for documentation purpose. The basic format of this clause is

RECORDING MODE is mode

The mode is specified either by F (fixed logical record size), U (unspecified; however, records must be unblocked), or V (logical records are variable in length and "blocks" may contain more than one logical record).

RECORD CONTAINS clause

The RECORD CONTAINS clause is used to specify the size of the logical record within a file. This clause is really never required since the actual size of each record is completely defined within the record-description entry. However, the programmer usually includes this clause in the coding for purposes of documentation. The exact format of the RECORD CONTAINS clause is

[RECORD CONTAINS[integer-1 TO]integer-2 CHARACTERS]

Example 3

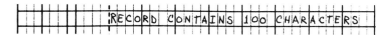

Example 4

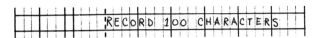

Example 5

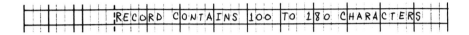

LABEL RECORDS clause

The LABEL RECORDS clause is the only clause required in the FD entry. This clause has been discussed in Chapter 4. However, it should be stressed that when

is coded, it indicates that labels exist for the file, and such labels conform to the installation's standard specification. However, if

is used, then it specifies that either

(1) no explicit labels to be created exist for the file, or
(2) the labels are nonstandard and the user wishes that the system would not invoke the standard procedure to process such labels. (Thus in this case, labels must be processed as data records if so desired.)

Example 6

A SALES-FILE is recorded on a magnetic tape. It contains SALES-REC, which is organized as 10 records per block with each record containing 80 characters. This file has no explicit label records. A complete FD and record description entry is shown in the following:

```
        DATA DIVISION.
   FD   SALES-FILE
        BLOCK CONTAINS 10 RECORDS
        RECORD CONTAINS 800 CHARACTERS
        LABEL RECORDS ARE OMITTED
        DATA RECORDS ARE SALES-REC.
   01   SALES-REC PIC X(80).
```

VALUE OF clause

The VALUE OF clause is used to specify the description of an item in the label records associated with a file. It takes the general form

11.4 COBOL Instructions for Processing Tape Files

$$\underline{\text{VALUE}} \; \underline{\text{OF}} \; \text{implementor-name-1 is} \; \begin{Bmatrix} \text{data-name-1} \\ \text{literal-1} \end{Bmatrix}$$
$$\left[, \text{implementor-name-2 is} \; \begin{Bmatrix} \text{data-name-2} \\ \text{literal-2} \end{Bmatrix} \dots \right]$$

where data-name-1 and data-name-2 must be specified in the WORKING-STORAGE section.

The VALUE OF clause has been implemented differently in different computers. For example, for IBM 360/370 systems, this clause is optional and serves only as documentation. (Information concerning the labels is specified through the use of job control statements.) However, for UNIVAC 1108, the VALUE OF clause is required whenever standard labels are used. A typical example is shown in Fig. 11.6.

```
        VALUE OF IDENTIFICATION IS 'MASTER-FILE'
        DATE-WRITTEN IS 101574.
```

Fig. 11.6 Coding of VALUE OF clause for UNIVAC 1108.

In this figure, the VALUE OF clause specifies the label identification as 'MASTER-FILE' and creation date as 101574. When processing an input file, the system would check these values with the value written in the label records. If these values do not match, the program would automatically be terminated. For an output file, the system's label routine would create standard labels with the information as given. Since the VALUE OF clause varies from one computer system to another, the reader is urged to consult the local manual for further details.

PROCEDURE DIVISION

All files must be "opened" before they can be processed and must be "closed" after the processing of that file is completed. The general format of OPEN statements relating to the tape files is as follows:

$$\text{OPEN} \begin{bmatrix} \underline{\text{INPUT}} \; \text{file-name} \; \begin{bmatrix} \text{REVERSED} \\ \text{WITH} \; \underline{\text{NO}} \; \underline{\text{REWIND}} \end{bmatrix} \dots \\ \underline{\text{OUTPUT}} \; \text{file-name} \; [\text{WITH} \; \underline{\text{NO}} \; \underline{\text{REWIND}}] \dots \\ [\underline{\text{I-O}} \; \text{file-name} \dots] \end{bmatrix}$$

The NO REWIND option means that the tape reel should not be rewound when the file is "opened." Rewind would cause the tape to position itself at its beginning. The NO REWIND option is used when processing a multifile reel. If the option is omitted, then rewind would automatically take place.

The REVERSED option is used for processing records of a tape file in reverse order, starting from the last record. When this option is specified, the OPEN command would cause the file to be positioned at the end of the file.

If the clause LABEL RECORDS ARE STANDARD were specified in the FD entries of the DATA DIVISION, the OPEN statement would automatically perform checking and/or writing of tape labels. For IBM 360/370 systems, this means that header labels are checked to ensure the correct identity of the input tape file. For the output file, the OPEN statement would cause the writing of header labels. On the other hand, if the clause LABEL RECORDS ARE OMITTED were specified, the checking and/or writing of labels would automatically be bypassed.

Some examples of OPEN statements are

```
OPEN INPUT UPDATE-FILE.
OPEN INPUT M-FILE OUTPUT C-FILE.
OPEN OUTPUT W-FILE, S-FILE, T-FILE.
```

CLOSE statement

The CLOSE statement for the tape file has the following format:

$$\text{CLOSE file-name-1} \left\{ \begin{array}{c} \text{REEL} \\ \text{UNIT} \end{array} \right\} \left[\text{WITH} \left\{ \begin{array}{c} \text{NO REWIND} \\ \text{LOCK} \end{array} \right\} \right]$$

Just like the OPEN statement, the action generated by the CLOSE statement depends on the "specification" of the LABEL RECORDS clause. If the LABEL RECORDS are specified as standard, the CLOSE statement would automatically cause the computer to initiate the end-of-file procedures. For the output file, this means the writing (that is, creation) of trailer labels before terminating the processing of the file. For the input file, the trailer labels would be automatically checked by the computer. If LABEL RECORDS ARE OMITTED were specified, trailer-label checking routines would be bypassed.

The CLOSE statement without the WITH NO REWIND or LOCK option would automatically rewind the tape reel at the end of the processing. The NO REWIND option would prevent such rewinding. This option is often used when a tape reel contains more than one file (that is, a multifile reel).

The LOCK option would unload the tape reel from the tape drive after rewinding. Thus, it prevents further processing of the same tape file. The purpose of the LOCK option is to prevent the accidental opening and misuse of a file whose data have already been processed.

Example 7. Automatic Rewind

Example 8. No Rewind

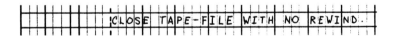

Example 9. Rewind and Unload

Here the tape file cannot be opened again within the same program.

READ/WRITE statements

The READ and WRITE statements are the same for tape files as for card or printer files. For a blocked tape file, the necessary blocking and deblocking functions are automatically taken care of by the computer without additional instructions from the programmer. For example, when a READ statement is executed for a blocked tape file, the first physical block is read from the tape into the computer storage area (this area is commonly known as the buffer area). However, only the first record of the block is made available to the program at this point. Each subsequent READ command will make the next sequential record in the buffer area (that is, storage area) available to the program as shown in Fig. 11.7. This process of making records in the buffer area available to the program will continue until all records in the buffer are processed. When this happens, the next READ command will again bring the next group of block records from the tape to the buffer area, repeating the deblocking process as outlined above.

The WRITE statement is executed exactly as the READ command except that it works in reverse order. When the first WRITE statement is executed, the record is transferred to the buffer area and no writing takes place on the tape. Subsequently WRITE commands for the same file will transfer more records to the buffer area. The actual writing on the tape reel takes place only when the buffer is full (that is, block reaches the desirable number of records) or the CLOSE statement is executed. In the latter case, the unfilled area in the block will be automatically padded by blanks before a physical tape write occurs.†

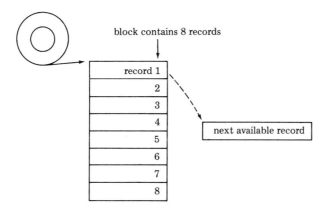

Fig. 11.7 Reading a block of records. Records are made available to the program one at a time in a sequential manner after each READ command.

11.5 VARIABLE-LENGTH RECORDS

The OCCURS . . . DEPENDING ON . . . Clause

All of the files described so far are of fixed length; that is, each record contained in the file has the same fixed length. However, there are times it is necessary to process records of different lengths in the same file. For instance, a major retail store may maintain a tape

---

† *Note:* To handle both nonstandard labels and READ/WRITE errors, one must use DECLARATIVE statements, which are beyond the scope of this text.

210   11 Magnetic Tape Processing

```
    FD  CUSTOMER-FILE
        LABEL RECORDS ARE STANDARD
        RECORDING MODE IS V
        BLOCK CONTAINS 20 RECORDS
        RECORD CONTAINS 7 TO 223 CHARACTERS
        DATA RECORD IS CUST-REC.
    01  CUST-REC.
        03 CUST-ID PIC X(5).
        03 UNPD-INV-N PIC 99.
        03 UNPD-INV-DATA OCCURS 0 TO 12 TIMES
                        DEPENDING ON UNPD-INV-N.
            05 DUE-DATE PIC 9(6).
            05 INV-ID PIC X(7).
            05 UNPD-AMT PIC S9(3)V99.
```

Fig. 11.8 File and record descriptions for variable-length file.

file containing the credit-card customers' records. Each of these records contains the customer's ID, followed by the due date and unpaid balance. The number of unpaid invoices varies from one customer to another, that is, some customers may have no unpaid balance while others may have as many as, say, twelve unpaid invoices. Certainly this file is best processed in a variable-length mode. The file and record description for this file might be as shown in Fig. 11.8. Note that the record length of each CUSTOMER-REC depends on the number of unpaid invoices (that is, UNPD-INV-N). However, this is specified by the clause

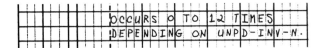

which has the general form

<u>OCCURS</u> integer-1 TO integer-2
<u>DEPENDING</u> ON data-name

where integer-1 and integer-2 represent the minimum and maximum number of times the data field may be repeated. Integer-1 may be zero, while integer-2 must be greater than zero and also greater than integer-1.

The DEPENDING ON option indicates that the exact number of times the data fields may be repeated is specified by the value of data-name. Thus, in Fig. 11.8, if the value of UNPD-INV-N is 3, then the data field UNPD-INV-DATA would repeat 3 times. The exact record layout in this case would have the form shown in Fig. 11.9.

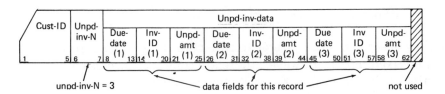

Fig. 11.9 An example of record layout specified by DEPENDING ON UNPD-INV-N.

11.6 SAMPLE PROGRAM 11A: CREATING A VARIABLE-LENGTH TAPE FILE

This sample program produces a file of variable-length records. These records contain the customer's identification, name, address, number of invoices outstanding, and a record of the invoices. The program does this by first reading a main record that contains the customer's ID, name, address, and the number of invoices that follow the main card. When the invoices are read, they contain the customer's ID, the sequence number of the card (01, 02, etc.), and the invoice data (due date, item ID, unpaid amount). The program then checks the invoice ID and sequence number. If they do not match the main record, data will be rejected with an error message. After all records are processed, the program will reopen the customer file to generate a printout.

Input Description: Main Record and Invoice Record

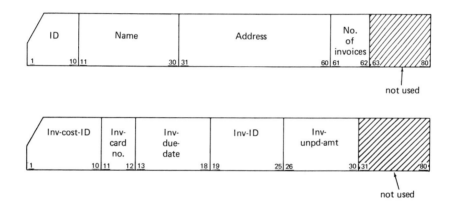

Sample Input

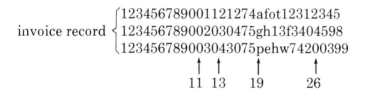

Source Listing

```
0C001            IDENTIFICATION DIVISION.
0C002            PROGRAM-ID.  'SAMPLE11A'.
0C003            AUTHOR.  LESTER THIERWECHTER.
CC004       ******************************************************************
CC005            ENVIRONMENT DIVISION.
C0006            CONFIGURATION SECTION.
0C007            SOURCE-COMPUTER.   IBM-370.
00008            OBJECT-COMPUTER.   IBM-370.
00009            INPUT-OUTPUT SECTION.
CC010            FILE-CONTROL.
00011                SELECT INVOICE-FILE ASSIGN TO UR-2501-S-CARDIN.
00012                SELECT CUSTOMER-FILE ASSIGN TO UT-2400-S-TAPEFILE.
CC013                SELECT PRINT-FILE ASSIGN TO UR-1403-S-PROUT.
CC014       ******************************************************************
```

```
00015           DATA DIVISION.
00016           FILE SECTION.
00017           FD  INVOICE-FILE
00018               LABEL RECORDS ARE OMITTED
00019               DATA RECORDS ARE MAIN-INVOICE-RECORD, INVOICE-RECORD.
00020           01  MAIN-INVOICE-RECORD.
00021               03  MAIN-INVOICE-ID         PIC X(10).
00022               03  MAIN-INVOICE-NAME       PIC X(20).
00023               03  MAIN-INVOICE-ADDRESS    PIC X(30).
00024               03  NUMBER-OF-INVOICES      PIC 99.
00025               03  FILLER                  PIC X(18).
00026           01  INVOICE-RECORD.
00027               03  INVOICE-CUSTOMER-ID     PIC X(10).
00028               03  INVOICE-CARD-NUMBER     PIC 99.
00029               03  INVOICE-DUE-DATE        PIC 9(6).
00030               03  INVOICE-ITEM-ID         PIC X(7).
00031               03  INVOICE-UNPAID-AMOUNT   PIC S9(3)V99.
00032               03  FILLER                  PIC X(50).
00033           FD  CUSTOMER-FILE
00034               LABEL RECORDS ARE STANDARD
00035               RECORDING MODE IS V
00036               BLOCK CONTAINS 20 RECORDS
00037               DATA RECORD IS CUSTOMER-RECORD.
00038           01  CUSTOMER-RECORD.
00039               03  CUSTOMER-ID             PIC X(10).
00040               03  CUSTOMER-NAME           PIC X(20).
00041               03  CUSTOMER-ADDRESS        PIC X(30).
00042               03  CUSTOMER-INVOICES       PIC 99.
00043               03  CUSTOMER-UNPD-DATA      OCCURS 0 TO 12 TIMES
00044                                           DEPENDING ON CUSTOMER-INVOICES.
00045                   05  CUSTOMER-DUE-DATE       PIC 9(6).
00046                   05  CUSTOMER-ITEM-ID        PIC X(7).
00047                   05  CUSTOMER-UNPAID-AMOUNT  PIC S9(3)V99.
00048           FD  PRINT-FILE
00049               LABEL RECORDS ARE OMITTED
00050               DATA RECORD IS PRINT-LINE.
00051           01  PRINT-LINE.
00052               03  FILLER                  PIC X.
00053               03  PRINT-AREA              PIC X(132).
00054           WORKING-STORAGE SECTION.
00055           77  KOUNTER                     PIC 99.
00056           77  CHECK-NUMBER                PIC 99.
00057           77  CHECK-ID                    PIC X(10).
00058      ****************************************************************
00059           PROCEDURE DIVISION.
00060               OPEN INPUT INVOICE-FILE, OUTPUT CUSTOMER-FILE.
00061           BEGIN.
00062               PERFORM READ-A-CARD.
00063           NEW-MAIN-INVOICE-CARD.
00064               MOVE SPACES TO CUSTOMER-RECORD.
00065               MOVE MAIN-INVOICE-ID TO CHECK-ID, CUSTOMER-ID.
00066               MOVE MAIN-INVOICE-NAME TO CUSTOMER-NAME.
00067               MOVE MAIN-INVOICE-ADDRESS TO CUSTOMER-ADDRESS.
00068               MOVE NUMBER-OF-INVOICES TO CHECK-NUMBER, CUSTOMER-INVOICES.
00069               PERFORM READ-A-CARD THRU MOVE-DATA
00070                   VARYING KOUNTER FROM 1 BY 1
00071                       UNTIL KOUNTER > CHECK-NUMBER.
00072               WRITE CUSTOMER-RECORD.
00073               GO TO BEGIN.
00074           READ-A-CARD.
00075               READ INVOICE-FILE AT END GO TO END-OF-JOB.
00076           MOVE-DATA.
00077               IF INVOICE-CARD-NUMBER NOT NUMERIC
00078                   DISPLAY '****NOT ENOUGH INVOICES****'
00079                   CUSTOMER-ID, '**', CUSTOMER-NAME, '**', CUSTOMER-ADDRESS,
00080                   '**', CUSTOMER-INVOICES, '**NUMBER READ = ', KOUNTER,
00081                   UPON SYSOUT,
00082                   WRITE CUSTOMER-RECORD, GO TO NEW-MAIN-INVOICE-CARD, ELSE
00083               IF INVOICE-CUSTOMER-ID NOT EQUAL TO CHECK-ID
00084                   DISPLAY '****ID CHECK FAILED****', CHECK-ID, '**',
00085                   INVOICE-RECORD UPON SYSOUT, ELSE
00086               IF INVOICE-CARD-NUMBER NOT EQUAL TO KOUNTER
00087                   DISPLAY '****SEQUENCE ERROR****', KOUNTER, '**',
00088                   INVOICE-RECORD UPON SYSOUT, ELSE
00089               MOVE INVOICE-DUE-DATE TO CUSTOMER-DUE-DATE (KOUNTER)
00090               MOVE INVOICE-ITEM-ID TO CUSTOMER-ITEM-ID (KOUNTER)
00091               MOVE INVOICE-UNPAID-AMOUNT TO
00092                   CUSTOMER-UNPAID-AMOUNT (KOUNTER).
00093           END-OF-JOB.
00094               SUBTRACT 1 FROM KOUNTER.
00095               IF KOUNTER NOT EQUAL CHECK-NUMBER
00096                   DISPLAY '****NOT ENOUGH INVOICES****'
00097                   CUSTOMER-ID, '**', CUSTOMER-NAME, '**', CUSTOMER-ADDRESS,
00098                   '**', CUSTOMER-INVOICES, '**NUMBER READ = ', KOUNTER,
00099                   UPON SYSOUT, WRITE CUSTOMER-RECORD.
00100               CLOSE INVOICE-FILE, CUSTOMER-FILE.
00101           OPEN-AGAIN.
00102               OPEN INPUT CUSTOMER-FILE, OUTPUT PRINT-FILE.
00103           READ-MORE.
00104               READ CUSTOMER-FILE INTO PRINT-AREA AT END
00105                   CLOSE CUSTOMER-FILE, PRINT-FILE, STOP RUN.
00106               WRITE PRINT-LINE AFTER ADVANCING 2 LINES.
00107               GO TO READ-MORE.
```

EXERCISES

1 What are the basic characteristics of magnetic tape? How is information recorded on it?

2 Define the following terms:
IBG,
TM,
load point,
bpi.

3 Compute the amount of tape for each of the following files:
  (a) file contains 60,000 records,
      80 characters per record,
      5 records per block,
      tape density is 800 bpi;
  (b) same as (a) except each block contains 20 records.

4 What are tape labels? Why they are necessary?

5 An inventory file is stored on a magnetic tape with a standard label. The file contains both order records and master records. Each block has 10 order records and 2 master records. Each order record contains 40 characters, whereas each master record has 80 characters. Write a complete file description for this file.

6 Write a program to create a master file on tape from data on punched cards. The file should be organized as 10 records per block. After the master file is created, reopen it and print a report as indicated below.

Input Description: Inventory Record

Column	Content
1–6	item number (numeric)
7–10	not used
11–30	item name
31–35	quantity on hand (numeric)
36–80	not used

(Input should be arranged in ascending order of item number.)

Output

(1)   Master Record (10 records per block)

Position	Content
1–6	item number
7–25	item name
26–30	quantity on hand

(2) Printed Report

INVENTORY REPORT

ITEM NO.	ITEM NAME	QUANTITY ON HAND
X⟷X	X⟷X	X⟷X

7 Write a program to update the master file as created in Exercise 7 by processing a deck of transaction records. These transaction records should be sorted in sequence as the tape records. There are two types of transaction records: type 1 requires adding the quantity, while type 2 requires subtracting the quantity. If the corresponding master record cannot be found for a transaction record, an appropriate error message should be displayed. Input and output descriptions of this program are given.

Input Description

(1) Master file (same as in Exercise 7)

(2) Transaction record (punched card)

Column	Content
1–6	item number
7	transaction code (must be either 1 or 2)
8–10	not used
11–15	quantity
16–80	not used

Output Description

(1) New master file (updated)

(2) Transaction report (printed)

TRANSACTION REPORT AS OF XX/XX/XX

ITEM NO	ITEM NAME	TRAN CODE	QUANTITY ON HAND	BALANCE
XXXXXX	X⟷X	X	XXXXX	XXXXX

12
Sorting and Searching

12.1 SORT FEATURE

In business data processing, sorting data according to a specific sequence is often a necessity. However, such a task is too complicated for an individual programmer to program. For this reason, most computer manufacturers supply a SORT/MERGE module (that is, program) for use in sorting data files. In COBOL, the programmer can gain direct access to the sorting capability of the system by including a SORT statement and other elements of the SORT feature in the source program.

To use the SORT feature, the programmer must provide additional information in the ENVIRONMENT, DATA, and PROCEDURE DIVISIONS of the source program. A brief discussion of the most commonly required information is presented here. However, the reader is urged to consult the local COBOL manual for more detailed specifications.

ENVIRONMENT DIVISION

In this division, the programmer must write SELECT statements for all files used as input and output for the SORT module and for each file to be sorted. (These are called sort-files.) The SELECT statement takes the same format as discussed in Chapter 3. In the format

```
          SELECT sort-file-name
              ASSIGN TO [integer-1] system-name-1
              [system-name-2] ...
```

sort-file-name identifies the sort-file to the compiler.

For example, the statement

```
          SELECT SORT-STUDENT-FILE
              ASSIGN TO UT-2400-S-TAPE1.
```

would assign the sort-student-file to a magnetic tape unit.

DATA DIVISION

For each file to be sorted, the programmer must include a sort-file-description (SD) entry and its associated record description entries in the FILE SECTION of the DATA DIVISION. These entries describe the physical structure, record names, and characteristics of the data files to be sorted. The basic format of these entries is

SD sort-file-name
  [DATA $\begin{Bmatrix} \underline{RECORD} \text{ IS} \\ \underline{RECORDS} \text{ ARE} \end{Bmatrix}$ data-name-1, data-name-2, . . .]
  [<u>RECORD</u> CONTAINS [integer-1 <u>TO</u>] integer-2 CHARACTERS]
  record-description entries . . .

The reader should note the following:

(1) The only required entry in the sort-file-description is

SD sort-file-name

where SD is the level indicator (a COBOL reserved word), which identifies the beginning of the sort-file-description and must precede the file-name.

(2) The LABEL clause is not required or permitted here (some COBOL compilers would treat the LABEL clause as a comment if present, but others would consider it an error).

(3) The format of the record-description-entry varies according to the type of record to be described. All rules for record-description entries as discussed in Chapter 4 apply here.

An example of these entries follows; other examples are given in Section 12.2.

Example: SD Entries

```
       DATA DIVISION.
       FILE CONTROL.
   FD  MASTER-FILE
           LABEL RECORDS ARE OMITTED.
   01  CARD-REC    PIC X(80).
   SD  TEMP-FILE
           DATA RECORDS ARE TEMP-REC.
   01  TEMP-REC.
       03  FILLER   PIC X(10)
       03  NAME-1   PIC X(20)
       03  FILLER   PIC X(50)
           (other FD entries)
```

Procedure Division

In this division, the programmer specifies a SORT statement providing information that controls the sorting operation. This information directs the sorting operation to obtain records to be sorted either from an input procedure or by transferring records from another file. At the completion of the sorting operation, it makes each record available in sorted order, either to an output procedure or by transferring them to another output file.

The general format of the SORT statement is

SORT file-name-1
  ON $\begin{Bmatrix} \underline{\text{DESCENDING}} \\ \underline{\text{ASCENDING}} \end{Bmatrix}$ KEY {data-name-1} ...
  $\left[\text{ON } \begin{Bmatrix} \underline{\text{DESCENDING}} \\ \underline{\text{ASCENDING}} \end{Bmatrix} \text{ KEY {data-name-2} ...}\right] ...$
  $\begin{Bmatrix} \underline{\text{USING}} \text{ file-name-2} \\ \underline{\text{INPUT PROCEDURE}} \text{ IS section-name-1}[\underline{\text{THRU}} \text{ section-name-2}] \end{Bmatrix}$
  $\begin{Bmatrix} \underline{\text{GIVING}} \text{ file-name-2} \\ \underline{\text{OUTPUT PROCEDURE}} \underline{\text{ IS}} \text{ section-name-3}[\underline{\text{THRU}} \text{ section-name-4}] \end{Bmatrix}$

In the general format, file-name-1 is the name given in the sort-file-description entry that describes the record to be sorted. The ASCENDING and DESCENDING options specify whether records are to be sorted in an ascending or descending sequence, based on one or more sort keys. Each key is specified by the data-name and must be described in the records associated with the sort-file-name.

The INPUT PROCEDURE option directs the sorting operation to obtain records for the sort-file by executing procedures or sections as specified (a RELEASE command must be used to transfer records to the sorted files—this command will be discussed in Section 12.3), while the USING option is used to obtain records for file-name-1 (that is, the sort-file) by transferring the entire file from file-name-2.

The OUTPUT PROCEDURE option specifies that at the completion of the sorting procedure, program control will automatically branch to the designated section so that the user can access the sorted-file and proceed to perform additional processing. (A RETURN command must be used to obtain the access of the sorted-file. This command will be discussed in Section 12.3.) However, if the GIVING option is used, records in sorted order will be automatically transferred to the designated file (that is, file-name-3) without any further work by the user. A complete sample program illustrating how these tasks are accomplished is given in Section 12.3.

There are many rules and restrictions governing the use of the SORT statement. These rules and restrictions are often hardware dependent. It is indeed desirable to consult the local system manual (that is, "COBOL Programmer's Guide") before embarking on any serious project involving sorting.

However, to clarify the use of the SORT statement somewhat, two complete programs will be presented.

12.2 SAMPLE PROGRAM 12A: COBOL SORT FEATURE WITH USING/GIVING OPTION

```
        PROCEDURE DIVISION.
        SORT-R SECTION.
            SORT WK-FILE
                ON DESCENDING KEY WK-BALANCE
                   ASCENDING KEY WK-ACCT-ID
                USING ACCT-FILE
                GIVING ACCT-REPORT
        COMP-R SECTION.
        END-JOB.
            DISPLAY '*** END-OF-SORT***'
            STOP RUN.
```

218 12 Sorting and Searching

In this program, the file to be sorted is the WK-FILE, which is created by transferring records from the ACCT-FILE. (This is specified by the USING clause, that is, USING ACCT-FILE.)

After this is accomplished, records on the WK-FILE are then sorted according to the descending order of WK-BALANCE, and then in the ascending order of WK-ACCT-ID. (Both of these data fields are specified in the record description of WK-FILE; see the source listing.)

After the sorting operation is completed, the sorted records are automatically transferred to the REPORT-FILE before displaying the '***END-OF-SORT***' message and STOP RUN.

It should be noted that there are no OPEN and CLOSE statements when the USING/GIVING options are used. The system SORT feature will automatically take care of these functions. In fact, it would be incorrect to specify the OPEN/CLOSE statements here.

Program Logic

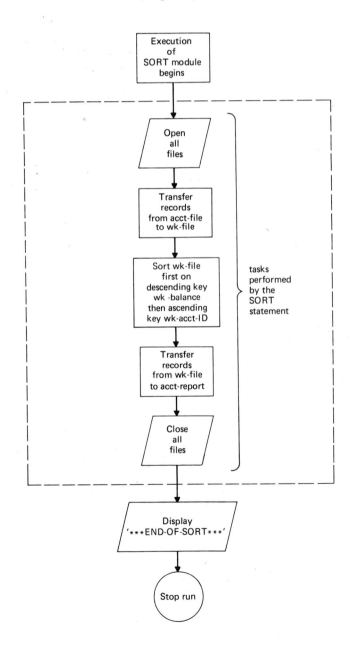

12.2 Sample Program 12A: COBOL SORT Feature with USING/GIVING Option

Source Listing

```
00001              IDENTIFICATION DIVISION.
00002              PROGRAM-ID. 'SAMPLE12A'
00003              AUTHOR. LESTER THIERWECHTER.
00004     ***************************************************************************
00005              ENVIRONMENT DIVISION.
00006              CONFIGURATION SECTION.
00007              SOURCE-COMPUTER. IBM-370.
00008              OBJECT-COMPUTER. IBM-370.
00009              INPUT-OUTPUT SECTION.
00010              FILE-CONTROL.
00011                  SELECT ACCT-FILE ASSIGN TO UR-2501-S-CARDIN.
00012                  SELECT ACCT-REPORT ASSIGN TO UR-1403-S-PROUT.
00013                  SELECT WK-FILE ASSIGN TO DA-2314-S-DSKFILE.
00014     ***************************************************************************
00015              DATA DIVISION.
00016              FILE SECTION.
00017              FD  ACCT-FILE
00018                  LABEL RECORDS ARE OMITTED
00019                  DATA RECORD IS ACCT-REC.
00020              01  ACCT-REC.
00021                  04  ACCT-ID     PIC  X(6).
00022                  04  FILLER      PIC  X(4).
00023                  04  AMT-REC     PIC  S9(5)V99.
00024                  04  FILLER      PIC  X(3).
00025                  04  BALANCE     PIC  S9(5)V99.
00026                  04  FILLER      PIC  X(53).
00027              FD  ACCT-REPORT
00028                  LABEL RECORDS ARE OMITTED
00029                  DATA RECORD IS PRINT-AREA.
00030              01  PRINT-AREA      PIC  X(121).
00031              SD  WK-FILE
00032                  DATA RECORD IS WK-REC.
00033              01  WK-REC.
00034                  04  WK-ACCT-ID  PIC  X(6).
00035                  04  FILLER      PIC  X(4).
00036                  04  WK-AMT-REC  PIC  S9(5)V99.
00037                  04  FILLER      PIC  X(3).
00038                  04  WK-BALANCE  PIC  S9(5)V99.
00039                  04  FILLER      PIC  X(53).
00040     ***************************************************************************
00041              PROCEDURE DIVISION.
00042              SORT-R SECTION.
00043                  SORT WK-FILE ON
00044                      DESCENDING KEY WK-BALANCE,
00045                      ASCENDING KEY WK-ACCT-ID,
00046                      USING ACCT-FILE,
00047                      GIVING ACCT-REPORT.
00048              COMP-R SECTION.
00049              END-SORT.
00050                  DISPLAY '***END OF SORT***' UPON CONSOLE.
00051                  STOP RUN.
```

Lines 00031–00039: SORT-FILE description

Lines 00043–00047: SORT command

Sample Output

```
J45676     2750174    9876543
W37173       85902    9876543
123456     1234567    9876543
343434     8912345    9876543
001234       91051      12389
001235      186395      12389
773454        3838        199
```

Job Control Statements for IBM 360/370 Systems SORT Feature

Since the COBOL SORT feature depends on the system's SORT/MERGE module, there are certain system requirements one must follow when the SORT feature is used. For the IBM OS system, the SORT/MERGE module requires a minimum of three working data sets, namely, SORTWK01, SORTWK02, and SORTWK03. These data sets must be specified in the JCL statements. Figure 12.1 presents a set of JCL cards that could be used with Sample Program 12A. Readers who use other computer systems should consult the local manual for appropriate job control cards.

```
//JOB CARD
//*PASSWORD NULLPASS
//EXEC COBACG,PARM='APOST,XREF'
//COB.SYSIN DD *
   (source program here)
/*
//GO.DSKFILE DD UNIT=SYSDA,SPACE=(TRK,2)
//GO.SORTWK01 DD UNIT=SYSDA,SPACE=(TRK,(200,20,2),,CONTIG)
//GO.SORTWK02 DD UNIT=SYSDA,SPACE=(TRK,(200,20,2),,CONTIG)
//GO.SORTWK03 DD UNIT=SYSDA,SPACE=(TRK,(200,20,2),,CONTIG)
//GO.SORTLIB DD DSNAME=SYS1.SORTLIB,DISP=SHR
//GO.PROUT DD SYSOUT=A
//GO.CARDIN DD *
   (input data cards here)
/*
//
```

Fig. 12.1 OS JCL statements for Sample Program 12A.

12.3 SAMPLE PROGRAM 12B: COBOL SORT FEATURE WITH INPUT/OUTPUT PROCEDURE OPTIONS

The sample program presented here is a slight modification of the preceding program (thus, only the PROCEDURE DIVISION is given in the source listing). The only difference is that in this example, the INPUT PROCEDURE option is used so that the program first reads the ACCT-FILE and transfers to the WK-FILE only those records whose BALANCE field contains a positive value. Also, the OUTPUT PROCEDURE option is specified to handle the printout after the desired sorting operation is completed.

The RELEASE Statement

The RELEASE statement transfers data from the computer memory onto the sort-file. It takes the form

   RELEASE sort-record-name [FROM identifier-1].

It may be used *only* within the range of an INPUT PROCEDURE associated with the SORT statement (in this case, the SELECT-ACCT-REC SECTION). The sort-record-name must be a record in the sort-file. When the FROM option is used, it makes the RELEASE statement equivalent to the statement

   MOVE identifier-1 TO sort-record-name

followed by the RELEASE statement. For instance, the statement

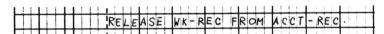

would have the same effect as

```
            MOVE ACCT-REC TO WK-REC.
            RELEASE WK-REC.
```

12.3 Sample Program 12B: COBOL SORT Feature with INPUT/OUTPUT PROCEDURE Options

The RETURN Statement

The RETURN statement obtains individual records in a sorted order from the sorted-file. Its general format is

<u>RETURN</u> sort-file-name RECORD [<u>INTO</u> identifier]
[AT <u>END</u> imperative-statement]

where sort-file-name is the name given in the sort-file description entry.

The RETURN statement works very much like a READ statement. For instance, the statement

```
           RETURN WK-FILE INTO TEMP-REC.
```

is essentially saying "read a record from WK-FILE and move it to TEMP-REC."

However, the difference is that the RETURN statement may only be applied to SORT-FILE within the range of an OUTPUT PROCEDURE. Also, the sort-file will be automatically "opened" and "closed" by the system sort feature. Thus it would be incorrect to write

```
           RETURN SORT-FILE INTO TEMP-REC
               AT END CLOSE SORT-FILE.
```

Program Description

This program produces a sorted listing of the input data using the internal SORT package with the INPUT and OUTPUT PROCEDURES options. It reads an account file whose records contain the account-id, amount received, and balance. Next the program sorts the records in descending order of balance and then in ascending order of account-id. After the records are sorted they are printed out.

Input Description: ACCT-REC

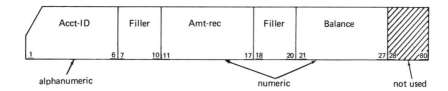

Sample Input

```
     1       6    10      17    21      27
     ↓       ↓    ↓       ↓     ↓       ↓
     343434       8912345        9876543
     w37173       0085902        9876543
     001234       0091051        0012389
     j45676       2750174        9876543
     001235       0186395        0012389
     773454       0003838        0000199
     123456       1234567        9876543
```

Source Listing

```
CC063              PROCEDURE DIVISION.
CC064              SORT-R SECTION.
00065                  SORT WK-FILE ON
CC066                      DESCENDING KEY WK-BALANCE,
CC067                       ASCENDING KEY WK-ACCT-ID,
00068                  INPUT PROCEDURE IS SELECT-ACCT-REC,
00069                       OUTPUT PROCEDURE IS PRINT-REPORT.
0C070              END-SORT.
00071                  DISPLAY '***END OF SORT***' UPON CONSOLE.
0C072                  STOP RUN.
00073              SELECT-ACCT-REC SECTION.
00074              OPEN-1.
0C075                  OPEN INPUT ACCT-FILE.
0C076              READ-SELECT.
0C077                  READ ACCT-FILE AT END GO TO END-OF-INPUT.
00078                  IF BALANCE IS GREATER THAN ZERO THEN
00079                      RELEASE WK-REC FROM ACCT-REC.
00080                  GO TO READ-SELECT.
00081              END-OF-INPUT.
00082                  CLOSE ACCT-FILE.
00083              PRINT-REPORT SECTION.
00084              OPEN-2.
0C085                  OPEN OUTPUT ACCT-REPORT.
CC086                  MOVE CURRENT-DATE TO TODAY-DATE.
00087                  WRITE PRINT-AREA FROM REPORT-HEADING
00088                      AFTER ADVANCING NU-PAGE.
CC089                  WRITE PRINT-AREA FROM HEADING-1 AFTER ADVANCING 3 LINES.
0C090                  WRITE PRINT-AREA FROM SUB-1 AFTER ADVANCING 1 LINES.
00091              READ-PRINT.
00092                  RETURN WK-FILE AT END GO TO END-OF-OUTPUT.
00093                  MOVE WK-ACCT-ID TO ACCT-ID-P.
00094                  MOVE WK-AMT-REC TO AMT-REC-P.
00095                  MOVE WK-BALANCE TO BALANCE-P.
00096                  WRITE PRINT-AREA FROM LINE-1 AFTER ADVANCING 1 LINES.
00097                  GO TO READ-PRINT.
00098              END-OF-OUTPUT.
00099                  CLOSE ACCT-REPORT.
00100                  STOP RUN.
```

- Lines CC064–00069: SORT command
- Lines 00070–00082: INPUT procedure
- Lines 00083–00100: OUTPUT procedure

Sample Output

```
WEEKLY CHARGE ACCOUNT REPORT AS OF 06/17/75

ACCOUNT ID    AMOUNT RECEIVED        BALANCE
-------------------------------------------------
  J45676       $27,501.74          $98,765.43
  W37173       $     859.02        $98,765.43
  123456       $12,345.67          $98,765.43
  343434       $89,123.45          $98,765.43
  001234       $     910.51        $***123.89
  001235       $  1,863.95         $***123.89
  773454       $      38.38        $*****1.99
```

output description same as Sample Program 6A, p. 97

12.4 INDEXED NAME AND SET STATEMENT

The topics of table handling and subscripting were discussed in Chapter 9. In this section, an alternative notion, namely, indexing in table handling, will be presented.

To illustrate the use of indexing, consider the following tables:

```
01  VENDOR-LIST.
    03  VENDOR-ENTRY OCCURS 30 TIMES.
        05  ID PIC 9(5).
        05  NAME PIC X(25).
```

As discussed in Chapter 9, we know that entries of this table can be referred to by the use of subscripts. For instance, if SUB is defined as

```
77  SUB PIC 99.
```

with a value of 10, then ID (SUB) would refer to the tenth entry of the ID field.

The same table, however, can be referred to by using indexing. This can be accomplished through the use of the INDEXED BY clause as shown in the following:

```
01  VENDOR-TABLE.
    03  VENDOR-ENTRY OCCURS 30 TIMES
            INDEXED BY K.
        05  ID PIC 9(5).
        05  NAME PIC X(25).
```

In this particular example, K is an index-name defined by the INDEXED BY clause. This clause causes a field named K to be set aside automatically by the compiler for use as an index to the entries in the table. The expression ID (K) would refer to a particular entry in the table depending on the value in K. However, there is a distinct difference between the subscript and the index. The value in an index-name does not represent the actual subscript of the table; instead it represents a displacement from the beginning of the table in the actual internal machine storage layout. For instance, the storage layout for the VENDOR-TABLE may appear as in Fig. 12.2.

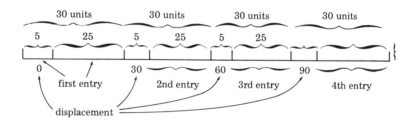

Fig. 12.2. Storage layout for VENDOR-TABLE.

Thus, a value of 30 in K would not refer to the 30th entry in the table; it really refers to the second entry in the table. The value of K for the nth entry is computed by the formula

$$(n-1) \times \text{(the length of a table entry)}.$$

Thus, for the VENDOR-TABLE, the subscript associated with the 4th entry is 4, while the index associated with it would have the value 90 (that is, $(4-1) \times 30$).

The use of the index-name on a table in general enhances the program execution and is definitely more efficient than the use of subscripts. Also, the index-name plays an indispensable role in the use of the SEARCH command, which will be discussed later.

SET Statement

The SET statement establishes reference points for table handling operations by setting index-names associated with table elements. The SET statement has two different formats:

Format 1

$$\underline{\text{SET}} \left\{ \begin{array}{l} \text{index-name-1} \\ \text{identifier-1} \end{array} \right\} \underline{\text{TO}} \left\{ \begin{array}{l} \text{index-name-2} \\ \text{identifier-2} \\ \text{literal-1} \end{array} \right\}$$

Format 2

$$\underline{\text{SET}} \text{ index-name-3} \left\{ \begin{array}{l} \underline{\text{UP}}\ \underline{\text{BY}} \\ \underline{\text{DOWN}}\ \underline{\text{BY}} \end{array} \right\} \left\{ \begin{array}{l} \text{identifier-3} \\ \text{literal-2} \end{array} \right\}$$

All identifiers must be either an index data item or an elementary numeric item described as an integer. When a literal is used, it must be a positive (or unsigned) integer. Index-names must be related to a given table through the INDEXED BY option of the OCCURS clause.

In format 1, the SET command is used to initialize the index-name or transfer values between index-names and other elementary data items. When this format is used, one of the operands (that is, index-name-1, identifier-1, index-name-2, identifier-2, or literal-1) must be an index-name.

Format 2 is used to alter the value of an index-name as specified as shown in the following examples:

(1) The statement SET K TO 10 would automatically set the value of K to the value referred to by the 10th entry in the table. Needless to say, K must be an index-name associated with one specific table.

(2) The statement SET K TO ACCT-ID would set the value of the index-name K to the value corresponding to the same entry as referred to by the data-name ACCT-ID. That is, if ACCT-ID contains value 5, then K would be set to the value corresponding to the 5th entry in the table. It should be noted that the statement MOVE ACCT-ID TO K would be incorrect since K is an index-name, and not a data name.

(3) The statement SET K BY 1 would automatically increment the index-name K by the length of a table entry. Thus K would have the value referred to in the next entry of a table. However, it would be incorrect to write ADD 1 TO K since K is an index-name.

12.5 SEARCH STATEMENT

The SEARCH verb is a special COBOL feature to facilitate searching through the entries of a table for an entry that satisfies a particular condition. There are two types of SEARCH commands: linear (sequential) and binary.

Linear (Sequential) Search

Linear search would search an entire table by checking each entry of the table, starting from the current index setting, one by one until a given condition is met. The format of the linear search is

$$\begin{array}{l} \underline{\text{SEARCH}} \text{ table-name} \\ \quad [\text{AT } \underline{\text{END}} \text{ imperative-statement-1}] \\ \quad \underline{\text{WHEN}} \text{ condition-1} \left\{ \begin{array}{l} \text{imperative-statement-2} \\ \underline{\text{NEXT SENTENCE}} \end{array} \right\} \\ \quad \left[\underline{\text{WHEN}} \text{ condition-2} \left\{ \begin{array}{l} \text{imperative-statement-2} \\ \underline{\text{NEXT SENTENCE}} \end{array} \right\} \right] \ldots \end{array}$$

where table-name is the name of the table to be searched. Condition-1, condition-2, etc., may be any condition as described in Chapter 8. The exact use of the SEARCH statement is perhaps best explained by the following example:

Suppose the following table were defined to contain 12 valid charge account numbers for a retail store:

```
       01  CHGE-ACCT-VALUES.
           03  FILLER PIC X(36)
               VALUE 'M51M61M7IM81M91N01N10N20N30N40X51X52'.
       01  CHGE-ACCT-TABLE REDEFINES CHGE-ACCT-VALUES.
           03  CHGE-ACCT OCCURS 12 TIMES
               INDEXED BY SUB
               PIC X(3).
```

Then the following coding could be used to search this table and to check whether an inputted charge number is one of the twelve valid account numbers (we assume that ACCT-ID is the data name containing the account number to be validated):

```
       PROCEDURE DIVISION.
            :
       ACCT-ID-VALIDATION.
           SET SUB TO 1.
           SEARCH CHGE-ACCT-TABLE
               AT END GO TO INVALID-ACCT-R,
               WHEN CHGE-ACCT (SUB) = ACCT-ID,
                   GO TO VALID-ACCT-R.
            :
       VALID-ACCT-R.
            :
       INVALID-ACCT-R.
            :
```

Here, the SET statement is used to initialize the index-name SUB to the value that would refer to the first entry of the table. The SEARCH statement would have the program compare the ACCT-ID with each of the charge account numbers in the table (starting with the first one) until a matching number is found. In this case, the program would branch to VALID-ACCT-NO-R. (Note that this is specified by the WHEN phrases.) If a matching number is not found when the end of the table is reached, the program would branch to INVALID-ACCT-R. The program flow chart for this routine is shown in Fig. 12.3.

Linear search is suitable for a table with relatively few entries. In case the table to be searched contains a large number of entries, the binary type of SEARCH statement should be utilized. This is discussed next.

Binary Search

The format of a binary search statement is very similar to that of linear search. It takes the form

$$\underline{\text{SEARCH ALL}}\ \text{table-name}$$
$$[\text{AT END imperative-statement-1}]$$
$$\underline{\text{WHEN}}\ \text{condition-1} \begin{Bmatrix} \text{imperative-statement-2} \\ \underline{\text{NEXT}}\ \underline{\text{SENTENCE}} \end{Bmatrix}$$
$$\left[\underline{\text{WHEN}}\ \text{condition-2} \begin{Bmatrix} \text{imperative-statement-3} \\ \underline{\text{NEXT}}\ \underline{\text{SENTENCE}} \end{Bmatrix}\right]$$

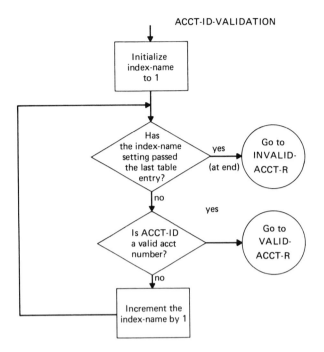

Fig. 12.3 Flowchart for linear search routine.

Notice that the only difference between the binary and the linear search formats is that a COBOL reserved word ALL is added to the word SEARCH. However, in order to implement a binary search statement, the elements of the table must be arranged in either ascending or descending order of a particular key (that is, element) to be searched. This requires the use of a special option in the OCCURS clause when defining a table. This special option takes the form

$$\underline{\text{OCCURS}} \text{ integer } \underline{\text{TIMES}} \left\{ \begin{array}{l} \underline{\text{ASCENDING}} \\ \underline{\text{DESCENDING}} \end{array} \right\}$$
$$\underline{\text{KEY}} \text{ IS key-name.}$$

To illustrate how this can be implemented, if we wish to use a binary search for the CHGE-ACCT-TABLE, we must make three changes from the linear search coding on p. 225 as follows: (1) the insertion of the ASCENDING key phase in the first coding; (2) the word ALL must follow the word SEARCH in the SEARCH statement in the second coding; and (3) the SET statement is deleted before the SEARCH statement. These changes are shown in the following coding:

```
01  CHGE-ACCT-TABLE REDEFINES CHG-ACCT-VALUES.
    03  CHGE-ACCT OCCURS 12 TIMES
            ASCENDING KEY IS CHG-ACCT
            INDEXED BY SUB
            PIC X(3).

    PROCEDURE DIVISION.

    ACCT-ID-VALIDATION.
        SEARCH ALL CHGE-ACCT-TABLE
            AT END GO TO INVALID-ACCT-R
            WHEN CHGE-ACCT (SUB) = ACCT-ID
                GO TO VALID-ACCT-R.
```

Binary search always starts the search operation at the midpoint of a table. In our example, the comparison would start at CHGE-ACCT (6). If ACCT-ID is lower, the next comparison would start at CHGE-ACCT (3), which is the middle term of the lower half of the table. If ACCT-ID is higher, the next comparison would start at the upper half of the table. Thus, after each comparison, if a matching entry is not found, the search operation would eliminate half of the remaining entries. Hence, for a table with 1000 entries, the binary search would reach any entry in the table in a maximum of 10 comparisons, while the linear search would require an average of 500 comparisons. For this reason the binary search is strongly recommended for searching large tables.†

EXERCISES

1. Give the SORT command as shown:

   ```
   SORT DK-FILE
        ASCENDING KEY SOC-SEC-NO
        USING STUDENT-FILE
        GIVING REPORT-A.
   ```

   (a) Which file contains the data to be sorted?
   (b) Which file is the sort-file?
   (c) Which file is described in an SD entry?
   (d) Which file contains the sorted data?

2. Given the following data, state the output that would be produced by the SORT command

   ```
   SORT SORT-FILE
        DESCENDING KEY AMT
        ASCENDING KEY DATA-1, ACCT-ID.
   ```

   (a) **Input**

DATE-1	AMT	ACCT-ID
113075	74231	12345
113075	21011	13456
093075	10012	11612
081075	74231	12344
113075	74231	10111

---

† The number 10 is arrived at by the fact that $2^{10} = 1024$. Thus a table with exactly 1024 entries would require a maximum of 10 comparisons in a binary search.

(b) Input

ACCT-ID	DATE-1	AMT
A 1234	061275	10050
O 1134	061275	10050
1134	061275	10050
B 1234	110175	81006
1234	110175	68100

3 Modify Sample Program 7A by using COBOL SORT features so that the report will list each department in ascending order.

4 Modify Programming Exercise 8-21 by using COBOL SORT features so that the report will list the students in alphabetical order.

5 The XXX medical center maintains its billing records on punched cards in the following format:

Column	Content
1–20	patient's name
21–29	patient's social security number
30	not used
31–40	last name of patient's doctor
41–47	amount due, XXXXX.XX
48–53	due date, mm/yy/dd
54–80	not used

Write a program to perform the following:

(a) Use the COBOL SORT feature to sort the billing record in alphabetical order according to doctor. Then the billing records for a given doctor should be sorted in ascending order of due date.

(b) Print a billing report. The billing report should be broken down by doctor as shown:

```
XXX         MEDICAL BILLING SUMMARY        PAGE XX
                  DOCTOR X⟵⟶X
    NAME        DUE DATE              $ AMOUNT
    X⟵⟶X       mm/dd/yy              $ XX,XXX.XX
      .            .                       .
      .            .                       .
    X⟵⟶X       mm/dd/yy              $ XX,XXX.XX
                              TOTAL  $XXX,XXX.XX
```

The program should also print a total amount for the entire report.

13
Program Checkout: Testing and Debugging

After a programmer has written a program, it is his responsibility to make sure that the program does what it is expected to, in any possible situation that it is likely to encounter. This phase of programming is called *program checkout*. The program is tested and if, as often will happen, it either fails to run, or does not run as it was intended, then we "debug" the program, that is, take steps to find and correct errors ("bugs").

The errors we encounter can be divided into two classes, based on their types. On the one hand, we can have language or *syntax* errors—for example, a reserved word misspelled or a paragraph name punched in the wrong margin. On the other hand, we can have a program that is syntactically correct, but when it runs it does not perform properly. Here we have a *logical* error, an error in program design.

We can also divide errors into two classes, depending on when the error makes itself known, that is, either during compilation or during actual running or execution of the program. *Compile-time* errors generally tend to be syntax errors, while *run-time* errors tend to be of the logical type. (Run-time errors are also called *object-time* errors since they occur during the execution of the machine language program, called an *object program*, produced by the compiler from the COBOL program, called the *source program*.)

13.1 COMPILE-TIME ERRORS[†]

These errors are the easiest to make, but since COBOL provides excellent diagnostic messages, they are also the easiest to find and correct.

In addition to producing the object program, the compiler gives a listing of the COBOL source program and following that a list of diagnostic messages, telling the programmer of the existence and location of syntax (and sometimes logical) errors encountered during compilation.

---

† Error messages explained in this chapter are IBM oriented. Readers who utilize other computers should consult local COBOL manuals.

13 Program Checkout: Testing and Debugging

```
OC001        IDENTIFICATION DIVISION.
OC002        PROGRAM-ID.  ERRORPGM.
OC003        AUTHOR.  ROBERT J. SMITH.
OC004        ENVIRONMENT DIVISION.
OC005        CONFIGURATION SECTION.
OC006        SOURCE-COMPUTER.  IBM-370.
OC007        OBJECT-COMPUTER.  IBM-370.           ← FILE-CONTROL paragraph name missing
OC008        INPUT-OUTPUT SECTION.
OC009            SELECT IN-FILE, ASSIGN TO UR-2540R-S-CARDIN.
OC010            SELECT OUT-FILE, ASSIGN TO UR-1403-S-PROUT.
OC011        DATA DIVISION.
OC012        FILE SECTION.
OC013        FD  IN-FILE
OC014            LABEL RECORDS ARE OMITTED.
00015        01  IN-RCD.                          ← period missing here
OC016            02  NAME-IN     PIC A(20).
OC017            02  NUMERIC-DATA-IN  PIC 9(4).
OC018            02  OTHER-DATA-IN    PIC X(56).
OC019        FD  OT-FILE                          ← OUT-FILE misspelled OT-FILE.
OC020            LABEL RECORDS ARE OMITTED.
OC021        01  OUT-RCD.
OC022            02  NAME-OUT    PIC A(20).
OC023            02  NUMERIC-DATA-OUT  PIC 9(4).
OC024            02  OTHER-DATA-OUT    PIC X(56).
OC025        WORKING-STORAGE SECTION.
OC026        77  IND-ITEM    PIC 9(1)  VALUE 5.
OC027        PROCEDURE DIVISION.
OC028        OPEN-UP.
OC029            OPEN INPUT IN-FILE, OUTPUT OUT-FILE.
OC030        READS.
OC031            READ IN-FILE, AT END GO TO END-OF-JOB.
OC032        MOVES.
OC033            MOVE NAME-IN TO NAME-OUT.
OC034            MOVE OTHER-DATA-IN TO OTHER-DATA-OUT.
OC035        COMPS.
OC036            COMPUTE NUMERIC-DATA-OUT = IND-ITEM * NUMERIC-DATA-IN.
OC037        WRITES.
OC038            WRITE OUT-RCD.
OC039            GO TO READS.
OC040        END-OF-JOB.
OC041            CLOSE IN-FILE, OUT-FILE, STOP RUN.
```

Fig. 13.1 Source listing with errors.

```
CARD   ERROR MESSAGE
 9     IKF1003I-W    FILE-CONTROL PARAGRAPH NAME MISSING. ASSUMED PRESENT.
16     IKF1043I-W    END OF SENTENCE SHOULD PRECEDE 02 . ASSUMED PRESENT.
20     IKF1056I-E    FILE-NAME NOT DEFINED IN A SELECT. DESCRIPTION IGNORED.
26     IKF1087I-W    ' IND-ITEM ' SHOULD NOT BEGIN A-MARGIN.
29     IKF3001I-E    OUT-FILE NOT DEFINED. DELETING TILL LEGAL ELEMENT FOUND.
33     IKF3001I-E    NAME-OUT NOT DEFINED. DISCARDED.
34     IKF3001I-E    OTHER-DATA-OUT NOT DEFINED. DISCARDED.
36     IKF3001I-E    NUMERIC-DATA-OUT NOT DEFINED. STATEMENT DISCARDED.
38     IKF3001I-E    OUT-RCD NOT DEFINED. STATEMENT DISCARDED.
41     IKF3001I-E    OUT-FILE NOT DEFINED. DELETING TILL LEGAL ELEMENT FOUND.
```

Fig. 13.2 Error messages for source listing of Fig. 13.1 (IBM ANS COBOL compiler).

For example, consider the program in Fig. 13.1. This is a very simple program that reads in a record from IN-FILE and moves the name and a miscellaneous data field to an output area. It then takes the quantity called NUMERIC-DATA-IN, multiplies it by an independent item called IND-ITEM, whose value is 5, and stores the result in the field called NUMERIC-DATA-OUT. Finally, the program prints the output record.

However, when running of the job was attempted, several errors were detected by the compiler. A listing of the error messages given by the compiler is shown in Fig. 13.2.

Each diagnostic consists of three parts. First is a number corresponding to a card number generated by the compiler for each card of the program. Ordinarily the number in the message is that of the card in which the error occurred. Occasionally, however, an error is not detected until information later in the program is processed, so it is possible that the card number is not exact.

After the card number comes an identifying number preceded by IKF. The IKF signifies that the message is from the IBM COBOL compiler. Each message the compiler prints has such a number. This identifying number is followed by a letter whose meaning is explained below.

Finally, there is the diagnostic message itself, telling what the error was and what, if any, corrective action the compiler took.

Each error has a *severity level* denoted by the letter W, C, E, or D following the message number. The severity levels for the IBM COBOL compiler are

W   Warning: indicates that an error was made in the source program. However, it is not serious enough to hinder the execution of the program.

C   Conditional: indicates that an error was made but that the compiler usually makes a corrective assumption. The statement containing the error is retained. Execution can be attempted for the debugging value.

E   Error: indicates that a serious error was made. Usually the compiler makes no corrective assumption. The statement containing the error is dropped. Execution of program should not be attempted.

D   Disaster: indicates that a serious error was made. Compilation is not completed. Results are unpredictable.

Associated with each severity level is a value of the *return code* issued to the operating system by the compiler after compilation:

  no error messages: 0
                W: 4
                C: 8
                E: 12
                D: 16

Now we take a closer look at Fig. 13.2. The first error is a warning. We forgot the FILE CONTROL paragraph name. This causes no problem—the compiler assumed it was there, and the error was not fatal.

The next error is an example of the card number not corresponding to the actual error. On card 15 we forgot to put a period after IN-RCD, but the compiler has no way of knowing that it should have been there until it has processed the next card. As a result, the error message refers to the *next* card number, 16. Again, however, it assumed the period was there and no harm was done.

But now in card 20 we have a serious error.† We have misspelled OUT-FILE as OT-FILE. This causes two problems. The first is an error right here since OT-FILE is not defined in a SELECT clause. We shall see the second problem presently.

The next error is a minor one in that we punched, in card 26, IND ITEM in column 11, within the A margin, instead of in column 12 or after. But the compiler treats it as if it were punched in column 12, so this error has no effect on the program.

We now see an example of how one error in COBOL can "snowball" into many error messages. Note that due to the fact that in card 20 we spelled OUT-FILE as OT-FILE the file description was ignored. Therefore, in the procedure division, every time we refer to the ignored file or to any data-item within that file, we get an error message saying that the item is not defined. Therefore, the beginner should not be discouraged on receiving a large number of error messages on his first attempted running of a program. In fact, in this program, the three warnings would not have hindered successful running, and there is actually *only one* real error, the misspelling of OUT-FILE. Fix it and *seven* error messages will disappear! (The same program, error free, is shown in Fig. 13.3.)

---

† Although the error is actually in line 19, the compiler reads it as line 20, which is the line containing a period at the end.

```
00001           IDENTIFICATION DIVISION.
00002           PROGRAM-ID.  ERRORPGM.
00003           AUTHOR.  ROBERT J. SMITH.
00004           ENVIRONMENT DIVISION.
00005           CONFIGURATION SECTION.
00006           SOURCE-COMPUTER.  IBM-370.
00007           OBJECT-COMPUTER.  IBM-370.
00008           INPUT-OUTPUT SECTION.
00009           FILE-CONTROL.
00010               SELECT IN-FILE, ASSIGN TO UR-2540R-S-CARDIN.
00011               SELECT OUT-FILE, ASSIGN TO UR-1403-S-PROUT.
00012           DATA DIVISION.
00013           FILE SECTION.
00014           FD  IN-FILE
00015               LABEL RECORDS ARE OMITTED.
00016           01  IN-RCD.
00017               02   NAME-IN     PIC A(20).
00018               02   NUMERIC-DATA-IN    PIC 9(4).
00019               02   OTHER-DATA-IN   PIC X(56).
00020           FD  OUT-FILE
00021               LABEL RECORDS ARE OMITTED.
00022           01  OUT-RCD.
00023               02   NAME-OUT    PIC A(20).
00024               02   NUMERIC-DATA-OUT    PIC 9(4).
00025               02   OTHER-DATA-OUT   PIC X(56).
00026           WORKING-STORAGE SECTION.
00027           77  IND-ITEM    PIC 9(2)    VALUE 5.
00028           PROCEDURE DIVISION.
00029           OPEN-UP.
00030               OPEN INPUT IN-FILE, OUTPUT OUT-FILE.
00031           READS.
00032               READ IN-FILE, AT END GO TO END-OF-JOB.
00033           MOVES.
00034               MOVE NAME-IN TO NAME-OUT.
00035               MOVE OTHER-DATA-IN TO OTHER-DATA-OUT.
00036           COMPS.
00037               COMPUTE NUMERIC-DATA-OUT = IND-ITEM * NUMERIC-DATA-IN.
00038           WRITES.
00039               WRITE OUT-RCD.
00040               GO TO READS.
00041           END-OF-JOB.
00042               CLOSE IN-FILE, OUT-FILE, STOP RUN.
```

Fig. 13.3 Source listing error free after corrections.

13.2 OBJECT-TIME ERRORS

Object- or run-time errors are often difficult to find, since we are not aided at this stage by elaborate diagnostic messages. Or possibly, as far as the computer is concerned, no error exists. For example, we may have incorrectly specified the size of a field and some digits or characters of a result do not get printed, or we may have incorrectly written

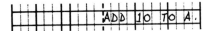

instead of

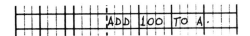

These are errors that would not be detected by the computer.

On the other hand, there are other object-time errors (that is, logical errors) that can be detected by the computer. When this happens, it results in immediate termination of program execution. Some examples of this type of errors are as follows:

(1) Read or write a file that has not been opened.
(2) Read a file that was opened as output.
(3) Perform calculation on a numeric field that contains nonnumeric data.
(4) The value of a subscript exceeds the size of a table as specified in an OCCURS clause.

To help the programmer debug any of these object-time errors, the COBOL compiler provides special features. The features include the TRACE, EXHIBIT, and ON statements. These comprise what is known as *debug language.* These statements can be used within the program, or in a special *debug packet* placed after its last statement. Programmers can use these features to trace the progress of the program and print the indicative information as they go along, eventually pinpointing the source of the problem.

When all else fails, we can resort to a *dump* of part of the computer's main storage, and by using this, determine the statement that was executing when failure occurred.

13.3 READY/RESET TRACE STATEMENT

This statement has the form

$$\left\{ \begin{array}{l} \underline{\text{READY}} \\ \underline{\text{RESET}} \end{array} \right\} \underline{\text{TRACE}}$$

After the statement READY TRACE is executed, each time the execution of a section or paragraph name begins, the compiler-generated card number of that paragraph or section name is printed out.

Since we may only need the tracing function for a particular section or paragraph that we suspect of causing a problem, we can place the READY TRACE in such a position that it gets executed just before control passes to the name of interest. Once control has left the area being investigated, if we see to it that a RESET TRACE statement gets executed, this stops the functioning of the previous READY TRACE.

```
0C001          IDENTIFICATION DIVISION.
0C002          PROGRAM-ID.  ERRORPGM.
0C003          AUTHOR.  ROBERT J. SMITH.
0C004          ENVIRONMENT DIVISION.
0C005          CONFIGURATION SECTION.
0C006          SOURCE-COMPUTER.  IBM-370.
0C007          OBJECT-COMPUTER.  IBM-370.
0C008          INPUT-OUTPUT SECTION.
0C009          FILE-CONTROL.
0C010              SELECT IN-FILE, ASSIGN TO UR-2540R-S-CARDIN.
0C011              SELECT OUT-FILE, ASSIGN TO UR-1403-S-PROUT.
0C012          DATA DIVISION.
0C013          FILE SECTION.
0C014          FD  IN-FILE
0C015              LABEL RECORDS ARE OMITTED.
0C016          01  IN-RCD.
0C017              02  NAME-IN    PIC A(20).
0C018              02  NUMERIC-DATA-IN  PIC 9(4).
0C019              02  OTHER-DATA-IN    PIC X(56).
0C020          FD  OUT-FILE
0C021              LABEL RECORDS ARE OMITTED.
0C022          01  OUT-RCD.
0C023              02  NAME-OUT   PIC A(20).
0C024              02  NUMERIC-DATA-OUT  PIC 9(4).
0C025              02  OTHER-DATA-OUT    PIC X(56).
0C026          WORKING-STORAGE SECTION.
0C027          77  IND-ITEM   PIC 9(2)   VALUE 5.
0C028          PROCEDURE DIVISION.
0C029          OPEN-UP.
0C030              OPEN INPUT IN-FILE, OUTPUT OUT-FILE.
0C031          READS.
0C032              READ IN-FILE, AT END GO TO END-OF-JOB.
0C033              READY TRACE.                              ←——— TRACE statement
0C034          MOVES.
0C035              MOVE NAME-IN TO NAME-OUT.
0C036              MOVE OTHER-DATA-IN TO OTHER-DATA-OUT.
0C037          COMPS.
0C038              COMPUTE NUMERIC-DATA-OUT = IND-ITEM * NUMERIC-DATA-IN.
0C039          WRITES.
0C040              RESET TRACE.
0C041              WRITE OUT-RCD.
0C042              GO TO READS.
0C043          END-OF-JOB.
0C044              CLOSE IN-FILE, OUT-FILE, STOP RUN.
```

Fig. 13.4a Source program with the READY TRACE statement.

Fig. 13.4b Results of the READY TRACE statement.

Figure 13.4a shows a program with the tracing function added to the PROCEDURE DIVISION. We have inserted the READY TRACE just before the MOVES paragraph. We stop tracing by a RESET TRACE just after the WRITES paragraph to demonstrate that each time we go beyond this card tracing stops and only begins again after we go back to the READS paragraph.

Figure 13.4b shows the results of the trace. We can see that we passed card number 39, the WRITES paragraph, three times before failure, indicating that for this run we had bad data in the fourth card.

Note that the output listing for the TRACE statement is on the system logical output device, as explained in the next section on the EXHIBIT statement.

EXHIBIT Statement

The EXHIBIT statement, in any of its three forms, allows us to display the value of one or more data items, and/or one or more nonnumeric literal messages.

The format for the EXHIBIT statement is

$$\text{EXHIBIT} \begin{Bmatrix} \underline{\text{NAMED}} \\ \underline{\text{CHANGED NAMED}} \\ \underline{\text{CHANGED}} \end{Bmatrix} \begin{Bmatrix} \text{identifier-1} \\ \text{nonnumeric-} \\ \text{literal-1} \end{Bmatrix} \begin{Bmatrix} \text{identifier-2} \\ \text{nonnumeric-} \\ \text{literal-2} \end{Bmatrix} \dots$$

Any nonnumeric literal will be displayed followed by a blank.

Each time an EXHIBIT NAMED statement is executed, the name of each data item (its identifier) in the statement and an equals sign will be printed, followed by the present value of the item. Any nonnumeric literal message in the EXHIBIT statement will also be printed.

Consider the following program segment:

```
        IF-PARA.
            ADD YEARLY-SALARY TO SALARY-TOTAL.
            IF YEARLY-SALARY IS NOT LESS THAN 100000.00
              ADD 1 TO BIG-SHOT-COUNTER.
            EXHIBIT NAMED
                 'WE ARE IN IF-PARA'
                  BIG-SHOT-COUNTER
                  SALARY-TOTAL.
        NEXT-PARA.
```

13.3 READY/RESET TRACE Statement

```
0C001            IDENTIFICATION DIVISION.
0C002            PROGRAM-ID.  JOBNO-5.
CC003            AUTHOR.  FRANCES PALMIERI.
0C004            ENVIRONMENT DIVISION.
0C005            CONFIGURATION SECTION.
0C006            SOURCE-COMPUTER.  IBM-370.
0C007            OBJECT-COMPUTER.  IBM-370.
0C008            INPUT-OUTPUT SECTION.
0C009            FILE-CONTROL.
0C010                SELECT IN-FILE, ASSIGN TO UR-2540R-S-CARDIN.
0C011                SELECT OUT-FILE, ASSIGN TO UR-1403-S-PROUT.
CC012            DATA DIVISION.
0C013            FILE SECTION.
CC014            FD   IN-FILE
0C015                LABEL RECORDS ARE OMITTED.
0C016            01   IN-RCD.
0C017                02  PERSON-ID    PIC X(4).
0C018                02  YEARLY-SALARY   PIC 9(6)V9(2).
0C019                02  FILLER       PIC X(68).
0C020            FD   OUT-FILE
0C021                LABEL RECORDS ARE OMITTED.
0C022            01   OUT-RCD.
0C023                02  FILLER    PIC X.
0C024                02  OUT-LINE  PIC X(120).
0C025            WORKING-STORAGE SECTION.
CC026            77   BIG-SHOT-COUNTER   PIC 9(3)    VALUE ZERO.
CC027            01   SALARY-LINE.
0C028                02  SALARY-TOTAL   PIC 9(7)V9(2)   VALUE ZEROS.
0C029                02  FILLER         PIC X(111)      VALUE SPACES.
0C030            PROCEDURE DIVISION.
0C031            OPEN-UP.
CC032                OPEN INPUT IN-FILE, OUTPUT OUT-FILE.
0C033            CLEARS.
0C034                MOVE SPACES TO OUT-RCD.
0C035            READS.
0C036                READ IN-FILE, AT END GO TO END-OF-JOB.
0C037            IF-PARA.
0C038                ADD YEARLY-SALARY TO SALARY-TOTAL.
0C039                IF YEARLY-SALARY IS NOT LESS THAN 100000.00
0C040                    ADD 1 TO BIG-SHOT-COUNTER.
0C041                EXHIBIT NAMED
0C042                    'WE ARE IN IF-PARA'       ⎫
CC043                    BIG-SHOT-COUNTER          ⎬  EXHIBIT statement
CC044                    SALARY-TOTAL.             ⎭
0C045            NEXT-PARA.
0C046                GO TO READS.
CC047            END-OF-JOB.
0C048                MOVE SALARY-LINE TO OUT-LINE.
CC049                WRITE OUT-RCD.
0C050                MOVE SPACES TO OUT-LINE.
0C051                WRITE OUT-RCD.
0C052                MOVE BIG-SHOT-COUNTER TO OUT-LINE.
CC053                WRITE OUT-RCD.
0C054            CLOSE-UP.
CC055                CLOSE IN-FILE, OUT-FILE.
0C056                STOP RUN.
```

Fig. 13.5a Source program with the EXHIBIT NAMED statement.

```
WE ARE IN IF-PARA BIG-SHOT-COUNTER = 000 SALARY-TOTAL = 000650000
WE ARE IN IF-PARA BIG-SHOT-COUNTER = 000 SALARY-TOTAL = 002835300
WE ARE IN IF-PARA BIG-SHOT-COUNTER = 001 SALARY-TOTAL = 012835325
WE ARE IN IF-PARA BIG-SHOT-COUNTER = 002 SALARY-TOTAL = 038198025
WE ARE IN IF-PARA BIG-SHOT-COUNTER = 002 SALARY-TOTAL = 038765546
WE ARE IN IF-PARA BIG-SHOT-COUNTER = 002 SALARY-TOTAL = 039887646
WE ARE IN IF-PARA BIG-SHOT-COUNTER = 002 SALARY-TOTAL = 046011229
WE ARE IN IF-PARA BIG-SHOT-COUNTER = 003 SALARY-TOTAL = 056011229
WE ARE IN IF-PARA BIG-SHOT-COUNTER = 003 SALARY-TOTAL = 066011228
WE ARE IN IF-PARA BIG-SHOT-COUNTER = 003 SALARY-TOTAL = 066825449
```

Fig. 13.5b Results of the EXHIBIT NAMED statement.

A source listing with the EXHIBIT NAMED statement is shown in Fig. 13.5a, and the output caused by the EXHIBIT NAMED might be as shown in Fig. 13.5b.

There are times when we might want to display a value only if that value has changed since the last time it was printed. In such cases we can use the EXHIBIT CHANGED NAMED. For example,

```
    IF-PARA.
        ADD YEARLY-SALARY TO SALARY-TOTAL.
        IF YEARLY-SALARY IS NOT LESS THAN 100000.00.
            ADD 1 TO BIG-SHOT-COUNTER.
        EXHIBIT CHANGED NAMED 'WE ARE IN IF-PARA'
            BIG-SHOT-COUNTER SALARY-TOTAL.
    NEXT-PARA.
        :
```

Note in Fig. 13.6 that BIG-SHOT-COUNTER only got printed on those occasions when it changed. So did SALARY-TOTAL, but it changed with each piece of input data. Note also that the literal message will get printed each time, even if neither BIG-SHOT-COUNTER nor SALARY-TOTAL were to change.

The third form of the EXHIBIT statement, EXHIBIT CHANGED, will cause any literal in the statement to be printed each time the statement is executed, and the present value of each identifier in the statement, provided that its value has changed. However, the identifier itself, that is, the data item's name, will not be printed. We can tell which item's value has been printed, since the printout will have a fixed column format, unlike EXHIBIT CHANGED NAMED, the columns corresponding to the order of the identifiers in the EXHIBIT CHANGED statement. For example,

```
    IF-PARA.
        ADD YEARLY-SALARY TO SALARY-TOTAL.
        IF YEARLY-SALARY IS NOT LESS THAN 1000000.00
            ADD 1 TO BIG-SHOT-COUNTER.
        EXHIBIT CHANGED 'WE ARE IN IF-PARA' BIG-SHOT-COUNTER
            SALARY-TOTAL.
    NEXT-PARA.
        :
```

The output is shown in Fig. 13.7. Note that if there are no literals in an EXHIBIT CHANGED statement and none of the identifiers have changed value, a blank line will be printed. For an EXHIBIT CHANGED NAMED, no action at all is taken. Some additional comments on EXHIBIT:

```
WE ARE IN IF-PARA BIG-SHOT-COUNTER = C00 SALARY-TOTAL = 000650000
WE ARE IN IF-PARA SALARY-TOTAL = 002835300
WE ARE IN IF-PARA BIG-SHOT-COUNTER = C01 SALARY-TOTAL = 012835325
WE ARE IN IF-PARA BIG-SHOT-COUNTER = C02 SALARY-TOTAL = 038198025
WE ARE IN IF-PARA SALARY-TOTAL = 038765546
WE ARE IN IF-PARA SALARY-TOTAL = 039887646
WE ARE IN IF-PARA SALARY-TOTAL = 046011229
WE ARE IN IF-PARA BIG-SHOT-COUNTER = C03 SALARY-TOTAL = 056011229
WE ARE IN IF-PARA SALARY-TOTAL = 066011228
WE ARE IN IF-PARA SALARY-TOTAL = 066825449
```

Fig. 13.6 Results of the EXHIBIT CHANGED NAMED statement.

```
WE ARE IN IF-PARA C00 000650000
WE ARE IN IF-PARA     002835300
WE ARE IN IF-PARA C01 012835325
WE ARE IN IF-PARA C02 038198025
WE ARE IN IF-PARA     038765546
WE ARE IN IF-PARA     039887646
WE ARE IN IF-PARA     046011229
WE ARE IN IF-PARA C03 056011229
WE ARE IN IF-PARA     066011228
WE ARE IN IF-PARA     066825449
```

Fig. 13.7 Results of the EXHIBIT CHANGED without NAMED.

(1) The maximum length for each nonnumeric literal is 120 characters.
(2) The maximum length for each identifier, including any qualifiers required, is also 120 characters.
(3) The maximum value for each identifier is 256 bytes.
(4) On the first execution of an EXHIBIT CHANGED or EXHIBIT CHANGED NAMED statement, each identifier is considered changed and gets printed.

For IBM S/360/370 OS computer systems the EXHIBIT (and TRACE) statements require a SYSOUT DD statement in the JCL cards. For example

//GO.SYSOUT DD SYSOUT=A

Since this data set is separate from your output data set, the listing for the EXHIBIT and TRACE statements will more than likely be separate from your program's output.

For debugging, EXHIBIT statements, like TRACE statements, allow you to follow program flow. In addition, they also allow you to see the actual values of certain data items. This can be very helpful in determining why a program is not performing as expected.

ON (Count-Conditional) Statement

The ON statement is a conditional statement that allows the statements it contains to be executed only under specified condition. Its format is

$$\underline{\text{ON}} \text{ integer-1 } \underline{\text{AND EVERY}} \text{ integer-2 } \underline{\text{UNTIL}} \text{ integer-3}$$
$$\left\{ \begin{array}{lll} \text{imperative statement} & \underline{\text{ELSE}} & \text{statement} \ldots \\ \underline{\text{NEXT SENTENCE}} & \underline{\text{OTHERWISE}} & \underline{\text{NEXT SENTENCE}} \end{array} \right\}$$

An example would be

```
        ON 15 AND EVERY 3 UNTIL 24
          ADD A-COUNT TO B-COUNT,
          GO TO READ-PAR ELSE ADD C-COUNT TO D-COUNT
          GO TO COMPS-PAR.
```

The ON statement works as follows: A counter is set up before execution for each ON statement and initialized to zero. Each time control passes through an ON statement, 1 is added to its counter. If the count-condition, which is integer-1 + (integer-2 * K), for K = 0, 1, 2, etc., is satisfied, that is, if the counter is equal to integer-1 + (integer-2 * K) and not greater than integer-3, then the first imperative statement is executed.

In the example shown, the first 14 times the ON statement is passed, C-COUNT is added to D-COUNT and control passes to COMPS-PAR. But on the 15th, 18th, 21st and 24th times, A-COUNT gets added to B-COUNT and control passes to READ-PAR. On the intervening counts (16, 17, 19, 20, 22, 23) and on all passes from the 25th on, C-COUNT is again added to D-COUNT and control goes to COMPS-PAR.

Some further points:

Integer-1, integer-2, and integer-3 must be positive and not greater than 16,777,216. The ELSE/OTHERWISE may be omitted if it immediately follows the period for the ON sentence. For example,

```
          ON 3 AND EVERY 2 UNTIL 9 GO TO OUT-PAR.
```

238 13 Program Checkout: Testing and Debugging

Not all integers need be specified. Some possibilities are

If only integer-1 is specified, then the count-condition is satisfied only when control passes the ON statement integer-1 times. For example,

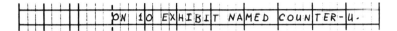

If integer-1 and integer-3 are specified, integer-2 is assumed to be 1. For example,

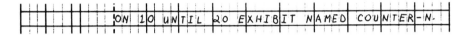

COUNTER-N gets displayed on the 10th through 20th passes inclusive.

If integer-1 and integer-2 are specified then no upper limit is assumed to exist. For example,

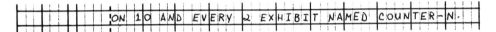

COUNTER-N gets displayed on the 10th pass and every even number thereafter.

Note that one or both imperative statements can actually be composed of several statements, as in our first example.

Although the imperative statements can be any valid COBOL statements, most of the time the ON statements will be used for debugging and will be concerned with TRACE and EXHIBIT statements. For example, suppose we know that we are having trouble processing data after the 500th record. We might use

```
            ON 500 AND EVERY 10 READY TRACE.
            ON 501 AND EVERY 10 RESET TRACE.
```

These statements will cause a trace on the 500th record, the 510th record, 520th record, etc.

One other point: If we should happen to make an error in an ON statement, the diagnostic message we receive may refer not to the ON statement itself, but to the card number of the statement immediately preceding it.

13.4 COMPILE-TIME DEBUGGING PACKET†

If we wish to insert some statements into a program temporarily for testing or debugging purposes, it is not always necessary to go through the entire program deck inserting a card here and there, as necessary, and then later going through the deck again to remove the temporary cards. Often all or at least most of the cards used for this purpose can be added to the deck together in what is known as a *debug* or *debugging packet*.

Each debug packet refers to a specific section or paragraph name in the PROCEDURE DIVISION. Following this, we place the statements we wish to add to that section or paragraph, punched in the *correct margins,* exactly as if they were in the main body of the

---

† Debugging packet is an IBM-oriented feature. Readers who utilize non-IBM machines may skip this section.

13.4 Compile-Time Debug Packet

program. They will then be compiled as if they were actually at that location. The format is

> DEBUG location
>   statements to be added after location in the program

Location is the name (qualified if necessary) of a section or paragraph in the main program.

Example

Suppose we have a program in which a counter called A-COUNTER is being incremented. Further, suppose that the next paragraph executed after the one in which the incrementing takes place is named COMPS-PAR, and that the program looks like this:

```
        COMPS-PAR.
            MOVE C-ITEM TO C-OUT.
            ADD 1 TO Q-ITEM.
            COMPUTE C-ITEM = X-ITEM + 5
        NEXT PAR.
```

If we add a debug packet at the end of the program,

```
        DEBUG COMPS-PAR
            EXHIBIT NAMED A-COUNTER.
```

the program will be executed as if it were written

```
        COMPS-PAR.
            EXHIBIT NAMED A-COUNTER.
            MOVE C-ITEM TO C-OUT.
            ADD 1 TO Q-ITEM.
            COMPUTE C-ITEM = X-ITEM + 5.
        NEXT-PAR.
```

Some things to note:

(1) The word DEBUG followed by location can be punched anywhere on the card from column 1 to 72. There can be no other text on this card.
(2) The DEBUG card and packet are placed immediately after the last statement of the program.
(3) There can be more than one debug packet, each with its own DEBUG card used with a program, but the same location name cannot be used on more than one DEBUG card.
(4) You can actually add section or paragraph names to the program by placing them inside a debug packet, but the added names cannot themselves be used as locations for other DEBUG cards.

240   13 Program Checkout: Testing and Debugging

(5) The statements you use may be any that you might use in the main body of a program, but keep the following in mind:
   (a) A PERFORM or ALTER† statement in a debug packet *may* refer to a procedure-name in any debug packet or in the main body of the program.
   (b) a GO TO statement in a debug packet *may not* refer to a procedure-name in another debug packet, but it *may* refer to a procedure-name in the main body of the PROCEDURE DIVISION.

Since the statements in the debug packet are executed as if they were actually in the program just after the section or paragraph name, if the added lines are not to be executed as the first lines of the section or paragraph, then it will be necessary in the debug packet to reproduce the entire section or paragraph including these added statements. This should then be followed by a GO TO referring to the next section or paragraph in the main body to which control is to be transferred. Figure 13.8a shows a job with a debug packet added and Fig. 13.8b gives the results. Since we wanted the READ to be executed before the ON statement, we had to repeat it in the debug packet. Can you see why we then had to add the GO TO IF-PARA in order that two cards would not be read on each pass through READS, one by the READ in the debug packet and one by the READ in the main body? Since statements added by a debug packet are only added to the PROCEDURE DIVISION, it is sometimes necessary to add some cards to the main body of the program in addition to using a debug

```
00030              PROCEDURE DIVISION.
00031              OPEN-UP.
00032                  OPEN INPUT IN-FILE, OUTPUT OUT-FILE.
00033              CLEARS.
00034                  MOVE SPACES TO OUT-RCD.
00035              READS.
00036                  READ IN-FILE, AT END GO TO END-OF-JOB.
00037              IF-PARA.
00038                  ADD YEARLY-SALARY TO SALARY-TOTAL.
00039                  IF YEARLY-SALARY IS NOT LESS THAN 100000.00
00040                      ADD 1 TO BIG-SHOT-COUNTER.
00041              NEXT-PARA.
00042                  GO TO READS.
00043              END-OF-JOB.
00044                  MOVE SALARY-LINE TO OUT-LINE.
00045                  WRITE OUT-RCD.
00046                  MOVE SPACES TO OUT-LINE.
00047                  WRITE OUT-RCD.
00048                  MOVE BIG-SHOT-COUNTER TO OUT-LINE.
00049                  WRITE OUT-RCD.
00050              CLOSE-UP.
00051                  CLOSE IN-FILE, OUT-FILE.
00052                  STOP RUN.
00053      DEBUG   READS                                              ⎫
00054                  READ IN-FILE, AT END GO TO END-OF-JOB.         ⎬ debug packet
00055                  ON 5 AND EVERY 5 EXHIBIT NAMED IN-RCD.         ⎭ is added here
00056                  GO TO IF-PARA.
```

Fig. 13.8a Source program with a debug packet.

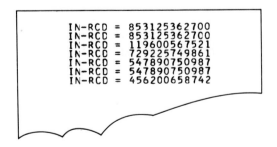

Fig. 13.8b Results of using the debug packet.

† The ALTER statement is discussed in Chapter 16.

packet. For example, if we wished to set up, for test purposes, a counter, while we could use a DISPLAY or EXHIBIT statement in a debug packet to display its value, we would still need a card in the WORKING-STORAGE SECTION to define it (most likely as a 77-level item). Or we might wish to take a program that ordinarily gets its input from a tape unit and test it using data from the card reader. We could use the debug packet to bypass opening of the tape unit for input by a GO TO, and use an ACCEPT statement for input of the data, but we would still need to add one or more cards (again, in the WORKING-STORAGE SECTION, but probably not at the 77-level) into which to put the data obtained by the ACCEPT statement.

13.5 THE USE OF DUMPS FOR DEBUGGING

As we mentioned earlier, when all methods of debugging fail to determine the source of our problem, we can always resort to a complete dump of that part of the computer's memory concerned with our program. Such a "core" dump can be readily obtained by including a proper job control statement. However, we will not pursue the matter further here since:

(1) The JCL required to obtain the dump and associated information varies from system to system. For the IBM 360/370 OS systems, the required JCL may be

//GØ.SYSUDUMP DD SYSØUT=A

(2) The interpretation of the dump requires knowledge of some areas of computer operation, the discussion of which, while certainly not beyond the average COBOL programmer's ability to understand, would require a prohibitive amount of space to cover.

(3) The debugging features that we have covered are sufficient to find the problem in all but the most sophisticated or unusual cases.

Suffice it to say that a dump is available if you should ever need it, and can be obtained and interpreted with assistance from your data-center personnel.

14

Direct-Access Devices

14.1 DIRECT DATA SETS AND FILES

The terms "file" and "data set" can often be used interchangeably. "Data set" is more often used when we are referring to a group of related data as the computer's operating system† sees it, that is, without regard to whether or not a COBOL program was used to create it or will be used to access it. On the other hand, we more often will use the term "file" when we are discussing the group of data as it is related to the program (COBOL) with which it is being used.

There are several ways of organizing a data set. By organization we mean the relation that each record on the data set has to the other records in the data set, and how we would go about accessing that particular record. For example, a deck of data cards is a data set, a *sequential* data set. Another sequential data set would be a COBOL file written onto a magnetic tape. If we compare the records in their logical sequence and in their physical sequence, we find that the two agree; that is, the record that is logically first in our scheme of things is also first in its physical location on the tape, and so on.

Such a sequential data set is simple to create and read, but it has limitations. For example, suppose we are using such a data set to keep a list of customers' names and addresses to be used as a mailing list. The main characteristic of a sequential data set is that in order, for example, to get to the 100th record, we have to process the first 99: thus the term "sequential." In using such a mailing list, where we ordinarily would run through the entire list at one time, this poses no problem—it is not usually necessary to access any particular record.

Now suppose instead of a mailing list we have a list of bank customers along with the balance in each person's account. When a customer makes a withdrawal, we would like to be able to go *directly* to his record in the data set and update it without having to process all the records that physically precede his. Another way of saying this is that we would like to have the ability to process records at *random*. Hence what we need is a *direct* or *random* access method. We are not able to do this using magnetic tape. We will have to resort to another storage medium.

† An operating system is a collection of programs that manages the overall operations of a computer. These programs are usually supplied by the computer manufacturer.

14.2 MAGNETIC DISK UNITS

While there are several devices that we can use to obtain direct access (sometimes called *mass-storage* devices) such as magnetic drums and data cells, the most common by far is the *magnetic disk unit*.

A disk unit (see Fig. 14.1) is a device containing one or more *disk packs*. These disk packs can be removed from a disk unit and put aside in a protective cover. There are several types of disk packs, differing in physical size, storage capacity, and access speed. A typical disk pack (for example, IBM 2314, see Fig. 14.2) may consist of 11 disks. Each of these disks is 14 inches in diameter and is made of metal with a magnetic oxide coating on both sides. Thus, data may be recorded on both sides of the disk. However, the top surface of the top disk and the bottom surface of the bottom disk are not used for recording, because these are the surfaces most likely to be scratched in handling and thereby rendered useless. For the IBM 2314 there are 20 recording surfaces, as shown in Fig. 14.2.

Recording of Data Tracks

The recording surface of each disk is divided into many concentric tracks. For IBM 2314 disk units, there are 203 tracks for each surface, numbered from 000 to 202 as shown in Fig. 14.3. However, only 200 of the 203 tracks are used for storing data. The remaining three are reserved as alternates in case any track is damaged.

Data are recorded on the track in the form of bits (as described in Chapter 11.) Eight bits are grouped to represent one character or byte. Each track can contain up to 7294 characters. Thus, a disk pack such as the IBM 2314 can store approximately 29.1 million characters of information (20 surfaces × 200 tracks × 7294 characters).

Access Mechanism

Each disk unit is equipped with a comb-type access mechanism so that data can be transferred to and from the unit. For the IBM 2314, the access mechanism consists of a group of ten access arms that move as one single entity horizontally to the different positions on the disk.

Each access arm has a pair of READ/WRITE heads, giving a total of 20 heads, one for each recording surface (see Fig. 14.4). However, only one head at a time can transfer data.

When the disk pack is in the disk unit (we call this part of the disk unit the disk drive), the disks rotate at about 40 revolutions per second. The access arm can move laterally and position itself at any specific track. Thus, to access any information from the disk all we have to do is to specify a track number and the READ/WRITE head number that services the track.

Cylinder Concept

There is an alternate method we can use to specify particular tracks. Consider, for example, on each disk the track numbered 005. All such 005 tracks on the disk pack can be considered to form a *cylinder* (see Fig. 14.5). If each surface has 203 tracks, then the disk pack has 203 cylinders. Therefore, to specify a particular track, we could do so by specifying a cylinder number and a READ/WRITE head number.

244 14 Direct-Access Devices

Fig. 14.1 Direct-access storage facility.

11 metal disks, 20 recording surfaces, 14 inches in diameter

Fig. 14.2 IBM 2314 disk pack.

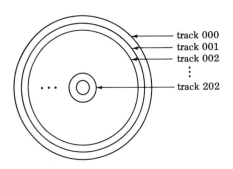

track 000
track 001
track 002
track 202

Fig. 14.3 Tracks on a disk surface.

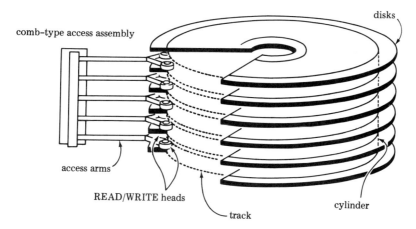

Fig. 14.4 Comb-type access mechanism.

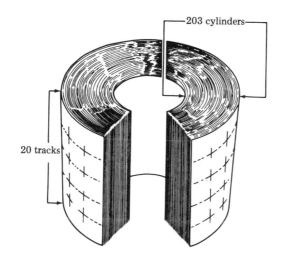

Fig. 14.5 IBM 2314 cylinders.

Suppose that we have a data set that requires ten tracks. If the tracks are not all in the same cylinder, then as we go from one track to another, there will first be a delay while the access arm moves laterally. Then there is another delay while the disk rotates until the beginning of the track is under the READ/WRITE head. (The electrical delay when a particular head is turned on is negligible.) On the other hand, if all ten tracks are in the same cylinder, as we go from track to track we do not have to wait for the access mechanism to move—it remains stationary. Thus, significant amounts of access time can be saved.

14.3 DIRECT FILES

We will discuss two methods of file organization that allow such direct access to each record: the *direct file* and the *indexed sequential* file.

Let us take a look at how our file will be stored on a disk unit for a directly organized file in IBM 360/370 systems. Fig. 14.6 shows part of a track.

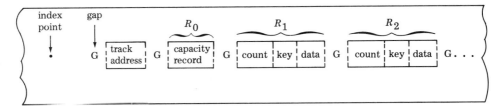

Fig. 14.6 Directly organized data as they appear on a disk (IBM 360/370 systems).

Index point: There is one index point on each track. As the track rotates under the READ/WRITE head, this informs the unit where the track begins.

Gaps: These separate areas of data on the track.

Track address: This tells the system the physical location of this track, that is, its cylinder and READ/WRITE head numbers.

R_0, *capacity record:* This tells the system how much unused space is left on this track. Its value is not available to the user.

$R_1, R_2, \ldots, R_K$: These are the physical records on the track. Each one consists of three parts:

(a) *Count area:* This contains control information.
(b) *Key:* This field identifies the record we are looking at. It contains the RECORD IDENTIFIER (1–255 bytes) specified by the programmer in the ACTUAL KEY clause (to be discussed later).
(c) *Data:* The data that were moved into the program's FD just before a WRITE was executed—in other words, the actual data of the record.

One thing to take note of is that for a direct file the records are stored individually, that is, there is *no blocking of records* allowed for direct files.

COBOL Description for Direct File Organization

In COBOL, direct file processing utilizes a relative track addressing scheme. With this scheme, if we require 500 tracks, it is not necessary for us to know the actual number of a track on the disk pack; the computer system numbers the tracks 0 to 499, and we can refer to the track by these numbers in our program.

However, to identify the position of each record in a file the COBOL programmer must specify an ACTUAL KEY clause along with the SELECT clause for that file in the ENVIRONMENT DIVISION.

The following is the SELECT statement for processing a direct file:

SELECT file-name
    ASSIGN TO system-name
    ACCESS IS RANDOM
    ACTUAL KEY IS data-name
    TRACK-LIMIT IS integer $\begin{Bmatrix} \text{TRACK} \\ \text{TRACKS} \end{Bmatrix}$.

(1) System-name is usually machine dependent. For instance, for the IBM 360/370 systems, the standard system-name for a direct file is

DA-2314-D-ddname.

14.3 Direct Files

The reader should consult the local manual or Appendix A for an appropriate system-name.

(2) ACCESS IS RANDOM: This entry specifies that the file is to be processed by a random method (that is, nonsequential). This entry is required whenever a direct file is organized.

(3) ACTUAL KEY IS data-name: The ACTUAL KEY clause is used to identify the physical position of each record in a file. Data-name can be any fixed item from 5 to 259 bytes in length and must be specified either in the FILE SECTION, WORKING-STORAGE SECTION, or LINKAGE SECTION. It will always consist of two parts:

Track identifier: This tells the system on which relative track data are located. It is always four bytes long, always has a PICTURE of S9(5) COMP SYNC, that is, a 5-digit binary item, *synchronized*. (Note that five digits binary is four bytes.) Its maximum value can not exceed 65,535.

The SYNC clause is required here to ensure correct alignment for the internal data structure. (See the local manual for more detailed information.)

Record identifier: This remaining portion of the data-name being used as the ACTUAL KEY can be from 1 to 255 bytes in length. This is what is contained in the KEY field of each physical record in Fig. 14.6. It identifies a particular record on a track. The following coding provides an example:

```
ENVIRONMENT DIVISION.
    SELECT A-FILE
        ASSIGN TO DA-2314-D-MASTER
        ACCESS IS RANDOM
        ACTUAL KEY IS THE-ACTUAL-KEY
        TRACK-LIMIT IS 500.
DATA DIVISION.
FILE SECTION.
FD  DIRECT-FILE.
    LABEL RECORDS ARE STANDARD.
01  REC-1       PIC X(200).

WORKING-STORAGE SECTION.
01  THE-ACTUAL-KEY.
    05  TRACK-ID    PIC S9(5) COMP SYNC.
    05  RECORD-ID   PIC X(3).
```

In writing a record, the system will go to whichever relative track is specified by the current value of TRACK-ID (the track identifier), and write the record in the first available location, putting the current value of RECORD-ID (the record identifier) into the KEY field, and REC-1 into the data field. (It also writes control information into the control field.)

In retrieving a record, the system will go to the relative track specified by the present value of TRACK-ID, and then search for the first record whose KEY field matches the present value of RECORD-ID. If found, the value of the data field of that record becomes the new value of REC-1.

Note that all records in a particular track will be referred to by the same value of TRACK-ID.

(4) The TRACK-LIMIT clause in the ENVIRONMENT DIVISION requires some explanation. Its use is optional and its format is

$$\underline{\text{TRACK-LIMIT IS}} \text{ integer } \left\{ \begin{array}{l} \underline{\text{TRACK}} \\ \underline{\text{TRACKS}} \end{array} \right\}$$

Integer specifies the relative number of the last track to be initialized during creation of a direct file. Initialization means that even if no records are written on the track by our program, the system will fill the track with dummy records, which can be replaced by us at a later date with new, real additions to the file.

If we do not use the TRACK-LIMIT clause, the number of tracks will be determined by the primary allocation in the SPACE parameter of our DD card. It is best to use TRACK-LIMIT and an integer large enough to allow for any possible future expansion of the file.

14.4 CREATING A DIRECT FILE

In creating a direct file, it is up to the programmer to see to it, prior to a WRITE, that the two elements of the ACTUAL KEY, the track identifier and the record identifier, contain the proper values for that particular record. How does one do this? Ordinarily we move some part of the record itself to the record identifier. For example, a customer's name or social security number, which is part of the record itself, might also, through the record identifier, become the KEY that identifies that particular record.

But how about the track identifier? Its value determines which track a particular record will be placed on. How do we decide that? First, we must use a method that calculates the track identifier from something in the record itself, because then we can use the same method to locate that particular record when we wish to access it. In other words, we need a method that is *consistent*; we cannot just assign records to tracks haphazardly. Second, we would like to have a method that distributes the records of our file evenly on all our assigned tracks, not bunched on just a few tracks.

One technique for such "randomizing" (also called "hashing") is called the *division/remainder* method. First we take some field that forms part of the record and divide it by a prime number.† We then use the remainder of this division as the track identifier. The field we use can be the same as the one we are using for the record identifier; if it is an alphabetic field, we first move it to an area designated as numeric to convert it to numeric by stripping its zone fields.

It is obvious that if we divide by a number, say K, then the remainders will be in the range 0 to $K-1$. We can also see that it is entirely possible that more than one record will yield the same remainder. Such records are called *synonyms*. We want to satisfy two criteria: (1) Every possible KEY must randomize to an address in our designated range; (2) we want to distribute the records across all our tracks as evenly as possible, that is, we want as few synonyms as possible.

One way to reduce the number of synonyms is to assign more disk storage space than the file actually requires. The extra allotted space will certainly reduce the probability that two KEYS will have the same track address.

---

† A prime number is a number divisible only by itself and 1.

Example

Suppose a company is planning to create an inventory file on a 2314 disk storage device. There are 8000 different inventory parts each identified by an 8-character part number. Using an 80% *packing factor,* 10,000 record positions are allocated to store the data file. We will assume that each record is 80 bytes in length.

(1) We consult a table† showing track capacity for a 2314 disk unit. In the section for records with keys, we find that each track can hold 31 records of length 88 bytes (80 bytes for the record, 8 bytes for the key). The count area is fixed in length and automatically accounted for by the table. By a calculation, we find that, putting 31 records on each track, we need 323 tracks to give us 10,000 record positions.

(2) By consulting a table of prime numbers, we find that the largest prime not greater than 323 is 313.

(3) Therefore we divide each zone-stripped part number by 313 to determine its track identifier. For example, if the part number is 253514F4, upon clearing of zones we obtain 25351464. If we had 253514W4, this too would become 25351464, a synonym. Dividing by 313 we obtain a remainder of 29. Therefore both of these records go on relative track number 29.

14.5 SAMPLE PROGRAM 14A: CREATING A DIRECT FILE

This program creates a direct file. Note that in the ASSIGN clause (00010) we have DA-2314-D-MASTER; the *device class* that the 2314 disk unit belongs to is DA (direct access) and the *file organization* is D (direct).

Note also that in the READS paragraph (00040–00046) we make good use of the REMAINDER option of the DIVIDE verb to put the remainder in TRACK-ID. SAVE and QUOTIENT are specified as COMP SYNC in the WORKING-STORAGE SECTION.

One other addition to note is the INVALID KEY clause used with the WRITE clause (00049 and 00050). This clause should be used whenever we have a READ or WRITE acting on a direct file. It tells the system what to do if the track identifier calculated falls outside the limits of our file on a READ or WRITE. We follow the words INVALID KEY with an imperative statement, telling the system what course of action to follow. Here, we would EXHIBIT the faulty record and then go on to the next one.

---

† Such a table can be found in "COBOL Programmer's Guide," IBM publication GC28-6399.

Sample Input

```
2504000000000000000
2504031300000000000
250403a300000000000
250403j300000000000
2504062600000000000
250406b600000000000
250406k600000000000
250406s600000000000
1878000000000000000
187800a100000000000
187800z600000000000
1878016700000000000
187801w700000000000
1878030000000000000
187802n900000000000
```

Source Listing

```
00001            IDENTIFICATION DIVISION.
00002            PROGRAM-ID.  'SAMPLE14A'.
00003            AUTHOR.  FRANCES R. PALMIERI.
00004            ENVIRONMENT DIVISION.
00005            CONFIGURATION SECTION.
00006            SOURCE-COMPUTER.  IBM-370.
00007            OBJECT-COMPUTER.  IBM-370.
00008            INPUT-OUTPUT SECTION.
00009            FILE-CONTROL.
00010                SELECT D-FILE ASSIGN TO DA-2314-D-MASTER       ⎫
00011                    ACCESS IS RANDOM                           ⎬ ASSIGN clause
00012                    ACTUAL KEY IS ACT-KEY                      ⎪
00013                    TRACK-LIMIT IS 323.                        ⎭
00014                SELECT IN-FILE ASSIGN TO UR-2540R-S-CARDIN.
00015            DATA DIVISION.
00016            FILE SECTION.
00017            FD  D-FILE
00018                LABEL RECORDS ARE STANDARD.
00019            01  D-REC.
00020                02  PART-NUM    PIC X(8).
00021                02  NUM-ON-HAND PIC 9(4).
00022                02  PRICE       PIC 9(5)V99.
00023                02  FILLER      PIC X(61).
00024            FD  IN-FILE
00025                LABEL RECORDS ARE OMITTED.
00026            01  IN-REC.
00027                02  PART-NUM    PIC X(8).
00028                02  NUM-ON-HAND PIC 9(4).
00029                02  PRICE       PIC 9(5)V99.
00030                02  FILLER      PIC X(61).
00031            WORKING-STORAGE SECTION.
00032            77  SAVE     PIC S9(8)    COMP   SYNC.             ⎫ SYNCHRONIZE clause used to ensure
00033            77  QUOTIENT PIC S9(5)    COMP   SYNC.             ⎭ proper internal data alignment
00034            01  ACT-KEY.                                       ⎫ track identifier and
00035                02  TRACK-ID  PIC S9(5)  COMP  SYNC.           ⎬
00036                02  RECORD-ID PIC X(8).                        ⎭ record identifier
00037            PROCEDURE DIVISION.
00038            OPENS.
00039                OPEN INPUT IN-FILE, OUTPUT D-FILE.
00040            READS.
00041                READ IN-FILE AT END GO TO EOJ.
00042                MOVE CORRESPONDING IN-REC TO D-REC.
00043                MOVE PART-NUM OF IN-REC TO
00044                    RECORD-ID, SAVE.
00045                DIVIDE SAVE BY 313 GIVING QUOTIENT             ⎫ use division remainder method
00046                    REMAINDER TRACK-ID.                        ⎭ to obtain TRACK-ID
00047            WRITES.
00048                EXHIBIT NAMED TRACK-ID, IN-REC.
00049                WRITE D-REC INVALID KEY EXHIBIT CHANGED        ⎫ WRITE statement for
00050                    'INVALID KEY', ACT-KEY, IN-REC.            ⎭ creating a direct file
00051                GO TO READS.
00052            EOJ.
00053                CLOSE IN-FILE, D-FILE.
00054                STOP RUN.
```

Sample Output

```
                                      input record
                                   ┌──────────────────┐
        TRACK-ID = 00000  IN-REC = 250400C0C000C0000000
        TRACK-ID = 00000  IN-REC = 25040313000C0000000
        TRACK-ID = 00000  IN-REC = 250403A3000C0000000
        TRACK-ID = 00000  IN-REC = 250403J3000C0000000
        TRACK-ID = 00000  IN-REC = 25040626000C0000000
        TRACK-ID = 00000  IN-REC = 250406B600CC0000000
        TRACK-ID = 00000  IN-REC = 250406K600C0C0000C0
        TRACK-ID = 00000  IN-REC = 250406S6000C0000000
        TRACK-ID = 00000  IN-REC = 1878CC0000C0000C00
        TRACK-ID = 00011  IN-REC = 187800A100000000000
        TRACK-ID = 00096  IN-REC = 1878002600000000000
        TRACK-ID = 00167  IN-REC = 187801670000C0000C0
        TRACK-ID = 00167  IN-REC = 187801W7000C0000000
        TRACK-ID = 00300  IN-REC = 187903000000C000000
        TRACK-ID = 00259  IN-REC = 187802N9000C000C0C0
```

14.6 SAMPLE PROGRAM 14B: UPDATING A DIRECT FILE

This is a program for updating records of a direct file. We omit the TRACK-LIMIT clause since it only has meaning during creation of a direct file. We open the disk file I-O (input-output, 00034), which allows us to update any particular record in place, an action only possible with a file stored on a mass-storage device such as the disk unit.

We calculate from the transaction record the ACTUAL KEY of the record we are looking for (00037-00039). (We must know the prime number that was used as a division in creating the file.) We then access the DISK-REC by using the READ statement (00040-00042). When we want to update the record, we use the WRITE statement (00044-00046). The fact that the ACTUAL KEY has not changed since the last READ causes the new DISK-REC to replace the one on the direct file.

Sample Input

```
250406b612340000567
187801w710750002253
187801w500270015031  ← invalid record, exceeds track limit
250403j300050007142
187802n905630001123
```

Source Listing

```
00001           IDENTIFICATION DIVISION.
00002           PROGRAM-ID.  'SAMPLE14B'.
00003           AUTHOR.  FRANCES R. PALMIERI.
00004           ENVIRONMENT DIVISION.
00005           CONFIGURATION SECTION.
00006           SOURCE-COMPUTER.  IBM-370.
00007           OBJECT-COMPUTER.  IBM-370.
00008           INPUT-OUTPUT SECTION.
00009           FILE-CONTROL.
00010               SELECT DISK-FILE ASSIGN TO DA-2314-D-MASTER    ⎫
00011                   ACCESS IS RANDOM                           ⎬ ASSIGN clause
00012                   ACTUAL KEY IS ACT-KEY.                     ⎭
00013               SELECT TRANS-FILE ASSIGN TO UR-2540R-S-CARDIN.
00014           DATA DIVISION.
00015           FILE SECTION.
00016           FD  DISK-FILE
00017               LABEL RECORDS ARE STANDARD.
00018           01  DISK-REC     PIC X(80).
00019           FD  TRANS-FILE
00020               LABEL RECORDS ARE OMITTED.
00021           01  TRANS-REC.
00022               02  PART-NUM     PIC X(8).
00023               02  NUM-ON-HAND  PIC 9(4).
00024               02  PRICE        PIC 9(5)V99.
00025               02  FILLER       PIC X(61).
```

```
0C026              WORKING-STORAGE SECTION.
0C027              77  SAVE      PIC S9(8)   COMP    SYNC.
00028              77  QUOTIENT  PIC S9(5)   COMP    SYNC.
CC029              01  ACT-KEY.
00030                  02  TRACK-ID    PIC S9(5)    COMP    SYNC.     ⎫ track identifier and
00031                  02  RECORD-ID   PIC X(8).                      ⎬ record identifier
CC032              PROCEDURE DIVISION.
00033              OPENS.
0C034                  OPEN INPUT TRANS-FILE, I-O DISK-FILE.          ← DISK—FILE is "opened" as I-O file
00035              READS.
CC036                  READ TRANS-FILE AT END GO TO EOJ.
0C037                  MOVE PART-NUM TO RECORD-ID, SAVE.              ⎫
00038                  DIVIDE SAVE BY 313 GIVING QUOTIENT             ⎬ division/remainder method
0C039                      REMAINDER TRACK-ID.                        ⎭
0C040                  READ DISK-FILE INVALID KEY EXHIBIT CHANGED     ← access the disk-file
0C041                      'INVALID READ', ACT-KEY, TRANS-REC,
CC042                      GO TO READS.
0C043              WRITES.
CC044                  WRITE DISK-REC FROM TRANS-REC INVALID KEY      ← update the disk-rec
00045                      EXHIBIT CHANGED 'INVALID WRITE', ACT-KEY,
CC046                      TRANS-REC, GO TO READS.
CC047                  EXHIBIT NAMED TRACK-ID, TRANS-REC.
0C048                  GO TO READS.
00049              EOJ.
00050                  CLOSE TRANS-FILE, DISK-FILE.
0C051                  STOP RUN.
```

Sample Output

```
TRACK-ID = 00C00  TRANS-REC = 250406B6123400C0567
TRACK-ID = 00167  TRANS-REC = 187801W710750002253
INVALID READ 9992187801W5 187801W500270015031
TRACK-ID = 00C00  TRANS-REC = 250403J3C0050007142
TRACK-ID = 00259  TRANS-REC = 187802N905630001123
```

14.7 INDEXED SEQUENTIAL FILES

There are circumstances in which data will be stored in a file: sometimes it is necessary to access the data directly, while at other times it is more important to go through the file sequentially. A direct file fulfills the first requirement but cannot be accessed sequentially conveniently. However, we have at our disposal another type of file organization, the *indexed sequential* file.

An indexed sequential file is created sequentially. Then it can be accessed either sequentially or directly. The records are stored in *ascending order* based on the contents of a field that is part of each record itself, called the RECORD KEY. The operating system then keeps tables of *indexes,* which inform it as to what range of keys is stored in a particular area of the file. For sequential access, the file is run through much the same as any sequential file. For direct access, we tell the system which record we are looking for by putting a value into a field we call the NOMINAL KEY. The system will then consult its index tables to determine approximately where that record is. It then makes a short sequential search of that area and retrieves the desired record.

We shall first look at how records and indexes are physically handled; then with this knowledge, we shall discuss the logic of the programming involved.

As we mentioned briefly, no blocking of records is allowed in direct organization of files. With indexed sequential files (often just called *indexed files* or *indexed organization*) however, we can block or not block records as we choose.

We choose a particular data field in our record, described in the FD, to be used as the key that determines the location for the record (in ascending order). This data-name can be at fixed lengths, from 1 to 255 bytes. It must be (except in special circumstances) defined to exclude the first byte of the record. We define data-name by adding the following to our ASSIGN sentence.

<u>RECORD</u> KEY IS data-name

14.7 Indexed Sequential Files

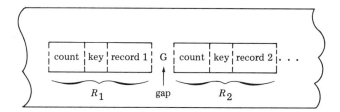

Fig. 14.7 Unblocked records on an indexed file.

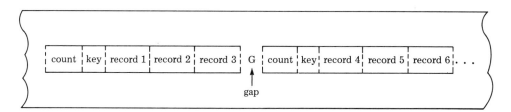

Fig. 14.8 Blocked records on an indexed file.

If the records are unblocked, they will be stored as shown in Fig. 14.7. The count area contains control information for the system's use, DATA contains our entire record, and KEY contains a copy of the data-name in our record, which we have designated as the RECORD KEY.

Blocked records are stored as shown in Fig. 14.8. Here, the key is a copy of the RECORD KEY of the last record in the block. You can see how blocking of records makes for more efficient use of disk space, by storing only one key for several records and also by eliminating some interrecord gaps.

For our purposes, when we request space for an indexed file, we must do so in cylinders, not by tracks. The system then maintains two sets of indexes for our file.

Track Index

There is one track index for each cylinder of our file and it tells which records are on which track and where the *overflow area* for each track is (in case more records should be added to a track than it can hold). Consider the track index shown in Fig. 14.9.

Home address: This defines the physical location (cylinder, READ/WRITE head) of the track in which the cylinder appears.

COCR—cylinder overflow control record: If a cylinder overflow area is requested (to be discussed later) R_0 is used to keep track of overflow records and make available overflow space.

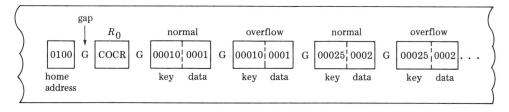

Fig. 14.9 Track index (IBM 360/370 systems).

Normal entry: There is one normal and one overflow entry for each usable track in the cylinder. The normal entry contains two areas: (1) *key,* the key of the highest record on the track specified in the data area, and (2) *data,* the home address of one of the prime tracks (see below) in the cylinder.

Overflow entry: The overflow entry is originally the same as the normal entry. If a track "overflows," then this entry is changed to keep track of the location of overflow records so that the logical sequence can be maintained even if the physical sequence is not.

In Fig. 14.9 we see that neither track 1 nor track 2 has overflowed, and that the highest record on track 1 has RECORD KEY 00010 and the highest record on track 2 has RECORD KEY 00025.

Cylinder Index

If our file requires more than one cylinder, then a *cylinder index* will be maintained by the system. An example is shown in Fig. 14.10. Here we see that cylinder 0 of our file holds records up to RECORD KEY 500, cylinder 1 holds records up to RECORD KEY 945, and cylinder 2 holds records up to RECORD KEY 1550.

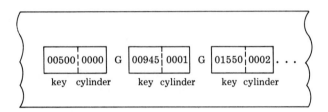

Fig. 14.10 Cylinder index (IBM 360/370 systems).

There is a third type of index possible, a *master index.* If our cylinder index gets too large and unwieldy we can, in effect, split it up. It is even possible to split up master indexes and the index to the indexes. We will not have need in our work to use any master indexes.

There is some additional index terminology to cover:

Prime area: This is the area that contains the data records when the file is created. At the beginning of each cylinder of the prime area will be found the track index for that cylinder.

Index area: This area contains the cylinder indexes if they exist, and the master indexes if they are requested. It will also be in the prime area unless specifically requested otherwise.

Overflow area: The overflow area is the area in which space is allocated for records forced from their original (prime) tracks by insertion of new records. Overflow areas can be allocated in one of three ways:

(1) A number of tracks on each cylinder can be used to hold overflow for *that* cylinder. This is a *cylinder overflow area.*
(2) We may ask for all the overflow from all cylinders to be lumped together anywhere on the device we are using or on another unit of the same type. This is an *independent overflow area.*

(3) If the prime area is not filled completely when the file is created, some of the space remaining on the last cylinder in which data were written will be designated automatically by the system as an independant overflow area.

Two other points are worthy of comment: First, if we decide to block the records in a file when we create it, then we must specify the block size in every subsequent program utilizing that file, no matter whether the subsequent programs use sequential or random access. For example, if we decide to use a block of 50 records, then we must have in the FD of the indexed file BLOCK CONTAINS 50 RECORDS in each program associated with that file.

Second, dummy records, that is, records only written to reserve space, are identified to the system by placing the figurative constant HIGH-VALUE in the first byte of the record. Also, if we wish during file updating to delete a record from a file, we do so by moving HIGH-VALUE to the first byte.

The system responds as follows: If we READ a file using sequential access, records with HIGH-VALUE are skipped, and not made available. In using random access, however, if a record is searched for and found, it will be made available even though it contains HIGH-VALUE. In this case, it is the programmer's responsibility to inspect the first byte to determine if it is a valid record or not.

Records having HIGH-VALUE as the first byte, whether by being set up as dummy records during file creation, or by being designated as deleted records during file updating, will not be physically deleted, and will be available for use until one of two things occurs. Ordinarily if a track "overflows," that is, if a record being written forces an existing one off the track, the one forced off will be stored in an overflow area. However, if this record has HIGH-VALUE, it will be physically deleted. The other case where a record will be physically deleted is if we request reorganization of our file. (Consult your local system manual for details.)

It is not always mandatory, but it is advisable to reserve the first byte of your record specifically to be used as a deletion indicator. A common practice is to move LOW-VALUE to this byte of each active record when it is written on the file.

14.8 SAMPLE PROGRAM 14C: CREATING AN INDEXED SEQUENTIAL FILE

Now that we have an idea of what is physically going on, we look at a program to create an indexed file.

In the ASSIGN clause (00010–00012) we have stated that the data organization is I for indexed sequential. Since an indexed file is *always* created sequentially, we have stated this by ACCESS IS SEQUENTIAL. In the same sentence we notify the system that the RECORD KEY is the data-item called CUST-ID-D. In the FD for IS-FILE we have used the BLOCK CONTAINS clause (00018).

In the PROCEDURE DIVISION we used the INVALID KEY option (00044). This option will be taken if an attempt is made to write a record whose RECORD KEY is equal to or less than the last one written since (and remember it well) during file *creation* the RECORD-KEYS presented to the system must be *unique* and in *ascending order*.

Sample Input

```
01A 185753        out of sequence → 35F 389346
01P 162921                           351 363743
34D 711254                           352 341571
34M 712767                           363 413722
344 712767                           521 741510
35F 363223                           634 262921
35G 342939                           859 791715
35H 357186
```

Source Listing

```
00001      IDENTIFICATION DIVISION.
00002      PROGRAM-ID.  'SAMPLE14C'.
00003      AUTHOR.  FRANCES R. PALMIERI.
00004      ENVIRONMENT DIVISION.
00005      CONFIGURATION SECTION.
00006      SOURCE-COMPUTER. IBM-370.
00007      OBJECT-COMPUTER. IBM-370.
00008      INPUT-OUTPUT SECTION.
00009      FILE-CONTROL.
00010          SELECT IS-FILE, ASSIGN TO DA-2314-I-MASTER          ⎫ ASSIGN clause for
00011              ACCESS IS SEQUENTIAL,                           ⎬ creating an ISAM file
00012              RECORD KEY IS CUST-ID-D.                        ⎭
00013          SELECT INPUT-FILE, ASSIGN TO UR-2540R-S-CARDIN.
00014      DATA DIVISION.
00015      FILE SECTION.
00016      FD  IS-FILE
00017          LABEL RECORDS ARE STANDARD
00018          BLOCK CONTAINS 5 RECORDS.        ←——— BLOCK CONTAINS clause
00019      01  IS-REC.
00020          02  DELETION-CODE   PIC X.
00021          02  CARD-COPY.
00022              04  CUST-ID-D   PIC X(5).
00023              04  BAL-DUE-D   PIC 9(3)V9(2).
00024              04  FILLER      PIC X(70).
00025      FD  INPUT-FILE
00026          LABEL RECORDS ARE OMITTED.
00027      01  INPUT-REC.
00028          02  CUST-ID-IN   PIC X(5).
00029          02  BAL-DUE-IN   PIC 9(3)V9(2).
00030          02  FILLER       PIC X(70).
00031      WORKING-STORAGE SECTION.
00032      77  RECORD-COUNTER   PIC 9(3)   VALUE ZERO.
00033      77  SAVE-KEY         PIC X(5).
00034      PROCEDURE DIVISION.
00035      OPENS.
00036          OPEN INPUT INPUT-FILE, OUTPUT IS-FILE.
00037      READS.
00038          READ INPUT-FILE AT END GO TO EOJ.
00039      MOVES.
00040          MOVE LOW-VALUE TO DELETION-CODE.
00041          MOVE INPUT-REC TO CARD-COPY.
00042          MOVE CUST-ID-D TO SAVE-KEY.
00043      WRITES.
00044          WRITE IS-REC INVALID KEY GO TO INVALID-R.   ←——— INVALID KEY clause
00045          ADD 1 TO RECORD-COUNTER.                              in WRITE statement
00046          GO TO READS.
00047      EOJ.
00048          EXHIBIT NAMED RECORD-COUNTER.
00049          CLOSE INPUT-FILE, IS-FILE.
00050          STOP RUN.
00051      INVALID-R.
00052          EXHIBIT NAMED 'OUT OF SEQUENCE OR DUPLICATE KEY',
00053              INPUT-REC.
00054          GO TO READS.
```

Sample Output

```
OUT OF SEQUENCE OR DUPLICATE KEY INPUT-REC = 35F389346
RECORD-COUNTER = 014
```

14.9 SAMPLE PROGRAM 14D: SEQUENTIAL ACCESS OF INDEXED FILES

This program accesses our indexed file sequentially and writes out each active record. There is not much difference compared to accessing a file having sequential organization. We specify in the ASSIGN clause that data organization is "I." The access method is SEQUENTIAL (00011). We do have to specify RECORD-KEY (00012). In the DATA DIVISION we must specify BLOCK CONTAINS 5 RECORDS since we used this same block size during file creation (00018).

Note that in the PROCEDURE DIVISION, the READ statement (00030) for the indexed file uses the AT END option as with any sequential file, rather than the INVALID KEY option. There is no such thing as an INVALID KEY during sequential access.

We will mention one further action that can be taken in sequentially accessed indexed files, which is starting the reading of the file at other than the first record by using the START verb. We will discuss this after we introduce NOMINAL KEY in the next section.

Source Listing

```
00001         IDENTIFICATION DIVISION.
00002         PROGRAM-ID. 'SAMPLE14D'.
00003         AUTHOR. FRANCES R. PALMIERI.
00004         ENVIRONMENT DIVISION.
00005         CONFIGURATION SECTION.
00006         SOURCE-COMPUTER. IBM-370.
00007         OBJECT-COMPUTER. IBM 370.
00008         INPUT-OUTPUT SECTION.
00009         FILE-CONTROL.
00010             SELECT IS-FILE, ASSIGN TO DA-2314-I-MASTER     } ASSIGN clause
00011                 ACCESS IS SEQUENTIAL,
00012                 RECORD KEY IS CUST-ID-D.
00013             SELECT OUT-FILE, ASSIGN TO UR-1403-S-PROUT.
00014         DATA DIVISION.
00015         FILE SECTION.
00016         FD  IS-FILE
00017             LABEL RECORDS ARE STANDARD                     } LABEL and BLOCK
00018             BLOCK CONTAINS 5 RECORDS.                      } CONTAINS clauses
00019         01  IS-REC.
00020             02  DELETION-CODE   PIC X.
00021             02  DATA-PART.
00022                 04  CUST-ID-D   PIC X(5).
00023                 04  FILLER      PIC X(75).
00024         FD  OUT-FILE
00025             LABEL RECORDS ARE OMITTED.
00026         01  OUT-REC PIC X(100) JUST RIGHT.
00027         PROCEDURE DIVISION.
00028         OPENS.
00029             OPEN INPUT IS-FILE  OUTPUT OUT-FILE.
00030         READS.
00031             READ IS-FILE AT END GO TO END-JOB.    ← READ statement for accessing
00032             WRITE OUT-REC FROM DATA-PART.            an ISAM file sequentially
00033             GO TO READS.
00034         END-JOB.
00035             CLOSE IS-FILE OUT-FILE.
00036             STOP RUN.
```

Sample Output

```
01A185753
01P162921
34D711254
34M712767
344712767
35F363223
35G342939
35H357186
351363743
352341571
363413722
521741510
634262921
859791715
```

14.10 RANDOM ACCESS OF INDEXED FILES

Indexed files can be accessed randomly for record retrieval or update. As usual, we use the RECORD KEY clause to tell the system where, in the record, the key lies. In addition, we must tell the system what value RECORD KEY has for the particular record we desire. This value is placed prior to a READ in a data-name we designate as the NOMINAL KEY:

NOMINAL KEY is data-name

Data-name must be an item in the WORKING-STORAGE SECTION of a fixed length of 1 to 255 bytes. If data-name is not an independent item, then it must be a fixed distance from the beginning of the record that contains it (that is, it cannot be subsequent to an entry using an OCCURS DEPENDING ON clause).

Before we go on to random access, we back track to sequential access for a moment. If we wish to start accessing a file sequentially at other than the first record, we may say

START file-name [INVALID KEY imperative-statement]

After opening the indexed file, we would put the value of the key of the record at which we wish to start processing into the data-name specified as NOMINAL KEY. Then we use the START statement. File-name is the indexed file. Processing begins with the record whose key matches NOMINAL KEY and continues until the end of the file, a CLOSE statement for the file, or another START statement (which thus allows us to skip parts of the file).

Returning now to random access, we must specify in the SELECT sentence that ACCESS IS RANDOM and NOMINAL KEY IS data-name. Having done this, there are three ways in which we can open the file: INPUT, OUTPUT, or I-O (input-output).

If we open the file as INPUT, we can use only the READ verb with the INVALID KEY option after placing the key of the record we want into NOMINAL KEY. The system finds the record we want and makes it available to us (if it is there). As mentioned before, if the record is found, even if it has HIGH-VALUE as the first byte, it becomes available. Note that an INVALID KEY condition will exist only if no matching record can be found.

If we open the file for OUTPUT, we will, after putting a value into NOMINAL KEY, execute a WRITE statement. If the record is a new one and the system does not find a match, then the system inserts the record in the file in a location such that the sequence of the keys is maintained. If insertion causes overflow and an overflow area exists, then the record bumped off the track goes to the overflow area unless it has HIGH-VALUE, in which case it gets physically deleted. In adding such a new record, no INVALID KEY condition can result.

If the key of the insertion record matches the key of a record in the file and that record is a dummy record (HIGH-VALUE) then the insertion record replaces the dummy record. If, on the other hand, a match is found and it is not a dummy record, then an INVALID-KEY condition exists. Whenever a WRITE statement is executed, the contents of RECORD KEY and NOMINAL KEY must be identical. As we saw, except for dummy records, this value must be unique in the file.

The third way we can open a file is I-O. This allows us to use the READ and WRITE much as has been described above. In addition, I-O allows us to use the REWRITE statement for updating a record in place. We do this by putting the key value of the desired record into NOMINAL KEY. We then READ the record. Then we can move into the FD for the file, the new values of the fields of the record that are to be updated. We then execute the REWRITE statement and this updates the record.

The REWRITE statement's format is

<u>REWRITE</u> record-name [<u>FROM</u> identifier]

Two things must be remembered: First, before a REWRITE can be executed for a record, a READ must have been executed to that same record. Second, after that READ and prior to the REWRITE, we must be careful not to change the value in either NOMINAL KEY or RECORD KEY, since whenever a REWRITE statement is executed the value contained in NOMINAL KEY and RECORD KEY must be identical.

14.11 SAMPLE PROGRAM 14E: RANDOM UPDATING AN ISAM FILE

This program combines several concepts. Note that in the SELECT sentence we have specified RECORD KEY and NOMINAL KEY (00012 and 00013). The program reads in a card from the card reader and then updates this record on the file if it is already there, or adds it if it is an entirely new record.

When the READ of the indexed file is executed, if the record is present (even if marked with HIGH-VALUE), control goes to the REWRITE-OLD paragraph (00045). Here LOW-VALUE is moved to the deletion indicator just in case the record was a dummy (00047). We then move the update information in and REWRITE the record (00049). We have included the optional INVALID KEY in a REWRITE, although from the logic of the program it should never be needed.

If, upon the execution of the READ of the indexed file, the INVALID KEY option is taken, this means that the record was not found. In this case we go to the WRITE-NEW paragraph (00054), where LOW-VALUE is moved to the deletion indicator, the new data moved to the disk record, and the new record written. Again, the logic of the program dictates that the INVALID KEY for this WRITE should never occur. We have included it here since for some compilers it is mandatory.

We also have added two counters, UPDATE-COUNTER and ADD-COUNTER, whose values are exhibited at the end of the program to tell us how many records were updated or added, respectively.

One last thing: You might wonder why we have added SAVE-THE-KEY and moved the same data to this field as we moved to NOMINAL KEY. The reason for this is that we wished to EXHIBIT the value of NOMINAL KEY. But if one tries this after the execution of a WRITE or REWRITE the results are unpredictable. Instead we exhibit SAVE-THE-KEY, a field that should contain the same data as NOMINAL KEY. (Actually the same type of situation holds for a field in any program when you try to use the field after a WRITE has been executed. You might wish to experiment by taking any program with a simple WRITE statement in it and insert, immediately following it, an identical WRITE statement.)

Sample Input

```
001 597614
35H353322
371 852115
521 742792
971 658597
```

Records on Disk before Updating

```
01A 185753
01P 162921
34D 711254
34M 712767
344 712767
35F 363223
35G 342939
35H 357186
351 363743
352 341571
363 413722
521 741510
634 262921
859 791715
```

Source Listing

```
00001           IDENTIFICATION DIVISION.
00002           PROGRAM-ID.  'SAMPLE14E'.
00003           AUTHOR. FRANCES R PALMIERI.
00004           ENVIRONMENT DIVISION.
00005           CONFIGURATION SECTION.
00006           SOURCE-COMPUTER.  IBM-370.
00007           OBJECT-COMPUTER.  IBM-370.
00008           INPUT-OUTPUT SECTION.
00009           FILE-CONTROL.
00010               SELECT DISK-FILE ASSIGN TO DA-2314-I-MASTER      ⎫  ASSIGN clause (both RECORD
00011                   ACCESS IS RANDOM                             ⎬  KEY and NOMINAL KEY are
00012                   RECORD KEY IS ID-D                           ⎪  required here)
00013                   NOMINAL KEY IS NOM-KEY.                      ⎭
00014               SELECT IN-FILE ASSIGN TO UR-2540R-S-CARDIN.
00015           DATA DIVISION.
00016           FILE SECTION.
00017           FD  DISK-FILE
00018               LABEL RECORDS ARE STANDARD
00019               BLOCK CONTAINS 5 RECORDS.
00020           01  DISK-REC.
00021               02 DELETE-CODE PIC X.
00022               02 MAIN-DATA.
00023                   04 ID-D PIC X(5).
00024                   04 BAL-DUE-D PIC 9(3)V9(2).
00025                   04 FILLER PIC X(70).
00026           FD  IN-FILE
00027               LABEL RECORDS ARE OMITTED.
00028           01  IN-REC.
00029               02 ID-IN PIC X(5).
00030               02 BAL-DUE-IN PIC 9(3)V9(2).
00031               02 FILLER PIC X(70).
00032           WORKING-STORAGE SECTION.
00033           77  NOM-KEY PIC X(5).
00034           77  SAVE-THE-KEY PIC X(5).
00035           77  UPDATE-COUNTER PIC 9(3) VALUE ZERO.
00036           77  ADD-COUNTER PIC 9(3) VALUE ZERO.
00037           PROCEDURE DIVISION.
00038           OPENS.
00039               OPEN INPUT IN-FILE, I-O DISK-FILE.    ←———        DISK-FILE is "opened"
00040           READ-IN.                                              as I-O file
00041               READ IN-FILE, AT END GO TO EOJ.
00042           READ-DSK.
00043               MOVE ID-IN TO NOM-KEY.                       ⎫  set up NOMINAL KEY
00044               READ DISK-FILE INVALID KEY GO TO WRITE-NEW.  ⎬  before READ DISK-FILE
00045           REWRITE-OLD.                                     ⎭
00046               MOVE LOW-VALUE TO DELETE-CODE.
00047               MOVE IN-REC TO MAIN-DATA.
00048               REWRITE DISK-REC INVALID KEY          ←———        use REWRITE statement
00049                   EXHIBIT NAMED 'INVALID REWRITE'                to update DISK-FILE
00050                   IN-REC, SAVE-THE-KEY,
00051                   GO TO READ-IN.
00052               ADD 1 TO UPDATE-COUNTER.
00053               GO TO READ-IN.
```

```
00054          WRITE-NEW.
00055              MOVE LOW-VALUE TO DELETE-CODE.
00056              MOVE IN-REC TO MAIN-DATA.
00057              WRITE DISK-REC INVALID KEY
00058                  EXHIBIT NAMED 'INVALID WRITE'
00059                      IN-REC, SAVE-THE-KEY,
00060                      GO TO READ-IN.
00061              ADD 1 TO ADD-COUNTER.
00062              GO TO READ-IN.
00063          EOJ.
00064              CLOSE IN-FILE, DISK-FILE.
00065              EXHIBIT NAMED UPDATE-COUNTER, ADD-COUNTER.
00066              STOP RUN.
```
} write a new record.

Sample Output

UPDATE-COUNTER = 002 ADD-COUNTER = 003

Records on Disk after Updating

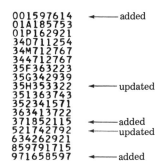

EXERCISES

Write the ENVIRONMENT DIVISION entries according to the following specifications:

1 Create a direct file called MASTER-FILE, with INVT-N as the key. The file also requires 300 tracks.

2 Create an indexed sequential file called CUSTOMER-FILE with standard labels. The key is CUSTOMER-ID.

3 Random update an existing indexed sequential file called WK-PAYROLL, which is in the sequence of SOC-SEC-NO. However, in this program, this file will be accessed according to ACCT-CODE.

4 Briefly explain the following terms:

track	record identifer
cylinder	ACTUAL KEY
index point	TRACK LIMIT
track address	REWRITE
count area	INVALID KEY
track identifier	

5 Use the division/remainder method to create a direct file according to the following file characteristics:
   (a) Maximum number of records: 4000; record length: 80 bytes.
   (b) Packing factor: 80%.
   (c) Record identifier: ACCOUNT-ID (8 alphanumeric characters).
   (d) Storage device: one disk pack.

   Input Description: ACCT-REC (punched cards)

Column	Content
1–8	account identification (alphanumeric)
9	account type
10–30	customer name
31–60	address
61–64	purchase date, mm/yy
65–70	balance, XXXX.XX
71–80	not used

   Processing

   Each ACCT-REC must contain an M in column 9. If not, display an error message upon console and skip to read next ACCT-REC. Otherwise, compute track identification and use it to write ACCT-REC on disk.

   Output Description

   (1) ACCT-MASTER-FILE: on disk pack—has same format as input.
   (2) Printed report: must print one line for each data card with appropriate headers.

6 Write a program to update ACCT-FILE as created in Exercise 5 by reading a deck of purchase records. There are three types of purchase records:
   (1) Type 1 indicates that the amount purchased on the card be added to the balance on the disk record, and updates the purchase-date.
   (2) Type 2 indicates that the information on the disk be replaced by the same information from the card.
   (3) Type 3 records are new records. These records should be added to the disk file.

Input Description

Column	Content
1–8	account identification (alphanumeric)
9	type code
10–30	customer name
31–60	address
61–64	purchase date, mm/yy
65–70	balance, XXXX.XX
71–80	not used

The output report should contain one line for each purchase record processed with appropriate headers.

7 Modify Programming Exercise 8-12 so that the program will create a master student file on disk. The master file should be organized as an indexed sequential file with standard labels. The blocking factor is 20 and the social security number is the key field.

8, 9 Modify Programming Exercises 10-7 and 10-8 so that the master file will be indexed sequentially, organized on a disk pack. (Keep everything else the same.)

15

Report Writer Feature

Producing a printed report is perhaps one of the most indispensable tasks in business programming. However, such tasks as printing the report heading and the page headings, calculating totals and subtotals, and performing proper spacing are often tedious and cumbersome. Fortunately, in COBOL there is a report writer module that allows programmers to produce complicated reports by describing the physical appearance of a report in the DATA DIVISION with just a few statements in the PROCEDURE DIVISION. To use this feature the programmer must follow some basic rules and learn a few new entries. At first these rules and entries appear somewhat complex and awkward. However, they are very similar in nature. Thus, with some practice, they should become relatively routine.

15.1 BASIC CONCEPTS

In the report writer module, every line in a printed report is classified as one of the seven printed classes. These classes, known as report groups, are

(1) *Report heading:* This group of lines is produced only once at the beginning of a report.
(2) *Page heading:* This group is produced at the beginning of each new page.
(3) *Control heading,* and
(4) *Control footing:* These are two control groups that are printed whenever the content of a specific data field (designated as the group) changes. The control heading is printed at the beginning of a control group, while the control footing is printed at the end of a control group.
(5) *Detail group:* This group of lines constitutes the main body of the report.
(6) *Page footing:* This group is printed at the bottom of each page.
(7) *Report footing:* This group is printed only at the termination of a report.

The relationship between these printed groups is shown in Fig. 15-1.

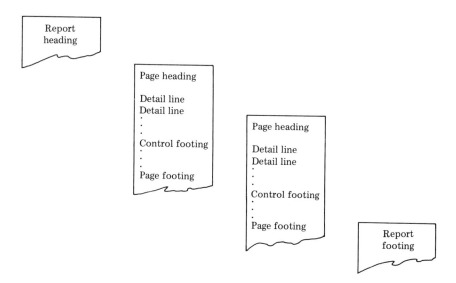

Fig. 15.1 Relationships between report headings, page headings, detail lines, control footings, page footings, and report footings.

The report writer module automatically maintains two special registers for keeping track of page numbers and line numbers in a printed page. These registers are known as PAGE-COUNTER and LINE-COUNTER, respectively. They also maintain numerous SUM counters that produce totals and subtotals when appropriate.

15.2 DATA DIVISION—REPORT SECTION

In order to utilize the report writer, the programmer must provide a detailed specification of the physical format of the desired report. These specifications must be coded in the REPORT SECTION of the DATA DIVISION. The best way to explain how this task can be accomplished is perhaps by an illustration.

Consider Sample Program 15A (page 271), which reads the EMPLOYER-FILE and produces a WEEKLY PAYROLL REPORT as shown in the sample output (page 273). The following programming notes should explain features of the report writer:

1. The EMPLOYEE-FILE is an input file that is not processed by the report writer; therefore, all entries pertaining to the description of this file are unchanged. (It is the same as in Chapter 4.)

2. The FD entry for the REPORT-FILE contains a REPORT clause (00031). This clause specifies that the name of the report to be produced by the report writer is PAYROLL-REPORT. Its format is

<u>REPORT</u> IS report-name.

where report-name is a programmer-supplied name and must be specified in the REPORT SECTION.

The REPORT clause is a required entry of the FD whenever the report writer is invoked.

3. There are no 01 record-description entries for the REPORT-FILE. Such entries are not required since the description of the REPORT-FILE will be handled by the REPORT SECTION.

4. The REPORT SECTION (00035-00080) contains two types of entries: the report description entry (RD), and the report group description entry. These entries will be discussed in the following.

5. The report description entry contains information pertaining to the physical appearance of the report. It is used to specify

(a) maximum number of lines per printed page,
(b) names of data items that act as control,
(c) the starting line number in which the header group should be printed, and
(d) the starting line number in which the first detail group should be printed.

The format of the report description entry is

$$\underline{\text{RD}} \text{ report-name}$$
$$\text{CONTROL CLAUSE}$$
$$\text{PAGE CLAUSE}$$

CONTROL Clause

This clause is used to indicate which data item is the designated control, and when such control breaks should occur. It has the following format:

$$\left\{ \begin{array}{l} \underline{\text{CONTROL IS}} \\ \underline{\text{CONTROLS}} \text{ ARE} \end{array} \right\} \left\{ \begin{array}{l} \text{identifier} \\ \underline{\text{FINAL}} \\ \underline{\text{FINAL}} \text{ identifier} \end{array} \right\}$$

If the CONTROL IS identifier is specified, it means that the report writer will always check the contents of the identifier after each detailed group is printed. If the value in the identifier is changed, a control break will be invoked, causing the automatic printing of the appropriate control group. On the other hand, if CONTROL IS FINAL is used, then it will print totals at the end of a report. If the clause

CONTROL IS FINAL identifier

is specified, then the clause will print the final total at the end of the report, and print the control group when the value in the identifier is changed.

In Sample Program 15A, the clause (00036)

would cause the subtotals (see sample output, page **273**) to be printed whenever there is a change in the value of the DEPT-NO. The word FINAL causes the subtotals to be printed for the last department as shown the sample output. If FINAL is omitted here, then there will be no subtotals for the last department processed.

PAGE LIMIT Clause

The PAGE LIMIT clause specifies the physical format of a page. It has the following format:

15.2 DATA DIVISION: REPORT SECTION

$$\underline{\text{PAGE}} \left\{ \begin{array}{l} \underline{\text{LIMIT IS}} \\ \underline{\text{LIMITS}} \text{ ARE} \end{array} \right\} \text{integer-1} \left\{ \begin{array}{l} \underline{\text{LINE}} \\ \underline{\text{LINES}} \end{array} \right\}$$
$$[\underline{\text{HEADING}} \text{ integer-2}]$$
$$[\underline{\text{FIRST DETAIL}} \text{ integer-3}]$$
$$[\underline{\text{LAST DETAIL}} \text{ integer-4}]$$
$$[\underline{\text{FOOTING}} \text{ integer-5}]$$

where integer-1 indicates the maximum number of lines per printed page, integer-2 the starting line number on which the heading group is to be printed, integer-3 the line number on which the first detail group is to be printed, and integer-4 the last line number on which a detail group is permitted to be printed.

In Sample Program 15A, the PAGE LIMIT clause (00037) is

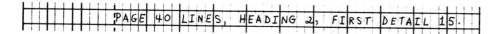

which indicates that there is a maximum of 40 lines per page. The heading group is started on line 2 and the first detail group is started on line 15.

Report Group Description Entries

The rest of the REPORT SECTION comprises several report group description entries. A report group is a printed line or series of lines considered one unit. There are four distinct formats that can be used to describe various report groups.

Format-1

        01   data-name
                LINE clause
                NEXT GROUP clause
                TYPE clause.

Format-1 is used to indicate a report group. It must begin with an 01 level number and must be the first entry for a report group. The data-name entry has special meaning for describing a detail group or control group and is an optional entry here.

The LINE clause is used to specify the relative or absolute line number of the group to be printed. It has the following format:

$$\underline{\text{LINE}} \underline{\text{NUMBER}} \text{ IS} \left\{ \begin{array}{l} \text{integer-1} \\ \underline{\text{PLUS}} \text{ integer-2} \\ \underline{\text{NEXT PAGE}} \end{array} \right\}$$

where integer-1 indicates the beginning line number on which the report group is to be printed.

The PLUS integer-2 option specifies the relative line position of the report group. It indicates that the first line of this report group is to be printed some number of lines (integer-2) past the last line printed on.

The NEXT PAGE option indicates that this report group is to be printed on a new page.

NEXT GROUP Clause

The NEXT GROUP clause is used to specify how far the printer should advance for the next report group after the last line of the present report group is printed. Options for this clause are very similar to those of the LINE clause. The format for the NEXT GROUP clause is as follows:

$$\underline{\text{NEXT GROUP}} \text{ IS} \begin{Bmatrix} \text{integer-1} \\ \underline{\text{PLUS}} \text{ integer-2} \\ \underline{\text{NEXT PAGE}} \end{Bmatrix}$$

TYPE Clause

The TYPE clause is always a required entry in Format-1. It has the following general format:

$$\underline{\text{TYPE}} \text{ IS} \begin{Bmatrix} \begin{Bmatrix} \underline{\text{REPORT HEADING}} \\ \underline{\text{RH}} \end{Bmatrix} \\ \begin{Bmatrix} \underline{\text{PAGE HEADING}} \\ \underline{\text{PH}} \end{Bmatrix} \\ \begin{Bmatrix} \underline{\text{CONTROL HEADING}} \\ \underline{\text{CH}} \end{Bmatrix} \begin{Bmatrix} \text{identifier-1} \\ \underline{\text{FINAL}} \end{Bmatrix} \\ \begin{Bmatrix} \underline{\text{DETAIL}} \\ \underline{\text{DE}} \end{Bmatrix} \\ \begin{Bmatrix} \underline{\text{CONTROL FOOTING}} \\ \underline{\text{CF}} \end{Bmatrix} \begin{Bmatrix} \text{identifier-2} \\ \underline{\text{FINAL}} \end{Bmatrix} \\ \begin{Bmatrix} \underline{\text{PAGE FOOTING}} \\ \underline{\text{PF}} \end{Bmatrix} \\ \begin{Bmatrix} \underline{\text{REPORT FOOTING}} \\ \underline{\text{RF}} \end{Bmatrix} \end{Bmatrix}$$

Note that there are seven possible options associated with the TYPE clause. These options have been explained previously. It should be stressed that the TYPE clause is primarily used to determine when a report group should be generated as output by the report writer. If the REPORT HEADING (RH) or REPORT FOOTING (RF) is specified, then this report group is to be produced only once at the beginning or end of a report. If the PAGE HEADING (PH) or PAGE FOOTING (PF) is specified, then this report is to be printed once at the beginning or bottom of a report.

The DETAIL or DE option specifies that the report group constitutes the main body of the report. In this case, each detail report must have a unique data-name at the 01 level. The data-name must be referred to by a GENERATE statement, which will be discussed in the PROCEDURE DIVISION. The GENERATE statement will cause the actual printing of a detail group.

If a report group contains totals or subtotals, then CONTROL HEADING (CH) or CONTROL FOOTING (CF) should be specified together with either an identifier or the word FINAL. When the identifier is specified, the report group is printed whenever the value in the identifier changes. On the other hand, when FINAL is indicated, the report group is produced at the end of the entire report.

In Sample Program 15A, there is one PAGE HEADING (00038-00052), one DETAIL LINE (00053-00059), two CONTROL FOOTINGS (00060-00068), (00069-00080). Note

15.2 DATA DIVISION: REPORT SECTION

that these report groups all begin with 01 level numbers and only the detail group has a data-name, namely, WAGE-LINE. The rest of the report groups have no data-name entries.

Format-2

                level-number   LINE clause

This format is used to represent a group item with a level number from 02 through 49. It is used when a printed line contains more than one elementary item as shown in 00054-00059 of Sample Program 15A.

Format-3

           level-number   [data-name]
              COLUMN NUMBER IS integer-1
              PICTURE clause
              [JUSTIFIED clause]
              [GROUP INDICATE]

$$\left\{ \begin{array}{l} \underline{\text{SOURCE}} \text{ IS identifier-1} \\ \underline{\text{VALUE}} \text{ IS literal} \\ \underline{\text{SUM}} \text{ IS identifier-2} \end{array} \right\}$$

Format-3 is used to describe an elementary item that is part of a printed line. The level number may be any number ranging from 02 through 49.

The COLUMN clause indicates the column printed position of the elementary item. Thus, the clause COLUMN 34 would cause the elementary item to be printed from left to right starting at column 34.

The PICTURE, JUSTIFIED, and VALUE clauses are the same as those used to describe an elementary item in the DATA DIVISION.

SOURCE Clause

The SOURCE clause specifies the data field whose value is to be printed here. For example, the statement

                03   COLUMN 5   PIC 9(9)
                      SOURCE identifier-1

would cause the value in identifier-1 to be printed from left to right starting in column 5 of the printed form. Identifier-1 must be either an elementary item or a special register such as PAGE-COUNTER or LINE-COUNTER.

SUM Clause

The SUM clause is used to obtain the summation of a series of data and may appear in an elementary item entry of a control footing report group. When this clause is specified, a special SUM counter is automatically established by the report writer.

The format of the SUM clause is

                    SUM IS identifier-2

Identifier-2 must be either an elementary numeric item specified in a SOURCE clause or a data-name in a SUM COUNTER. For instance, in Sample Program 15A, the statement (00060-00068)

```
        01  TYPE CONTROL FOOTING DEPT-NO.
            05 SUB-TOTAL-HRS-WK COLUMN 70 PIC ZZZ.99
                SUM HOURS-WORKED.
```

establishes a SUM counter: SUB-TOTAL-HRS-WK for HOURS-WORKED. This counter would be automatically incremented every time the detail group WAGE-LINE is printed. (Note that HOURS-WORKED is an elementary numeric item specified in a SOURCE clause—of WAGE-LINE, 00058.) This SUM counter would be automatically reset to zero each time this CONTROL group is printed.

The data-name of a SUM counter can also be used as the identifier for another SUM counter. For example, in sequence 00069-00074 of Sample Program 15A, we have

```
        01  TYPE IS CONTROL FOOTING FINAL.
            05 COLUMN 78 PIC Z,ZZZ.99 SUM SUB-TOTAL-HRS-WK.
```

which defines an unnamed SUM counter. This SUM counter would be incremented each time before SUB-TOTAL-HRS-WK is reset to zero.

GROUP INDICATE Clause

This clause specifies that this elementary item is to be printed only once within each control or page break. Its format is <u>GROUP</u> INDICATE. For example, the statements

```
        01  WAGE-LINE TYPE IS DETAIL LINE PLUS 2.
            03 COLUMN 8 PIC X(5) SOURCE DEPT-NO GROUP INDICATE.
```

print DEPT-NO only once for each control break as shown in Sample Program 15A.

The <u>GROUP</u> INDICATE clause may be used only with a DETAIL report group at the elementary item level.

15.3 PROCEDURE DIVISION

There are only a few statements that the programmer must supply in order to use the report writer. These statements, with pertinent comments, are as follows:

(1) Just like any other output file, the report-file must be opened before any processing can be initiated.
(2) To begin the processing of a report-file, the statement

INITIATE report-name.

must be executed. This statement essentially resets the PAGE-COUNTER, the LINE-COUNTER, and all appropriate SUM counters to zeros.

(3) To print each detail line in the report, the statement

GENERATE data-name.

must be used, where data-name is the name of a detail group.

The GENERATE statement would also cause the report header, page header, or various control breaks to be printed.

(4) To terminate the processing of the report, the statement

TERMINATE report-name.

should be invoked. This statement also causes the final control footing and report footing to be printed.

We should mention that the TERMINATE statement does not close the file. A CLOSE statement for the report-file should be issued before STOP RUN.

This completes our discussion of the report writer. It should be noted that the report writer comprises a multitude of options. The discussion in this chapter has been limited to the basic ideas and elementary features of the report writer. Any interested reader should consult a standard COBOL reference manual for more details.

15.4 SAMPLE PROGRAM 15A: REPORT WRITER

This program produces a payroll report using the report writer feature of COBOL. The program reads in a payroll file that contains the employee's department number, social security number, name, hourly rate of pay, and hours worked. The program then computes his weekly wage and prints out a report. The report is by department, with the total wages and hours worked for each department. The program also prints out the total wages and hours worked for the entire report.

Input Description: Weekly Time Card

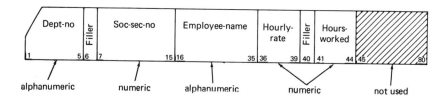

Sample Input

```
1    5         7        15   16              35  36          41
↓    ↓         ↓         ↓    ↓               ↓   ↓           ↓
12345          098389761      lester thierwechter  1010       4000
12345          047581922      al chai              3728       5350
12345          625373634      mike elliott         1350       3500
29481          029157293      john james doe       0250       2000
local          375838374      tim daly             1054       4000
local          618482944      dave brookside       0888       4000
local          121212121      robert smithe        2478       4500
local          948573848      frank williams       0850       4000
comp           374518459      sue ann gladdings    4958       4000
comp           010173572      red baron            1975       4750
comp           987654321      henry jones          0625       3950
```

Source Listing

```
00001              IDENTIFICATION DIVISION.
00002              PROGRAM-ID.  'SAMPLE15A'.
00003              AUTHOR.  LESTER THIERWECHTER.
00004              DATE-WRITTEN.  JUNE 10,1975.
00005         ************************************************************
00006              ENVIRONMENT DIVISION.
00007              CONFIGURATION SECTION.
00008              SOURCE-COMPUTER.  IBM-370.
00009              OBJECT-COMPUTER.  IBM-370.
00010              INPUT-OUTPUT SECTION.
00011              FILE-CONTROL.
00012                  SELECT PAYROLL-FILE ASSIGN TO UR-2501-S-CARDIN.
00013                  SELECT REPORT-FILE ASSIGN TO UR-1403-S-PROUT.
00014         ************************************************************
00015              DATA DIVISION.
00016              FILE SECTION.
00017              FD  PAYROLL-FILE
00018                  LABEL RECORDS ARE OMITTED
00019                  DATA RECORD IS WKLY-TIME-CARD.
00020              01  WKLY-TIME-CARD.
00021                  05   DEPT-NO           PIC X(5).
00022                  05   FILLER            PIC X.
00023                  05   SOC-SEC-NO        PIC 9(9).
00024                  05   EMPLOYEE-NAME     PIC X(20).
00025                  05   HOURLY-RATE       PIC 99V99.
00026                  05   FILLER            PIC X.
00027                  05   HOURS-WORKED      PIC 99V99.
00028                  05   FILLER            PIC X(36).
00029              FD  REPORT-FILE
00030                  LABEL RECORDS ARE OMITTED
00031                  REPORT IS PAYROLL-REPORT.
00032              WORKING-STORAGE SECTION.
00033              77  WEEKLY-WAGE           PIC S9(3)V99.
00034              77  TODAY-DATE            PIC X(8).        ←── report specification begins here
00035              REPORT SECTION.
00036              RD  PAYROLL-REPORT CONTROL FINAL DEPT-NO,
00037                  PAGE 40 LINES, HEADING 2, FIRST DETAIL 15.
00038              01  TYPE PAGE HEADING.
00039                  03  LINE PLUS 2  COLUMN 10  PIC X(65)  VALUE ALL '*'.
00040                  03  LINE PLUS 2.
00041                      05  COLUMN 15  PIC X(30)
00042                          VALUE 'WEEKLY PAYROLL REPORT AS OF '.
00043                      05  COLUMN 47  PIC X(8)  SOURCE TODAY-DATE.
00044                      05  COLUMN 57  PIC X(4)  VALUE 'PAGE'.
00045                      05  COLUMN 62  PIC ZZ9   SOURCE PAGE-COUNTER.   ⎫
00046                  03  LINE PLUS 2.                                    ⎬ page heading
00047                      05  COLUMN  6  PIC X(10) VALUE 'DEPARTMENT'.    ⎪
00048                      05  COLUMN 21  PIC X(10) VALUE 'SOC-SEC-NO'.
00049                      05  COLUMN 36  PIC X(15) VALUE 'EMPLOYEE-NAME'.
00050                      05  COLUMN 60  PIC X(4)  VALUE 'RATE'.
00051                      05  COLUMN 71  PIC X(5)  VALUE 'HOURS'.
00052                      05  COLUMN 81  PIC X(4)  VALUE 'WAGE'.          ⎭
00053              01  WAGE-LINE TYPE IS DETAIL  LINE PLUS 2.
00054                  03  COLUMN  8  PIC X(5)  SOURCE DEPT-NO  GROUP INDICATE. ⎫
00055                  03  COLUMN 20  PIC XXXBXXBXXXX  SOURCE SOC-SEC-NO.       ⎪
00056                  03  COLUMN 36  PIC X(20)  SOURCE EMPLOYEE-NAME.          ⎬ detail line
00057                  03  COLUMN 59  PIC $Z9.99  SOURCE HOURLY-RATE.           ⎪
00058                  03  COLUMN 71  PIC Z9.99  SOURCE HOURS-WORKED.
00059                  03  COLUMN 80  PIC ZZZ.99  SOURCE WEEKLY-WAGE.           ⎭
00060              01  TYPE CONTROL FOOTING DEPT-NO.
00061                  03  LINE PLUS 2  COLUMN 55  PIC X(31) VALUE ALL '*'.     ⎫
00062                  03  LINE PLUS 2.                                         ⎪
00063                      05  COLUMN 55  PIC X(10) VALUE 'SUBTOTALS '.         ⎪
00064                      05  SUB-TOTAL-HRS-WK  COLUMN 70  PIC ZZZ.99          ⎬ control footing
00065                          SUM HOURS-WORKED.                                ⎪ (by dept-no)
00066                      05  SUB-TOTAL-WAGE    COLUMN 78  PIC Z,ZZZ.99        ⎪
00067                          SUM WEEKLY-WAGE.
00068                  03  LINE PLUS 2  COLUMN 55  PIC X(31)  VALUE ALL '*'.    ⎭
00069              01  TYPE IS CONTROL FOOTING FINAL.
00070                  03  LINE PLUS 3  COLUMN 45  PIC X(41)  VALUE ALL '*'.    ⎫
00071                  03  LINE PLUS 3.                                         ⎪
00072                      05  COLUMN 45  PIC X(30)                             ⎪
00073                          VALUE '**** TOTAL HOURS WORKED ****'.
00074                      05  COLUMN 78  PIC Z,ZZZ.99  SUM SUB-TOTAL-HRS-WK.   ⎬ final control footing
00075                  03  LINE PLUS 2.                                         ⎪
00076                      05  COLUMN 45  PIC X(30)                             ⎪
00077                          VALUE '**** TOTAL WEEKLY WAGE   ****'.
00078                      05  COLUMN 76  PIC $**,***.99  SUM SUB-TOTAL-WAGE.   ⎭
00079                  03  LINE PLUS 2.
00080                      05  COLUMN 69  PIC X(20)  VALUE 'END OF THE REPORT'.
00081         ************************************************************
00082              PROCEDURE DIVISION.
00083              BEGIN.
00084                  OPEN INPUT PAYROLL-FILE,           ⎫ open all files
00085                       OUTPUT REPORT-FILE.           ⎭ (including report file)
00086                  MOVE CURRENT-DATE TO TODAY-DATE.
00087                  INITIATE PAYROLL-REPORT.           ←── initiate report
00088              GEN-REPORT.
00089                  READ PAYROLL-FILE AT END GO TO END-JOB.
00090                  COMPUTE WEEKLY-WAGE ROUNDED = HOURLY-RATE * HOURS-WORKED.
00091                  GENERATE WAGE-LINE.                ←── generate detail lines
00092                  GO TO GEN-REPORT.
00093              END-JOB.
00094                  TERMINATE PAYROLL-REPORT.          ←── terminate report
00095                  CLOSE PAYROLL-FILE, REPORT-FILE.
00096                  STOP RUN.
```

Sample Output

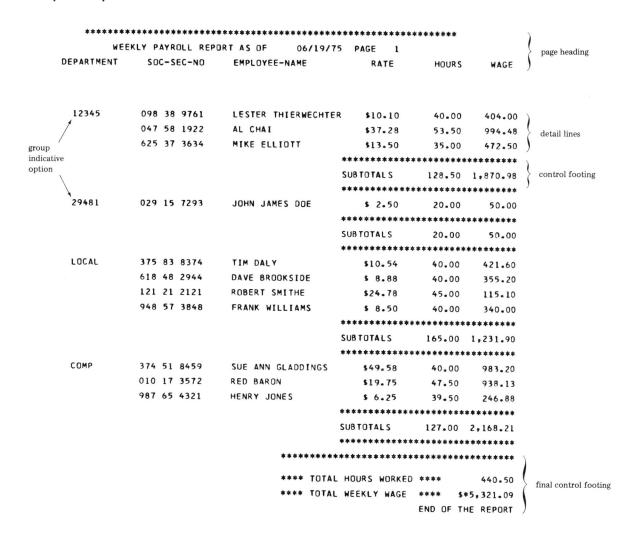

15.5. SAMPLE PROGRAM 15B: REPORT WRITER WITH SORT FEATURE

This program produces a payroll report using the report writer feature of COBOL. The program reads in a payroll file that contains the employee's department number, social security number, name, hourly rate of pay, and hours worked. The program then computes his weekly wage and prints out a report. The report is by department with the total wages and hours worked for each department. The program also prints out the total wages and hours for the entire report. (The input description for this program is identical to that of Sample Program 15A.)

This program also uses the internal SORT package to sort the records, which is done by ascending department number and then by ascending employee name. This allows the data records to be in any order, but the program will group all employees of the same department together for the report.

Sample Input

1 5	7 15	16 35	36	41
12345	098389761	lester thierwechter	1010	4000
local	121212121	robert smithe	2478	4500
29481	029157293	john james doe	0250	2000
12345	047581922	al chai	3728	5350
local	375838374	tim daly	1054	4000
local	948573848	frank williams	0850	4000
12345	625373634	mike elliott	1350	3500
comp	374518459	sue ann gladdings	4858	4000
comp	010173572	red baron	1975	4750
comp	987654321	henry jones	0625	3950
local	618482944	dave brookside	0888	4000

Source Listing

```
00001      IDENTIFICATION DIVISION.
00002      PROGRAM-ID.  'SAMPLE15B'.
00003      AUTHOR.  LESTER THIERWECHTER.
00004      DATE-WRITTEN.  JUNE 10,1975.
00005  ************************************************************************
00006      ENVIRONMENT DIVISION.
00007      CONFIGURATION SECTION.
00008      SOURCE-COMPUTER.  IBM-370.
00009      OBJECT-COMPUTER.  IBM-370.
00010      INPUT-OUTPUT SECTION.
00011      FILE-CONTROL.
00012          SELECT PAYROLL-FILE ASSIGN TO UR-2501-S-CARDIN.
00013          SELECT SORT-FILE ASSIGN TO DA-2314-S-DSKFILE.
00014          SELECT REPORT-FILE ASSIGN TO UR-1403-S-PROUT.
00015          SELECT TEMP-FILE ASSIGN TO DA-2314-S-TEMPFILE.
00016  ************************************************************************
00017      DATA DIVISION.
00018      FILE SECTION.
00019      FD  PAYROLL-FILE
00020          LABEL RECORDS ARE OMITTED
00021          DATA RECORD IS WKLY-TIME-CARD.
00022      01  WKLY-TIME-CARD       PIC  X(80).
00023      SD  SORT-FILE
00024          DATA RECORD IS SORT-RECORD.
00025      01  SORT-RECORD.
00026          05  SORT-DEPT-NO     PIC  X(5).
00027          05  FILLER           PIC  X(10).       ⎫
00028          05  SORT-NAME        PIC  X(20).       ⎬ SORT-FILE
00029          05  FILLER           PIC  X(45).       ⎭
00030      FD  TEMP-FILE
00031          LABEL RECORDS ARE STANDARD
00032          BLOCK CONTAINS 10 RECORDS
00033          DATA RECORD IS TEMP-RECORD.
00034      01  TEMP-RECORD.
00035          05  DEPT-NO          PIC  X(5).
00036          05  FILLER           PIC  X.
00037          05  SOC-SEC-NO       PIC  9(9).
00038          05  EMPLOYEE-NAME    PIC  X(20).
00039          05  HOURLY-RATE      PIC  99V99.
00040          05  FILLER           PIC  X.
00041          05  HOURS-WORKED     PIC  99V99.
00042          05  FILLER           PIC  X(36).
00043      FD  REPORT-FILE
00044          LABEL RECORDS ARE OMITTED
00045          REPORT IS PAYROLL-REPORT.
00046      WORKING-STORAGE SECTION.
00047      77  WEEKLY-WAGE          PIC  S9(3)V99.
00048      77  TODAY-DATE           PIC  X(8).
00049      REPORT SECTION.
00050      RD  PAYROLL-REPORT CONTROL FINAL DEPT-NO,
00051          PAGE 40 LINES, HEADING 2, FIRST DETAIL 15.
00052      01  TYPE PAGE HEADING.
00053          03  LINE PLUS 2 COLUMN 10 PIC X(65)  VALUE ALL '*'.
00054          03  LINE PLUS 2.                                       ⎫
00055              05  COLUMN 15  PIC X(30)                           ⎪
00056                      VALUE 'WEEKLY PAYROLL REPORT AS OF '.      ⎪
00057              05  COLUMN 47  PIC X(8)   SOURCE TODAY-DATE.       ⎬ page heading
00058              05  COLUMN 57  PIC X(4)   VALUE 'PAGE'.            ⎪
00059              05  COLUMN 62  PIC ZZ9   SOURCE PAGE-COUNTER.      ⎪
00060          03  LINE PLUS 2.                                       ⎪
00061              05  COLUMN  6  PIC X(10) VALUE 'DEPARTMENT'.       ⎪
00062              05  COLUMN 21  PIC X(10) VALUE 'SOC-SEC-NO'.       ⎪
00063              05  COLUMN 36  PIC X(15) VALUE 'EMPLOYEE-NAME'.    ⎪
00064              05  COLUMN 60  PIC X(4)  VALUE 'RATE'.             ⎪
00065              05  COLUMN 71  PIC X(5)  VALUE 'HOURS'.            ⎪
00066              05  COLUMN 81  PIC X(4)  VALUE 'WAGE'.             ⎭
```

15.5 Sample Program 15B: Report Writer with SORT Feature

```
00067      01  WAGE-LINE  TYPE IS DETAIL  LINE PLUS 2.             ⎫
00068          03   COLUMN   8   PIC X(5)    SOURCE DEPT-NO  GROUP INDICATE. ⎪
00069          03   COLUMN  20   PIC XXXBXXBXXXX   SOURCE SOC-SEC-NO.         ⎪
00070          03   COLUMN  36   PIC X(20)   SOURCE EMPLOYEE-NAME.            ⎬ detail line
00071          03   COLUMN  59   PIC $Z9.99  SOURCE HOURLY-RATE.              ⎪
00072          03   COLUMN  71   PIC Z9.99   SOURCE HOURS-WORKED.             ⎪
00073          03   COLUMN  80   PIC ZZZ.99  SOURCE WEEKLY-WAGE.              ⎭
00074      01  TYPE CONTROL FOOTING DEPT-NO.                       ⎫
00075          03   LINE   PLUS 2    COLUMN 55    PIC X(31) VALUE ALL '*'.    ⎪
00076          03   LINE   PLUS 2.                                            ⎪
00077              05   COLUMN 55  PIC X(10) VALUE 'SUBTOTALS '.              ⎪
00078              05   SUB-TOTAL-HRS-WK   COLUMN 70   PIC ZZZ.99             ⎬ control footing
00079                   SUM HOURS-WORKED.                                     ⎪ (by dept-no)
00080              05   SUB-TOTAL-WAGE     COLUMN 78   PIC Z,ZZZ.99           ⎪
00081                   SUM WEEKLY-WAGE.                                      ⎪
00082          03   LINE   PLUS 2    COLUMN 55    PIC X(31) VALUE ALL '*'.    ⎭
00083      01  TYPE IS CONTROL FOOTING  FINAL.                     ⎫
00084          03   LINE   PLUS 3    COLUMN 45    PIC X(41) VALUE ALL '*'.    ⎪
00085          03   LINE   PLUS 3.                                            ⎪
00086              05   COLUMN 45   PIC X(30)                                 ⎪
00087                   VALUE '**** TOTAL HOURS WORKED ****'.                 ⎪
00088              05   COLUMN 78   PIC Z,ZZZ.99   SUM SUB-TOTAL-HRS-WK.      ⎬ final control
00089          03   LINE   PLUS 2.                                            ⎪ footing
00090              05   COLUMN 45   PIC X(30)                                 ⎪
00091                   VALUE '**** TOTAL WEEKLY WAGE  ****'.                 ⎪
00092              05   COLUMN 76   PIC $**,***.99 SUM SUB-TOTAL-WAGE.        ⎪
00093          03   LINE   PLUS 2.                                            ⎪
00094              05   COLUMN 69   PIC X(20)  VALUE 'END OF THE REPORT'.     ⎭
00095  ****************************************************************
00096   PROCEDURE DIVISION.
00097       SORT SORT-FILE ON                                       ⎫
00098            ASCENDING KEY SORT-DEPT-NO,                        ⎪
00099            ASCENDING KEY SORT-NAME,                           ⎬ SORT command
00100          USING PAYROLL-FILE,                                  ⎪
00101          GIVING TEMP-FILE.                                    ⎭
00102   BEGIN.
00103       OPEN INPUT TEMP-FILE,
00104            OUTPUT REPORT-FILE.
00105       MOVE CURRENT-DATE TO TODAY-DATE.
00106       INITIATE PAYROLL-REPORT.                      ← initiate report
00107   GEN-REPORT.
00108       READ TEMP-FILE AT END GO TO END-JOB.
00109       COMPUTE WEEKLY-WAGE ROUNDED = HOURLY-RATE * HOURS-WORKED.
00110       GENERATE WAGE-LINE.                           ← generate detail lines
00111       GO TO GEN-REPORT.
00112   END-JOB.
00113       TERMINATE PAYROLL-REPORT.                     ← terminate report
00114       CLOSE TEMP-FILE, REPORT-FILE.
00115       STOP RUN.
```

Sample Output

```
          ****************************************************************
          WEEKLY PAYROLL REPORT AS OF    06/19/75   PAGE   1
DEPARTMENT    SOC-SEC-NO    EMPLOYEE-NAME        RATE      HOURS      WAGE


   COMP       987 65 4321   HENRY JONES         $ 6.25     39.50     246.88
              010 17 3572   RED BARON           $19.75     47.50     938.13
              374 51 8459   SUE ANN GLADDINGS   $48.58     40.00     943.20
                                                *******************************
                                                SUBTOTALS            127.00   2,128.21
                                                *******************************
   LOCAL      618 48 2944   DAVE BROOKSIDE      $ 8.88     40.00     355.20
              948 57 3848   FRANK WILLIAMS      $ 8.50     40.00     340.00
              121 21 2121   ROBERT SMITHE       $24.78     45.00     115.10
              375 83 8374   TIM DALY            $10.54     40.00     421.60
                                                *******************************
                                                SUBTOTALS            165.00   1,231.90
                                                *******************************
   12345      047 58 1922   AL CHAI             $37.28     53.50     994.48
              098 38 9761   LESTER THIERWECHTER $10.10     40.00     404.00
              625 37 3634   MIKE ELLIOTT        $13.50     35.00     472.50
```

```
                                    ****************************
                                    SUBTOTALS    128.50   1,870.98
                                    ****************************
29481       029 15 7293  JOHN JAMES DOE  $ 2.50    20.00      50.00
                                    ****************************
                                    SUBTOTALS     20.00      50.00
                                    ****************************
                                    ****************************
                                    **** TOTAL HOURS WORKED ****      440.50
                                    **** TOTAL WEEKLY WAGE  ****   $*5,281.09
                                                        END OF THE REPORT
```

EXERCISES

Answer exercises 1–5 (true or false) by referring to the following coding:

```
       RD  SALES-REPORT-FILE
           PAGE LIMIT 40 LINES
           HEADING 2 FIRST DETAIL 11 LAST DETAIL 35.
       01  TYPE PAGE HEADING.
           05 COLUMN 20 PIC X(30)
              VALUE 'MONTHLY SALES REPORT'.
```

1 SALES-REPORT-FILE is the name of the report. It must be specified in a SELECT clause in the ENVIRONMENT DIVISION.

2 The phrase HEADING 2 means that the page heading has 2 lines.

3 The phrase FIRST DETAIL 11 LAST DETAIL 35 means that there are 25 detail lines to be specified in one page.

4 There will be no control break in this report.

5 The page heading will be printed on the record line.

6 Explain the significance of the following terms:

    SOURCE   PAGE-COUNTER
    DETAIL   INITIATE
    GROUP INDICATE   TERMINATE
    SUM

7, 8 Rewrite at least two of the following reports by using the report writer feature:

  (a) Sample Program 4A.
  (b) Sample Program 5A or 5C.
  (c) Sample Program 6A or 7A.
  (d) Sample Program 8A or 8C.
  (e) Sample Program 9A or 9B.
  (f) Programming Exercise 8-12, 8-13, or 8-14.
  (g) Programming Exercise 9-5.
  (h) Programming Exercise 10-22.
  (i) Programming Exercise 12-5.

16
Additional Features

16.1 COPY STATEMENT

The COPY statement can be used to reduce a considerable amount of coding. It allows the programmer to include prewritten DATA DIVISION entries, ENVIRONMENT DIVISION clauses, and PROCEDURE DIVISION procedures in the source program.

The general format of the COPY statement is

$$\underline{\text{COPY}} \text{ library-name } [\underline{\text{SUPPRESS}}]$$
$$\left[\underline{\text{REPLACING}} \text{ word-1 BY } \begin{Bmatrix} \text{word-2} \\ \text{literal-1} \\ \text{identifier-1} \end{Bmatrix} \right]$$

where library-name is the name of a prewritten text contained in the user's library. (The COPY library can usually be created by using the installation's utility program.)

For example, if the library entry RECLIB1 consists of the coding

```
       01  REC-A.
           03  NAME PIC X(25).
           03  STREET-ADDRESS PIC X(25).
           03  CITY-STATE-ZIP PIC X(25).
           03  NOT-USED PIC X(5).
```

then the programmer can use the COPY statement as follows:

```
       01  CUSTOMER-REC COPY RECLIB1.
```

After the program is compiled the resulting source listing of the program would be shown as

```
01  CUSTOMER-REC.
    03  NAME PIC X(25).
    03  STREET-ADDRESS PIC X(25).
    03  CITY-STATE-ZIP PIC X(25).
    03  NOT-USED PIC X(5).
```

The REPLACING option permits the programmer to change part (or all) of the data-names within the library entry. For instance, the coding

```
            01  CUSTOMER-REC COPY RECLIB1
                REPLACING NAME BY CUSTOMER-NAME
                NOT-USED BY CUSTOMER-ID.
```

would produce a resulting source listing as shown:

```
01  CUSTOMER-REC.
    03  CUSTOMER-NAME PIC X(25).
    03  STREET-ADDRESS PIC X(25).
    03  CITY-STATE-ZIP PIC X(25).
    03  CUSTOMER-ID PIC X(5).
```

It should be mentioned that the REPLACING option does not change any data-name in the library, but only affects the program source listing.

The SUPPRESS option is used when data names in the library entry are not to be listed. This option is used for data security and file protection.

Option 1 (within the CONFIGURATION SECTION):
    SOURCE-COMPUTER.   COPY statement.
    OBJECT-COMPUTER.   COPY statement.
    SPECIAL-NAMES.   COPY statement.

Option 2 (within the INPUT–OUTPUT SECTION):
    FILE-CONTROL.   COPY statement.
    I-O-CONTROL.   COPY statement.

Option 3 (within the FILE SECTION):
    FD file-name COPY statement.
    SD sort-file-name COPY statement.

Option 4 (within the REPORT SECTION):
    RD report-name COPY statement.
    RD report-name [WITH CODE menomic-name] COPY statement.

Option 5 (within a file or SORT description entry, or within the
    WORKING-STORAGE SECTION or the LINKAGE SECTION):
    01 data-name COPY statement.

Option 6 (within a report group):
    01 [data-name] COPY statement.

Option 7 (within the PROCEDURE DIVISION):
    section-name SECTION [priority-number]. COPY statement.
    paragraph-name. COPY statement.

Fig. 16.1 Permissible COPY options.

16.1 COPY Statement

The COPY statement certainly is not limited to the record description entry of the DATA DIVISION. It is available to other entries. Figure 16-1 presents a summary of permissible COPY options.

Setting Up a COBOL COPY Library: An Example

In order to set up a COBOL COPY library, the programmer may utilize the utility programs of certain systems. Figure 16-2 presents an example showing how such a COPY library can be set up under the IBM OS operating system.

```
/*PASSWORD NULLPASS
//STEP2    EXEC  PGM=IEBUPDTE,PARM=NEW              ←——— IBM utility program used here
//SYSUT2   DD    DSN=MSC.SC000701.APPLICAT.CHAIPC,
//               VOL=SER=EIS105,UNIT=3330,
//               DISP=(NEW,KEEP),SPACE=(TRK,(10,5,2)),
//               DCB=(LRECL=80,BLKSIZE=80,RECFM=F,DSORG=PO)
//SYSPRINT  CD   SYSOUT=A
//SYSIN     DD   *
./     ADD NAME=STREC,LEVEL=00,SOURCE=0,LIST=ALL
./     NUMBER NEW1=10,INCR=10
       01 STUDENT-REC.
          03  NAME1.
              05  LAST1      PIC    X(11).
              05  FIRST1     PIC    X(9).
              05  INITIAL1   PIC    X.
          03  ADDRESS1.
              05  STREET     PIC    X(14).
              05  CITY       PIC    A(9).
              05  STATE      PIC    A(2).
              05  ZIP-CODE   PIC    9(5).
          03  SEX            PIC    A.
          03  SOC-SEC-NO.
              05  S1         PIC    999.
              05  S2         PIC    99.
              05  S3         PIC    9999.
          03  MAJOR-CODE     PIC    9.
          03  CLASS-CODE     PIC    9.
          03  CR-HRS-MATH    PIC    99.
          03  CS-CODE        PIC    9.
          03  CR-HRS-CS      PIC    99.
          03  YEAR           PIC    99.
          03  SEMESTER       PIC    A.
          03  COURSE-NO      PIC    999.
          03  SECT-NO        PIC    99.
          03  FILLER         PIC    XXX.
./     ENDUP
/*
```

Fig. 16.2a Setting up a COBOL COPY library.

```
// EXEC COBUCG,PARM='APOST,XREF'
//SYSLIB    CD   DSN=MSC.SC000701.APPLICAT.CHAIPC,
//               VOL=SER=EIS105,UNIT=3330,
//               DISP=OLD
//CCB.SYSIN CD   *
       IDENTIFICATION DIVISION.
       PROGRAM-ID.    COPYA.
       ENVIRONMENT DIVISION.
       CONFIGURATION SECTION.
       SOURCE-COMPUTER. IBM-370.
       OBJECT-COMPUTER. IBM-370.
       DATA DIVISION.
       WORKING-STORAGE SECTION.
       01  STUDENT-RECORD COPY STREC.          ←——— COPY statement
       PROCEDURE DIVISION.
       BEGIN-A.
           DISPLAY 'END OF JOB'.
           DISPLAY 'END OF JOB' UPON CONSOLE.
           STOP RUN.
/*
//
```

Fig. 16.2b Source program using a COPY statement.

16.2 GO TO ... DEPENDING STATEMENT

This statement has the format

> GO TO procedure-name-1 [procedure-name-2 ...]
>   DEPENDING ON identifier

It is used to branch to one of a series of procedures depending on the value of the identifier.

For example, in the coding

```
        GO TO PARA-A, PARA-B, PARA-C, PARA-D
            DEPENDING ON ID.
```

the program would branch to PARA-A if the identifier ID has the value 1, PARA-B if ID has the value 2, and so forth. If the value of the identifier is anything other than 1 through n (in our example, n is 4) the GO TO statement is ignored and the program automatically continues with the next sequential statement. For the GO TO ... DEPENDING statement to have any effect, the identifier must represent a positive or unsigned integer.

16.3 ALTER STATEMENT

The ALTER statement is used to change the procedure-name (that is, transfer point) specified in a GO TO statement. It has the format

> ALTER procedure-name-1
>   TO PROCEED TO procedure-name-2

where procedure-name-1, procedure-name-2, ... must be the names of paragraphs that contain only one sentence consisting of a GO TO statement without the DEPENDING option.

To illustrate how the ALTER statements can be used, consider the following coding:

```
        PARA-1.
            GO TO SKIP-1.
        PARA-2.
            .
            .
        SKIP-1.
            .
            ALTER PARA-1 TO PROCEED TO PARA-3.
            .
        PARA-3.
            .
```

When the program first executes PARA-1, the GO TO statement transfers control to SKIP-1. However, when PARA-1 is encountered again, after execution of the ALTER statement, the GO TO statement causes the program to branch to PARA-3.

16.4 SUBPROGRAMS

In Chapter 10 we have shown by using the PERFORM statement that the programmer can organize the program as a collection of subroutines. These subroutines are procedures within the program. They must be coded, compiled, and debugged with the program. In COBOL, there is a way to organize subroutines as subprograms, which can be coded, compiled, and debugged separately from the main program. Subprograms are one of the most powerful features of computer programming. In this section, we present a brief discussion of this subject related to the IBM ANS compiler.

Coding a Subprogram: LINKAGE SECTION and EXIT Program Statement

COBOL subprograms are very much like regular programs. They contain all four COBOL divisions. However, in order to pass information between a subprogram and a main program, the subprogram must contain a LINKAGE SECTION within a DATA DIVISION. The LINKAGE SECTION describes data items that will be made available from/to another program. Also, to terminate the execution of the subprogram so that control will be returned to the main program, the statement EXIT PROGRAM or GO BACK can be used. If EXIT PROGRAM is used, it must be preceded by a paragraph name and be the only statement in the paragraph.

The coding in Fig. 16.3 shows how these features can be used to create a subprogram. Note that the subprogram is identified as SUB1. The LINKAGE SECTION provides names and a description of the data fields that are assumed to exist in the main program. The format for the LINKAGE SECTION is basically the same as for the WORKING-STORAGE SECTION. The level 01 heading must be preceded by the level 77 entry. However, the VALUE clause can not be specified except for level 77.

The USING clause associated with the PROCEDURE DIVISION header specifies the names of the data fields that are to be received from the main program. These data fields must be defined in the LINKAGE SECTION.

```
       IDENTIFICATION DIVISION.
       PROGRAM-ID. SUB1.
       ENVIRONMENT DIVISION.
       DATA DIVISION.
       WORKING-STORAGE SECTION.
       77 KOUNTER PIC S99 VALUE ZEROS.
       LINKAGE SECTION.
       77 WAGE PIC S9(4)V99.
       01 PAY-INFOR.
           05 RATE PIC S99V99.
           05 HOURS PIC S99V99.

       PROCEDURE DIVISION USING PAY-INFOR, WAGE.
           ADD 1 TO KOUNTER.
           COMPUTE WAGE = HOURS * RATE.
           DISPLAY KOUNTER.
       OUT. EXIT PROGRAM.
```

Fig. 16.3 A subprogram (called program).

Coding a Main Program: CALL Statement

In order to utilize the subprogram shown in Fig. 16-3, the main program must invoke a CALL statement. An example of such a main program is shown in Fig. 16-4. Note that this program is written as usual up to the CALL statement.

```
        IDENTIFICATION DIVISION.
        PROGRAM-ID 'MAIN'
        ENVIRONMENT DIVISION.

        DATA DIVISION.

        WORKING-STORAGE SECTION.
        77 GROSS PIC S9(4)V99.

        01 PAYROLL-DATA
            02 HRLY-RATE PIC S99V99.
            02 HRS-WK PIC S99V99.

        PROCEDURE DIVISION.

            CALL 'SUB1' USING PAYROLL-DATA GROSS.
```

Fig. 16.4 A main (calling) program.

The CALL statement permits a main program (known as the calling program) to communicate with a subprogram (known as the called program). It has the format

<u>CALL</u> literal-1 <u>USING</u> [identifier-1, identifier-2]

where literal-1 is the name of the subprogram that is being called. The identifiers specified in the USING option of the CALL statement indicate that those data fields are shared with the subprogram.

The programmer has the option of using different data names in the subprogram. However, for these identifiers, if more than one identifier is specified in the USING clause, the order in which they are coded must correspond to the order in which they appeared in the subprogram. Also, the PICTURE clause for each of the identifiers must correspond to that of the subprogram. (Note that in Figs. 16-3 and 16-4, PAYROLL-DATA corresponds to PAY-INFOR and GROSS corresponds to WAGE.)

When the CALL statement is executed, the program will automatically branch to the named subprogram. It will perform the operation as specified in the subprogram until an EXIT statement or a GO BACK statement is encountered. The EXIT statement or the GO BACK statement would return the control to the statement directly following the CALL statement in the main program.

16.5 SAMPLE PROGRAM 16A: COBOL MAIN PROGRAM TO CALL A SUBPROGRAM

This sample program consists of a main program and a subprogram identified as 'SUBP1'. The main program handles all the input/output processing, including reading the CUSTOMER-REC and printing the WEEKLY CHARGE ACCOUNT REPORT.

16.5 Sample Program 16A: COBOL Main Program to Call a Subprogram

Subprogram 'SUBP1' has an internal MONTH-TABLE that converts the payment due date from the numeric date to the calendar month (that is, 10 would be converted to OCT).

Input Description: CUSTOMER-REC (punched card)

Column	Content
1–20	name
21–40	street address
41–60	city, state, zip code
61–76	payment information
61–66	due date, mmddyy
67–71	amount due, XXX.XX
72–76	amount received, XXX.XX
77–80	not used

Program Logic

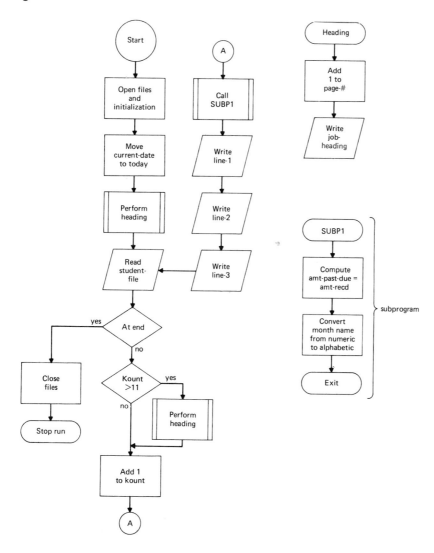

Sample Input

```
1                    21              41                    61       67    72
↓                    ↓               ↓                     ↓        ↓     ↓
W A CHAI             555 JACKSON AVE NEW YORK, NY 10019    1116745050544545
ANNA W MARCINKO      123 BROADWAY    NEW YORK, NY 10020    1116744057954545
GARY SCARCELLA       MEADOW LANE     ANDOVER, NJ 07821     1029740899914050
```

Source Listing: Main Program

```
00001            IDENTIFICATION DIVISION.
00002            PROGRAM-ID.  'SAMPL16A'.
00003            ENVIRONMENT DIVISION.
00004            CONFIGURATION SECTION.
00005            SOURCE-COMPUTER. IBM-370.
00006            OBJECT-COMPUTER. IBM-370.
00007            SPECIAL-NAMES.
00008                C01 IS TO-TOP-OF-PAGE.
00009            INPUT-OUTPUT SECTION.
00010            FILE-CONTROL.
00011                SELECT STUDENT-FILE
00012                    ASSIGN TO UR-2540R-S-CARDIN.
00013                SELECT PRINT-FILE
00014                    ASSIGN TO UR-1403-S-PROUT.
00015           ***********************************************
00016            DATA DIVISION.
00017            FILE SECTION.
00018            FD  STUDENT-FILE
00019                LABEL RECORDS ARE OMITTED.
00020            01  CUSTOMER-REC.
00021                05 NAME   PIC X(20).
00022                05 STREET  PIC X(20).
00023                05 CITY-STATE-ZIP  PIC X(20).
00024                05 PAYMENT-INFO.
00025                    08 DUE-DATE.
00026                        10 MM  PIC 99.
00027                        10 DD  PIC 99.
00028                        10 YY  PIC 99.
00029                    08 AMOUNT-DUE   PIC S9(3)V99.
00030                    08 AMOUNT-RECD  PIC S9(3)V99.
00031                05 FILLER PIC X(4).
00032            FD  PRINT-FILE
00033                LABEL RECORDS ARE OMITTED.
00034            01  PRINT-AREA  PIC X(133).
00035            WORKING-STORAGE SECTION.
00036            77  AMOUNT-PAST-DUE  PIC S9(3)V99 VALUE ZEROS.
00037            77  MONTH-S   PIC AAA.
00038            77  LINE-KOUNT         PIC 99 COMP VALUE ZERO.
00039            77  PAGE-KOUNT         PIC 999 VALUE ZERO.
00040            01  JOB-HEADING.
00041                05 FILLER  PIC X(20) VALUE SPACES.
00042                05 FILLER PIC X(35)
00043                    VALUE 'WEEKLY CHARGE ACCOUNT REPORT AS OF
00044                05 TODAY-DATE  PIC X(8).
00045                05 FILLER   PIC X(10) VALUE 'PAGE  ' JUST RIGHT.
00046                05 PAGE-NO  PIC ZZ9.
00047            01  LINE-1.
00048                05 FILLER PIC X(5) VALUE SPACES.
00049                05 NAME-OUT  PIC X(20) VALUE SPACES.
00050            01  LINE-2.
00051                05 FILLER PIC X(5) VALUE SPACES.
00052                05 STREET-OUT  PIC X(20).
00053                05 FILLER   PIC X(5) VALUE SPACES.
00054                05 FILLER   PIC X(18) VALUE 'AMOUNT RECEIVED
00055                05 AMT-RECD-OUT  PIC $$$$.99.
00056            01  LINE-3.
00057                05 FILLER PIC X(5) VALUE SPACES.
00058                05 C-S-Z-OUT  PIC X(20).
00059                05 FILLER   PIC X(5) VALUE SPACES.
00060                05 FILLER   PIC X(22) VALUE 'AMOUNT PAST DUE AS OF
00061                05 MONTH-OUT  PIC AAA.
00062                05 DAY-OUT   PIC ZZ9.
00063                05 FILLER  PIC X(3) VALUE ',19'.
00064                05 YR-OUT   PIC 99.
00065                05 FILLER   PIC XXX VALUE SPACES.
00066                05 AMT-PAST-DUE-OUT   PIC $$$$.99.
00067           ***********************************************
00068            PROCEDURE DIVISION.
00069            BEGIN.
00070                OPEN INPUT STUDENT-FILE, OUTPUT PRINT-FILE.
00071                MOVE SPACES TO PRINT-AREA.
00072                MOVE CURRENT-DATE TO TODAY-DATE.
00073                PERFORM PAGE-HEADING.
```

16.5 Sample Program 16A: COBOL Main Program to Call a Subprogram

```
0C074          READ-PRINT.
0C075              READ STUDENT-FILE AT END GO TO END-JOB.
0C076              IF LINE-KOUNT > 11 PERFORM PAGE-HEADING.
0C077              ADD 1 TO LINE-KOUNT.
0C078              CALL 'SUBP1' USING PAYMENT-INFO, AMOUNT-PAST-DUE, MONTH-S.    ← CALL
0C079              MOVE NAME TO NAME-OUT.                                         SUBPROGRAM
0C080              WRITE PRINT-AREA FROM LINE-1 AFTER ADVANCING 3 LINES.
0C081              MOVE STREET TO STREET-OUT.
0C082              MOVE AMOUNT-RECD TO AMT-RECD-OUT.
0C083              WRITE PRINT-AREA FROM LINE-2 AFTER ADVANCING 1 LINES.
0C084              MOVE CITY-STATE-ZIP TO C-S-Z-OUT.
0C085              MOVE MONTH-S TO MONTH-OUT.
0C086              MOVE DD TO DAY-OUT.
0C087              MOVE YY TO YR-OUT.
0C088              MOVE AMOUNT-PAST-DUE TO AMT-PAST-DUE-OUT.
0C089              WRITE PRINT-AREA FROM LINE-3 AFTER ADVANCING 1 LINES.
0C090              GO TO READ-PRINT.
0C091          END-JOB.
0C092              CLOSE STUDENT-FILE, PRINT-FILE.   STOP RUN.
0C093          PAGE-HEADING.
0C094              MOVE SPACES TO PRINT-AREA.
0C095              ADD 1 TO PAGE-KOUNT.
0C096              MOVE PAGE-KOUNT TO PAGE-NO.
0C097              WRITE PRINT-AREA FROM JOB-HEADING
0C098                  AFTER ADVANCING TO-TOP-OF-PAGE.
0C099              MOVE ZEROS TO LINE-KOUNT.
```

Source Listing: Subprogram

```
0C001          IDENTIFICATION DIVISION.
0C002          PROGRAM-ID. SUBP1.
0C003          AUTHOR. GARY SCARCELLA.
0C004          ENVIRONMENT DIVISION.
0C005          CONFIGURATION SECTION.
0C006          SOURCE-COMPUTER. IBM-370.
0C007          OBJECT-COMPUTER. IBM-370.
0C008          DATA DIVISION.
0C009          WORKING-STORAGE SECTION.
0C010          01  MONTH-VALUE   PIC X(36)
0C011                  VALUE 'JANFEBMARAPRMAYJUNJULAUGSEPOCTNOVDEC'.
0C012          01  MONTH-TABLE REDEFINES MONTH-VALUE.
0C013              05 MONTH  PIC X(3)  OCCURS 12 TIMES.
0C014          ****************************************************
0C015          LINKAGE SECTION.
0C016          77  AMOUNT-PAST-DUE  PIC S9(3)V99.
0C017          77  MONTH-S  PIC AAA.                                    ⎫
0C018          01  PAYMENT-INFO.                                        ⎪
0C019              08  DUE-DATE.                                        ⎪
0C020                  10  MM   PIC 99.                                 ⎬  LINKAGE
0C021                  10  DD   PIC 99.                                 ⎪  SECTION
0C022                  10  YY   PIC 99.                                 ⎪
0C023              08  AMOUNT-DUE   PIC S9(3)V99.                       ⎪
0C024              08  AMOUNT-RECD  PIC S9(3)V99.                       ⎭
0C025          ****************************************************
0C026          PROCEDURE DIVISION USING PAYMENT-INFO, AMOUNT-PAST-DUE, MONTH-S.
0C027          BEGIN.
0C028              COMPUTE AMOUNT-PAST-DUE = AMOUNT-DUE - AMOUNT-RECD.
0C029              MOVE MONTH (MM) TO MONTH-S.
0C030          EXIT-R.  EXIT PROGRAM.
```

Sample Output

```
W A CHAI
555 JACKSON AVE           AMOUNT RECEIVED    $445.45
NEW YORK, NY   10019      AMOUNT PAST DUE AS OF NOV 16,1974    $505.05

ANNA W MARCINKO
123 BROADWAY              AMOUNT RECEIVED    $545.45
NEW YORK, NY   10020      AMOUNT PAST DUE AS OF NOV 16,1974    $405.79

GARY SCARCELLA
MEADOW LANE               AMOUNT RECEIVED    $140.50
ANDOVER, NJ   07821       AMOUNT PAST DUE AS OF OCT 29,1974    $89.99
```

EXERCISES

1. Use your system utility routine to set up at least one of the following COBOL entries as a part of your COBOL COPY library. Then access the library by using the COPY statement.
   - (a) EMPLOYEE-CARD-REC in Sample Program 7B.
   - (b) VENDOR-REC and line 1 in Sample Program 8C.
   - (c) TASK-3 in Sample Program 8C.
   - (d) Salesman's commission rate table in Programming Exercise 9-6.
   - (e) PRINT-REPORT SECTION in Sample Program 12A.

2. Modify Sample Program 8A so that the statements related to the tax computation will be organized as a subprogram identified as 'TAX-R'.

3. Modify Sample Program 8B so that the salesman's commission rate determination routine will be organized as a subprogram identified as 'COMRATE'.

4. Modify any one of the following Programming Exercises so that the print routine will be organized as a subprogram:
   - (a) 6-5 or 7-11.
   - (b) 8-12, 8-13, or 8-14.
   - (c) 9-5, 9-6, or 9-7.
   - (d) 10-8, 11-7, 11-8, or 12-5.
   - (e) 14-5, 14-6, 14-7, or 14-8.

17

Structured Programming

Structured programming is perhaps one of the most recent major intellectual developments in the field of computer programming. It is generally agreed that it was first introduced by E. W. Dijkstra in a series of publications beginning in 1968. Since then, structured programming has been advocated by many leading computer scientists with various interpretations and connotations. This chapter presents a very brief glimpse of structured programming from the COBOL programmer's point of view. The interested reader should consult the references listed at the end of this chapter for further study.

17.1 WHY WE NEED STRUCTURED PROGRAMMING: PROGRAM CORRECTNESS AND READABILITY

One of the most important objectives of the computer programmer is to develop a correct program. *Correctness* means a program actually performing what it is supposed to perform. But how do we know that we have written a correct program? One way is to run the program with test data. If the results of these runs show no errors, then the program is considered to be correct (that is, debugged). Such a procedure may work well for a simple program. However, when a large and complicated program is to be validated, test runs can only show the presence but never the absence of errors since most of these test data only can represent a very small sample of the program input. To ensure the correctness of the program by testing, we must test the program with all possible input conditions. Such a task can be rather absurd, if not altogether impossible.

Structured programming basically deals with the methodologies of developing correct as well as more readily understood programs. It recognizes that the problem of writing large programs correctly is mainly one of complexity and deals with this problem by providing specific guidelines in program design. By following these guidelines, programmers can systematically break down a complex program into a collection of small and simpler modules. These modules should be organized in a top to bottom format, where top-level modules can invoke lower-level modules. Thus, program correctness can be established by testing each module from top down. However, in order to keep each module simple, structured programming permits the programmer to use only three types of control structures: linear sequence, selection pattern, and conditional iteration. These three basic structures are discussed in the next section.

17.2 THE THREE BASIC CONTROL STRUCTURES

Linear Sequence

Linear sequence represents a series of actions to be performed by the program. In the program flowchart, this type of structure is represented by a series of process symbols as shown in Fig. 17-1.

In COBOL, almost all imperative statements with the exception of the GO TO statement can be viewed as an acceptable linear sequence. For example, the following sequence of statements is a linear sequence:

```
        MOVE SPACES TO PRINT-AREA.
        ADD A-FIELD TO B-FIELD.
        WRITE REC-B.
```

Selection Pattern

This type of control structure directs the program to select the next set of instructions based on the result of a test, as shown in Fig. 17-2. In COBOL, the IF ... THEN ... ELSE statement represents this type of control structure.

Conditional Iteration—The Loop

The conditional iteration is often known as a "do-while" or "do-until" control. In COBOL the PERFORM statement with the VARYING/UNTIL option essentially specifies a conditional iteration as shown in the following coding:

```
        PERFORM COMP-R VARYING I FROM 1 BY 1 UNTIL I > 10.
        ⋮
COMP-R.
        MOVE X (I) TO SAVE (I).
        ADD   X (I) TO TOTAL-X.
        ADD   Y (I) TO SAVE (I).
```

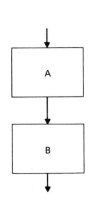

Fig. 17.1 Linear sequence.

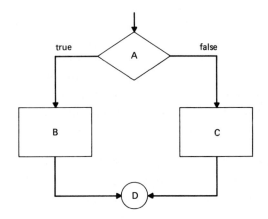

Fig. 17.2 Selection pattern.

17.3 BASIC RULES OF STRUCTURED PROGRAMMING

In designing a program under structured programming, one must organize the program flow by repeatedly using only these three basic control structures. However, in order to ensure a degree of success, the following rules must be strictly followed:

(1) The entire program should be organized as a collection of routines, and there should be a single main-line routine that monitors the overall execution of the program.
(2) Each routine may have its own secondary control routine. To activate any secondary routine the PERFORM statement should be used.
(3) Do not use the GO TO statement unless it is a last resort, such as an error or terminal exit. The GO TO statement is considered harmful since it causes the program control to jump around and makes the program logic difficult to follow and understand.
(4) Each routine should have only one entry point and one exit. It should never activate another routine on its own level.
(5) The program logic for each routine including the main line routine should be organized from top down. Therefore, the program can be "read" like a book and the source program statement would automatically reflect the actual program execution flow.

As we can see there are no "magical" or "highly sophisticated tricks" in structured programming. It merely introduces the concept of building programs by modularization with a limited number of control structures. By following these guidelines diligently, experience has shown that the programmer can make his programs and flowcharts more manageable. Therefore, it enhances program readability and reliability, and hence makes the program easier to debug, modify, and maintain.

17.4 SAMPLE PROGRAM 17A: A STRUCTURED PROGRAM

This program represents an example of a program that is developed according to the rules of structured programming. Note that the program is organized as a collection of small modules, including

(1) One main-line routine that controls the overall execution of the program.
(2) Four secondary-level routines.
(3) Three third-level routines.
(4) One termination routine.

None of these routines is activated by another routine within the same level. This relationship is depicted in Fig. 17-3.

17 Structured Programming

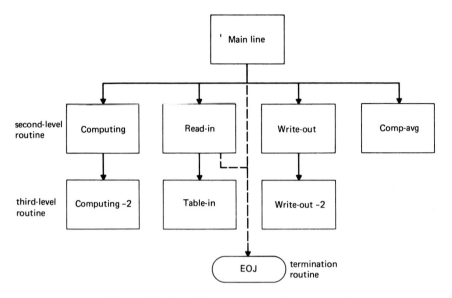

Fig. 17.3 Hierarchical modular structure of a structured program.

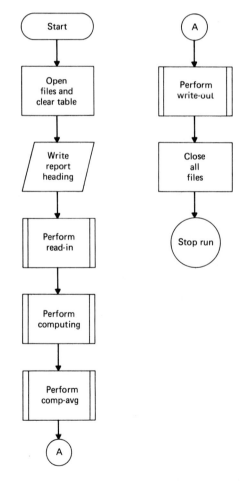

Fig. 17.4 Control structure for the main-line routine.

Source Listing

```
                PROCEDURE DIVISION.
                MAINLINE.
                  OPEN INPUT IN-FILE, OUTPUT OUT-FILE.
                  MOVE ZEROS TO TEST-TABLE.
main-line         WRITE OUT-LINE FROM HEADER AFTER ADVANCING 3.
routine           PERFORM READ-IN VARYING I FROM 1 BY 1 UNTIL I > 5.
                  PERFORM COMPUTING VARYING I FROM 1 BY 1 UNTIL I > 5.
                  PERFORM COMP-AVG VARYING I FROM 1 BY 1 UNTIL I > 5.
                  PERFORM WRITE-OUT VARYING I FROM 1 BY 1 UNTIL I > 6.

termination     EOJ.
routine           CLOSE IN-FILE, OUT-FILE.
                  STOP RUN.

                READ-IN.
                  READ IN-FILE INTO CARD-MASK
first-              AT END DISPLAY '****NOT ENOUGH DATA****' UPON CONSOLE
level               GO TO EOJ.
routine           MOVE ZEROS TO COL-TOTAL (I).
                  MOVE ZEROS TO ROW-TOTAL (I).
                  MOVE STUDENT-ID TO S-ID (I).
                  PERFORM TABLE-IN VARYING J FROM 1 BY 1 UNTIL J > 5.   ← invoke a lower-level routine.

second-         TABLE-IN.
level
routine           MOVE TEST-IN (J) TO TEST (I, J).

first-level     COMPUTING.
routine           PERFORM COMPUTING-2 VARYING J FROM 1 BY 1 UNTIL J > 6.   ← invoke a lower-level routine

second-         COMPUTING-2.
level             ADD TEST (I, J) TO COL-TOTAL (J).
routine           ADD TEST (I, J) TO ROW-TOTAL (I)

first-level     COMP-AVG.
routine           COMPUTE TEST (I, 6) = ROW-TOTAL (I) / 5.
                  COMPUTE TEST (6, I) = COL-TOTAL (I) / 5.

                WRITE-OUT.
first-level       PERFORM WRITE-OUT-2 VARYING J FROM 1 BY 1 UNTIL J > 6.   ← invoke a lower-level routine
routine           IF I > 6 THEN MOVE S-ID (I) TO STUDENT-ID-OUT
                  ELSE MOVE 'AVER' TO STUDENT-ID-OUT.
                  WRITE OUT-LINE FROM PRINT-MASK AFTER ADVANCING 3.

second-         WRITE-OUT-2.
level             MOVE TEST (I, J) TO TEST-OUT (J).
routine           MOVE SPACES TO FILL-OUT (J).
```

process modules: control logic that processes each module is organized from top to bottom, and only the permissible control structures are used in the entire program

Also note that the main control logic that processes each routine is organized from top to bottom as shown in Fig. 17-4, and only the basic permissible control structures are used. It is rather self-evident that the entire program is easy to read and understand.

REFERENCES

Dahl, O.-J., Dijkstra, E. W., and Hoare, A. R., "Structured Programming." Academic Press, New York, 1972.

Dijkstra, E. W., GO TO Statement Considered Harmful, *Comm. ACM* **11,** 147–148 (1968).

Dijkstra, E. W., The Humble Programmer. 1972 ACM Turing Award Lecture, *Comm. ACM* **15,** 859–866 (1972).

Knuth, D. E., Structured Programming with GO TO Statements, Stanford Computer Science Department Report STAN-CS-74-416 (1976).

McGowan, C. L., and Kelly, J. R., "Top-Down Structured Programming Techniques." Petrocelli/Charter, New York, 1975.

"Programming." *Special Issue, ACM Computing Survey* **6,** 4 (1974).

Stevenson, H. P., *Proc. Symp. Structured Programming in COBOL—Future and Present*, ACM, 1975.

Appendix A
ENVIRONMENT DIVISIONS
for Various Systems

Burroughs-5500

    CONFIGURATION SECTION.
    SOURCE-COMPUTER. B-5500.
    OBJECT-COMPUTER. B-5500.
    INPUT-OUTPUT SECTION.
    FILE-CONTROL.
        SELECT file-name
            ASSIGN TO { READER (card reader)
                          PRINTER (line printer)
                          TAPE (tape drive)
                          SORT-TAPES (sort-tape)
                          PUNCH (card punch)
                          MESSAGE-PRINTER (console)
                          KEYBOARD (console)
                          DISK (disk pack)
                          SORT-DISK (sort disk) }

A ENVIRONMENT DIVISIONS for Various Systems

Control Data 6400, 6500, 6600

    CONFIGURATION SECTION.
    SOURCE-COMPUTER. $\left\{\begin{array}{l}6400.\\6500.\\6600.\end{array}\right\}$
    OBJECT-COMPUTER.
    INPUT-OUTPUT SECTION.
    FILE-CONTROL.
        SELECT file-name
            ASSIGN TO $\left\{\begin{array}{l}\text{INPUT (card reader)}\\\text{OUTPUT (line printer)}\\\text{PUNCH (card punch)}\\\text{TAPE01 (tape drive)}\dagger\\\text{DISK01 (disk)}\dagger\end{array}\right.$

Honeywell 200

    CONFIGURATION SECTION.
    SOURCE-COMPUTER. H-200.
    OBJECT-COMPUTER. H-200.
    SPECIAL-NAMES.
        PAGE IS mnemonic-name (for printer control—skip to top of new page)
    INPUT-OUTPUT SECTION.
    FILE-CONTROL.
        SELECT file-name
            ASSIGN TO $\left\{\begin{array}{l}\text{CARD-READER}\\\text{CARD PUNCH}\\\text{PRINTER}\\\text{TAPE-UNIT}\\\text{MSD (mass-storage device)}\end{array}\right.$

IBM 360/370

    CONFIGURATION SECTION.
    SOURCE-COMPUTER. $\left\{\begin{array}{l}\text{IBM-370.}\\\text{IBM-360.}\end{array}\right\}$
    OBJECT-COMPUTER.
    SPECIAL-NAMES.
        C01 IS mnemonic-name (for printer control—skip to top of new page)
    INPUT-OUTPUT SECTION.
    FILE-CONTROL.
        SELECT file-name
            ASSIGN TO

---

† For tape or disk file, TAPE01 or DISK01 can be any programmer-supplied name beginning with a letter, no more than seven characters long, containing only letters or numbers.

294 A ENVIRONMENT DIVISIONS for Various Systems

(a) Under OS

$$\left\{\begin{array}{l}\text{UR-S-ddname (card reader)}\\ \text{UR-2501-S-ddname (card reader)}\\ \text{UR-S-ddname (line printer)}\\ \text{UR-1403-S-ddname (line printer)}\\ \text{UR-S-ddname (card punch)}\\ \text{UR-1540P-S-ddname (card punch)}\\ \text{UT-S-ddname (tape)}\\ \text{UT-2400-S-ddname (tape)}\\ \text{DA-D-ddname (direct-file disk)}\\ \text{DA-2314-D-ddname (direct-file disk)}\\ \text{DA-I-ddname (indexed sequential file)}\\ \text{DA-2314-I-ddname (indexed sequential file)}\\ \text{DA-S-ddname (sequential disk file)}\\ \text{DA-2314-S-ddname (sequential disk file)}\end{array}\right.$$

Here ddname is a unique external-name as it appears in the DD card of JCL. The ddname must begin with a letter and may center in 1 to 8 characters.

(b) Under DOS

$$\left\{\begin{array}{l}\text{SYSnnn-UR-2501-S (card reader)}\\ \text{SYSnnn-UR-1403-S (printer card punch)}\\ \text{SYSnnn-UR-2540P-S (printer card punch)}\\ \text{SYSnnn-UT-2400-S (tape)}\\ \text{SYSnnn-DA-2314-D (direct file)}\\ \text{SYSnnn-DA-2314-I (indexed sequential file)}\\ \text{SYSnnn-DA-2314-S (sequential disk file)}\end{array}\right.$$

Here nnn is a number between 000 and 321.

IBM 1130

```
        CONFIGURATION SECTION.
        SOURCE-COMPUTER. IBM-1130.
        OBJECT-COMPUTER. IBM-1130.
        INPUT-OUTPUT SECTION.
        FILE-CONTROL.
            SELECT file-name
                ASSIGN TO
```

$$\left\{\begin{array}{l}\text{RD-1442 (card reader)}\\ \text{RD-2501 (card reader)}\\ \text{PU-1442 (card punch)}\\ \text{PR-1403 (printer)}\\ \text{PR-1132 (printer)}\\ \text{DF-fffff-rrrrr (disk)}\end{array}\right.$$

Here fffff is a file number and rrrrr a record number. Both of these numbers must be between 1 and 32767.

UNIVAC 1106, 1108

    CONFIGURATION SECTION.
    SOURCE-COMPUTER. { UNIVAC-1108.
    OBJECT-COMPUTER. { UNIVAC-1106. }
    SPECIAL-NAMES.
        TOP-OF-PAGE IS mnemonic-name (for printer control—skip to top of new page)
    INPUT-OUTPUT SECTION.
    FILE-CONTROL.
        SELECT file-name
            ASSIGN TO { CARD-READER.
                          CARD-PUNCH
                          PRINTER
                          UNISERVO (tape drive)
                          MASS-STORAGE (disk)

XDS SIGMA

    CONFIGURATION SECTION.
    SOURCE-COMPUTER. XDS-SIGMA.
    OBJECT-COMPUTER. XDS-SIGMA.
    INPUT-OUTPUT SECTION.
    FILE-CONTROL.
        SELECT file-name
            ASSIGN TO { CARD-READER
                          CARD-PUNCH
                          PRINTER
                          MAGNETIC-TAPE
                          DISC

RCA SPECTRA 70

    CONFIGURATION SECTION.
    SOURCE-COMPUTER. RCA-SPECTRA.
    OBJECT-COMPUTER. RCA-SPECTRA.
    INPUT-OUTPUT SECTION.
    FILE-CONTROL.
        SELECT file-name
            ASSIGN TO { SYSIN (system card reader)
                          SYSINT (system input tape)
                          SYSOUT (printer)
                          SYSPUNCH (card punch)
                          SYSOPT (output tape)

Appendix B

Job Control Statements for IBM 360/370 Systems

An operating system is a collection of vendor-developed programs that manages the overall utilization of a computer system. In order to have a program compiled and executed by the computer, programmers must provide instructions to the operating system. These instructions are entered by means of job control statements. In this appendix, we will present a brief introduction to the job control statements for IBM 360/370 OS and DOS operating systems. Readers are urged to consult local system manuals for further study.

B.1 JOB CONTROL STATEMENTS FOR OS

The most commonly required job control statements for programmers are

JOB statement: // JOB
EXEC statement: // EXEC
DD STATEMENT (data definition): // DD
delimiter statement: /*
null statement: //
comment statement: //*

A brief discussion of these statements follows.

JOB Statement

The JOB statement marks the beginning of a new job and thus must be the first statement of every job. The general format of the statement is

//job-name JOB operands comments

The job-name identifies the job. It must begin in column 3 and may contain up to 8 alphanumeric characters, but the first character must be a letter.

The operand field contains parameters such as account number, the programmer or user name (these are positional parameters), job priority, time limit, job class, message class and level, and main storage allocation (for MVT). (These are keyword parameters.) These parameters govern the manner in which a job is processed.

Example 1

This is an example of a standard JOB card, using all job defaults:

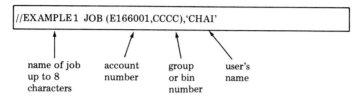

Example 2

A JOB card requesting 100K of main storage and 1 minute, 20 seconds, of CPU time might take the form

Example 3

This is a JOB card requesting 150K of main storage, and detailing the printout of job control statements and system messages:

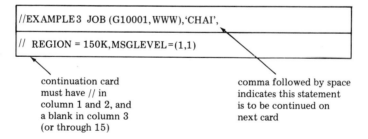

Example 4

An example of a nonstandard JOB statement is

```
//LT JOB CCC SC000701.OPSYS N=CHAI,REG=100
```

EXEC Statement

The EXEC statement is the first statement of a job step. It identifies the processing program to be executed or the name of a catalogued procedure to be used. The general format of the EXEC statement is

//step-name EXEC operands comments

The step-name identifies the job step and can be referred to in other JCL statements. The operand field contains both positional parameters (such as program name) and keyword parameters (such as region size and time limit).

Example 5

To execute an IBM standard catalogued procedure compiling a COBOL source program, either

```
//STEP1  EXEC COBUC,PARM=APOST
```

or

```
// EXEC COBAC  PARM=APOST
```

can be used, where APOST indicates that in the COBOL source program, apostrophes (') are used to define nonnumeric literals.

Example 6

To execute a program called PAYPRG1, which requires 150K of main storage and 2 hours of CPU time, we use

```
//BIGSTEP EXEC PGM=PAYPRG1, TIME=(120,0),REGION=150K
```

DD Statement

The DD statement is used to provide a description of a data set. Under the operating system, every data set that is to be processed by the job step must be defined through the DD statement. The DD statement for a job step must follow the EXEC statement and takes the form

//ddname DD operands comments

The ddname connects the data set with the COBOL source program's unit name in the ASSIGN clause. For instance, if the user's COBOL program contains

... ASSIGN TO UR-2540R-S-INFILE.

then the corresponding DD statement would have INFILE as the ddname, that is,

```
//INFILE DD ...
```

The DD statement must also provide information such as data set disposition (DISP), data set name (DSN), IO unit, and volume specification (VOL). This information must be coded in the operand field of the DD statement (separated by commas).

Example 7

An example of the DD statement is

```
//DISKFLE DD DSNAME=MASTER,UNIT=2314,DISP=(NEW,KEEP)
```

Delimiter Statement

The delimiter statement

/* comments

is used to separate the data from subsequent control statements. If data cards appear in the input stream, a delimiter statement must be presented to signify the end of such a data set.

Null Statement

The null statement

// comments

is used to indicate the end of a job stream. Every job must have the null statement as the last job control statement in its job stream.

Comment Statement

The statement

//* comments

can be inserted before or after any control statements. It is used to contain information deemed helpful by the person who codes the control statements. Comments can be coded in columns 4 through 80.

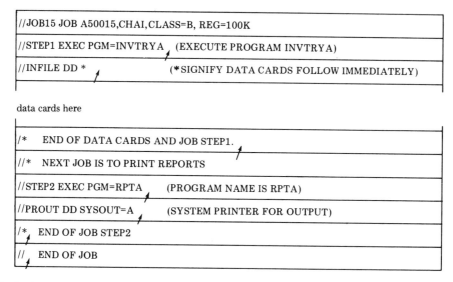

Fig. B-1 A single job stream. Short arrows indicate that comments must be separated by at least one blank space.

Figure B-1 illustrates a typical job stream consisting of a two-job step. Notice that in this example almost every job statement contains comments. These comments must be separated from the operand by at least one blank space.

B.2 COMPILING AND EXECUTING A COBOL PROGRAM UNDER OS

After a COBOL program has been coded and keypunched, it must be translated into machine language before the computer is able to execute the instructions. Such translation is performed by the COBOL compiler, which produces an object module.

The object module must then be processed by the *linkage editor* before it is ready for execution. Thus, in order for a COBOL source program to be compiled and executed, the following steps must be accomplished:

(1) The job of compiling the program must be defined through the job card.
(2) The COBOL compiler must be loaded into the main core storage in order to translate the source program into an object module. This is accomplished through the use of an EXEC control card.
(3) The COBOL source deck must be read by the compiler.
(4) The end of the source program must be indicated to the compiler. The delimiter control statement /* is used for this purpose.
(5) If the program is to be executed, it must call upon the linkage editor to resolve any external reference and form a load module that may then be loaded into the main storage for execution.
(6) Input/output or working files that are to be processed by the program must be specified for the operating system. This is accomplished by using the DD control cards.

Using the IBM Catalogued Procedures

The simplest way to process a COBOL program is to utilize the IBM-supplied catalog procedures. These procedures are distributed by IBM with the operating system and are usually available at any OS installation. These procedures are

(1) COBUC or COBAC for compilation.
(2) COBUCG or COBACG for compilation and loading (that is, execution).
(3) COBUCL or COBACL for compilation and linkage editing.
(4) COBUCLG or COBACLG for compilation, linkage editing, and execution.
(5) LKEDG, COBULG, or COBALG for linkage editing and execution.

Note that the letter U stands for version 2 and letter A for version 4 of the IBM COBOL compilers.

Complete job streams for compiling and executing COBOL source programs are given in the following examples.

B.2 Compiling and Executing a COBOL Program under OS

Example 1: Compiling and executing a single source program

```
//TESTA JOB (A001, CCCC),'CHAI', MSGLEVEL=(1, 1),REGION=100K
```
```
/*PASSWORD NULLPASS
```
```
//STAPA EXEC COBUCG, PARM=(APOST,XREF)
```
```
//COB.SYSIN DD *
```
```
    COBOL source deck here
```
```
/*
```
```
//GO.PROUT DD SYSOUT=A
```
```
//GO.INFILE DD *
```
```
    data cards here
```
```
/*
```
```
//
```

Note: It is assumed that in the user's source program, PROUT and INFILE must appear as the last entries in the ASSIGN clause, that is

> SELECT xxxxx ASSIGN TO UR-2540R-S-INFILE.
> SELECT yyyyy ASSIGN TO UR-1403-S-PROUT.

Explanation: This example illustrates how an IBM catalogued procedure COBUCG can be used to compile and execute a single COBOL source program. The COBUCG is a two-step procedure, commonly known as "compile and load."

In our JCL setups, we assume that the source program is to read a batch of data cards, then list the output on the printer.

JCL Description

(1) The JOB statement

```
//TESTA JOB (A001, CCCC),'CHAI', MSGLEVEL=(1, 1),REGION=100K
```

must be the first statement in a job stream. In this example, the job is identified as TESTA, the account number as A001, and the programmer's name as CHAI. The job is to be executed with 100K of the main core storage (REGION=100k). The MSGLEVEL=(1,1) parameter specifies that all of the job control and data set allocation messages are to be printed.

(2) The PASSWORD statement

```
/*PASSWORD NULLPASS
```

identifies the PASSWORD of this job as NULLPASS.

(3) The EXEC statement

```
//STEPA EXEC COBUCG,PARM=(APOST, XRFF)
```

directs the operating system to execute the job step (identified as STEPA) according to the catalogued procedure COBUCG.

The APOST entry in the PARM parameter specifies that apostrophes are used to define nonnumeric literals in the source program. If this entry is deleted, the compiler would take the default option, which assumes that quotation marks (") are used to define nonnumeric literals. The XREF entry indicates that a cross-reference listing is to be produced by the compiler.

(4) The first DD statement

```
//COB. SYSIN DD *
```

signifies that the source program that serves as the input to the procedure COBUCG follows immediately.

(5) The delimiter card (/*) signifies the end of the source deck.

(6) The DD statement for printer output is

```
//GO. PROUT DD SYSOUT=A
```

In this statement, the operand SYSOUT=A indicates that the output is to be placed in an output class A. In most installations, the value of an output class can be any letter A through Z. However, traditionally the letter A is reserved for the printer. Also, the ddname PROUT must correspond to the ddname entry in the ASSIGN clause of the source program, that is,

SELECT xxxxx ASSIGN TO UR-1403-S-PROUT

If the programmer changes the above clause to

SELECT xxxxx ASSIGN TO UR-1403-S-PAYRPT

the ddname on the corresponding JCL DD card must be changed accordingly to

```
//GO.PAYRPT DD SYSOUT=A
```

Furthermore, the ddname entry PROUT is preceded by the word GO and these words are separated by a period. An entry such as GO is required whenever a catalogued procedure such as COBUCG is invoked.

(7) The DD statement for the input data card file is

```
//GO.INFILE DD *
```

The symbol * is used to indicate that input data cards follow after the DD statement in the job stream.

The ddname INFILE, as in the case of PROUT, must correspond to the ddname entry of the source program. That is, the programmer must have the following ASSIGN clause in the source program:

SELECT xxxxx ASSIGN TO UR-2540R-S-INFILE.

Example 2: Program and subprogram—compile-link-GO

//TESTB JOB (CL12345, MMMM), 'MARCINKO',REGION=150K,TIME=2 ← indicates 2 minutes of CPU time
//STEP1 EXEC COBUC,PARM=APOST
//COB.SYSIN DD *
SOURCE PROGRAM 1
/*
//STEP2 EXEC COBUCLG,PARM=APOST
//COB.SYSIN DD *
SOURCE PROGRAM 2
/*
//LKED.SYSIN DD *
ENTRY MAINP
/*
//GO.PROUT DD SYSOUT=A
//GO.CARDIN DD *
DATA CARDS
/*
//

Explanation: This example illustrates how a COBOL main program and a subprogram can be compiled and executed together as a single program. The first EXEC statement specifies that a source program A will be compiled only (no execution). Source program A could be either a main program or a subprogram. The second EXEC statement calls for the execution of COBUCLG, which is a three-step procedure: compile, link, and GO.

The statement

//LKED.SYSIN DD *
ENTRY MAINP
/*

specifies that the program execution should start in the main program. (Here we assume that the name of the main program is MAINP. This name may be specified in the program-ID entry of the source program, that is, PROGRAM-ID. 'MAINP'.)

B.3 DD STATEMENTS FOR PROCESSING DISK FILES UNDER OS

Creating a Temporary Sequential File on Disk

```
//GO.DSKFILE DD UNIT=SYSDA, SPACE=(TRK, 2)
```

Explanation

(a) DSKFILE is a ddname that must correspond to the ddname used by the programmer in the source program, for example, SELECT ... ASSIGN TO DA-2314-S-DSKFILE.
(b) The UNIT parameter indicates that a system direct access device is being used.
(c) The SPACE parameter requests the system to allocate two tracks of disk storage.

Creating a Sequential File on Disk for Future Use

```
//GO.ddname DD DSN=FILEA,UNIT=3330,VOL=SER=EIS105,
//DISP=(NEW, KEEP),SPACE=(TRK,(10, 2))
```

Explanation

(a) The DSN (DSNAME) parameter identifies the data set name as FILEA.
(b) The UNIT parameter indicates that a 3330 disk pack is being used.
(c) The VOL parameter specifies that a file be placed on a disk pack that has the serial number EIS105.
(d) The DISP parameter indicates that this file is to be created (NEW) and should be kept after the completion of the job.
(e) The SPACE parameter requests the system initially allocate five tracks. If that is not enough, two additional tracks will be provided, up to 16 allocations of two tracks (that is, $5 + 32 = 37$ tracks in all).

Retrieving a Sequential File on Disk

```
//GO.ddname DD DSN=FILEA,UNIT=3330,VOL=SER=EIS105,DISP=OLD
```

Explanation: To retrieve a file from the disk, the DISP parameter must be specified as OLD. If such a file is to be deleted after the completion of the job, the DISP parameter should be coded as DISP=(OLD,DELETE).

Creating a Direct File

```
//GO.MISTR DD DSN=E10001.CHAI.FILE1,
// UNIT=3330,VOL=SER=EIS105,
// SPACE=(TRK,(10, 2),RLSE),
// DCB=(DSORG=DA,RECFM=F,LRECL=80,BLKSILE=80),
// DISP=(NEW,CATLG)
```

Explanation

(a) The DSN specifies the name of the data set (notice that we are using a qualified name that contains three levels: E10001 (account-ID), CHAI (programmer's name), and FILE1 (data set name). These levels are separated by a period.

(b) The SPACE parameter specifies that any unused tracks will be released back to the system.

(c) The DCB parameter provides the necessary information concerning file characteristics. It contains four subparameters:

DSORG=DA: specifies that this file is a direct file. If this parameter is omitted, the system would assume the file to be sequential.
RECFM=F: specifies that records are a fixed length.
LRECL=80: specifies that each logical record contains 80 characters.
BLKSIZE=80: specifies that each block of records contains 80 characters.

(d) The DISP parameter specifies that this is a new file and it should be catalogued at the end of the job.

Retrieving and Updating a DIRECT FILE

```
//GO.UPDATE1 DD DSN=E10001.CHAI.FILE1,
// DCB=(DSORG=DA,RECFM=F,LRECL=80,BLKSIZE=80),
// DISP=OLD
```

Explanation: To retrieve or update an existing file that was previously catalogued, the programmer can omit both UNIT and VOL parameters. Also note that the DISP=OLD is specified here.

Creating an ISAM File

```
//GO.ISFILE DD DSN=E50001.SMITH.MASTER1,
// UNIT=2314,VOL=SER=123456,
// SPACE=(CYL,(5,2)),
// DCB=(DSORG=IS,RECM=F,LRECL=80,BLKSIZE=800),
// DISP=(NEW,CATLG)
```

Explanation: The DD statement for processing an ISAM file is very similar to the DD statement used for the direct file, except that the SPACE parameter must be specified as cylinders and the DSORG (which is a subparameter of DCB) must be specified as IS.

The SPACE parameter

```
// SPACE=(CYL,(5, 2)), . . .
```

indicates that five cylinders should be allocated to the file initially. If this is not enough, an additional 32 (2 × 16) cylinders will be made available to the file.

Updating or Retrieving an ISAM File

```
// GO.MYFILE DD DSN=E50001.SMITH.MASTERS,
// SPACE=(CYL,(5,2)),
// DCB=(DSORG=IS,RECFM=F,LRECL=80,BLKSIZE=800),
// DISP=OLD
```

Explanation: Here again we assume that the ISAM file was previously catalogued. Thus both UNIT and VOL parameters are omitted.

B.4 JOB CONTROL STATEMENTS FOR DOS

Compiling a COBOL Source Program

```
// JOB card
// EXEC FCOBOL
      COBOL
      source program here
/*
/&
```

Compiling and Link Editing a COBOL Source Program

```
// JOB card
// OPTION LINK
// EXEC FCOBOL
     COBOL source deck here
/*
// EXEC LNKEDT
/*
/&
```

Compiling, Link Editing, and Executing a COBOL Source Program

```
// JOB card
// OPTION LINK
// EXEC FCOBOL
     COBOL
     source program here
```

B.4 Job Control Statements for DOS   307

```
/*
// EXEC LNKEDT
// ASSGN SYS005,SYSRDR  (System reader)
// ASSGN SYS005,SYSLST  (System printer)
// EXEC
input data cards here
/*
/&
```

(a) It is assumed that the following entries appear in the source program:

SELECT xxxxxx ASSIGN TO SYS0005-UR-2501-S.
SELECT yyyyy ASSIGN TO SYS0006-UR-1403-S.

(b) In some installations, the same SYSRDR or SYSLST may be replaced by X'OOC' or X'OOE'.

Test Run for Processing a Tape File (Using Standard Labels)

```
// JOB card
// OPTION LINK
// EXEC FCOBOL
   COBOL source program here
/*
// LBLTY TAPE (required for standard label)
// EXEC LNKEDT
// ASSIGN SYS005,X'OOE' (output printer)
// ASSIGN SYS007,X'180' (tape file)
// TLBL TPMASTER,'CUSTOMER A',75/300,120011
// EXEC
/*
/&
```

(a) The LBLTY card is required whenever the standard labels are used. They must appear prior to the EXEC LNKEDT statement as shown.

(b) The TLBL statement contains the information on the tape label. It identifies the FILE-ID as 'CUSTOMER A', the expiration date of the file as 75/300, where the first number represents the year 1975 and the second the Julian day of the year (for example, Jan. 24, 1976 would be written 76/024), and the volume serial number of the tape as 120001. This information will be automatically checked by the operating system when the file is opened. If this information does not check, the operating system will terminate the job with an error message. Also, the name

TPMASTER is the ddname that appears in the source program as shown:

SELECT . . . ASSIGN TO SYS007-UT-2400-S-TPMASTER

Test Run for Creating an ISAM File from Data Cards

// JOB card
// OPTION LINK
// EXEC FCOBOL
source program here
/*
// LBLTYP NSD (02)
// EXEC LNKEDT
// ASSIGN SYS005,X'00C'
// ASSIGN SYS010,X'131'
// DLBL ISFILE,'MY ISAM FILE',100,ISC
// EXTENT SYS010,EIS105,4,1,200,1
// EXTENT , ,1,2,220,60
// EXEC
input data cards here
/*
/&

(a) The LBLTYP card specifies that this is a nonsequential disk file with a maximum of two extents.

(b) The DLBL card specifies the information that will be part of the standard labels. It identifies the FILE-ID as 'MY ISAM FILE', which should be retained for 100 days (that is, this file may be scratched after 100 days). The word ISC indicates that the program is creating an ISAM file.

(c) The first EXTENT card specifies that the file is to be placed on a disk pack that has the serial number EIS105. Only one track is assigned to the cylinder index (track 1 of cylinder 10—assume that IBM 2314 is used here).

(d) The second EXTENT card specifies that 60 tracks are assigned to the prime data area. These 60 tracks begin in cylinder 11 of EIS105.

(e) The name ISFILE is the ddname as it appears in the source program, that is,

SELECT . . . ASSIGN TO SYS010-DA-2314-I-ISFILE

(f) When retrieving the above ISAM file, the programmer only has to change the word ISC to ISE:

// DLBL ISFILE,'MY ISAM FILE,' 100,ISE

Appendix C

COBOL Reserved Words

Words with an asterisk are special reserved words for the IBM COBOL compiler. These words may not have meaning to any other computer system.

ACCEPT	*CBL	COPY
ACCESS	CF	*CORE-INDEX
ACTUAL	CH	CORR
ADD	*CHANGED	CORRESPONDING
ADDRESS	CHARACTERS	*CSP
ADVANCING	CLOCK-UNITS	CURRENCY
AFTER	CLOSE	*CURRENT-DATE
ALL	COBOL	*CYL-INDEX
ALPHABETIC	CODE	*CYL-OVERFLOW
ALTER	COLUMN	*C01
ALTERNATE	COMMA	*C02
AND	COMP	*C03
*APPLY	*COMP-1	*C04
ARE	*COMP-2	*C05
AREA	*COMP-3	*C06
AREAS	*COMP-4	*C07
ASCENDING	COMPUTATIONAL	*C08
ASSIGN	*COMPUTATIONAL-1	*C09
AT	*COMPUTATIONAL-2	*C10
AUTHOR	*COMPUTATIONAL-3	*C11
	*COMPUTATIONAL-4	*C12
*BASIS	COMPUTE	
BEFORE	*COM-REG	DATA
BEGINNING	CONFIGURATION	*DATE
BLANK	*CONSOLE	DATE-COMPILED
BLOCK	CONSTANT	DATE-WRITTEN
BY	CONTAINS	*DAY
	CONTROL	DE
CALL	CONTROLS	*DEBUG
CANCEL	CONVERSION	*DEBUG-SUB-1

*DEBUG-SUB-2
*DEBUG-SUB-3
*DEBUGGING
DECIMAL-POINT
DECLARATIVES
*DELIMITED
DEPENDING
DESCENDING
*DELIMITER
DETAIL
*DISP
DISPLAY
*DISPLAY-ST
DIVIDE
DIVISION
DOWN
DUPLICATES
DYNAMICS

*EJECT
ELSE
END-OF-PAGE
*ENDING
ENTER
*ENTRY
ENVIRONMENT
EOP
EQUAL
EQUALS
ERROR
EVERY
EXAMINE
EXCEEDS
*EXHIBIT
EXIT
EXTEND
*EXTENDED-SEARCH

FILE
FILE-CONTROL
FILE-LIMIT
FILE-LIMITS
FILLER
FIRST
FOOTING
FOR
FROM

GENERATE
GIVING
*GOBACK
GREATER
GROUP

HEADING
HIGH-VALUE
HIGH-VALUES

*ID
IDENTIFICATION
INDEX
INDEXED
INDICATE
*INITIATE
INPUT
INPUT-OUTPUT
INSTALLATION
INTO
INVALID
I-O
I-O-CONTROL

JUST
JUSTIFIED

KEY
KEYS

LABEL
*LABEL-RETURN
LAST
LEADING
*LEAVE
LEFT
LESS
LIMIT
LIMITS
LINAGE
LINAGE-COUNTER
LINE
LINE-COUNTER
LINES
LINKAGE

LOCK
LOW-VALUE
LOW-VALUES

MASTER-INDEX
MEMORY
MODE
MODULES
*MORE-LABELS
MOVE
MULTIPLE
MULTIPLY

NAMED
NEGATIVE
NEXT
NOMINAL
NOT
NOTE
NUMBER
NUMERIC

OBJECT-COMPUTER
OCCURS
OMITTED
OPEN
OPTIONAL
ORGANIZATION
*OTHERWISE
OVERFLOW

PAGE
PAGE-COUNTER
PERFORM
PF
PH
PIC
PICTURE
PLUS
POSITION
*POSITIONING
POSITIVE
PRINT-SWITCH
PROCEDURE

C COBOL Reserved Words

PROCEED	SELECT	TERMINATE
PROCESSING	SELECTED	THAN
PROGRAM	SENTENCE	*THEN
PROGRAM-ID	SEQUENCED	THROUGH
	SEQUENTIAL	THRU
*QUEUE	SET	TIME
QUOTE	SIGN	*TIME-OF-DAY
QUOTES	SIZE	TIMES
	*SKIP1	TO
RANDOM	*SKIP2	TOP
RD	*SKIP3	*TOTALED
READ	SORT	*TOTALING
*READY	*SORT-CORE-SIZE	*TRACE
RECORD	*SORT-FILE-SIZE	*TRACK
*RECORD-OVERFLOW	*SORT-MODE-SIZE	*TRACK-AREA
*RECORDING	*SORT-RETURN	*TRACK-LIMIT
RECORDS	SOURCE	TRAILING
REDEFINES	SOURCE-COMPUTER	*TRANSFORM
REEL	SPACE	TYPE
RELATIVE	SPACES	
RELEASE	SPECIAL-NAMES	UNIT
REMAINDER	STANDARD	UNSTRING
REMARKS	START	UNTIL
RENAMES	STATUS	UP
*REORG-CRITERIA	STOP	UPON
REPLACING	STRING	*UPSI-1
REPORT	SUB-QUEUE-1	*UPSI-2
REPORTING	SUB-QUEUE-2	*UPSI-3
REPORTS	SUB-QUEUE-3	*UPSI-4
*REREAD	SUBTRACT	*UPSI-5
RERUN	SUM	*UPSI-6
RESERVE	SUPERVISOR	*UPSI-7
RESET	SUPPRESS	USAGE
RETURN	SUSPEND	USE
*RETURN-CODE	SYMBOLIC	USING
REVERSED	SYNC	
REWIND	SYNCHRONIZED	VALUE
*REWRITE	*SYSIN	VALUES
RF	*SYSIPT	VARYING
RH	*SYSLST	
RIGHT	*SYSOUT	WHEN
ROUNDED	*SYSPCH	WITH
RUN	*SYSPUNCH	WORDS
	*S01	WORKING-STORAGE
SAME	*S02	WRITE
SD		*WRITE-ONLY
SEARCH	TABLE	*WRITE-VERIFY
SECTION	TALLY	
SECURITY	TALLYING	ZERO
SEGMENT-LIMIT	TAPE	ZEROES
		ZEROS

Appendix D

Standard COBOL Statements and Instruction Formats

COBOL statements pertinent to the IBM systems are identified by shaded areas. These statements may not have meaning to any other COBOL compilers.

IDENTIFICATION DIVISION – BASIC FORMATS

{IDENTIFICATION DIVISION.}
{ID DIVISION.}
PROGRAM-ID. program-name.
AUTHOR. [comment-entry] . . .
INSTALLATION. [comment-entry] . . .
DATE-WRITTEN. [comment-entry] . . .
DATE-COMPILED. [comment-entry] . . .
SECURITY. [comment-entry] . . .
REMARKS. [comment-entry] . . .

ENVIRONMENT DIVISION – BASIC FORMATS

ENVIRONMENT DIVISION.
CONFIGURATION SECTION.
SOURCE-COMPUTER. computer-name.
OBJECT-COMPUTER. computer-name [MEMORY SIZE integer {WORDS / CHARACTERS / MODULES}]
    [SEGMENT-LIMIT IS priority-number].
SPECIAL-NAMES. [function-name IS mnemonic-name] . . .
    [CURRENCY SIGN IS literal]
    [DECIMAL-POINT IS COMMA].
INPUT-OUTPUT SECTION.
FILE-CONTROL.
    {SELECT [OPTIONAL] file name
    ASSIGN TO [integer-1] system-name-1 [system-name-2] . . .
    [FOR MULTIPLE {REEL / UNIT}]
    RESERVE {NO / integer-1} ALTERNATE [AREA / AREAS]
    {FILE-LIMIT IS / FILE-LIMITS ARE} {data-name-1 / literal-1} THRU {data-name-2 / literal-2}
    [{data-name-3 / literal-3} THRU {data-name-4 / literal-4}] . . .
    ACCESS MODE IS {SEQUENTIAL / RANDOM}
    PROCESSING MODE IS SEQUENTIAL
    ACTUAL KEY IS data-name
    NOMINAL KEY IS data-name
    RECORD KEY IS data-name
    TRACK-AREA IS {data-name / integer} CHARACTERS
    TRACK-LIMIT IS integer [TRACK / TRACKS] .}. . .

I-O-CONTROL.
    RERUN ON system-name EVERY [integer RECORDS / [END OF] {REEL / UNIT}] OF file-name
    SAME [RECORD / SORT] AREA FOR file-name-1 {file-name-2} . . .
    MULTIPLE FILE TAPE CONTAINS file-name-1 [POSITION integer-1]
      [file-name-2 [POSITION integer-2]] . . .
    APPLY WRITE-ONLY ON file-name-1 [file-name-2] . . .
    APPLY CORE-INDEX ON file-name-1 [file-name-2] . . .
    APPLY RECORD-OVERFLOW ON file-name-1 [file-name-2] . . .
    APPLY REORG-CRITERIA TO data-name ON file-name . . . .
NOTE: Format 2 of the RERUN Clause (for Sort Files) is included with Formats for the SORT feature.

DATA DIVISION – BASIC FORMATS

DATA DIVISION.
FILE SECTION.
FD file-name
    BLOCK CONTAINS [integer-1 TO] integer-2 {CHARACTERS / RECORDS}
    RECORD CONTAINS [integer-1 TO] integer-2 CHARACTERS
    RECORDING MODE IS mode
    LABEL {RECORD IS / RECORDS ARE} {OMITTED / STANDARD / data-name-1 [data-name-2] . . . [TOTALING AREA IS data-name-3 TOTALED AREA IS data-name-4]}
    VALUE OF data-name-1 IS {literal-1 / data-name-2} [data-name-3 IS {literal-2 / data-name-4}] . . .
    DATA {RECORD IS / RECORDS ARE} data-name-1 [data-name-2] . . . .
NOTE: Format for the REPORT Clause is included with Formats for the REPORT WRITER feature.

01-49 {data-name-1 / FILLER}
    REDEFINES data-name-2
    BLANK WHEN ZERO
    {JUSTIFIED / JUST} RIGHT
    {PICTURE / PIC} IS character string
    [SIGN IS] {LEADING / TRAILING} [SEPARATE CHARACTER] (Version 3 & 4)
    {SYNCHRONIZED / SYNC} [LEFT / RIGHT]

D Standard COBOL Statements and Instruction Formats

$$[\text{USAGE IS}] \left\{ \begin{array}{l} \text{INDEX} \\ \text{DISPLAY} \\ \text{COMPUTATIONAL} \\ \text{COMP} \\ \text{COMPUTATIONAL-1} \\ \text{COMP-1} \\ \text{COMPUTATIONAL-2} \\ \text{COMP-2} \\ \text{COMPUTATIONAL-3} \\ \text{COMP-3} \\ \text{COMPUTATIONAL-4} \\ \text{COMP-4} \\ \text{DISPLAY-ST} \end{array} \right\} \text{(Version 3 \& 4)}$$

88 condition-name $\left\{\begin{array}{l}\underline{\text{VALUE IS}}\\\underline{\text{VALUES ARE}}\end{array}\right\}$ literal-1 [THRU literal-2]

[literal-3 [THRU literal-4]] ...

66 data-name-1 RENAMES data-name-2 [THRU data-name-3].

NOTE: Formats for the OCCURS Clause are included with Formats for the TABLE HANDLING feature.

WORKING-STORAGE SECTION.

77 data-name-1

01-49 $\left\{\begin{array}{l}\text{data-name-1}\\\text{FILLER}\end{array}\right\}$

REDEFINES data-name-2

BLANK WHEN ZERO

$\left\{\begin{array}{l}\text{JUSTIFIED}\\\text{JUST}\end{array}\right\}$ RIGHT

$\left\{\begin{array}{l}\text{PICTURE}\\\text{PIC}\end{array}\right\}$ IS character string

[SIGN IS] $\left\{\begin{array}{l}\text{LEADING}\\\text{TRAILING}\end{array}\right\}$ [SEPARATE CHARACTER]   (Version 3 & 4)

$\left\{\begin{array}{l}\text{SYNCHRONIZED}\\\text{SYNC}\end{array}\right\}\left[\begin{array}{l}\text{LEFT}\\\text{RIGHT}\end{array}\right]$

$$[\text{USAGE IS}] \left\{ \begin{array}{l} \text{INDEX} \\ \text{DISPLAY} \\ \text{COMPUTATIONAL} \\ \text{COMP} \\ \text{COMPUTATIONAL-1} \\ \text{COMP-1} \\ \text{COMPUTATIONAL-2} \\ \text{COMP-2} \\ \text{COMPUTATIONAL-3} \\ \text{COMP-3} \\ \text{COMPUTATIONAL-4} \\ \text{COMP-4} \\ \text{DISPLAY-ST} \end{array} \right\} \text{(Version 3 \& 4)}$$

VALUE IS literal

88 condition-name $\left\{\begin{array}{l}\underline{\text{VALUE IS}}\\\underline{\text{VALUES ARE}}\end{array}\right\}$ literal-1 [THRU literal-2]

[literal-3 [THRU literal-4]] ...

66 data-name-1 RENAMES data-name-2 [THRU data-name-3].

NOTE: Formats for the OCCURS Clause are included with Formats for the TABLE HANDLING feature.

LINKAGE SECTION.

77 data-name-1

01-49 $\left\{\begin{array}{l}\text{data-name-1}\\\text{FILLER}\end{array}\right\}$

REDEFINES data-name-2

BLANK WHEN ZERO

$\left\{\begin{array}{l}\text{JUSTIFIED}\\\text{JUST}\end{array}\right\}$ RIGHT

$\left\{\begin{array}{l}\text{PICTURE}\\\text{PIC}\end{array}\right\}$ IS character string

[SIGN IS] $\left\{\begin{array}{l}\text{LEADING}\\\text{TRAILING}\end{array}\right\}$ [SEPARATE CHARACTER]   (Version 3 & 4)

$\left\{\begin{array}{l}\text{SYNCHRONIZED}\\\text{SYNC}\end{array}\right\}\left[\begin{array}{l}\text{LEFT}\\\text{RIGHT}\end{array}\right]$

$$[\text{USAGE IS}] \left\{ \begin{array}{l} \text{INDEX} \\ \text{DISPLAY} \\ \text{COMPUTATIONAL} \\ \text{COMP} \\ \text{COMPUTATIONAL-1} \\ \text{COMP-1} \\ \text{COMPUTATIONAL-2} \\ \text{COMP-2} \\ \text{COMPUTATIONAL-3} \\ \text{COMP-3} \\ \text{COMPUTATIONAL-4} \\ \text{COMP-4} \\ \text{DISPLAY-ST} \end{array} \right\} \text{(Version 3 \& 4)}$$

88 condition-name $\left\{\begin{array}{l}\underline{\text{VALUE IS}}\\\underline{\text{VALUES ARE}}\end{array}\right\}$ literal-1 [THRU literal-2]

[literal-3 [THRU literal-4]] ...

66 data-name-1 RENAMES data-name-2 [THRU data-name-3].

NOTE: Formats for the OCCURS Clause are included with Formats for the TABLE HANDLING feature.

PROCEDURE DIVISION — BASIC FORMATS

$\left\{\begin{array}{l}\underline{\text{PROCEDURE DIVISION}}.\\\underline{\text{PROCEDURE DIVISION}} \ \underline{\text{USING}} \ \text{identifier-1 [identifier-2] ...}\end{array}\right\}$

ACCEPT Statement

FORMAT 1

ACCEPT identifier [FROM $\left\{\begin{array}{l}\text{SYSIN}\\\text{CONSOLE}\\\text{mnemonic-name}\end{array}\right\}$]

FORMAT 2 (Version 4)

ACCEPT identifier FROM $\left\{\begin{array}{l}\text{DATE}\\\text{DAY}\\\text{TIME}\end{array}\right\}$

ADD Statement

FORMAT 1

ADD $\left\{\begin{array}{l}\text{identifier-1}\\\text{literal-1}\end{array}\right\}\left\{\begin{array}{l}\text{identifier-2}\\\text{literal-2}\end{array}\right\}$ ... TO identifier-m [ROUNDED]

[identifier-n [ROUNDED]] ... [ON SIZE ERROR imperative-statement]

FORMAT 2

ADD $\left\{\begin{array}{l}\text{identifier-1}\\\text{literal-1}\end{array}\right\}\left\{\begin{array}{l}\text{identifier-2}\\\text{literal-2}\end{array}\right\}\left[\begin{array}{l}\text{identifier-3}\\\text{literal-3}\end{array}\right]$ ... GIVING

identifier-m [ROUNDED] [ON SIZE ERROR imperative-statement]

FORMAT 3

ADD $\left\{\begin{array}{l}\text{CORRESPONDING}\\\text{CORR}\end{array}\right\}$ identifier-1 TO identifier-2 [ROUNDED]

[ON SIZE ERROR imperative-statement]

ALTER Statement

ALTER procedure-name-1 TO [PROCEED TO] procedure-name-2

[procedure-name-3 TO [PROCEED TO] procedure-name-4] ...

Call Statement

Format 1

CALL literal-1 [USING identifier-1 [identifier-2] ...]

Format 2 (Version 4)

CALL identifier-1 [USING identifier-2 [identifier-3] ...]

CANCEL Statement (Version 4)

CANCEL $\left\{\begin{array}{l}\text{literal-1}\\\text{identifier-1}\end{array}\right\}\left[\begin{array}{l}\text{literal-2}\\\text{identifier-2}\end{array}\right]$ ...

CLOSE Statement

FORMAT 1

CLOSE file-name-1 $\left[\begin{array}{l}\text{REEL}\\\text{UNIT}\end{array}\right]$ [WITH $\left\{\begin{array}{l}\text{NO REWIND}\\\text{LOCK}\end{array}\right\}$]

[file-name-2 $\left[\begin{array}{l}\text{REEL}\\\text{UNIT}\end{array}\right]$ [WITH $\left\{\begin{array}{l}\text{NO REWIND}\\\text{LOCK}\end{array}\right\}$]] ...

FORMAT 2

CLOSE file-name-1 [WITH $\left\{\begin{array}{l}\text{NO REWIND}\\\text{LOCK}\\\text{DISP}\end{array}\right\}$]

[file-name-2 [WITH $\left\{\begin{array}{l}\text{NO REWIND}\\\text{LOCK}\\\text{DISP}\end{array}\right\}$]] ...

FORMAT 3

CLOSE file-name-1 $\left\{\begin{array}{l}\text{REEL}\\\text{UNIT}\end{array}\right\}$ [WITH $\left\{\begin{array}{l}\text{NO REWIND}\\\text{LOCK}\\\text{POSITIONING}\end{array}\right\}$]

[file-name-2 $\left\{\begin{array}{l}\text{REEL}\\\text{UNIT}\end{array}\right\}$ [WITH $\left\{\begin{array}{l}\text{NO REWIND}\\\text{LOCK}\\\text{POSITIONING}\end{array}\right\}$]] ...

COMPUTE Statement

COMPUTE identifier-1 [ROUNDED] = $\left\{\begin{array}{l}\text{identifier-2}\\\text{literal-1}\\\text{arithmetic-expression}\end{array}\right\}$

[ON SIZE ERROR imperative-statement]

DECLARATIVE Section

PROCEDURE DIVISION.

DECLARATIVES.

{section-name SECTION. USE sentence.

{paragraph-name. {sentence} ...} ...} ...

END DECLARATIVES.

DISPLAY Statement

DISPLAY $\left\{\begin{array}{l}\text{literal-1}\\\text{identifier-1}\end{array}\right\}\left[\begin{array}{l}\text{literal-2}\\\text{identifier-2}\end{array}\right]$ ... [UPON $\left\{\begin{array}{l}\text{CONSOLE}\\\text{SYSPUNCH}\\\text{SYSOUT}\\\text{mnemonic-name}\end{array}\right\}$]

DIVIDE Statement

FORMAT 1

DIVIDE $\left\{\begin{array}{l}\text{identifier-1}\\\text{literal-1}\end{array}\right\}$ INTO identifier-2 [ROUNDED]

[ON SIZE ERROR imperative-statement]

FORMAT 2

DIVIDE $\left\{\begin{array}{l}\text{identifier-1}\\\text{literal-1}\end{array}\right\}\left\{\begin{array}{l}\text{INTO}\\\text{BY}\end{array}\right\}\left\{\begin{array}{l}\text{identifier-2}\\\text{literal-2}\end{array}\right\}$ GIVING identifier-3

[ROUNDED] [REMAINDER identifier-4] [ON SIZE ERROR imperative-statement]

ENTER Statement

ENTER language-name [routine-name].

ENTRY Statement

ENTRY literal-1 [USING identifier-1 [identifier-2] . . .]

EXAMINE Statement

FORMAT 1

EXAMINE identifier TALLYING $\begin{Bmatrix} \text{UNTIL FIRST} \\ \text{ALL} \\ \text{LEADING} \end{Bmatrix}$ literal-1

[REPLACING BY literal-2]

FORMAT 2

EXAMINE identifier REPLACING $\begin{Bmatrix} \text{ALL} \\ \text{LEADING} \\ \text{FIRST} \\ \text{UNTIL FIRST} \end{Bmatrix}$ literal-1 BY literal-2

EXIT Statement

paragraph-name. EXIT [PROGRAM].

GOBACK Statement

GOBACK.

GO TO Statement

FORMAT 1

GO TO procedure-name-1

FORMAT 2

GO TO procedure-name-1 [procedure-name-2] . . . DEPENDING ON identifier

FORMAT 3

GO TO.

IF Statement

IF condition THEN $\begin{Bmatrix} \text{statement-1} \\ \text{NEXT SENTENCE} \end{Bmatrix}$ $\begin{Bmatrix} \text{ELSE} \\ \text{OTHERWISE} \end{Bmatrix}$ $\begin{Bmatrix} \text{statement-2} \\ \text{NEXT SENTENCE} \end{Bmatrix}$

MOVE Statement

FORMAT 1

MOVE $\begin{Bmatrix} \text{identifier-1} \\ \text{literal-1} \end{Bmatrix}$ TO identifier-2 [identifier-3] . . .

FORMAT 2

MOVE $\begin{Bmatrix} \text{CORRESPONDING} \\ \text{CORR} \end{Bmatrix}$ identifier-1 TO identifier-2

MULTIPLY Statement

FORMAT 1

MULTIPLY $\begin{Bmatrix} \text{identifier-1} \\ \text{literal-1} \end{Bmatrix}$ BY identifier-2 [ROUNDED]

[ON SIZE ERROR imperative-statement]

FORMAT 2

MULTIPLY $\begin{Bmatrix} \text{identifier-1} \\ \text{literal-1} \end{Bmatrix}$ BY $\begin{Bmatrix} \text{identifier-2} \\ \text{literal-2} \end{Bmatrix}$ GIVING identifier-3

[ROUNDED] [ON SIZE ERROR imperative-statement]

NOTE Statement

NOTE character string

OPEN Statement

FORMAT 1

OPEN [INPUT {file-name [REVERSED / WITH NO REWIND]} . . .]

[OUTPUT {file-name [WITH NO REWIND]} . . .]

[I-O {file-name} . . .]

Format 3

OPEN [INPUT {file-name [REVERSED / WITH NO REWIND] [LEAVE / REREAD / DISP]} . . .]

[OUTPUT {file-name [WITH NO REWIND] [LEAVE / REREAD / DISP]} . . .]

[I-O {file-name} . . .]

PERFORM Statement

FORMAT 1

PERFORM procedure-name-1 [THRU procedure-name-2]

FORMAT 2

PERFORM procedure-name-1 [THRU procedure-name-2] $\begin{Bmatrix} \text{identifier-1} \\ \text{integer-1} \end{Bmatrix}$ TIMES

FORMAT 3

PERFORM procedure-name-1 [THRU procedure-name-2] UNTIL condition-1

FORMAT 4

PERFORM procedure-name-1 [THRU procedure-name-2]

VARYING $\begin{Bmatrix} \text{index-name-1} \\ \text{identifier-1} \end{Bmatrix}$ FROM $\begin{Bmatrix} \text{index-name-2} \\ \text{literal-2} \\ \text{identifier-2} \end{Bmatrix}$ BY $\begin{Bmatrix} \text{literal-3} \\ \text{identifier-3} \end{Bmatrix}$ UNTIL condition-1

[AFTER $\begin{Bmatrix} \text{index-name-4} \\ \text{identifier-4} \end{Bmatrix}$ FROM $\begin{Bmatrix} \text{index-name-5} \\ \text{literal-5} \\ \text{identifier-5} \end{Bmatrix}$ BY $\begin{Bmatrix} \text{literal-6} \\ \text{identifier-6} \end{Bmatrix}$ UNTIL condition-2

[AFTER $\begin{Bmatrix} \text{index-name-7} \\ \text{identifier-7} \end{Bmatrix}$ FROM $\begin{Bmatrix} \text{index-name-8} \\ \text{literal-8} \\ \text{identifier-8} \end{Bmatrix}$ BY $\begin{Bmatrix} \text{literal-9} \\ \text{identifier-9} \end{Bmatrix}$ UNTIL condition-3]]

READ Statement

READ file-name RECORD [INTO identifier]

$\begin{Bmatrix} \text{AT END} \\ \text{INVALID KEY} \end{Bmatrix}$ imperative-statement

REWRITE Statement

REWRITE record-name [FROM identifier] [INVALID KEY imperative statement]

SEEK Statement

SEEK file-name RECORD

START Statement

Format 1

START file-name [INVALID KEY imperative statement]

Format 2

START file-name

USING KEY data-name $\begin{Bmatrix} \text{EQUAL TO} \\ = \end{Bmatrix}$ identifier

[INVALID KEY imperative statement]

STOP Statement

STOP $\begin{Bmatrix} \text{RUN} \\ \text{literal} \end{Bmatrix}$

SUBTRACT Statement

FORMAT 1

SUBTRACT $\begin{Bmatrix} \text{identifier-1} \\ \text{literal-1} \end{Bmatrix}$ $\begin{bmatrix} \text{identifier-2} \\ \text{literal-2} \end{bmatrix}$ . . . FROM identifier-m [ROUNDED]

[identifier-n [ROUNDED]] . . . [ON SIZE ERROR imperative-statement]

FORMAT 2

SUBTRACT $\begin{Bmatrix} \text{identifier-1} \\ \text{literal-1} \end{Bmatrix}$ $\begin{bmatrix} \text{identifier-2} \\ \text{literal-2} \end{bmatrix}$ . . . FROM $\begin{Bmatrix} \text{identifier-m} \\ \text{literal-m} \end{Bmatrix}$ GIVING identifier-n

[ROUNDED] [ON SIZE ERROR imperative-statement]

FORMAT 3

SUBTRACT $\begin{Bmatrix} \text{CORRESPONDING} \\ \text{CORR} \end{Bmatrix}$ identifier-1 FROM identifier-2 [ROUNDED]

[ON SIZE ERROR imperative-statement]

TRANSFORM Statement

TRANSFORM identifier-3 CHARACTERS FROM $\begin{Bmatrix} \text{figurative-constant-1} \\ \text{nonnumeric-literal-1} \\ \text{identifier-1} \end{Bmatrix}$

TO $\begin{Bmatrix} \text{figurative-constant-2} \\ \text{nonnumeric-literal-2} \\ \text{identifier-2} \end{Bmatrix}$

USE Sentence

FORMAT 1

Option 1:

USE $\begin{Bmatrix} \text{BEFORE} \\ \text{AFTER} \end{Bmatrix}$ STANDARD [BEGINNING] $\begin{Bmatrix} \text{REEL} \\ \text{FILE} \\ \text{UNIT} \end{Bmatrix}$

LABEL PROCEDURE ON $\begin{Bmatrix} \text{\{file-name\} . . .} \\ \text{OUTPUT} \\ \text{INPUT} \\ \text{I-O} \end{Bmatrix}$.

Option 2:

USE $\begin{Bmatrix} \text{BEFORE} \\ \text{AFTER} \end{Bmatrix}$ STANDARD [ENDING] $\begin{Bmatrix} \text{REEL} \\ \text{FILE} \\ \text{UNIT} \end{Bmatrix}$

LABEL PROCEDURE ON $\begin{Bmatrix} \text{\{file-name\} . . .} \\ \text{OUTPUT} \\ \text{INPUT} \\ \text{I-O} \end{Bmatrix}$.

FORMAT 2

USE AFTER STANDARD ERROR PROCEDURE

ON $\begin{Bmatrix} \text{\{file-name-1\} [file-name-2] . . .} \\ \text{INPUT} \\ \text{OUTPUT} \\ \text{I-O} \end{Bmatrix}$

[GIVING data-name-1 [data-name-2]].

NOTE: Format 3 of the USE Sentence is included in Formats for the REPORT WRITER feature.

WRITE Statement

FORMAT 1

    WRITE record-name [FROM identifier-1] [{BEFORE/AFTER} ADVANCING

        {identifier-2 LINES / integer LINES / mnemonic-name}] [AT {END-OF-PAGE/EOP} imperative-statement]

FORMAT 2

    WRITE record-name [FROM identifier-1] AFTER POSITIONING {identifier-2/integer} LINES

        [AT {END-OF-PAGE/EOP} imperative-statement]

FORMAT 3

    WRITE record-name [FROM identifier-1] INVALID KEY imperative-statement

SORT — BASIC FORMATS

Environment Division Sort Formats

FILE-CONTROL PARAGRAPH — SELECT SENTENCE

SELECT Sentence (for GIVING option only)

    SELECT file-name

        ASSIGN TO [integer-1] system-name-1 [system-name-2] ...

        OR system-name-3 [FOR MULTIPLE {REEL/UNIT}]

        [RESERVE {integer-2/NO} ALTERNATE [AREA/AREAS]].

SELECT Sentence (for Sort Work Files)

    SELECT sort-file-name

        ASSIGN TO [integer] system-name-1 [system-name-2] ...

I-O-CONTROL PARAGRAPH

RERUN Clause

    RERUN ON system-name

SAME RECORD/SORT AREA Clause

    SAME {RECORD/SORT} AREA FOR file-name-1 {file-name-2} ...

Data Division Sort Formats

SORT-FILE DESCRIPTION

    SD sort-file-name

        RECORDING MODE IS mode

        DATA {RECORD IS/RECORDS ARE} data-name-1 [data-name-2] ...

        RECORD CONTAINS [integer-1 TO] integer-2 CHARACTERS

        [LABEL {RECORD IS/RECORDS ARE} {STANDARD/OMITTED}] (Version 4)

Procedure Division Sort Formats

RELEASE Statement

    RELEASE sort-record-name [FROM identifier]

RETURN Statement

    RETURN sort-file-name RECORD [INTO identifier]

        AT END imperative-statement

SORT Statement

    SORT file-name-1 ON {DESCENDING/ASCENDING} KEY {data-name-1} ...

    [ON {DESCENDING/ASCENDING} KEY {data-name-2} ...] ...

    {INPUT PROCEDURE IS section-name-1 [THRU section-name-2]/USING file-name-2}

    {OUTPUT PROCEDURE IS section-name-3 [THRU section-name-4]/GIVING file-name-3}

REPORT WRITER — BASIC FORMATS

Data Division Report Writer Formats

NOTE: Formats that appear as Basic Formats within the general description of the Data Division are illustrated there.

FILE SECTION — REPORT Clause

    {REPORT IS/REPORTS ARE} report-name-1 [report-name-2] ...

REPORT SECTION

    REPORT SECTION.

    RD report-name

        WITH CODE mnemonic-name

        {CONTROL IS/CONTROLS ARE} {FINAL/identifier-1 [identifier-2] ... / FINAL identifier-1 [identifier-2] ...}

        PAGE {LIMIT IS/LIMITS ARE} integer-1 {LINE/LINES}

        [HEADING integer-2]

        [FIRST DETAIL integer-3]

        [LAST DETAIL integer-4]

        [FOOTING integer-5].

REPORT GROUP DESCRIPTION ENTRY

FORMAT 1

    01 [data-name-1]

        LINE NUMBER IS {integer-1/PLUS integer-2/NEXT PAGE}

        NEXT GROUP IS {integer-1/PLUS integer-2/NEXT PAGE}

        TYPE IS {REPORT HEADING/RH / PAGE HEADING/PH / CONTROL HEADING/CH {identifier-n/FINAL} / DETAIL/DE / CONTROL FOOTING/CF {identifier-n/FINAL} / PAGE FOOTING/PF / REPORT FOOTING/RF}

        USAGE Clause.

FORMAT 2

    nn [data-name-1]

        LINE Clause — See Format 1

        USAGE Clause.

FORMAT 3

    nn [data-name-1]

        COLUMN NUMBER IS integer-1

        GROUP INDICATE

        JUSTIFIED Clause

        LINE Clause — See Format 1

        PICTURE Clause

        RESET ON {identifier-1/FINAL}

        BLANK WHEN ZERO Clause

        SOURCE IS {TALLY/identifier-2}

        SUM {TALLY/identifier-3} [{TALLY/identifier-4}] ... [UPON data-name]

        VALUE IS literal-1

        USAGE Clause.

FORMAT 4

    01 data-name-1

        BLANK WHEN ZERO Clause

        COLUMN Clause — See Format 3

        GROUP Clause — See Format 3

        JUSTIFIED Clause

        LINE Clause — See Format 1

        NEXT GROUP Clause — See Format 1

        PICTURE Clause

        RESET Clause — See Format 3

        {SOURCE Clause / SUM Clause / VALUE Clause} See Format 3

        TYPE Clause — See Format 1

        USAGE Clause.

Procedure Division Report Writer Formats

GENERATE Statement

    GENERATE identifier

INITIATE Statement

    INITIATE report-name-1 [report-name-2] ...

TERMINATE Statement

    TERMINATE report-name-1 [report-name-2] ...

USE Sentence

    USE BEFORE REPORTING data-name.

TABLE HANDLING — BASIC FORMATS
Data Division Table Handling Formats
OCCURS Clause

Format 1
OCCURS integer-2 TIMES
[{ASCENDING/DESCENDING} KEY IS data-name-2 [data-name-3]...]...
[INDEXED BY index-name-1 [index-name-2]...]

Format 2
OCCURS integer-1 TO integer-2 TIMES [DEPENDING ON data-name-1]
[{ASCENDING/DESCENDING} KEY IS data-name-2 [data-name-3]...]...
[INDEXED BY index-name-1 [index-name-2]...]

Format 3
OCCURS integer-2 TIMES [DEPENDING ON data-name-1]
[{ASCENDING/DESCENDING} KEY IS data-name-2 [data-name-3]...]...
[INDEXED BY index-name-1 [index-name-2]...]

USAGE Clause
[USAGE IS] INDEX

Procedure Division Table Handling Formats
SEARCH Statement

Format 1
SEARCH identifier-1 [VARYING {index-name-1/identifier-2}]
[AT END imperative-statement-1]
WHEN condition-1 {imperative-statement-2/NEXT SENTENCE}
[WHEN condition-2 {imperative-statement-3/NEXT SENTENCE}]...

Format 2
SEARCH ALL identifier-1 [AT END imperative-statement-1]
WHEN condition-1 {imperative-statement-2/NEXT SENTENCE}

SET Statement

Format 1
SET {index-name-1 [index-name-2].../identifier-1 [identifier-2]...} TO {index-name-3/identifier-3/literal-1}

Format 2
SET index-name-4 [index-name-5]... {UP BY/DOWN BY} {identifier-4/literal-2}

SEGMENTATION — BASIC FORMATS
Environment Division Segmentation Formats

OBJECT-COMPUTER PARAGRAPH
SEGMENT-LIMIT Clause
SEGMENT-LIMIT IS priority-number

Procedure Division Segmentation Formats
Priority Numbers
section-name SECTION [priority-number].

SOURCE PROGRAM LIBRARY FACILITY
COPY Statement
COPY library-name [SUPPRESS]
[REPLACING word-1 BY {word-2/literal-1/identifier-1} [word-3 BY {word-4/literal-2/identifier-2}]...].

Extended Source Program Library Facility

BASIS Card
BASIS   library-name

INSERT Card
INSERT   sequence-number-field

DELETE Card
DELETE   sequence-number-field

DEBUGGING LANGUAGE — BASIC FORMATS
Procedure Division Debugging Formats
EXHIBIT Statement
EXHIBIT {NAMED/CHANGED NAMED/CHANGED} {identifier-1/nonnumeric-literal-1} [identifier-2/nonnumeric-literal-2]...

ON (Count-Conditional) Statement
Format 1
ON integer-1 [AND EVERY integer-2] [UNTIL integer-3]
{imperative-statement/NEXT SENTENCE} [ELSE/OTHERWISE] {statement.../NEXT SENTENCE}

Format 2 (Version 3 & 4)
ON {integer-1/identifier-1} [AND EVERY {integer-2/identifier-2}] [UNTIL {integer-3/identifier-3}]
{imperative-statement/NEXT SENTENCE} [ELSE/OTHERWISE] {statement.../NEXT SENTENCE}

TRACE Statement
{READY/RESET} TRACE

Compile-Time Debugging Packet
DEBUG Card
DEBUG   location

Appendix E

Revision of ANS COBOL: COBOL 1968 versus COBOL 1974

There are several changes called for in the 1974 version of ANS COBOL. They are listed in publication X3.23-1974 of the American National Standard Institute. In case the reader only has access to the 1968 version compiler, we herewith present those changes pertinent to this book:

(1) REMARKS paragraph of IDENTIFICATION DIVISION is deleted. An asterisk in position 7 now identifies any line as a comment line. The comment line may appear in any division. (In the 1968 version, comments can also be expressed in a NOTE statement. However, this statement is also deleted in the latest version.)
(2) A slash in column 7 causes page ejection of the compilation listing.
(3) Two contiguous quotation marks may be used to represent a single quotation mark character in a nonnumeric literal.
(4) Mnemonic-name must have at least one alphabetic character. (The 1968 version had no such restriction.)
(5) Level 77 items need not precede level 01 items in the WORKING-STORAGE SECTION.
(6) GIVING identifier series has been added to the arithmetic statement.
(7) Identifier series has been added to the COMPUTE statement.
(8) In a MULTIPLY statement, the BY identifier series is added.
(9) In a DIVIDE statement, the INTO identifier series has been added.
(10) In a DIVIDE statement, the remainder item can be numeric edited.
(11) An index can be set up or down by a negative value.
(12) In a GO TO statement, the word TO is not required.
(13) The slash symbol is permitted as an editing character.
(14) The punctuation rules with regard to spaces have been relaxed; for example, space may now optionally precede the comma or period. These symbols may optionally precede or follow a left parenthesis.
(15) PICTURE character-string is limited to 30 characters. (In the 1968 version, the limit was restricted to 30 symbols where one symbol could have been two characters.)
(16) In a WRITE statement, INVALID KEY phrase is deleted.

(17) In a WRITE statement, BEFORE/AFTER PAGE and END-OF-PAGE phases are added to provide the ability to skip to the top of a page.
(18) LINKAGE SECTION is added.
(19) The USING phrase is added in the PROCEDURE DIVISION header.
(20) The CALL identifier statement and the CALL identifier ON OVERFLOW statement are new added features.
(21) The EXIT PROGRAM statement is a new added feature in a COBOL subprogram.
(22) The COPY statement may appear anywhere whenever a COBOL word appears.

Appendix F

Operating the IBM 029 Keypunching Machine

The keypunching machine is a device for punching cards as well as printing characters on the cards. The keyboard of a keypunching machine is very similar to a typewriter (see Fig. F.1) and easy to operate. The following are basic step-by-step operating instructions:

(1) Place enough unpunched (blank) cards in the input card hopper. Cards must be placed in the hopper face forward with the 9 edge down. (The input card hopper is located at the upper right-hand corner of the machine, see Fig. F.2.)
(2) Turn on the machine switch located on the front side of the cabinet under the keyboard.
(3) Set all keyboard switches to the off position (see Fig. F.3) except the PRINT switch, which must be turned on if characters are to be printed on the card.

Fig. F.1 An 029 keyboard.

F Operating the IBM 029 Keypunching Machine

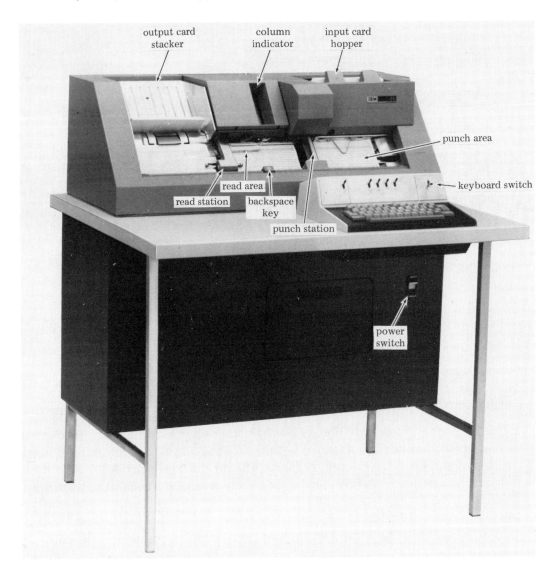

Fig. F.2 IBM 029 keypunching machine.

(4) Press the FEED key once. A card from the input card hopper will "feed" into the punch area.

(5) Press the REG key, which causes the card in the punch area to move toward the left so that its leftmost edge is slightly under the punch station. This process is called registering the card.

(6) Now, begin the process of keypunching as follows:

    (a) Press the space bar to skip a column (that is, leaving a column blank).

    (b) Press a key to keypunch an alphabetic letter or a character as it appears in the lower portion of the keyboard. (Note that there are no lowercase letters. All letters are capitals.)

    (c) Keep the NUMERIC key depressed in order to keypunch a number or a character in the upper portion of the keyboard.

F Operating the IBM 029 Keypunching Machine   321

Fig. F.3 Keyboard switches.

(7) When the keypunching of a card is done, press the REL key to move the card from the punch station to the read area. This process is called releasing the card.

(8) After a card is released, press the FEED key to feed another card from the input hopper to the punching area.

(9) Press the REG key. This moves the first card to the output card stacker and registers the second card for punching.

(10) Repeat step 6 for the second card.

Clear Punch/Read Stations—CLEAR Switch

To clear cards from punch or read stations, either press REL and REG keys or flip the CLEAR switch.

Duplicating Cards—DUP Key

Place the punched cards in the READ station and a blank card in the PUNCH station. Make sure that both are properly registered. Press the DUP key until all of the data are punched into the second card. Then flip the CLEAR switch to clear areas.

BACKSPACE Key

The BACKSPACE key can be used to move back columns one at a time.

Column Indicator

This indicator is located directly below the drum window. It indicates which column the machine is ready to punch.

AUTO FEED Switch

If the AUTO FEED switch is on, a second card will automatically feed into the PUNCH area when the REG key is pressed. This switch is often used to speed up the feeding process when many cards are to be keypunched.

ERROR RESET Switch

The ERROR RESET switch is used to unlock the keyboard. The keyboard is locked whenever multiple keys are pressed. The ERROR RESET switch will automatically reset the keyboard, so the normal keypunching operation can be assumed.

Glossary

Access arm: A mechanical part of a disk storage unit used to position the reading and writing mechanisms.

Access method: A method for moving data between input/output devices and main storage.

ACTUAL KEY: A data item of 5 to 259 bytes in length, used by the system to locate logical records on a direct access device.

Alphabetic character: A character that is one of the 26 characters of the alphabet, or a space. In COBOL, the term does *not* include any other characters.

Alphanumeric character: Any character in the computer's character set.

Alphanumeric edited character: A character within an alphanumeric character string that contains at least one B or 0.

Arithmetic expression: A statement containing any combination of data-names, numeric literals, and figurative constants, joined together by one or more arithmetic operators in such a way that the statement as a whole can be reduced to a single numeric value. It is used to specify the computation of a numerical value.

Arithmetic operator: A symbol that directs the system to perform an arithmetic operation. The following shows arithmetic operators:

Meaning	Symbol
Addition	+
Subtraction	−
Multiplication	*
Division	/
Exponentiation	**

Assumed decimal point: A decimal point position that does not occupy an actual space in storage, but is used by the compiler to align a value properly for calculation. In COBOL, the PICTURE symbol V is used for this purpose.

Block: A group of characters or records treated as a single entity when moved into or out of the computer synonymous with the term physical record.

Buffer: A portion of main storage reserved for transmitting data from or to the computer. Synonymous with I/O area.

Byte: A sequence of eight adjacent binary bits. When properly aligned, two bytes form a half word, four bytes a full word, and eight bytes a double word.

Channel: A device that directs the flow of information between the computer main storage and the input/output devices.

Character: A letter, digit or other symbol used to represent information.

Character set: The complete character set for COBOL consists of the following 51 characters:

Character	Meaning	Character	Meaning
0,1,...,9	digit	,	comma
A,B,...,Z	letter	;	semicolon
	space	.	period (decimal point)
+	plus sign	" or '	quotation mark†
−	minus sign (hyphen)	(	left parenthesis
*	asterisk	)	right parenthesis
/	stroke (virgule, slash)	>	"greater than" symbol
=	equal sign	<	"less than" symbol
$	currency sign		

Character string: A connected sequence of characters.

Checkpoint: A reference point in a program at which information about the contents of core storage can be recorded. Checkpoint is used to restart the program at that point if necessary.

Class condition: A statement used to determine whether or not a data item is strictly alphabetic or numeric.

Clause: A set of consecutive COBOL words whose purpose is to specify an attribute of an entry. There are three types of clauses: data, environment, and file.

COBOL character: Any of the 51 valid characters in the character set.

Collating sequence: The arrangement of all valid characters in the order of their relative precedence. The collating sequence of a computer is part of the computer design—each acceptable character has a predetermined place in the sequence. A collating sequence is used primarily in comparison operations.

Collating sequence for COBOL characters:

EBCDIC collating sequence		ASCII collating sequence	
1.	(space)	1.	(space)
2. .	(period)	2. "	(quotation mark)
3. <	(less than)	3. $	(currency symbol)
4. (	(left parenthesis)	4. '	(apostrophe, single quotation mark)
5. +	(plus symbol)	5. (	(left parenthesis)
6. $	(currency symbol)	6.)	(right parenthesis)
7. *	(asterisk)	7. *	(asterisk)
8.)	(right parenthesis)	8. +	(plus symbol)
9. ;	(semicolon)	9. ,	(comma)
10. -	(hyphen, minus symbol)	10. -	(hyphen, minus symbol)
11. /	(stroke, virgule, slash)	11. .	(period, decimal point)
12. ,	(comma)	12. /	(stroke, virgule, slash)
13. >	(greater than)	13–22.	0 through 9
14. '	(apostrophe, single quotation mark)	23. ;	(semicolon)
15. =	(equal sign)	24. <	(less than)
16. "	(quotation mark)	25. =	(equal sign)
17–42.	A through Z	26. >	(greater than)
43–52.	0 through 9	27–52.	A through Z

COLUMN clause: A COBOL clause used to identify a specific position within a report line.

Comment: An annotation in the IDENTIFICATION DIVISION or PROCEDURE DIVISION of a COBOL source program. A comment is ignored by the compiler. As an IBM extension, comments may be included at any point in a COBOL source program. A comment must have an asterisk punched in column 7.

† *Note:* IBM compiler's default option for the quotation mark is the apostrophe ('). Unless the default option is overridden, the quotation mark (") may not be used. If conformance with the standard COBOL character set is desired, the programmer must specify the quotation mark (") through an EXEC card at compile time. If the quotation mark is thus specified, the apostrophe (') may not be used.

Compile time: The time during which a COBOL source program is translated by the COBOL compiler into a machine language object program.

Compiler: A program that translates a program written in a higher level language (such as COBOL) into a machine language object program.

Compiler directing statement: A COBOL statement that causes the compiler to take a specific action at compile time, rather than the object program to take a particular action at execution time.

Compound condition: A statement that tests several conditions.

Conditional statement: A statement that determines the truth value of a condition. The subsequent action of the program is dependent on this truth value.

Conditional variable: A data item that can assume more than one value. The value(s) it assumes has a condition-name assigned to it.

Condition-name: A name preceded by an 88-level number. It is a name assigned to a specific value or set of values within a conditional variable.

Condition-name condition: A conditional statement involving the use of the condition-name.

CONFIGURATION SECTION: A section of the ENVIRONMENT DIVISION of the COBOL program. It describes the overall specifications of computers.

Connective: A word or a punctuation character that does one of the following:

associates a data-name or paragraph-name with its qualifier;
links two or more operands in a series;
forms a conditional expression.

CONSOLE: A COBOL mnemonic-name associated with the console typewriter.

Contiguous items: Consecutive elementary or group items in the DATA DIVISION that have a definite relationship with each other.

Control break: A recognition of a change in the contents of a control data item that governs a hierarchy.

Control data item: A data item that is tested each time a report line is to be printed. If the value of the data item has changed, a control break occurs and special actions are performed before the line is printed.

Control footing: A report group that occurs at the end of the control group of which it is a member.

Control group: An integral set of related data that is specifically associated with a control data item.

Control heading: A report group that occurs at the beginning of the control group of which it is a member.

Control hierarchy: A designated order of specific control data items. The highest level is the final control; the lowest level is the minor control.

Core storage: Storage within the central processing unit of the computer, so called because this storage exists in the form of magnetic cores.

Data description entry: An entry in the DATA DIVISION used to describe the characteristics of a data item. It consists of a level number, followed by an optional data-name, followed by data clauses that fully describe the format the data will take. An elementary data description entry (or item) cannot logically be subdivided further. A group data description entry (or item) is made up of a number of related group and/or elementary items.

DATA DIVISION: One of the four main component parts of a COBOL program. The DATA DIVISION describes the files to be used in the program and the records contained within the files. It also describes any internal WORKING-STORAGE records that will be needed.

Data item: A unit of recorded information that can be identified by a symbolic name or by a combination of names and subscripts. Elementary data items cannot logically be subdivided. Group data items are made up of logically related group and/or elementary items, and can be a logical group within a record or can itself be a complete record.

Data-name: A name assigned by the programmer to a data item in a COBOL program. It must contain at least one alphabetic character.

Device number: The reference number assigned to any external device.

Digit: Any of the numerals from 0 through 9.

DIVISION: One of the four major portions of a COBOL program:

IDENTIFICATION DIVISION, which names the program.
ENVIRONMENT DIVISION, which indicates the machine equipment and equipment features to be used in the program.
DATA DIVISION, which defines the nature and characteristics of data to be processed.
PROCEDURE DIVISION, which consists of statements directing the processing of data in a specified manner at execution time.

Division header: The beginning of a particular division of a COBOL program. The four division headers are

IDENTIFICATION DIVISION.
ENVIRONMENT DIVISION.
DATA DIVISION.
PROCEDURE DIVISION.

Division-name: The name of one of the four divisions of a COBOL program.

EBCDIC character: Any one of the symbols included in the eight-bit EBCDIC (Extended Binary-Coded-Decimal Interchange Code) set. All 51 COBOL characters are included.

Editing character: A single character or a fixed two-character combination used to create proper formats for output reports.

Elementary item: A data item that cannot logically be subdivided.

Entry: Any consecutive set of descriptive clauses terminated by a period, written in the IDENTIFICATION, ENVIRONMENT, or PROCEDURE DIVISIONS of a COBOL program.

Entry-name: A programmer-specified name that establishes an entry point into a COBOL subprogram.

ENVIRONMENT DIVISION: One of the four main component parts of a COBOL program. The ENVIRONMENT DIVISION describes the computers upon which the source program is compiled and those on which the object program is executed, and provides a linkage between the logical concept of files and their records, and the physical aspects of the devices on which files are stored.

Execution time: The time at which an object program actually performs the instructions coded in the PROCEDURE DIVISION, using the actual data provided.

Exponent: A number, indicating how many times another number (the base) is to be repeated as a factor. Positive exponents denote multiplication, negative exponents denote division, fractional exponents denote a root of a quality. In COBOL, exponentiation is indicated with the symbol ** followed by the exponent.

F-mode records: Records of a fixed length. Blocks may contain more than one record.

Figurative constant: A reserved word that represents a numeric value, a character, or a string of repeated values or characters. The word can be written in a COBOL program to represent the values or characters without being defined in the DATA DIVISION.

FILE-CONTROL: The name and header of an ENVIRONMENT DIVISION paragraph in which the data files for a given source program are named and assigned to specific input/output devices.

File description: An entry in the FILE SECTION of the DATA DIVISION that provides information about the identification and physical structure of a file.

File-name: A name assigned by the programmer to a set of input data or output data. A file-name must include at least one alphabetic character.

FILE SECTION: A section of the DATA DIVISION that contains descriptions of all externally stored data (or files) used in a program. Such information is given in one or more file description entries.

Floating-point literal: A numeric literal whose value is expressed in floating-point notation, that is, as a decimal number followed by an exponent that indicates the actual placement of the decimal point.

Function-name: A name that identifies system logical units, printer and card punch control characters, and report codes. When a function-name is associated with a mnemonic name in the ENVIRONMENT DIVISION, the mnemonic-name may then be substituted in any format in which such substitution is valid.

Group item: A data item made up of a series of logically related elementary items. It can be part of a record or a complete record.

Header label: A record that identifies the beginning of a physical file or a volume.

High-order: The leftmost position in a string of characters.

IDENTIFICATION DIVISION: One of the four main component parts of a COBOL program. The IDENTIFICATION DIVISION identifies the source program and the object program and, in addition, may include such documentation as the author's name, the installation where written, and date written.

Identifier: A data-name, unique in itself, or made unique by the syntactically correct combination of qualifiers, subscripts, and/or indexes.

Imperative-statement: A statement consisting of an imperative verb and its operands, which specifies that an action be taken, unconditionally. An imperative-statement may consist of a series of imperative-statements.

Index: A computer storage position or register, the contents of which identify a particular element in a table.

Index data item: A data item in which the contents of an index can be stored without conversion to subscript form.

Index-name: A name given by the programmer for an index of a specific table. An index-name must contain at least one alphabetic character. It is one word (4 bytes) in length.

Indexed data-name: A data-name identifier subscripted with one or more index-names.

INPUT-OUTPUT SECTION: In the ENVIRONMENT DIVISION, the section that names the files and external media needed by an object program. It also provides information required for the transmission and handling of data during the execution of an object program.

Input procedure: A set of statements that is executed each time a record is released to the sort file. Input procedures are optional; whether they are used or not depends upon the logic of the program.

Integer: A numeric data item or literal that contains a whole number without a decimal point. When the term integer appears in a format, it must be a numeric literal, not a data item.

INVALID KEY condition: A condition that may arise at execution time in which the value of a specific key associated with a mass-storage file does not result in a correct reference to the file (see the READ, REWRITE, START, and WRITE statements for the specific error conditions involved).

I-O-CONTROL: The name, and the header, for an ENVIRONMENT DIVISION paragraph in which object program requirements for specific input/output techniques are specified. These techniques include rerun checkpoints, sharing of same areas by several data files, and multiple-file storage on a single tape device.

KEY: One or more data items, the contents of which identify the type or the location of a record, or the ordering of data.

Key word: A reserved word whose employment is essential to the meaning and structure of a COBOL statement. In this text, key words are indicated in the formats of statements by underscoring. Key words are included in the reserved word list.

Level indicator: Two alphabetic characters that identify a specific type of file, or the highest position in a hierarchy. The level indicators are FD, RD, SD.

Level number: A numeric character or two-character set that identifies the properties of a data description entry. Level numbers 01 through 49 define group items, the highest level being identified as 01, and the subordinate data items within the hierarchy being identified with level numbers 02 through 49. Level numbers 66, 77, and 88 identify special properties of a data description entry in the DATA DIVISION.

Library-name: The name of a member of a data set containing COBOL entries, used with the COPY statement.

LINKAGE SECTION: A section of the DATA DIVISION that describes data made available from another program.

Literal: A character string whose value is implicit in the characters themselves. For example, the numeric literal 7 expresses the value 7, and the nonnumeric literal CHARACTERS expresses the value CHARACTERS.

Logical operator: A COBOL word that defines the logical connections between relational operators. The three logical operators and their meanings are

OR (logical inclusive—either or both)
AND (logical connective—both)
NOT (logical negation)

Logical record: The most inclusive data item, identified by a level-01 entry. It consists of one or more related data items.

Low-order: The rightmost position in a string of characters.

Main program: The highest level COBOL program involved in a step. (Programs written in other languages that follow COBOL linkage conventions are considered COBOL programs in this sense.)

Mass storage: A storage medium—disk, drum, or data cell—in which data can be collected and maintained in a sequential, direct, indexed, or relative organization.

Mass-storage file: A collection of records assigned to a mass-storage device.

Mnemonic-name: A programmer-supplied word associated with a specific function-name in the SPECIAL-NAMES paragraph of the ENVIRONMENT DIVISION.

Mode: The manner in which records of a file are accessed or processed.

Name: A word composed of not more than 30 characters, which defines a COBOL operand.

Noncontiguous item: A data item in the WORKING-STORAGE SECTION of the DATA DIVISION, which bears no relationship to other data items.

Nonnumeric literal: A character string bounded by quotation marks or apostrophes. For example, 'CHARACTER' is the literal for, and means, CHARACTER. The string of characters may include any characters in the computer's set, with the exception of the quotation mark. Characters that are not COBOL characters may be included.

Numeric character: One of the digits 0 through 9.

Numeric edited character: A character that may be used in a printed output, such as digit, decimal point, comma, and dollar sign.

Numeric item: A data item whose description restricts its contents to numeric digits.

Numeric edited character: A numeric character in such a form that it may be used in a printed output. It may consist of external decimal digits 0 through 9, the decimal point, commas, the dollar sign, etc.

Numeric item: An item whose description restricts its contents to a value represented by characters chosen from the digits 0 through 9; if signed, the item may also contain a + or −, or other representation of an operational sign.

Numeric literal: A numeric character or string of characters whose value is implicit in the characters themselves. Thus, 777 is the literal as well as the value of the number 777.

OBJECT-COMPUTER: The name of an ENVIRONMENT DIVISION paragraph describing the computer upon which the object program will be run.

Object program: The set of machine language instructions that is the output from the compilation of a COBOL source program. The actual processing of data is done by the object program.

Object time: The time during which an object program is executed.

Operand: The "object" of a verb or an operator, that is, the data governed or directed by a verb or operator.

Operational sign: An algebraic sign associated with a numeric data item, which indicates whether the item is positive or negative.

Optional word: A reserved word included in a specific format only to improve the readability of a COBOL statement. If the programmer wishes, optional words may be omitted.

Output procedure: A set of programmer-defined statements that is executed each time a sorted record is returned from the sort file. Output procedures are optional; whether they are used or not depends upon the logic of the program.

Overflow condition: In a MOVE statement, a condition that occurs when the sending field (that is, source field) contains more characters than the receiving field.

Page: A physical separation of continuous data in a report. The separation is based on internal requirements and/or the physical characteristics of the reporting medium.

Page footing: A report group at the end of a report page, which is printed before a page control break is executed.

Page heading: A report group printed at the beginning of a report page, after a page control break is executed.

Paragraph: A set of one or more COBOL sentences, making up a logical processing entity, and preceded by a paragraph-name or a paragraph header.

Paragraph header: A word followed by a period that identifies and precedes all paragraphs in the IDENTIFICATION DIVISION and ENVIRONMENT DIVISION.

Paragraph-name: A programmer-defined word that identifies and precedes a paragraph.

Parameter: A variable that is given a specific value for a specific purpose or process. In COBOL, parameters are most often used to pass data values between calling and called programs.

Physical record: A physical unit of data, synonymous with a block. It can be composed of a portion of one logical record, of one complete logical record, or of a group of logical records.

Print group: An integral set of related data within a report.

Procedure: One or more logically connected paragraphs or sections within the PROCEDURE DIVISION, which direct the computer to perform some action or series of related actions.

PROCEDURE DIVISION: One of the four main component parts of a COBOL program. The PROCEDURE DIVISION contains instructions for solving a problem. The PROCEDURE DIVISION may contain imperative-statements, conditional statements, paragraphs, procedures, and sections.

Procedure-name: A word that precedes and identifies a procedure, used by the programmer to transfer control from one point of the program to another.

Process: Any operation or combination of operations on data.

Program-name: A word in the IDENTIFICATION DIVISION that identifies a COBOL source program.

Punctuation character: A comma, semicolon, period, quotation mark, left or right parenthesis, or a space.

Qualifier: A group data-name that is used to reference a nonunique data-name at a lower level in the same hierarchy, or a section-name that is used to reference a nonunique paragraph. In this way, the data-name or the paragraph-name can be made unique.

Random access: An access mode in which specific logical records are obtained from or placed into a mass-storage file in a nonsequential manner.

Record: A set of one or more related data items grouped for handling either internally or by the input/output systems.

Record description: The total set of data description entries associated with a particular logical record.
Record-name: A data-name that identifies a logical record.
REEL: A module of external storage associated with a tape device.
Relation character: A character that expresses a relationship between two operands, for example, >—greater than, <—less than, or =—equal to.
Relation condition: A statement that the value of an arithmetic expression or data item has a specific relationship to another arithmetic expression or data item. The statement may be true or false.
Relational operator: A reserved word, or a group of reserved words, or a group of reserved words and relation characters. A relational operator plus programmer-defined operands make up a relational expression.
Report: A presentation of a set of processed data described in a report file.
Report description entry: An entry in the REPORT SECTION of the DATA DIVISION that names and describes the format of a report to be produced.
Report file: A collection of records, produced by the report writer, that can be used to print a report in the desired format.
Report footing: A report group that occurs, and is printed, only at the end of a report.
Report group: A set of related data that makes up a logical entity in a report.
Report heading: A report group that occurs, and is printed, only at the beginning of a report.
Report line: One row of printed characters in a report.
Report-name: A data-name that identifies a report.
REPORT SECTION: A section of the DATA DIVISION that contains one or more report description entries.
Reserved word: A word used in a COBOL source program for syntactical purposes. It must not appear in a program as a user-defined operand.
Routine: A set of statements in a program that causes the computer to perform an operation or series of related operations (same as procedure).
Run unit: A set of one or more object programs that function, at object time, as a unit to provide problem solutions. This compiler considers a run unit to be the highest level calling program plus all called subprograms.
Section: A logically related sequence of one or more paragraphs. A section must always be named.
Section header: A combination of words that precedes and identifies each section in the ENVIRONMENT, DATA, and PROCEDURE DIVISIONS.
Section-name: A word specified by the programmer that precedes and identifies a section in the PROCEDURE DIVISION.
Sentence: A sequence of one or more statements, the last ending with a period followed by a space.
Separator: An optional word or character that improves readability.
Sequential access: An access mode in which logical records are obtained from or placed into a file in such a way that each successive access to the file refers to the next subsequent logical record in the file. The order of the records is established by the programmer when creating the file.
Sequential processing: The processing of logical records in the order in which records are accessed.
Sign condition: A statement that the algebraic value of a data item is less than, equal to, or greater than zero. It may be true or false.
Simple condition: An expression that can have two values, and causes the object program to select between alternate paths of control, depending on the value found. The expression can be true or false.
Sort file: A collection of records that is sorted by a SORT statement. The sort file is created and used only while the sort function is operative.
Sort-file-description entry: An entry in the FILE SECTION of the DATA DIVISION that names and describes a collection of records that is used in a SORT statement.
Sort-file-name: A data-name that identifies a sort file.
Sort-key: The field within a record on which a file is sorted.
Sort-work-file: A collection of records involved in the sorting operation as this collection exists on intermediate device(s).
Source: In teleprocessing, the symbolic identification of the originator of a transmission to a queue.
Source computer: The name of an ENVIRONMENT DIVISION paragraph. It describes the computer upon which the source program will be compiled.
Source program: A program written in COBOL or any other higher level programming language.
Special characters: A character that is neither numeric nor alphabetic. Special characters in COBOL include the space ( ), the period (.), as well as the following: +, −, *, /, =, $, ,, ;, ",), (.
SPECIAL-NAMES: The name of an ENVIRONMENT DIVISION paragraph relating the mnemonic-name specified by the programmer with the system's function-name.

Special register: Compiler-generated storage areas primarily used to store information produced with the use of specific COBOL features. The special registers are TALLY, LINE-COUNTER, PAGE-COUNTER, CURRENT-DATE, TIME-OF-DAY, LABEL-RETURN, RETURN-CODE, SORT-RETURN, SORT-FILE-SIZE, SORT-CORE-SIZE, and SORT-MODE-SIZE.

Statement: A syntactically valid combination of words and symbols written in the PROCEDURE DIVISION. A statement combines COBOL reserved words and programmer-defined operands.

Subject of entry: A data-name or reserved word that appears immediately after a level indicator or level number in a DATA DIVISION entry. It serves to reference the entry.

Subprogram: A COBOL program that is invoked by another COBOL program. (Programs written in other languages that follow COBOL linkage conventions are COBOL programs in this sense.)

Subscript: An integer or a variable whose value references a particular element in a table.

SYSIN: IBM system logical input device.

SYSOUT: IBM system logical output device.

SYSPUNCH: IBM system logical punch device.

System-name: A name that identifies any particular external device used with the computer, and characteristics of files contained within it.

Table: A collection and arrangement of data in a fixed form for ready reference. Such a collection follows some logical order, expressing particular values (functions) corresponding to other values (arguments) by which they are referenced.

Table element: A data item that belongs to the set of repeated items comprising a table.

Test condition: A statement that, taken as a whole, may be either true or false, depending on the circumstances existing at the time the expression is evaluated.

Trailer label: A record that identifies the ending of a physical file or of a volume.

Unary operator: An arithmetic operator (+ or −) that can precede a single variable, a literal, or a left parenthesis in an arithmetic expression. The plus sign multiplies the value by +1; the minus sign multiplies the value by −1.

V-mode records: Records of variable length. Blocks may contain more than one record. Each record contains a record length field, and each block contains a block length field.

Variable: A data item whose value may be changed during execution of the object program.

Verb: A COBOL reserved word that expresses an action to be taken by a COBOL compiler or an object program.

Volume: A module of external storage. For tape devices it is a reel; for mass storage devices it is a unit.

Word: (1) In COBOL, a string of not more than 30 characters, chosen from the following: the letters A through Z, the digits 0 through 9, and the hyphen (-). The hyphen may not appear as either the first or last character. (2) In System 360/370 a full word is four bytes of storage; a double word is eight bytes of storage; a half word is two bytes of storage.

Word boundary: Any particular storage position at which data must be aligned for certain processing operations in System 360/370. The half word boundary must be divisible by 2, the full word boundary must be divisible by 4, the double word boundary must be divisible by 8.

WORKING-STORAGE SECTION: A section-name (and the section itself) in the DATA DIVISION. The section describes records and noncontiguous data items that are not part of external files, but are developed and processed internally. It also defines data items whose values are assigned in the source program.

Solutions to Selected Exercises

Chapter 1

3 (a) False
    (b) True
    (c) False
    (d) True
    (e) True
    (f) True
    (g) True

Chapter 2

1 The COBOL language consists of six types of elements:

    (a) Programmer-supplied names
    (b) Reserved words
    (c) Symbols
    (d) Literals
    (e) Level numbers
    (f) Pictures

2 (a) False
    (b) True
    (c) True
    (d) True
    (e) False
    (f) False
    (g) False
    (h) True
    (i) True

Chapter 3

4 The following are answers for the IBM 360/370 systems. Consult your local manual or Appendix A for other computer systems.

```
            SELECT  DATA-FILE
                ASSIGN  TO  UR-2501-S-CARDIN.
            SELECT  WKLY-REPORT
                ASSIGN  TO  UR-1403-S-PRINTER.
            SELECT  TAPE-IN
                ASSIGN  TO  UT-2400-S-TAPEIN.
```

5 IDENTIFICATION DIVISION

PROGRAM-ID. PROBLEMS.
ENVIRONMENT DIVISION.
CONFIGURATION SECTION.
SOURCE-COMPUTER. IBM-370.
OBJECT-COMPUTER. IBM-370.
INPUT-OUTPUT SECTION.
FILE CONTROL.
    SELECT CARDFILE, ASSIGN TO UR-2540R-S-CARDIN.
    SELECT PAYROLL-FILE ASSIGN TO UT-2400-S-TAPE1.
    SELECT MASTER-FILE ASSIGN TO UT-2400-S-TAPE2.
    SELECT PRINTFILE ASSIGN TO UR-1403-S-PROUT.

6 (a) False
   (b) True
   (c) False
   (d) True
   (e) False
   (f) True
   (g) False
   (h) False

Chapter 4

4 (a) False
   (b) False
   (c) True
   (d) True
   (e) True
   (f) True
   (g) False
   (h) False
   (i) False
   (j) True

7 01 STUDENT-RECORD.
    05 ID   PIC 9(9).
    05 NAME.
       10 LAST   PIC A(11).
       10 FIRST   PIC A(9).
       10 INITIAL   PIC A.
    05 ADDRESS.
       10 STREET   PIC X(15).
       10 CITY   PIC X(10).
       10 STATE   PIC AA.
       10 ZIP   PIC 9(5).
    05 DEPT.
       10 MAJOR   PIC 9999.
       10 MINOR   PIC 9999.
    05 FILLER   PIC X(10).

9 WORKING-STORAGE SECTION.
   77 BONUS-A PICTURE S9(3)V99 VALUE 275.5.
   01 HEADING-1.
      02 FILLER PICTURE X(11) VALUE SPACES.
      02 FILLER PICTURE X(25)
          VALUE 'SOCIAL SECURITY'.
      02 FILLER PICTURE X(25)
          VALUE 'EMPLOYEE NAME'.
      02 FILLER PICTURE X(71) VALUE 'BONUS'.

Chapter 5

3 (a) OPEN INPUT A-FILE, OUTPUT B-FILE.
   (b) READ A-FILE AT END GO TO END-JOB.
   (c) WRITE B-REC.
   (d) WRITE B-REC.
   (e) MOVE A-REC TO B-REC.
   (f) READ A-FILE INTO B-REC.
   (g) CLOSE A-FILE, B-FILE.
   (h) WRITE statement must begin at B-margin (position 12).
   (i) DISPLAY 'RECORD B'.
   (j) ACCEPT A-REC.

Chapter 6

1 (a) 12.34   (b) 706   (c) *12.34   (d) 1,234,567
       01.23   1.50   **012   1 2 34
       46.00   12.34   ***12   1002034
       23.45   .00   ****   12 345678
       00.00   .04   invalid picture
       1.23   0.04   invalid picture

   (e) $0012   (f) −$1234   (g) 23
        $12 $1234DB   00123
        $012 $1234CR   AB
        $**12 $1,234.56DB   ABC
        $12,345.67 $12.34+   23.45
        invalid picture   invalid picture   000123.45
        invalid picture   ABC
                                                                 invalid

3 (b) Permissible, but result may be unpredictable.
   (c) Invalid, numeric data to alphabetic data.

Chapter 7

1

	A	B	C
(a)	—	—	8.00
(b)	8.	—	—
(c)	—	—	3.78
(d)	—	—	−4.00
(e)	—	—	12.00
(f)	—	9.9	—
(g)	—	3.0	—
(h)	—	—	0.33
(i)	—	1.5	2.00
(j)	—	—	4.00
(k)	1.	—	—

2 (a) COMPUTE B = (1 + R) ** N.
   (b) COMPUTE FICA = 0.0585 + NET-INCOME.
   (c) COMPUTE A = 150 + 2.5 * Q ** 2 + 6.0 * S.
   (d) COMPUTE T = (A + B + R   S   2) / W.

Chapter 8

1 (a) Incorrect, must change '100' to 100.
   (b) Incorrect, since the ADD statement would never be executed. (The ADD statement should be placed before the GO TO statement.)
   (c) Incorrect, CLASS-CODE needs a PICTURE clause, for example,
       04 CLASS-CODE PIC X.
       88 SENIOR VALUE 'S'.
   (d) Delete EQUAL TO 'NJ' from the IF statement.
   (e) Correct as is.
   (f) Incorrect, X cannot be compared with both numeric and nonnumeric literals. Therefore, one of the literals must be changed, for example, IF X > 100 OR X EQUAL TO 200 GO TO R1.

3 IF A > B MOVE B TO C.
   ADD 1 TO A.

5 IF A NOT EQUAL TO B
       ADD A TO D
       SUBTRACT B FROM C
   ELSE
       ADD A TO C
       ADD B TO D.
   GO TO R1.

7 IF A > 50
       IF B > 40 ADD 1 TO J
       ELSE
           ADD 2 TO K
           ADD C TO D
   ELSE ADD 3 TO L.
   GO TO P1.

9 IF A > B OR C < D OR E = D
       GO TO X1
   ELSE GO TO X2.

Chapter 9

1 (a) Incorrect, the OCCURS clause cannot appear at the 01 level.
   (b) Incorrect, the level number of C cannot be the same as B.
   (c) Incorrect, the OCCURS clause cannot appear at the 77 level.
   (d) Incorrect, B is a two-dimensional data name. It needs two subscripts.
   (e) Incorrect, the subscript J must not contain a decimal point.
   (f) Incorrect, the REDEFINES clause cannot apply to a data name with a different level number.
   (g) Correct.

3 02 SALES-COMMISSION-VALUE PIC X(15)
       VALUE '010035070105120'.
   02 SALES-COMMISSION-RATE REDEFINE SALES-COMMISSION
       03 RATE PICTURE SV999 OCCURS 5 TIMES.

Chapter 10

1 (a) 99 (b) 100 (c) 0

3
    MOVE LOW-VALUES TO X-MAX.
    PERFORM FIND-MAX VARYING J FROM
    1 BY 1 UNTIL J > N.
       ⋮

FIND-MAX-X.
    IF X (J) GREATER THAN X-MAX
      MOVE X (J) TO X-MAX
      MOVE J TO K.

Index

A

A, in PICTURE clause, 48, 49, 88
ACCEPT, 69-70
Access mechanism, 243
ACCESS MODE clause,
  random, 246-247
  sequential, 255-256
ACTUAL KEY clause, 246-247
ADD, 106-110
  GIVING option, 108
  ON SIZE ERROR, 109-110
  ROUNDED option, 108, 109
ADD CORRESPONDING, 151-152
ADVANCING, 67-68
AFTER, 67-69
ALL, literal figurative constant, 55
Alphabetic data, moving, 93-94
Alphabetic test, 140-141
Alphanumeric data,
  moving, 93-94
  PICTURE symbol X, 48, 49
ALTER, 280
A margin, 19
AND (logical operator), 143-144
ANS COBOL, 15
ANSI, 15
Arithmetic logic unit, 8
Arithmetic expressions, 116, 117
Arithmetic symbols, 32
ASCENDING, 219
ASCII, 324
Assembly level language, 9
ASSIGN, 38, 39
Assumed decimal point (V), 49-51
Asterisk (*),
  in arithmetic expressions, 116-118
  in PICTURE clause (check protect symbol), 51, 87, 88
AT END, 66-68, 221-222
AUTHOR, 36-37

B

B, used in PICTURE clause, 51, 90
Bit, 200
Blanks, insertion of, 87, 88
BLOCK CONTAINS clause, 204-205
Block records, 200-201
B margin, 19
bpi, 200
Braces ({ }), 34
Brackets ([ ]), 34
Byte, 7, 200

C

CALL, 282
Capitalized words in format, 34
Card,
  COBOL statement on, 18, 19
  general descriptions, 12, 13
  punched, 12, 13, 319-322
  reader, 6
Cathode-ray tube (CRT), 7
Central processing unit (CPU), 8
Character set, 324
Characters, 323
  editing, 86-95
  floating, 93
  insertion of, 87-90
  replacement, 277-278
CHANNEL-1, 69
Check protection symbol (*), 51, 87, 88

Class test, 140, 141
CLOSE, 65, 208
COBOL,
    acronym, 15
    ANS, 15
    basic elements, 30
    coding sheet, 18–19
    program structure, 16–18
    punctuation symbols, 32
    reserved words list, 309–312
    rules for writing program, 23, 24
COCR (cylinder overflow control record), 253
CODASYL, 15
Coding sheet,
    rules for, 19
    sample, 18
Collating sequence,
    ASCII, 324
    EBCDIC, 324
COLUMN, 269
Comma,
    used in PICTURE clause, 88, 89
    used in source program, 32, 33
Comment lines, in coding sheet, 19
COMMUNICATION SECTION, 43
COMP (USAGE IS), 188–189
Comparison,
    nonnumeric operands, 137–138
    numeric operands, 138–139
Compilation, errors in, 229–232
Compiler, 15–16
Compound test, 142–144
COMPUTATIONAL (USAGE IS), 188–189
COMPUTE, 116–118
Computer name,
    OBJECT-COMPUTER, 38, 39
    SOURCE-COMPUTER, 38, 39
Computer system, 3–8
Condition-name (level 88), 47, 141–142
Condition-name test, 141–142
Conditional statement,
    examples, 132
    IF, 131–145
CONFIGURATION SECTION, 38–39
Constants,
    figurative, 54–55
    literal, 53–54
Continuation,
    indicator in COBOL coding sheet, 19
    JCL statement, 297
CONTROL, 264–268
    FINAL, 264, 266, 268
    FOOTING, 264, 268
    HEADING, 264, 268
    report group, 264, 267–270
Control cards, JCL, 29, 296–308
Control unit, 8
Control of SORT procedure, 218
Core memory, 7

COPY, 277–279
    JCL for COPY library, 279
CORRESPONDING, 151–152
Count area, 246
CPU, 8
CR, used in PICTURE clause, 51, 90
Creating files,
    direct (random access), 249, 250
    indexed, 255, 256
    tape, 211
Credit symbol (CR), 51, 90
CRT, 7
CURRENT-DATE, 79, 83
Cylinder, disk, 243–245
Cylinder index, 254
C01, . . . , C12 (system-names), 69

D

Data cards,
    alphabetic, punching of, 319–322
    description of, 12–13
    numeric punching of, 49, 319–322
Data description entry, 47, 48
DATA DIVISION, 16, 43–56, 312–313
Data-names, 325
    qualification (duplication), 151
    rules for coding, see Programmer-supplied names
DATA RECORD, 45
Data set, 242
DATE-COMPILED, 36, 37
DATE-WRITTEN, 36, 37
DB (debit symbol), 51, 90
DD, 296, 298
Debug packet, 238–240
Debugging, 229–241
Decimal point (.), 51, 87
    assumed, 49–51
Density, tape, 200
DEPENDING ON option,
    of GO TO, 280
    of OCCURS, 209–210
DESCENDING, 219
DETAIL, 264, 265, 267, 268
    FIRST, 267
    LAST, 267
Direct-access device, 3, 7, 243
Direct files, 245–252
    examples, 248–252
Disk, 7, 243–245
    cylinder, 243, 245
    pack, 243
    READ/WRITE head, 243, 244
    track, 243, 244
Disk operating system (DOS) job control language, 306–308
Disk pack, 243
Disk unit, 243
DISPLAY, 70–71, 188–189

DIVIDE, 114–116
Division/remainder method, 248
DLBL, 308
Dollar sign ($), in PICTURE clause, 51, 88
Duplicate data names, 151

E

EBCDIC, 138, 324, 326
Editing, 86–95
88-level number, 47, 141, 142
Elementary item, 46, 47
11 punch, 13
Ellipsis (. . .), 34
ELSE clause, 132–133
End of reel markers, 202
End of tape markers, 202
ENVIRONMENT DIVISION, 16, 37–40
    for various computer systems, 292–295
EQUAL, 136
ERRORS,
    compilation, 229–232
    correcting of, 230, 231
    debugging, 229–241
    object-time, 232
EXEC statement,
    DOS, 306, 307
    OS, 296, 297–298
EXHIBIT, 234, 235
EXIT, 177–178
EXIT PROGRAM, 281
Exponentiation symbol (**), 117
Expression, arithmetic, 116, 117
EXTENT, 308

F

FD (file description), 45–46
Figurative constants, 54–55
File,
    concepts, 44
    direct (random access), 242–252
    indexed sequential (ISAM), 242, 252–261
    sequential, 242
FILE-CONTROL, 39
File description (FD), 45–46
FILE SECTION, 43, 45–46
FILLER, 47
FINAL CONTROL, 268
Fixed insertion editing, 88, 89
Floating insertion editing, 89, 90
Flowchart, 10–12
Footing, control, 264–266, 268
FORTRAN, 9
Function-name, 38

G

Gap,
    interblock, 200, 201

    interrecord, 200
GENERATE, 271–272
GIVING option, 108, 217, 219
GO TO, 72
GO TO DEPENDING, 280
GREATER THAN, 136
Group,
    items, 46
    moving a, 94–95
GROUP INDICATE clause, 270

H

Head, read/write, 243, 245
Header labels, 201–202
HEADING, REPORT, 264–265
    CONTROL, 266
    PAGE, 267
HIGH-VALUE(S), 54
Higher-level languages, 9
Hollerith code, 13

I

IBG, 200, 201
IDENTIFICATION DIVISION, 16, 36–37
Identifier, 326
IF statement, 131–145
Imperative statement, 131
Independent elementary item, 47
Index,
    cylinder, 253–254
    track, 252–253
Index area, 254
Index name, 222–225
Indexed by, 223
Indexed sequential file (ISAM), 242, 252–261
    examples, 256, 257, 260, 261
INITIATE, 270, 272
Input/output devices, 3–7
INPUT-OUTPUT SECTION, 38–41
INPUT PROCEDURE, 217, 219
Insertion characters (editing), 88–90
Interblock gap (IBG), 200, 201
Interrecord gap (IRG), 200
INVALID KEY, 249, 252, 255–258
I-O-CONTROL, 204
I/O device, see Input/output device
I-O file, 64
IRG, 200
ISAM, see Indexed sequential file

J

Job control statements (JCL),
    DOS, 306–308
    OS, 296–306
JUSTIFIED (JUST) RIGHT, 93–94

K

Key, ascending/descending, 217, 226
KEY, INVALID, 249, 252, 255–258
Keypunching machine, 319–322

L

LABEL RECORD, 45, 206
Labels, leader or trailer, 201, 202
Languages, programming, 8–10
    assembly level, 8, 9
    higher-level, 9, 10
    machine, 8, 9
Language translator, 10
LAST DETAIL, 267
LBLTYP, 307, 308
LESS THAN, 136
Level number,
    01–49, 77 levels, 47
    88 level, 47, 141, 142, 150
LINES, 67, 68
LINE-COUNTER, 265
LINKAGE SECTION, 281
Literal,
    nonnumeric, 54
    numeric, 53
Load point, 201
Logical record, 45
Loop, nested, 183–184
LOW-VALUE, 54

M

Main storage, 7
Machine language, 9
Magnetic core, 7
Magnetic disk units, 243, *see also* Disk
Magnetic tape, 6, 199–210
    access, rate, 200
    blocking, 200, 201
    density, 200
    end of reel marker, 201
    file processing (example), 211, 212
    interblock gap, 200, 201
    load point, 201
Mass storage device, *see* Direct-access device
Mnemonic-name, 69
MOVE, 65–66
    permissible, 90–91
MOVE CORRESPONDING, 152–153
MULTIPLE REEL, 203
MULTIPLY, 113–114

N

Names,
    programmer supplied, 31
    qualification, 151
Nested loops, 183–184
NEXT GROUP, 267, 268
NEXT SENTENCE, 135
9, used in PICTURE clause, 47
Nine-track tape, 199
Nonnumeric literal, 54
NO REWIND, 207, 208
NOT, 144–145
Numbers, signed and unsigned, 49
Numeric,
    editing, 87–90
    literal, 53
    moves, 91–93
    PICTURE, 48, 49
    test, 140, 141

O

OBJECT-COMPUTER, 38
Object program (deck), 10, 15
Object-time error, 232
OCCURS, 161–162
OCCURS . . . DEPENDING ON, 209, 210
01 level number, 47
ON (count-condition), 237, 238
ON SIZE ERROR, 109–110
OPEN, 63–65, 207–208
OR, 143
OS (operating system) job control language, 296–306.
Output device, 3–7
OUTPUT PROCEDURE, 217, 219
Overflow area, 255

P

P, used in PICTURE clause, 49–51
PAGE-COUNTER, 195
PAGE FOOTING (PF)/HEADING (PH), 264, 265
PAGE LIMIT, 266, 267
Paragraph, 17, 38, 63
Paragraph name, 17, 63
    definition, 328
Parentheses, in expression, 180–183
Parity bit, 199
PERFORM, 70–74, 176–189
POSITION, 69
PICTURE character
    9 (nine), 48, 49
    A, 48, 49, 88
    actual decimal point (.), 51, 87
    B, 51, 88
    comma (,), 88, 89
    CR, DB, 51, 90
    S, P, V, X, 48–51
    Z, 51, 87–88
    +, −, 51, 90
    0 (zero), 88
Printed report, 67–69, 264–274
Printing a table, 159
Printing (starting a new page), 69

PROCEDURE DIVISION, 17, 63-74
Procedure-name, *see* Paragraph-name
Program, 8
    coding sheet, 18
    debugging, 229-241
    flowchart, 10, 11, 12
PROGRAM-ID, 36
Programmer-supplied names, 31
Programming language one (PL/I), 9
Programming languages, 8-10
Punched card, 12-13
Punching data cards, 319-322
Punctuation symbols, 32-33

Q

Qualification, 151
QUOTE(S), 55

R

Random-access file, *see* Direct file
Random-access units, *see* Direct-access device
READ, 66-67, 209, 249, 259-260
Reader, card, 6
Reading without defining files (ACCEPT), 69-70
Read/write head, 243, 245
READY TRACE, 233
Record,
    blocked, 200-201
    data, 44-52
    variable-length, 209-210
RECORD CONTAINS, 205-206
RECORDING MODE clause, 265
REDEFINES, 163-164
REEL, MULTIPLE, 203
Relational test, 136-140
RELEASE, 220, 222
REMAINDER clause, 114-116
REMARKS, 36-37
REPLACING BY, 277-278
REPORT,
    description (RD), 266-270
    FOOTING/HEADING, 264-265, 268
Report writer, 254-275
RESERVE clause, 203-204
Reserved words, COBOL, 309-311
RESET TRACE, 233
RETURN, 221-222
REVERSED, 207
REWRITE, 258-260
ROUNDED, 108-109
RPG (report page generator), 9

S

S, used in PICTURE clause, 49
SD (SORT description entries), 215-216
SEARCH (linear or sequential), 224, 225
SEARCH ALL (binary search), 225-227
Sequence number (in coding sheet), 19

Sequential device, 4
7 track, 199
77 level number, 47
SET, 223-224
Sign test, 139-140
Signed numbers, 49
SIZE ERROR, 109-110
SORT, 215-227
    examples, 219, 222
    JCL statements, 220
Sort description (SD), 215, 216
SOURCE clause, 269
SOURCE-COMPUTER, 38
Source program (deck), 10, 15
SPACE, 54
SPECIAL-NAMES, 38, 82
START, 258
Statement, imperative, 131
STOP RUN, 72
Structured programming, 287-291
    controls, 288
    rules, 289
Subprogram, 281-285
Subscript, 163-169
    rules, 168-169
SUBTRACT, 110-112
    CORRESPONDING, 152
SUM clause, 269-270
SUPPRESS clause, 277-278
SYNCHRONIZE (SYNC), 247
System flowchart, 10, 11
System-hardware-unit, 38

T

Table, 161-169
    one-dimensional, 161-164
    two- or three-dimensional, 164-169
Tape, *see* Magnetic tape
TERMINATE, 271, 272
Test, IF,
    class, alphabetic/numeric, 140 141
    compound, 142-145
    condition name, 141-142
    relational (EQUAL, GREATER, LESS, . . .),
        136-139
    SIGN, 139-140
THRU,
    PERFORM, 176-177
    VALUE clause, 142
TIMES,
    OCCURS, 161-162, 209-210
    PERFORM, 178-179
TRACE, 233
Track,
    disk, 243
    tape, 199
Track identifier, 247
TRACK-LIMIT clause, 246-247
Trailer label, 202

12 punch, 13
TYPE clause, 268-269

U

Unit record, 4
UNTIL option of PERFORM, 179
USAGE clause, DISPLAY/COMPUTATIONAL, 188-189
USING option, sort feature, 217-219

V

V, used in PICTURE clause, 48-51
VALUE clause,
    figurative constants, 54-55
    nonnumeric literals, 54
    numeric literals, 53
VALUE OF clause, 206-207
Variable-length records, 209, 210

VARYING, option of PERFORM, 180-183
Volume label (header), 202

W

WHEN clause, 224-225
Words, COBOL reserved, 309-311
WORKING-STORAGE SECTION, 43, 53, 55-56
WRITE, 67-69, 209, 249-252, 255-256

X

X, used in PICTURE clause, 48-49

Z

Z, used in PICTURE clause, 51, 87-88
ZERO(S), 54
Zero suppression, 51, 87-88
Zone punches (11 or 12), 13